ASPEN PUBLISHERS

LEGAL REASONING, RESEARCH, AND WRITING FOR INTERNATIONAL GRADUATE STUDENTS

Second Edition

Nadia E. Nedzel, J.D., LL.M.
Southern University Law Center

AUSTIN BOSTON CHICAGO NEW YORK THE NETHERLANDS

Aspen Publishers
Attn: Permissions Department
76 Ninth Avenue, 7th Floor
New York, NY 10011-5201

To contact Customer Care, e-mail customer.care@aspenpublishers.com, call 1-800-234-1660, fax 1-800-901-9075, or mail correspondence to:

Aspen Publishers
Attn: Order Department
PO Box 990
Frederick, MD 21705

Printed in the United States of America.

2 3 4 5 6 7 8 9 0

ISBN 978-0-7355-6953-9

Library of Congress Cataloging-in-Publication Data

Nedzel, Nadia E., 1954–
Legal reasoning, research, and writing for international graduate students/Nadia E. Nedzel. — 2nd ed.
p. cm.
Includes index.
ISBN 978-0-7355-6953-9
1. Legal research — United States. 2. Law — Unites States — Methodology. 3. Legal composition. I. Title.

KF240.N43 2008
340.072′073 — dc22

2008002417

About Wolters Kluwer Law & Business

Wolters Kluwer Law & Business is a leading provider of research information and workflow solutions in key specialty areas. The strengths of the individual brands of Aspen Publishers, CCH, Kluwer Law International and Loislaw are aligned within Wolters Kluwer Law & Business to provide comprehensive, in-depth solutions and expert-authored content for the legal, professional and education markets.

CCH was founded in 1913 and has served more than four generations of business professionals and their clients. The CCH products in the Wolters Kluwer Law & Business group are highly regarded electronic and print resources for legal, securities, antitrust and trade regulation, government contracting, banking, pension, payroll, employment and labor, and healthcare reimbursement and compliance professionals.

Aspen Publishers is a leading information provider for attorneys, business professionals and law students. Written by preeminent authorities, Aspen products offer analytical and practical information in a range of specialty practice areas from securities law and intellectual property to mergers and acquisitions and pension/benefits. Aspen's trusted legal education resources provide professors and students with high-quality, up-to-date and effective resources for successful instruction and study in all areas of the law.

Kluwer Law International supplies the global business community with comprehensive English-language international legal information. Legal practitioners, corporate counsel and business executives around the world rely on the Kluwer Law International journals, loose-leafs, books and electronic products for authoritative information in many areas of international legal practice.

Loislaw is a premier provider of digitized legal content to small law firm practitioners of various specializations. Loislaw provides attorneys with the ability to quickly and efficiently find the necessary legal information they need, when and where they need it, by facilitating access to primary law as well as state-specific law, records, forms and treatises.

Wolters Kluwer Law & Business, a unit of Wolters Kluwer, is headquartered in New York and Riverwoods, Illinois. Wolters Kluwer is a leading multinational publisher and information services company.

To my husband, Nicholas Capaldi, for his encouragement; my children, Chantal and Michael, for their patience; and my LL.M. students, for their insight and comments.

SUMMARY OF CONTENTS

CONTENTS

PREFACE

This book was originally conceived as a response to a perceived need, and I have been delighted and gratified by students' enthusiasm about it, and by how widely it has been adopted. I hope this second, improved, edition proves to be even more successful. When I first began teaching Legal Reasoning, Research, and Writing to LL.M. candidates in 1999, I quickly found that the existing textbooks were inappropriate for this particular group of students. Despite their many virtues, textbooks designed for J.D. students presumed a reader unfamiliar with law. Thus, they seemed patronizing to LL.M. candidates, many of whom had already practiced law in their native countries. Additionally, they moved too slowly and corrected writing problems non-native English speakers were unlikely to have, and failed to address the reasoning, organizational, and writing problems my students were likely to face. Furthermore, those textbooks did not address the differences between civilian and common law methodology, something I understood well because of my background in comparative law and Louisiana's bi-jural law, which mixes elements of both legal systems. Already finding it difficult to read large amounts of material in their doctrinal classes, my students were further frustrated by having to use one textbook for writing and another for research, plus the Bluebook and a style book. As a result, they felt mired in extraneous reading and unnecessary detail, and were losing focus on the most important part of a LRR&W course, developing active common-law lawyering skills.

In the fall of 2000, I was faced with an additional, exciting challenge: teaching basic U.S. LRR&W in a distance program to law faculty at the *Instituto Technològico y de Estudios Superiores de Monterrey* (ITESM), in Mexico. Out of necessity, I reduced the number of assignments to a bare minimum: four research assignments, a closed-universe memo, one rewrite of it, and an open memo. Out of this core, a book slowly grew, and thanks to the wonderful suggestions of Aspen's anonymous commentators, the second edition is both updated and significantly improved. The first three chapters introduce the knowledge and skills an LL.M. candidate most needs in order to approach common-law courses effectively: (1) an understanding of how a common law system differs from traditional civilian legal systems, how to approach common law courses, and how to brief a case; (2) an understanding of how to locate authorities as needed, either in a library or on-line; and (3) an understanding of how to synthesize several sources into an operative legal rule through IRAC analysis and a short closed-universe memorandum. The new Chapter Four provides a simple introduction to U.S. Civil and Administrative Procedure, as the differences between civilian and common law civil procedure are probably more profound and significant than differences in subjects such as torts and contracts. Chapters Five through Eight further develop research, reasoning, and writing skills for secondary sources, case law, and legislative or administrative law. Chapters Nine through Twelve, introduce skills that, while extremely useful, may not be needed for all courses or all students: computer-assisted legal research, scholarly writing, advocacy, and preventive writing. The appendixes explain how to prepare for and do well on U.S.-style essay exams, and how to draft advisory memos on non-U.S. law for attorneys in the United States.

ACKNOWLEDGMENTS

I would like to thank Chancellor Freddie Pitcher of Southern University Law Center for the summer research stipend that allowed me to address this project, and I would like to thank Dean Hernàn Corral Talicani of the *Universidad de los Andes* (Santiago, Chile) for inviting me as a Fulbright Senior Specialist to teach both comparative contract law and a seminar on drafting advisory memos, thus leading to further insight into the needs of non-U.S. students studying U.S. law, as well as the new appendix. I would also like to thank my fellow faculty at SULC for their support and understanding with scheduling issues, and Professor Mark Wojcik of John Marshall Law School for his enthusiasm and continued support. Improvements could not have been made without the able assistance of Aspen editors Elizabeth Kenny and Kaesmene Banks, nor could they have been made without the sacrifices made by my husband, Nicholas Capaldi, or my children, Chantal and Michael San Miguel. Finally, I would like to thank LL.M. students of U.S. law all over the world, particularly Professors Humayoun Rahimi, Wali Mohammad Naseh, Menhajuddin Hamed, and Mohammad Haroon Mutasem of Kabul and Balkh Universities in Afganistan for their overwhelmingly warm reception of the book.

Nadia E. Nedzel
Southern University Law Center

January 2008

LEGAL REASONING, RESEARCH, AND WRITING FOR INTERNATIONAL GRADUATE STUDENTS

CHAPTER 1

United States Common Law

INTRODUCTION

The United States legal system and law school experience are unique. Because of its common law system, the United States is one of only a few countries that fully adopt judicial decisions as a major source of law and use them as precedent in deciding future cases. The influence of common law systems is much greater than the number of common law countries would indicate, and some scholars argue that the international trend is toward the adoption of case law.[1] Furthermore, jurists from different legal systems may disagree about legal theories, but often agree about the result of an individual decision. Therefore, an understanding of how to read, interpret, and synthesize case law is likely to become increasingly important to attorneys who have clients with ties to the United States or who practice in the global marketplace. United States law schools are among the few, even among common law jurisdictions, to use Socratic dialogue and case law in the classroom. Understanding and adjusting to these features and others is necessary for success in an American graduate legal studies program, and a course in United States legal research and writing is the course in which non-U.S. LL.M. candidates, as well as U.S. J.D. candidates, learn these skills.

This text, which is designed for just such a course, does not teach substantive law. Substantive U.S. law is taught elsewhere. Instead, this text teaches something infinitely more useful: a new way to think about law; new methods of researching law, both in a

[1] *See, e.g.*, Lawrence R. Helfer & Anne-Marie Slaughter, *Toward a Theory of Effective Supranatural Adjudication*, 107 Yale L.J. 273, 276, 280, 282 (1997) (describing the growing body of case law from the European Court of Justice and the European Court of Human Rights; the United Nations Human Rights Committee's increasingly court-like behavior; and projecting a global community of law developed by overlapping networks of national, regional, and global tribunals, respectively). *See also* David A. Westbrook, *Islamic International Law & Public International Law: Separate Expressions of World Order*, 33 Va. J. Int'l L. 819, 875 (1993) (describing trend of public international law: "[c]ourts publish opinions, refer to prior cases, and so forth, so that even where there is no formal doctrine of precedent, an expanding body of case law develops."); Marcelo Halpern & Ajay K. Mehrotra, *From International Treaties to Internet Norms: The Evolution of International Trademark Disputes in the Internet Age*, 21 U. Pa. J. Int'l Econ. L. 523, 533 (2000) (discussing "Internet Common Law").

law library and on computer; and ways to analyze and synthesize a number of legal sources so that they can be accurately applied to specific factual situations. Not only will these skills enhance your understanding of and performance in the substantive law courses of your LL.M. program, but also they will be skills that you are likely to use throughout your future career. In addition to teaching these reasoning and research skills, the text explains how to draft several kinds of commonly used documents: American-style law firm memoranda, scholarly articles, advocacy (court filings), and preventive writing (contracts). Attorneys in the United States draft these kinds of documents every day.

In the United States, an attorney's income is directly related to his or her skill in reasoning, research, and writing. A saying common among lawyers in the United States is that a case is won or lost "on the paper." Writing and analytical skills are mutually dependent: when one improves, so does the other. After an abbreviated and over-simplified comparative explanation of a few of the unique characteristics of the U.S. legal system and how they developed, this chapter will explain the most useful and practical method of reading and studying case law, a method that is used throughout U.S. law schools to help students study case law: the case brief.

I. THE NATURE OF U.S. COMMON LAW, AS COMPARED TO OTHER LEGAL SYSTEMS

Law is defined as a rule or a body of rules that governs behavior and is enforced by a governing authority.[2] Societies expect two things from the law: that it should be predictable, and that it should also be flexible.[3] Law should be predictable so that people can reasonably forecast the legal consequences of their behavior. Lawyers need to be able to give clients trustworthy advice about what they should and should not do. Law should also be flexible, so that it can adjust to different situations and changing times; and it should be accessible, so that anyone interested can find, read, and understand it.

A. U.S. Common Law Contrasted with Civilian Jurisdictions

One way of characterizing legal systems is to divide them into generic civilian and common law jurisdictions based on whether or not they wholeheartedly use court-made (common) law, as well as legislation, as a source of law. Under this classification, those countries that do not use case law, or that use it only to a limited extent and

[2] *See Black's Law Dictionary* 884 (6th ed., West Group 1990).

[3] *See* A.N. Yiannopoulos, *Jurisprudence and Doctrine in Louisiana and Frances, in The Role of Judicial Decisions and Doctrine in Civil Law and in Mixed Jurisdictions* 69, 75 (Joseph Dainow ed., LSU Press 1974); Mary Ann Glendon, Michael W. Gordon, & Christopher Osakwe, *Comparative Legal Traditions in a Nutshell* 139 (West 1982); Wael B. Hallaq, *Authority, Continuity, and Change in Islamic Law* at ix (Cambridge Univ. Press 2001).

emphasize legislation as the primary source of law, are termed *civilian* jurisdictions. As mentioned before, they outnumber common law jurisdictions. The majority of civilian jurisdictions have adopted civil codes based on or influenced by the European civil codes, because of the demands of trade or colonialism, or both.[4] Using this definition, the civilian world includes Europe, Latin America, parts of Africa, the Middle East, the new post-Soviet republics, Asia, and mixed-jurisdiction enclaves such as Quebec, Scotland, Louisiana, and Puerto Rico.[5]

As compared to common law jurisdictions, civilian jurisdictions favor predictability and stability, to the detriment of flexibility, because of a fundamental difference in the way civilian and common law lawyers think about their respective systems of law. At one time, the traditional European civilian typically believed, "almost as an article of faith," that a single, complete, coherent, and logical system of law to govern all legal relationships is possible, and that the human mind is capable of thinking it out.[6] As a logical and historical consequence of this Enlightenment principle, in traditional civilian jurisdictions there were only two sources of law: legislation and custom.[7] Law is primarily and characteristically regarded as a body of rules enacted by the state, to be found in the codes and (in ever-increasing measure) in legislation supplementary to the codes. Custom includes behavioral habits that develop over time and become part of expected behavior. Legislated law is by its very nature predictable. Once a law is written and passed, what was passed is the law and can be relied upon in predicting legal consequences.

However, because it is written and can be changed only by legislative act, legislated law is inflexible. In general, because legislation is the primary source of law, a civilian lawyer interprets it expansively so as to add the flexibility needed to apply that legislation to new situations. A civilian lawyer relies primarily on legislation, and generally regards a court's decisions as mere application of legislation to a particular instance, or (at most) gap-filling. Nevertheless, civilian jurisdictions and international tribunals are increasingly and to various extents recognizing that courts necessarily create law when they apply it, and lawyers in these jurisdictions make it their business to be informed of judicial trends.[8]

---

[4] John Henry Merryman, David S. Clark, & John O. Haley, *The Civil Law Tradition: Europe, Latin America, and East Asia* 508 (Michie 1994).

[5] *Id. See also* Gabor Hamza & András Földi, *Trends of the Development of Private Law in Europe* pt. III (discussing post-Soviet Eastern European civil codes).

[6] Woodfin L. Butte, *Doctrine and Jurisprudence in Mexico*, in *The Role of Judicial Decisions and Doctrine in Civil Law and in Mixed Jurisdictions* 311, 315 (Joseph Dainow ed., LSU Press 1974).

[7] *See, e.g.*, La. Civ. Code Ann. art. 1 (West 2000).

[8] Konrad Zweigert & Hein Kötz, *Introduction to Comparative Law* 268-69 (Tony Weir trans., 3d rev. ed., Oxford Univ. Press 1998); John Henry Merryman, *On the Convergence (and Divergence) of the Civil Law and the Common Law*, 17 Stan. J. Int'l L. 357 (1981) (as reprinted in John Henry Merryman et al., *The Civil Law Tradition: Europe, Latin America, and East Asia* 16, 18 (Michie 1994). *But see* I.C.J. Acts & Docs. ch. 5 (1978):

> The Decision — Since a decision of the Court affects the legal rights and interests solely of the parties to the case and only in that particular case, it follows that the principle of *stare decisis* (the binding nature of precedents) as it exists in Common Law countries has no place in international law. It is nevertheless reasonable to suppose that where the ICJ has decided a case it would have to have serious reasons for thereafter deciding in a similar case to adopt a different approach. (See http://www.icj-cij.org/rejwww/publications.htm for further information.)

The common law approach is quite different. With some justification, civilian lawyers traditionally regard common law as a huge, chaotic, and inconsistent mass of individual rules and cases.[9] The intensely pragmatic common law lawyer, by and large, has no concept of a final and definitive formulation, simply does not care whether or not such a system exists, and is even skeptical about the possibility and practicality of such a system.[10] For her, law is characteristically the uncodified, unlegislated law found in the decisions of the courts.[11] Although legislation will prevail if it conflicts with prior case law, in the past legislation was traditionally regarded with suspicion as a suspension of the common law.[12] Possibly because she still regards legislation as an encroachment on or displacement of common law, a common law lawyer interprets legislation narrowly, as compared to the civilian's more expansive interpretation.[13]

Paradoxically, although their interpretation of a particular statute may be narrower, common law courts typically have more latitude in interpreting legislation than do civilian courts. If a common law court finds a statute to be unreasonable, the court endeavors to interpret it in a fair and reasonable manner[14]—sometimes to the point that one can argue that the court has effectively changed the language of the statute, as shall be shown in the exercises following Chapter 7. In conclusion, in civilian jurisdictions legislation tends to have more authority and courts less. In common law jurisdictions, legislation has a bit less authority and courts have more.

Because each case is considered individually, common law is more flexible than legislation.[15] It has no concept of a final and definitive formulation. Predictability is provided by the concept known as *stare decisis*: the courts' policy to stand by *precedent* (previous decisions) and not to disturb a settled point. In other words, similar cases must be decided similarly. When faced with a client's legal problem, a common law attorney researches other cases with similar legal issues and similar facts, and compares the client's case to those earlier cases. If the case has the same legal issue and is factually similar to one or more earlier cases, it will be decided the same way. If, however, the facts of the case or the legal issue involved are substantially different from an earlier case or cases, then the decision will be different. This methodology requires that the lawyer constantly scrutinize judicial decisions to analyze which facts were determinative of the courts' decisions and why, as well as exactly what issue was being considered. It also requires that case law be both recorded and accessible.

Civilian reasoning tends to be more purely deductive, meaning beginning with a general premise and then working down to a specific instance. The lawyer begins with a

[9] J.W. Tubbs, *The Common Law Mind: Medieval and Early Modern Conceptions* 173 (Johns Hopkins Univ. Press 2002).

[10] *See* Butte, *supra* note 6, at 315.

[11] *See* Frederick Pollock & Frederic William Maitland, 1 *The History of English Law: Before the Time of Edward I* at xxv (2d ed., Little, Brown 1899).

[12] Roscoe Pound, *The Development of American Law and Its Deviation from English Law*, 67 Law Q. Rev. 49, 59 (1951).

[13] *See* Karl N. Llewellyn, *Remarks on the Theory of Appellate Decision and the Rules or Canons About How Statutes Are to Be Constructed*, 3 Vand. L. Rev. 395, 404 (1950); *see, e.g., Duncan v. Walker*, 533 U.S. 167, 121 S. Ct. 2120, 2125 (2001).

[14] Tubbs, *supra* note 9, at 185.

[15] *See* Zweigert & Kötz, *supra* note 8, at 269.

general principle, analyzes its major premises, then the minor premises, and concludes that the principle applies (or not) to the client's problem.[16] In contrast, the reasoning used by a common law attorney combines inductive, deductive, and analogical reasoning. Inductive reasoning is the reverse of deductive reasoning. It moves from specific observations to generalizations. Thus, a common law attorney uses the methods of empirical science to derive general principles from case law.[17] He then organizes those general principles using deductive logic. Finally, using analogical reasoning, he compares facts of different cases and infers that if the facts are similar in important respects, then the courts' decisions should be similar as well.[18]

To explain this another way, the *common law* is the law of the case, as interpreted by courts; *civil law* is the law provided by legislation and expounded upon by legal scholars. The result is that the civilian lawyer goes from the general legislated law to the specific case at hand, whereas, in contrast, the common law lawyer builds her legal reasoning from the specifics of prior cases to derive the general principles applicable to the situation at hand. Even where a statute is controlling, a common law attorney will begin with the statute, analyze the case law that has interpreted that statute, and then compare the specific facts of those cases to the facts of the situation at hand. The result is often the same or similar under both legal systems, but the reasoning process and methodology used are different.

Examination methods in U.S. law schools reflect this difference in logical reasoning. In general, the aim of an examination in a non-U.S. law course (or a non-law course in the United States) is to test whether the student read and understood theoretical principles. The questions may simply require the student to repeat the language of the course materials. In contrast, law school examinations in the United States typically test whether the student has mastered the reasoning and methodology of the topic and can apply it in a practical situation, using deduction, induction, and analogy. In other words, can the student use the material the way a practicing attorney would if a client walked in his office door?

A typical U.S. law school course exam presents a complicated hypothetical client problem and asks the student to analyze the strengths and weaknesses of the client's problem in light of the case law studied in the course. The student is to write an essay analysis of the problem in an organized and systematic fashion known as *IRAC* (Issue, Rule, Application, Conclusion) analysis, which will be explained in Chapter 3. IRAC analysis itself is used as the foundation for most legal documents in the United States; therefore, using it on an examination gives the student further practice with this type of analytical thinking. As part of IRAC analysis, the student writes a deductive/analogical explanation of the law based on the principles he learned through inductive analysis of the cases studied in class. Generally, these U.S. exam questions have no "right" or "correct" answer, because the professor wants to see if the student understands the material enough to be able to formulate arguments on both sides of the legal issues being tested. Looking for arguments instead of answers is something that makes most LL.M. candidates uncomfortable at first.

---

[16] *See* 1 *Webster's Third New International Dictionary* 589 (Merriam-Webster 1981).
[17] *See id.*, vol. 2, at 1155.
[18] *See id.*, vol. 1, at 77.

B. Background Norms of United States Law

1. *United States Law as Compared to Shar'ia (Islamic) Law*

The preceding discussion focused on civilian legal systems because civilian concepts are widespread throughout the world; most countries have derived at least some of their legislation from one of the civil codes or have been influenced by them. Most non–common law jurisdictions limit courts' authority to merely interpreting law. Therefore, most LL.M. students are conversant with some or all of these concepts and can profit from the comparison, including Islamic students; however, other characteristics of United States and other Western European legal systems are likely to be unfamiliar to attorneys from Islamic systems.

Modern common law distinguishes between law and morality, and recognizes that one might be morally obligated but not legally obligated to do or not do something.[19] One well-established principle of common law is that generally there is no duty to rescue another person, even if the potential rescuer realizes that some action on his or her part is necessary for the other's protection or aid, unless there is a special relationship between the two parties.[20] For example, suppose you see a blind man trying to cross the street and realize that an oncoming car will hit him unless you stop or warn him.[21] Common law imposes no duty on you to do either.[22] Most Americans would feel a *moral* obligation to warn the man, but common law has refused to impose a *legal* obligation because it is believed that to impose a duty to rescue would discourage rescuers: People would avoid situations in which they might be legally required to rescue someone.[23]

In addition to a conscious separation of law and morality, common law and Islamic law differ with regard to whether the law changes. It is understood that common law changes over time, as society and technology change. When courts find that the policy and societal reasons for a particular precedent no longer apply, they change the law, explaining and justifying their reasoning in lengthy case opinions. In contrast, Islamic law is regarded as the law revealed by God and is in principle immutable.[24] Society must adapt itself to the law rather than the other way around.[25]

---

[19] *See, e.g.*, John Austin, *The Province of Jurisprudence Determined* 163 (H.L.A. Hart ed., Wendenfeld & Nicholson 1954); Oliver Wendell Holmes, *The Path of the Law*, in *Collected Legal Papers* 172 (1920) ("What constitutes the law? . . . [I]f we take the view of our friend the bad man we shall find that he does not care two straws for the axioms or deductions, but he does want to know what the . . . courts are likely to do in fact. I am much of his mind. The prophecies of what the courts will do in fact, and nothing more pretentious, are what I mean by the law."). *See also* Lon L. Fuller, *The Morality of Law* 106 (rev. ed., Yale Univ. Press 1969) (indicating that Holmes's view is somewhat overstated); *Ronald Dworkin and Contemporary Jurisprudence* 1-73 (Marshall Cohen ed., Duckworth 1984) (presenting various views of the relation between law and morality).

[20] *See* Restatement (Second) of Torts §§ 314, 302.

[21] Restatement (Second) of Torts § 314, illus. 1.

[22] *Id.*

[23] Richard W. Wright, *Hand, Posner, and the Myth of the "Hand Formula,"* in *Negligence in the Law II*, 4 Theoretical Inquiries L.J. 145, 237-38 (2003).

[24] Zweigert & Kötz, *supra* note 8, at 304; Merryman, Clark, & Haley, *supra* note 4, at 8; Westbrook, *supra* note 1, at 859-60.

[25] Zweigert & Kötz, *supra* note 8, at 304.

Furthermore, Islamic law does not distinguish between moral and legal obligations because it regards law and religion as intimately connected.[26] Finally, because the only law is that given by God, "court judgments are seen as momentary, atomistic events with no precedential effect, even for the judge who issued them."[27] Consequently, Islamic LL.M. candidates in the United States may at first get the impression that the common law system is inconsistent, lacks historical grounds, and is amoral.

A historical explanation for the Western view is possible, however. In the classical view of ancient Rome and Greece, no distinction was made between law, ethics, religion, and politics. Even today, in some forms of Judaism, no distinction is made between law and religion. Then, in the fourth century C.E., Saint Augustine of Hippo introduced a distinction between two "cities": the City of God, which is the foundation of religion and morality; and the City of Man, which is the foundation of law and politics.[28] Augustine premised this distinction on a statement made by Christ, as stated in the Bible: "Render therefore unto Caesar the things that are Caesar's and unto God the things that are God's." Since Augustine, two different views of the relation between these two "Cities" have developed. The Platonic-Augustinian-Protestant tradition emphasizes the extent to which the City of Man should emulate but not try to install (instantiate) the City of God. In contrast, the Aristotelian-Thomistic view asserts the existence of a seamless web that encompasses law, ethics, religion, and politics. Modern European states and the United States have followed the Augustinian-Protestant model.

In the West, since the Protestant Reformation, it has been recognized that there is no consensus on an encompassing religious vision. Consequently, Westerners do not deduce their legal or political systems from a uniform religious vision. In that sense, Western societies are secular. They do not necessarily marginalize religion, but they do limit its role in defining governments and laws.

The underlying common law policy or principle is that law is an invention of society. Although it is generally hoped that law will agree with morality, law is an instrument of humankind, and can do harm. If, for example, law created a duty to rescue, and thereby discouraged people from rescuing each other, then law would be making society worse, not better. Therefore, law should govern only societal relations and behavior, and should avoid religious implications and impositions, so as to promote toleration of differences in religious beliefs and to maximize individual liberty. Law should interfere with individual liberty only when an individual has transgressed the liberty of another individual. Otherwise, morality, like religion, is a private concern. Nevertheless, anytime a common law court attempts to reach a "just" or "equitable" decision, it relies on fundamental precepts of morality, although it uses legal reasoning and norms of public policy to determine what is just or equitable.

---

[26] *See* S.H. Amin, *Middle East Legal Systems* 25-26 (Royston 1985).

[27] Westbrook, *supra* note 1, at 873-74.

[28] St. Augustine of Hippo, The City of God, especially Book XIV, chs. 1, 2, 8; Book XIV, ch. 17 (New York: Modern Library 1950).

2. *United States Law as Compared to Asian Legal Traditions*

Attorneys whose legal training reflects the philosophy of Confucianism may also be uncomfortable with common law.[29] Although China's and other Asian countries' current legal systems represent a break with Confucianism, attorneys have found that it is relatively easy to formally break with traditions, but very difficult to completely overcome the influence of a tradition that was practiced for centuries.[30] Therefore, a comparative discussion of some of the background norms of that tradition may help in understanding U.S. common law.

The adversarial nature of common law conflicts with Confucianism, as do the facts that in Western systems, important questions of social life are regulated by rules of objective law, and disputes in these areas are resolved in the courts.[31] In most legal systems of the Far East, disputes are traditionally resolved by techniques other than suits at law. In these systems, informal means of dispute resolution are enormously more important than they are in the West.[32] As Confucius taught, social relations are part of the natural order: humans and God, Heaven and earth, all things living and inert are organic parts of a harmoniously ordered and integrated universe.[33] Therefore, the goal of each member of humanity must be to keep his or her thoughts, feelings, and actions in perfect accordance with cosmic harmony, and conduct himself or herself so as not to disturb the natural balance of these relations.[34]

Traditionally, anyone who disturbed social tranquility by calling in a state court and trying to put a fellow citizen publicly in the wrong was regarded as a disruptive, boorish, and uncultivated person who lacked the virtues of modesty and readiness to compromise. Legislation was primarily concerned with criminal and administrative law; private law was comparatively unimportant.

In the United States and internationally, alternative and informal dispute resolution mechanisms are becoming increasingly important for both commerce and private disputes. The vast majority of suits (85%) are resolved without trial, using informal methods such as negotiation, mediation, and arbitration because they are faster, are less expensive, and (especially with negotiation and mediation) often lead to more satisfactory results. Therefore, it is important to remember that although the United States remains an extremely litigious society, most disputes are in fact settled without litigation.

Nevertheless, many attorneys from the Far East and even from civilian jurisdictions are uncomfortable with the adversarial nature of suits at common law. In non-common law trials, both parties present evidence to the judge and each tries to persuade the court that both the law and the facts are in that party's favor.[35] Neither

[29] *See* Chin Kim, *Selected Writings on Asian Law* 41-45 (F.B. Rothman 1982).
[30] Daniel C.K. Chow, *The Legal System of the People's Republic of China in a Nutshell* 62 (West Group 2003).
[31] Zwiegert & Kötz, *supra* note 8, at 286-87.
[32] *Id.*
[33] *Id.*
[34] *Id.*; David S. Clark, *Tracing the Roots of American Legal Education: A Nineteenth-Century German Connection*, in 1 *The History of Legal Education* 406-07 (Steve Sheppard ed., Salem Press 1999).
[35] *See generally* Clark, *supra* note 34, at 1013-60 (comparing civil procedure in various civilian jurisdictions to that in the United States).

party concerns himself or herself much with the other side's case. The judge (and only the judge) can question either party and is free to conduct his or her own inquiries. In the United States, trials are more like blood-free gladiatorial combats: Each party is responsible not only for presenting his or her own case but also for discrediting the adversary's case. To prepare for this combat (trial), the parties' lawyers have broad powers of discovery, and although he or she has supervisory power, the judge intervenes only when attorneys quarrel over discovery issues. The judge's role is more like that of a referee at a boxing match, who watches the combat, makes sure that the parties follow the rules, and then, at the end, declares victory for one side and defeat for the other. The underlying belief of the adversarial system is that setting the parties against each other encourages truth-telling and gives the trier of fact, whether judge or jury, a more complete explanation of what led to the parties' dispute. Each side is motivated to try to prove that the other side is not telling the truth, or is telling only part of the truth. One side or the other will be able to establish to the satisfaction of the judge that the other side lacks credibility. Though no legal system works perfectly, the adversarial system works often enough that many attorneys in the United States believe very strongly in and vocally defend its effectiveness.

3. United States Legal Philosophy as Compared to Marxist/Leninist Theories

The three most discussed and debated aspects of U.S. political and legal theory are probably market economy, limited government, and the rule of law. The nature of these three concepts has been the subject of countless dissertations and scholarly works, and limitations of space preclude much discussion here. Although there has been a major movement toward market economies and civilian legal systems since the fall of the Soviet Union, enough Marxist-Leninist tradition remains in some systems that it may still be useful to provide some comparison.

Generally speaking, Marxist-Leninist theory posits that humankind has become dysfunctional as a result of its socioeconomic and political environment.[36] The historical mission of socialist law was to cleanse humanity of this dysfunction and prepare it for the ultimate demise of law under communism. Marxist-Leninist thinking presumes a collective good to which the individual good is subservient. It also presumes the existence of an intellectual elite with knowledge of social science (usually members of the Communist Party). This knowledge entitles the intellectual elite to use law and government as an instrument to serve the collective good. Law, therefore, is regarded as an instrument wielded by the intellectual elite through the government with the aim of perfecting human beings and creating a new socialist man who sees himself in solidarity with his society.

Because law is regarded as an order emanating from the sovereign law-giver for the collective good, an individual citizen has no right to disobey it. The power of the sovereign to legislate is absolute, and there is no zone of individual privacy insulated from legal regulation. Similar to Islamic legal traditions, which do not separate law and

[36] Glendon, Gordon, & Osakwe, *supra* note 3, at 278-79 (1982).

morality, Marxist-Leninist theory makes no separation between law and politics. In addition to being regarded as an instrument of social engineering, law is considered to be determined by economics and the politics of class consciousness.

In contrast, the U.S. common law system rejects the concept of a collective good, focusing instead on the individual good.[37] This individual good is conceptualized in terms of natural rights theory, specifically a conception that the individual has certain rights that must be protected. As stated in the Declaration of Independence: "We hold these truths to be self-evident, that all men are created equal, that they are endowed by their Creator with certain unalienable Rights, that among these are Life, Liberty, and the pursuit of Happiness." Government's primary role is to preserve, protect, and enhance these individual rights.

The individual, in exchange for consent to be governed, agrees to abide by law.[38] The government, as well as the individual, must abide by the law, which applies to all, without discrimination: "A government of laws, not of men."[39] However, it is recognized that power tends to corrupt and that government must therefore be limited (controlled) by internal checks and balances.[40] An independent judiciary, the jury system, and judicial review are examples of checks on governmental power.[41] Nevertheless, despite such checks and balances, if a government becomes overly powerful and destructive of individual rights, then the people governed have the right to alter or abolish that government and institute a new one more in keeping with their safety and happiness.[42]

The United States was conceived as a commercial republic, based on Montesquieu's theories about the stability of compound republics.[43] The founders of the United States began with John Locke's theory that men have the right to possess those things they have produced through their own labor, and that encouraging production produces more and better products that will later be shared through trade.[44] A market economy and the effects of competition encourage this "Technological Project,"[45] thus gradually

[37] *See generally* William B. Ewald, *What's So Special About American Law?*, 26 Okla. City U. L. Rev. 1083 (2001) (discussing fundamental characteristics of American law).

[38] *See* Declaration of Independence ("[T]o secure these rights, governments are instituted among men, deriving their just powers from the consent of the governed. That, whenever any form of government becomes destructive of these ends, it is the right of the people to alter or to abolish it, and to institute new government").

[39] F.A. Hayek, *Planning and the Rule of Law*, in *The Road to Serfdom* ch. 6 (University of Chicago Press 1994); Michael Oakeshott, *The Rule of Law*, in *On History and Other Essays* 119-64 (Barnes & Noble 1983).

[40] *The Federalist* No. 51 (James Madison): "If men were angels, no government would be necessary. If angels were to govern men, neither external nor internal controls on government would be necessary. In framing a government which is to be administered by men over men, the great difficulty lies in this: you must first enable the government to control the governed; and in the next place oblige it to control itself."

[41] *The Federalist* Nos. 78, 79, 83 (Alexander Hamilton).

[42] Declaration of Independence.

[43] *The Federalist* No. 9 (Alexander Hamilton).

[44] John Locke, *The Second Treatise of Government: An Essay Concerning the Origin, Extent and End of Civil Government* (1690).

[45] Francis Bacon, *Essays, Advancement of Learning, New Atlantis, and Other Works, Essays* 13, 16-17 (New York: Classic Books 2000). René Descartes, *Discourse on Method* (Indianapolis: Hacket 1993) (3d trans. Donald A. Cress).

improving a society's general quality of life.[46] In a famous essay, James Madison posited that the multiplicity of economic interests that results from the Technological Project, if properly controlled by the rule of law, can stabilize a compound republic.[47] Individuality, described as "self interest, rightly understood" is a positive quality, beneficial to society.

In contrast with communist theory, human beings are not regarded as corrupted by their environment, but as having free will and the capacity to choose between right (self-government and the Protestant work ethic) and wrong (intruding on the rights of others).[48] Unbridled greed and immoral behavior in the marketplace are not generic characteristics of the capitalist system but merely instances in which human beings have exercised their free will to do wrong. Government, being a creation of humanity, is as likely to be corrupted as humans are, and therefore must be limited and controlled. Its primary functions include protection against outside attack and protection against those who violate others' unalienable rights. Government's domestic role is to discourage and punish serious wrongs that intrude on others' rights. Thus, the purpose of intellectual property, security regulations, antitrust, and other laws is to encourage trade and development among individuals while discouraging dishonesty and unethical marketplace behavior.

II. COMPARATIVE DEVELOPMENT OF WESTERN LEGAL SYSTEMS

A. The Civil Law Tradition

Civil law is the older of the two European systems. The crucial event in the development of the civil law tradition was Emperor Justinian's compilation of Roman law around 534 C.E. However, Justinian's Digest did not come to the forefront of European law until around 1050 C.E., when it was rediscovered by Italian universities and gradually developed into the *jus commune* (shared law) of Europe. The Digest was not the only law in effect: Law in individual European countries was typically a mixture of Roman law, local customs, canon (church) law, and the *lex mercatoria* (law merchant). In the 16th and 17th centuries, as the center of legal scholarship shifted from Italy to France and Holland, the methods of the French legal humanists and the Dutch natural law school replaced the methods of the Italian universities and commentators. Jurists such as Grotius, Domat, and Pothier updated the Digest, using a systematic theory of law grounded in what they conceived to be the universal law of nature.

---

[46] David Hume, *Of Commerce*, in *Essays, Moral, Political and Literary* (Eugene F. Miller ed., Liberty Classics 1987); Adam Smith, 1 *An Inquiry into the Nature and Causes of the Wealth of Nations* bk. I, chs. 1-4 (Indianapolis: Liberty Fund 1981).

[47] *The Federalist* No. 10 (James Madison).

[48] G.W.F. Hegel, *Elements of the Philosophy of Right* (Cambridge: Cambridge Univ. Press, 1991).

As political power became sufficiently centralized, public and national law developed rapidly, and nations codified their laws in the 17th and 18th centuries, incorporating the Justinian heritage. Two of those codes — the French Civil Code of 1804 and the German Civil Code of 1896 — have served as models for many other modern civil codes, though the Swiss and Austrian civil codes were influential as well.[49] The French Code was developed in the aftermath of the French Revolution, and was considered in the development of the German Civil Code. However, whereas the French Code was a product of the French Enlightenment and revolutionary thought, the German Code was influenced by the Pandectist School, which focused on a scientific and systematic approach to law. All four codes, however, were heavily influenced by the Romanist *jus commune* and grounded in 19th-century liberalism, embracing concepts such as individual autonomy, private property, and liberty of contract. Nevertheless, they each developed a different tone, which has influenced the law and legal practices of the adopting countries. All of these codes delineate a role for the judge in applying the law, but none of the legal systems based on them accord the judge the immense prestige and full law-making role characteristic of common law jurisdictions.[50]

B. The Anglo-American Development of Common Law

The creation and rise of the common law of England can be traced back to 1066 C.E., when England was conquered by the Norman King, William the Conqueror. The Norman kings desired to consolidate their power over England, and the common law rose out of this desire. It is because of the Norman Conquest that the legal terms used in common law countries are predominantly French: *plaintiff, defendant, contract, covenant, obligation, tort, trespass, court, action, claim,* and *suit.*[51] The few Anglo-Saxon terms that remain include *witness, writ,* and *oath.*[52]

1. The Founding of Circuit Courts, Separation of Law and Religion, and Stare Decisis

William the Conqueror's successor, Henry II (1154-1189 C.E.), was an able administrator who implemented a number of new ideas in government to further consolidate his power.[53] Originally, each county or borough had its own local court, directed by a local lord, which decided most local disputes. Disputes involving large amounts of land were traditionally decided by the king. Henry II, however, founded a permanent central tribunal of expert judges, and also established systematic visitation (circuits) of counties by judges he appointed.[54] The royal judges began to mete out justice even in

---

[49] *See generally* Zweigert & Kötz, *supra* note 8, at 157-79.
[50] *See* Carl Baudenbacher, *Some Remarks on the Method of Civil Law,* 34 Tex. Int'l L.J. 333, 348-54 (1999) (discussing use of case law in specific European jurisdictions).
[51] Pollock & Maitland, *supra* note 11, at 81.
[52] *See id.* at 57-59.
[53] *See id.* at 136; Frederick G. Kempin, Jr., *An Historical Introduction to Anglo-American Law in a Nutshell* 102 (2d ed. 1973).
[54] Pollock & Maitland, *supra* note 11, at 155.

cases in which the king had no interest other than "the King's Peace," cases in which English subjects had trouble getting justice from their local court or lord.[55] Possibly because the professional royal justice was perceived of as more reliable, less biased, and fairer than the local courts, it gradually became the preferred forum.[56] In addition to consolidating Norman power, this system helped the royal purse through the fees charged by the king's court for hearing cases.[57]

By the 13th century, the habit was to appoint judges from among the attorneys practicing before the courts—from the practicing bar.[58] This became the rule by 1400, thereby uniting bench and bar as members of the same legal order and preventing the growth of a civil service bench.[59] As a result of this tradition, in the United States, courts charge fees for hearing cases, judges and lawyers have the same legal background, and judges are still appointed (or elected) only after they have acquired some status as practitioners. Furthermore, in the United States, Supreme Court Justices originally "rode circuit," just as the king's judges did, traveling around to all 13 of the original states to decide cases. Though this is no longer the case (the United States Supreme Court sits in Washington, D.C.), each of the U.S. appellate courts is called a "Circuit Court of Appeals," and to a limited extent, U.S. appellate court judges regularly travel to hear oral argument.

Roman and canon (Catholic Church) law was influential in England until Henry II and his former Chancellor and Archbishop Thomas Becket quarreled; from then on, the lay courts, rather than the ecclesiastical courts (Courts of Canon Law), were victorious in every contest between canon and common law.[60] As the practice of common law took hold, English lawyers became impatient with theories, preferring practical experience instead. Thus, they did not embrace the cosmopolitan learning of the civilians, though at times they were certainly influenced by it.[61] In an effort to provide consistency and predictability, English courts started recording judges' decisions early on (by the 13th century), so that judges and lawyers could use past decisions as precedent for future cases. Judicial opinions in the United States, for both state and federal courts, are lengthy and detailed, and are published in series of books called "reporters," which contain finding tools to help judges and lawyers research case law.

As early as the 13th century, court opinions were recorded and regarded as evidence of the law and practice for the future. By the 15th century, judges used the word *precedent* and would follow precedents—previous decisions—for the sake of certainty, even if the reasons for those earlier decisions were not immediately apparent or no longer made sense. However, by the early 17th century, the need to temper this doctrine of stare decisis with reason was brought to the forefront in the work of the influential jurist Sir Edward Coke. "According to Coke, the law was a perfection of

[55] W.S. Holdsworth, 1 *A History of English Law* 27 (1903).
[56] *See generally id.* at 37-72.
[57] J.H. Baker, *An Introduction to English Legal History* 20 (1971); *see also* Pollock & Maitland, *supra* note 11, at 159.
[58] Baker, *supra* note 57, at 65.
[59] *Id.*
[60] *See generally* Baker, *supra* note 57, at 111-35.
[61] *Id.*

artificial reason, and the accretions of legal wisdom over the centuries were more valuable than the sentiments of individual lawyers. Nevertheless, Coke would disregard precedent when he thought it necessary in an attempt to bring reason and authority into harmony."[62] In the United States, courts are bound by precedent, and generally are careful to follow it. However, they sometimes reinterpret and distinguish prior cases when new factual situations seem to demand new developments in legal thinking. This ever-shifting balance between reason and authority means that U.S. common law is always changing.

2. *The Role of Scholars*

The British emphasis on practical experience over scholarship, which began with Henry II's quarrel with Becket, has been passed on to the U.S. legal community. Although law professors' theories and explanations may at times be influential in the United States, they are still regarded as *secondary authority*, not law, and are not binding on courts. Instead, as described by Karl Llewellyn, the original drafter of the Uniform Commercial Code (the UCC, adopted in various forms and to varying extent by all 50 states in the United States), the emphasis is on the concrete, practical experience of case law:

> We have discovered that rules *alone*, mere forms of words, are worthless. We have learned that the concrete instance, the heaping up of concrete instances, the present, vital memory of a multitude of concrete instances, is necessary in order to make any general proposition, be it rule of law or any other, *mean* anything at all. Without the concrete instances the general proposition is baggage, impedimenta, stuff about the feet. It not only does not help. It hinders. . . .
>
> [T]he main thing is seeing what officials do, do about disputes, or about anything else; and seeing that there is a certain regularity in their doing—a regularity which makes possible prediction of what they and other officials are about to do tomorrow.[63]

A constant tension remains in common law jurisdictions, including the United States, between the judge's duty to do justice according to the law, without the least departure from the rules laid down by his or her predecessors, and that same judge's instinct that the law should be cultivated as a living organism. For these activist judges, "the judicial office is to develop the law in such a way that it remains consonant with justice, preserving only the principles which ought to be preserved."[64]

3. *The Jury System*

In addition to founding the royal court, Henry II implemented the accusing jury, an idea he likely brought from his contact with Islamic law during the Crusades.[65] The

[62] Baker, *supra* note 57, at 104-05.

[63] K.N. Llewellyn, *The Bramble Bush of Our Law and Its Study* 2-4 (1985).

[64] *Id.* at 290-91.

[65] *See* John Makdisi, *The Islamic Origins of the Common Law*, 77 N.C. L. Rev. 1635, 1676-94, 1726-29 (1999).

accusing jury consisted of lay witnesses who would testify as to the ownership of property in dispute, accusing the defendant of taking property that belonged to the crown.[66] Over time, the function of the accusing jury changed, though it still consists of laypersons. Using more or less random selection methods, judicial systems in the United States periodically summon citizens to jury duty (a duty of citizenship that many try to avoid). Juries are used to decide issues of fact in both criminal and civil cases, but they are not expected to be experts on law. The judge gives the jury instructions as to the applicable law, which the jurors follow to the best of their ability in deciding whether the defendant is either *guilty* or *not guilty* in a criminal trial, *liable* or *not liable* in a civil trial.

Normally, criminal juries consist of 12 jurors, whereas civil juries may consist of either 12 or 6 jurors (the latter called a *petit* or *petty jury*). The Constitution guarantees the right to a jury trial in criminal cases involving felonies,[67] and also in civil cases,[68] though defendants can waive their right to have a jury. If they decide to waive that right, then the judge decides both the facts and the law. In this instance, the process is called a *bench trial.* In contrast to the jury involved in a jury trial, the grand jury still retains some of the original accusatory function. The *grand jury* decides whether a prosecuting attorney has enough evidence to prosecute a defendant for a serious crime, but it does not actually decide whether the defendant committed the crime.

The United States jury system limits governmental power.[69] In making their decisions, juries convene in secret: No one is allowed to enter the jury room while the jurors are discussing the case. Thus, juries are free to examine and discuss in private all of the evidence presented to them. In criminal trials, if they find that the prosecution (the government) did not prove to them "beyond a reasonable doubt" that the defendant was guilty, then they acquit the defendant. Sometimes the evidence of guilt may seem overwhelming, but the jury nevertheless acquits the defendant. The O.J. Simpson trial is likely an example of such *jury nullification.* O.J. Simpson, a former football star and celebrity, was accused of brutally killing his estranged wife and her friend. Many people in the United States believe that the jury found the investigation so tainted by racism that it refused to find him guilty, despite a large amount of evidence indicating that he probably killed both people. Reviewing courts usually do not overturn jury verdicts and, under the Constitution, cannot overturn an acquittal in a criminal case.

In non-criminal cases, U.S. lay juries can be notoriously plaintiff friendly, awarding vast amounts of money to plaintiffs, especially when the plaintiff is someone regarded as sympathetic (such as a little old lady) and the defendant has deep pockets (e.g., a large corporation). For example, in 1994 a sympathetic jury awarded $2.7 million in punitive damages, plus $160,000 in medical expenses, to an elderly lady who was injured when she spilled a cup of hot McDonald's coffee on herself.[70]

---

[66] *Id.*

[67] United States Const. amend. V.

[68] United States Const. amend. VII.

[69] *See The Federalist* No. 83 (Alexander Hamilton).

[70] Liebeck v. McDonald's Rests., P.T.S., Inc., Civ. No. CV-93-02419, 1995 WL 360309 (Albuquerque, N.M. 1994) (unpublished). Though some jurors originally thought the suit was frivolous, they found the facts were overwhelmingly against McDonald's. They were offended by testimony indicating that

Although originally the jury was skeptical about the claim, it eventually decided to award the plaintiff substantial punitive damages because it found that McDonald's had been callously disregarding the safety of customers. (Under recent Supreme Court precedent, when a reviewing court finds that the amount of punitive damages awarded is excessive, it must be reduced.[71] Nevertheless, the lay jury acts as a control on both government and large corporations.

4. *Common Law Civil Procedure: Writ Pleading, the Distinction between Law and Equity, and Its Effect on the Jury System*

The King's Court, founded by Henry II, eventually developed into three individual courts: the King's Bench, the Court of Common Pleas, and the Court of the Exchequer. Each court had the power to hear (*jurisdiction over*) specific kinds of cases, but the setting for each court was the same. The judges sat on a raised bench behind a table covered with green cloth, and counsel stood in front of the judges, behind a wooden bar.[72] Each of the three courts was within earshot of the others and speakers had to compete with the noise made by the throngs of suitors, attorneys, and shopkeepers. This system lasted through five centuries and two civil wars, and the courts were closed only in times of plague or flood.[73] To this day in the United States, judges duly elected or appointed are called *members of the bench*, and attorneys may practice law only after they have passed a state *bar exam* and joined their local *bar association.*

Another aspect of law in the King's Court still affects U.S. law: the writ pleading system and the distinction it created between law and equity. Originally, someone who wanted to bring a suit to the Court of Common Pleas, which decided ordinary disputes between private parties, first had to obtain a *writ.*[74] In principle, a writ was simply a royal order that authorized a court to hear a case and instructed a sheriff to secure the defendant's attendance.[75] Once a proper writ was secured, a case brought to the Court of Common Pleas could be tried by a jury.[76] Although the writ pleading system is no longer followed in the United States, the term still remains in two circumstances: A *writ of certiorari* is issued by a supreme court when it agrees to review a specific case; and

---

McDonald's was aware that its coffee was causing serious burns when spilled, and that most people would not realize that severe burns were possible with coffee that hot. Furthermore, McDonald's had received more than 700 reports of coffee burns ranging from mild to severe, and had settled such claims for amounts up to and exceeding $500,000, but had refused to settle the claim in this case. The parties later settled the case for an undisclosed lesser amount, rather than appealing the decision.

[71] State Farm Mut. Auto. Ins. Co. v. Campbell, 538 U.S. 408 (2003). *See also* Advocat, Inc. v. Sauer, 111 S.W.3d 346 (Ark. 2003) (reducing damages awarded for negligent care in nursing home); Reed v. City of N.Y., 757 N.Y.S.2d 244 (App. Div. 2003) (affirming amount awarded plaintiff for injuries when struck by police officer on motor scooter); Mississippi Power & Light Co. v. Cook, 832 So. 2d 474 (Miss. 2002) (reducing award for bad-faith denial of workers' compensation benefits); Teamann v. Zafris, 811 A.2d 52 (Pa. Commw. Ct. 2002) (reducing damages awarded for wrongful death of child in auto accident caused by negligent highway construction).

[72] Baker, *supra* note 57, at 29.

[73] *Id.*

[74] S.F.C. Milsom, *Historical Foundations of the Common Law* 22 (Butterworths 1969).

[75] *Id.* at 22-23.

[76] *See id.* at 75.

convicted criminals have the constitutional right to petition courts for a *writ of habeas corpus*, asking that the court review their convictions.

In England, the writ system eventually became too rigid and unworkable.[77] The king's chancellor controlled the issuance of original writs.[78] The types of writs were limited, allowed for only certain remedies (money damages) and certain causes of action (such as a *writ of debt* or a *writ of trespass*). Furthermore, writs became expensive, inconvenient, and time-consuming to obtain.[79] A plaintiff unable to obtain a proper writ, and therefore left with no remedy under the law of the Court of Common Pleas, could petition the chancellor for special relief or *equity*, once he demonstrated that there was no claim at common law that could provide him with fair and just relief.[80] Eventually, the Chancery developed into a separate court with separate procedures and remedies to deal with equity cases.[81]

In general, the United States no longer have separate courts for cases that sound in equity as opposed to law. However, the historical distinction between law and equity is still maintained to the extent that, in a civil trial, a right to trial by jury is guaranteed by the Seventh Amendment of the United States Constitution "in Suits at common law." Thus, despite the merger of law and equity in 1938, a party to a civil suit may demand a jury trial if the cause of action at issue (if the legal issue involved) is one "at common law," such as for money damages for tort or breach of contract.[82] In addition to common law issues, some statutes provide that a plaintiff can demand a jury trial.[83] However, there is still no right to a trial by jury for equitable claims such as actions for injunction or specific performance.[84] (An *injunction* is a court order demanding that someone either do or not do something. Similarly, an *order for specific performance* demands that a party perform a contractual obligation as promised.)

5. Legal Education

England lacked a formal system of legal education until the 19th century, and entrance into the practice was generally through an apprenticeship system. Because knowledge of precedent was valuable, as early as the 13th-century apprentices of the bench would sit in Westminster Hall and take notes of the pleadings they heard there. However, by the mid-13th century, when the common law had become extensive and intricate, lack of education was a problem. The Inns of Court were set up to provide an education for those who practiced in the courts; there students would read manuals

---

[77] *Id.*

[78] 1 Holdsworth, *supra* note 55, at 196.

[79] *See generally* Milsom, *supra* note 74, at 53-55.

[80] 1 Holdsworth, *supra* note 55, at 196; Glendon, Gordon, & Osakwe, *supra* note 3, at 150.

[81] *See* 1 Holdsworth, *supra* note 55, at 196-99.

[82] Charles Allen Wright, *Law of Federal Courts* 610-11 (4th ed. 1983); *see also* Fed. R. Civ. P. 38. *See, e.g.*, Marseilles Hydro Power, *LLC v. Marseilles Land & Water Co.*, 299 F.3d 643 (7th Cir. 2002); Adams v. Johns-Manville Corp., 876 F.2d 702 (9th Cir. 1989).

[83] *See, e.g.*, La. Code Civ. Proc. Ann. art. 1732 (West 1996); La. Rev. Stat. Ann. § 13 (West 1996); Del. Code. Ann. tit. 25, § 5713 (1975); N.Y. Uniform City Court Act § 1806 (McKinney 1964); Wash. Rev. Code Ann. § 126 (West 1984); N.M. Stat. Ann. § 34-8A-5 (Michie 1978).

[84] Wright, *supra* note 82, at 610.

and books, listen to arguments in court, and discuss law among themselves.[85] Concurrently, the Inns of Chancery were developed to train clerks in the framing of documents used in the courts of chancery.[86] Eventually, competition between the Inns of Court and the Inns of Chancery led to the British distinction between barristers and solicitors[87]—a distinction not maintained in the United States. In the United States, all lawyers who have passed a state bar examination are regarded as equally qualified both to counsel clients and to argue before a court of that state.

Although the United States may have rejected the British tradition of distinguishing between lawyers who deal with clients (solicitors), and lawyers who deal with courts (barristers), it adopted much more than it rejected. The U.S. legal system has inherited terms such as *bar, bench, witness, writ, oath, plaintiff, defendant,* and *claim* from Britain's common law system, and it has also inherited the distinction between law and equity, as reflected in the constitutional right to a jury trial in a civil action. It has inherited the habit of choosing judges only from the ranks of practicing attorneys. Most importantly, it has inherited background norms and practices, including a distrust of legal theory and a strong faith in legal practice, as evidenced by the doctrine of stare decisis. However, even this doctrine may be limited or ignored when a judge finds a need to temper either a statute or precedent with reason, to do justice both to the parties and to the proper development of law.

III. THE STUDY OF LAW IN THE UNITED STATES: THE CASE METHOD

Before the late 19th century, in the United States as in England, law was learned primarily on an apprenticeship basis. An apprentice in a law office would be expected to read British compilations (first Edward Coke's *First Institutes of the Laws of England,* and later William Blackstone's *Commentaries on the Laws of England*), in addition to performing tasks assigned by his employer.[88] Lawyers selected and sponsored young men for membership in the bar on the basis of a "personal assessment of their character," not on their formal educational achievements.[89] This informality and lack of structured training was very much in character with the nature of legal practice in early 19th-century America.

On the American frontier, the coming of the court to town was an occasion for social gathering and a form of entertainment.[90] An exciting trial was like a combination

[85] Baker, *supra* note 57, at 68-69.
[86] *Id.* at 69-70.
[87] *Id.* at 70-72.
[88] Steve Sheppard, *An Introductory History of Law in the Lecture Hall,* in 1 *The History of Legal Education in the United States* 11-13 (Steve Sheppard ed., Salem Press 1999).
[89] William R. Johnson, *Schooled Lawyers: A Study in the Clash of Professional Cultures* 24 (New York Univ. Press 1978).
[90] *Id.* at 28.

of a circus, a parade, a gospel meeting, and a dogfight.[91] As a result, a lawyer's eminence was based not on his credentials, but on his effectiveness as a courtroom advocate and orator. For example, Abraham Lincoln entered politics only after he had achieved renown for his oratorical skill as an advocate. The quality of his legal education was never at issue: Abraham Lincoln was largely self-taught.[92] Some might even argue that the American public still regards an exciting trial as a form of gladiatorial combat, and still reveres attorneys who primarily demonstrate oratorical skill (case in point: Johnny Cochran's defense of O.J. Simpson). In Lincoln's time, however, the few law schools in existence served no important professional purpose, and at best were viewed as a useful supplement to the apprenticeship experience.[93] Law schools had little to do either with certifying professional competence or with regulating entry into the legal profession.[94]

This started to change in the mid- to late 19th century at prominent U.S. universities such as Columbia and Harvard. Harvard's history is particularly illuminating. In 1869, Charles Eliot was appointed president of Harvard University.[95] Eliot had carefully studied the great German universities, which were world-renowned at the time, and which attracted many American law students. The ideal of systematic knowledge and science (*Wissenschaft*) promulgated a reaction against the Enlightenment's speculative philosophy and natural law and in favor of empirical investigation, verification, and inductive logic, as developed by legal scholars such as Friedrich Carl von Savigny. Law professors and judges, trained in legal science, fostered the idea that correct law is identical with the opinion and practices of the people in matters of right and justice, and is the product of gradual and organic growth, not arbitrary and deliberate actions—a theory that appealed to supporters of common law. In addition to the traditional German lecture hall, German law schools developed seminar courses in which the professor gave students a statement of facts for solution at home. Each student wrote out his solution for the case, which was corrected by the instructor and discussed at subsequent class meetings.[96]

Eliot wanted Harvard to develop the strengths of the European schools and to become a great seat of learning itself. In emulation of the prestigious German universities, he favored a classroom laboratory method with an inductive reasoning process, instead of the lecture and recitation methods of instruction already used in U.S. law schools. He also wanted a definite curriculum. He brought Christopher Columbus Langdell, a Harvard graduate and New York practitioner, to the law school to implement his ideas. As dean, and with Eliot's help, Langdell focused on study methods that would develop the reasoning skills needed for practice, as well as the development of a basic curriculum and credential system. He established a law school entrance examination,

---

[91] *Id.*

[92] *See* Christopher C. Faille, *Book Review*, 45 APR Fed. Law. 54, 55 (1998) (reviewing *Daniel Webster: The Man and His Time*, by Robert V. Remeni); Steve Sheppard ed., 1 *History of Legal Education* 489 (Salem Press 1999).

[93] *Id.* at 24.

[94] *Id.*

[95] Clark, *supra* note 34, at 495, 501.

[96] *Id.* at 500.

a three-year progressive curriculum, requisite annual examinations before students could proceed to the next year, and a research function similar to that existing in German universities.[97] U.S. law schools still maintain these same characteristics.

Langdell's most significant innovation was the introduction of an instructional method utilizing Socratic dialogue to discuss case law and thereby develop reasoning skills.[98] In the case or "Socratic" method of study, the students read reported cases and other materials collected in a casebook, and the class answers questions about them instead of listening to a lecture by the professor. Langdell argued that

> [l]aw, considered as a science, consists of certain principles of doctrines. . . . Each of these doctrines has arrived at its present state by slow degrees; in other words, it is a growth, extending in many cases through centuries. . . . [T]he only way of mastering the doctrine effectually is by studying the cases in which it is embodied. But the cases which are useful and necessary for this purpose at the present day bear an exceedingly small proportion to all that have been reported."[99]

Consequently, Langdell collected those cases he felt were most useful, edited them, and compiled them into the first casebook on contracts.

Langdell's teaching was organized around cases rather than treatises, and around the search for principles rather than their explication, illustration, and application.[100] Rather than starting with the principles, Langdell required his students to extract them.[101] His first class was well described:

> The class gathered in the old amphitheatre of Dane Hall—the one lecture room of the School—and opened their strange new pamphlets, reports bereft of their only useful part, the head-notes! The lecturer opened his.
>
> "Mr. Fox, will you state the facts in the case of *Payne v. Cave*?"
>
> Mr. Fox did his best with the facts of the case.
>
> "Mr. Rawle, will you give the plaintiff's argument?"
>
> Mr. Rawle gave what he could of the plaintiff's argument.
>
> "Mr. Adams, do you agree with that?"[102]

This questioning or *Socratic* technique is now standard in American law school classrooms whenever case law is discussed. Although the case method and Socratic questioning have been adopted at some institutions in England and other common law countries, it remains the predominant method of teaching only in the United States.

The advantage of the case method is that it allows students to read and discuss original authorities and derive for themselves the principles of the law, in much the

---

[97] *Id.* at 501.
[98] *Id.*
[99] *Id.* (quoting Christopher C. Langdell, *A Selection of Cases on the Law of Contracts, with References and Citations* (1871)).
[100] William P. LaPiana, *Logic and Experience: The Origin of Modern American Legal Education* 24-25 (1994).
[101] *Id.* at 25.
[102] *Id.* at 22 (quoting Samuel L. Batchelder, *Christopher C. Langdell*, 18 Green Bag 437, 440 (1906)).

same way that they will do in practice.[103] As mentioned earlier, scholarly treatises on the law, though persuasive, are not themselves law in the United States. Reading cases allows students to read primary law, rather than persuasive authority, and trains students in the kind of analytical and analogical thinking required in common law jurisdictions. The case method has the added advantage of emphasizing the characteristic feature of the common law: the evolution of principles from decisions in actual cases. It focuses the student's attention on the processes of analogy and distinction, and is designed to accustom the student to view the law not as a collection of rules, but as a living, dynamic, and always-changing web.

In its purest form, Socratic dialogue consists of the professor posing questions and asking students to respond, with little direct input from the professor. The question posed is based either on a case in the casebook, or on a hypothetical case designed to show the students how a principle of law operates. Students may "tune out" a traditional lecture, but Socratic dialogue forces students to pay closer attention to the classroom interaction because they know they may be called upon at any time. When the professor asks a question, every student mentally responds by comparing his or her answer with that given by the student who is responding orally. The constant questioning thus requires the student to develop his or her own analysis of the law. As with most things, the case method also has its disadvantages. It is slow and relatively time-consuming in relation to the amount of "hard" knowledge of law that can be imparted, because the professor attempts to force the class to derive the legal principles from the readings, rather than stating those principles himself. To return to the example given of Langdell's classroom dialogue, typically what happens is that neither Mr. Rawle nor Mr. Adams, nor even a third student, will properly present the plaintiff's argument.

Because of its disadvantages, generally only first-year law courses, such as contracts and torts, use Socratic dialogue exclusively (or almost exclusively). So, for example, in an instance where neither Mr. Rawle nor Mr. Adams presents the plaintiff's argument correctly, often the professor will present the argument himself rather than delaying the class still further. Upper-level courses, the ones usually taken by LL.M. students, generally use a mixture of lecture and the case method. Regardless of which method the professor uses, professors in U.S. law schools generally expect students to participate in classroom discussion. Such participation requires more intensive preparation than merely reading the course book, and your professor will be disappointed (at the least) or even peeved if you are unprepared — the professor counts on students' having thoroughly studied the material, and it is *much* more difficult for her to teach when the class is unprepared to participate in a discussion.

IV. BRIEFING CASES

Because of this active learning method, merely reading the assigned cases is not enough to prepare for class. Students in U.S law schools must prepare a *brief* of

[103] *See* LaPiana, *supra* note 100, at 26.

each case assigned. Briefing cases leads to a greater understanding of the case opinion and encourages one's memory of it.[104] To begin with, if you are called on in class to discuss a case, you will not have time to fumble around in your casebook for the correct answer—you need to have it right in front of you, in easily understood, concise language so that you can quickly answer the professor's questions. Second, even if you are not called on in class, your brief enables you to follow the classroom conversation and take notes on what the professor indicates is important. Furthermore, reading assignments are lengthy, and you will not have time to read the casebook again after class; therefore, case briefs (with the addition of your class notes) become a primary tool in preparing for the final exam. Whether you are one of the more active speakers in class, or you try to avoid speaking whenever possible, you will maximize your learning by preparing the material properly.

A case brief is a **one-page**, organized, written summary of the important elements of a judicial opinion, *in your own words.* It is the best way to distill what is important out of a case. In class, you will add notes to your brief as class discussion warrants. Within a few weeks, briefing becomes faster and easier, and after a while you may find yourself briefing your cases in the margins of your casebook, rather than on a separate piece of paper. Nevertheless, as a rule of thumb, plan on at least two to four hours of preparation time for each hour of class.

English is probably not your first language, and therefore, especially at the beginning of your LL.M. studies, you probably read more slowly in English than you do in your native language. *All the more reason to maximize the efficiency of your studying.* Before you tackle a reading assignment, look at its placement in your casebook, and at the table of contents: What are the legal concepts that this section will discuss? How are they organized? How do the cases fit into that structure? It is probably best to skim the cases before reading them carefully, just to gain some understanding of what legal concept they are illustrating. You may even want to consult a one-volume treatise or hornbook on the subject to gain some preliminary understanding and make your reading easier, and you might look up unfamiliar terms in a law dictionary. (*Black's Law Dictionary* is a good one.) Bear in mind that unlike Langdell, who used cases to illustrate certain major concepts, casebooks now include some cases primarily for historical purposes or to illustrate a minority position. You will not want to spend as much time on these kinds of cases. The primary mistake most students make at the beginning is to assume that they must "learn" each case presented in the casebook. They then get lost in the forest of cases, rather than learning how to use the concepts illustrated by the cases.[105] The professor will eventually be testing how well you use those concepts, *not* whether you remember each case.

---

[104] *See* Robert H. Miller, *Law School Confidential: The Complete Law School Survival Guide: By Students, for Students* 113 (1st ed., St. Martin's Griffin 2000).

[105] *See* Carolyn J. Nygren, *Starting off Right in Law School* 67-71 (1997); Ann M. Burkhart & Robert A. Stein, *How to Study Law and Take Law Exams in a Nutshell* 98-104 (1996); Richard Michael Fischl & Jeremy Paul, *Getting to Maybe: How to Excel on Law School Exams* 3-11 (1999).

A. Components of a Case Brief

After you have skimmed the case, and have some idea of the legal concept it is discussing, the first requirement in briefing a case is to **read the case carefully**. As you read, concentrate on the six elements of a case brief:

1. facts
2. procedural history (or *posture* of the case)
3. issue
4. holding
5. rationale (or reasoning or *ratio decidendi*)
6. rule

Then, on a piece of lined paper (or on your laptop), jot down the name of the case and the six elements, and fill in these headings according to the following guidelines. If you are doing this by hand and not on a laptop, you may want to write your brief on only the left half of your page, and reserve the other half (the right half) for class notes. First jot down the name of the case, the court in which it was decided, and the year of the decision (as well as the page of your casebook on which the case starts). You will need the information on the court and year to determine how current and important the case is (or was). The sections of a case brief are more fully described as follows:

TITLE, DECIDING COURT, YEAR

1. ***Facts*** The fact section should include a brief summary of the facts that gave rise to the litigation (who the parties are, and what happened), and the *relevant* or *legally significant facts*—the facts on which the writing court relied in reaching its decision. Exclude extraneous information. The particular facts of the case are much more important in the United States than in civilian systems, because they are essential in determining the fitness of the case as precedent for later cases. You might want to develop your own simple symbols for commonly used words: *Plaintiff* is often indicated as "P" or "Π" (pi), *defendant* can be indicated as "D" or "Δ" (delta). If there are a number of parties or causes, it might be best to use names to avoid confusion, rather than "P" or "D."

2. ***Procedural History*** The procedural history explains how the case came before the writing court. Most cases in casebooks are opinions written by higher-level courts, not the original trial court. Therefore, begin by stating the plaintiff's *cause of action* (the plaintiff's legal claim against the defendant), and the trial court's *disposition* (what the trial court decided); and then explain how the case got to the writing court (who is appealing and why).

3. ***Issue*** Usually in an opinion, the court itself states the legal issue. Very often, this statement appears early in the opinion, especially in a U.S. Supreme Court case. If so, it is quite simple to restate the issue in the case brief. If the opinion does not straightforwardly state the issue, then examine what the trial court allegedly did wrong. Ultimately, no matter how the opinion phrases it, the issue is whether the legal rule applies to the facts of the case. Once you discern it, state the issue as a

one-sentence question incorporating the key facts and the legal rule that is in controversy. There may be more than one issue. If so, number and list them.

4. *Holding or Judgment* The *holding* is the disposition of the appellate case you are briefing, and it answers the question asked by the issue. What did the writing court decide? Who won, who lost, and what remedy was given by the writing court? Be careful here: Some professors use the term *holding* to refer to the general legal principle upon which the court decided the case, although this text calls this *rule* of the case, as explained in item 6. As you become familiar with your professor's terminology, you will learn which she is asking for.

5. *Rationale* This may be the most important part of the brief. The rationale must explain why the writing court decided the way it did. A commonly used synonym is *ratio decidendi*: the reason for the decision. A court could base its decision on any number of rationales. The reasoning of the court is usually based on precedent, and the result may be the same (or different) as in the precedent because the facts of the case at hand are similar to (or different from) the facts of the precedential case. Sometimes decisions are based on equity (fairness or justice). Other decisions are based on policy interests and the interests of society as a whole; sometimes on logic and a desire to avoid inconsistencies in the law; and very often on a combination of two or more of these reasons. Sometimes the rationale for a decision is easy to find, but sometimes it must be teased out of the opinion. *All of these rationales, as well as the rules described in item 6, should become tools that you will take with you to help reason through questions on the final exam.* Therefore, it is important to understand them and learn how they affect the area of law you are studying.

6. *Rule* In simple, clear language, state the general principle that caused the court to decide the way it did, and which can be applied to future cases.

Once you have delineated these six sections, your brief is essentially done. However, before you move on, you should consider one or two more things. Consider whether there are any significant *obiter dicta*, observations made by the court directed at types of facts not present in the case.[106] Dicta are not necessary to the holding of the opinion but may nevertheless be interesting and contribute to your understanding of the law.

Consider also the contents of any *concurring* or *dissenting opinion.* Although a U.S. trial court usually has only one judge, a reviewing court consists of at least three judges (nine judges in the case of the United States Supreme Court). For an opinion to become law, a majority of these judges must agree on it. Sometimes a judge will agree with the opinion, but on a slightly different reasoning. That judge will write a concurring opinion, also called a *concurrence.* The rationale of that concurrence may add to your understanding of the law. Likewise, a deciding judge who strongly disagrees with the majority opinion may write a *dissent.* The *dissent* is the losing position, and therefore is not law, but you should still consider what the judge found objectionable about the majority opinion. Occasionally, the reasoning of a dissent will eventually triumph in a later case—remember, the hallmark of common law is its ability to change.

[106] Samuel Mermin, *Law and the Legal System, An Introduction* 289 (2d ed. 1982).

Finally, think again for a few minutes about why the case was assigned: Did it significantly change the law, does it illustrate an established principle, or was it assigned merely for historical reasons? The reason you had to read the case may or may not be immediately apparent, but it should become clear before the final examination. Additionally, be sure you described the case in your own words. Not only will this force you to develop your English-language skills, but also it will force you to determine exactly what the court said, which concepts and facts were essential to its decision, and the proper legal terminology and procedures. Simply copying parts of the case will not help, but if you can describe the concept in your own words, you can feel reasonably confident that you understand it and will be able to explain it orally in class (and in a concise manner on your exam).[107]

Sometimes you may find that you simply do not understand everything in the case — the rationale is confused, or you cannot formulate an appropriate rule, or the stated facts seem ambiguous or incomplete. In this situation, you might want to see whether the case is mentioned or discussed in a hornbook or treatise, or simply jot down what you understand as well as what is confusing to you. If the professor calls on you, you can then explain the limits of your understanding, as well as the source of your confusion. Do not be too concerned that you may not look like a genius in class: The point that puzzled you may be exactly the point the professor will want to discuss, and he may then applaud your insight. At the very least, remember that if you understood everything, you would be the professor, not a student. The most important thing is that you show the professor that you read the case and thought about it, not necessarily that you understood everything before the class even took place. After briefing your case, carefully examine the noted cases in the casebook, or the questions that follow it. Often these are as important to your understanding of the topic as the original case, or even more so.

Read the following case. As you read, identify the issue, holding, facts, rationale, and rule. Then read the following sample brief and compare it to the opinion.

JEROME JONES, JR., Plaintiff-Appellee v. ADRIEN SMITH, ET AL., Defendants-Appellants*

Court of Appeal of Louisiana, Ninth Circuit

April 14, 1976

JUDGES:

WATSON, HOLMES, and PETERS, JJ. HOLMES, J., dissents and assigns written reasons.

OPINION BY:

WATSON

[107] Burkhart & Stein, *supra* note 105, at 104-05.

* Adapted from *Bourque v. Duplechin*, 331 So. 2d 40 (La. Ct. App. 1976).

OPINION:

Plaintiff, Jerome Jones, Jr., filed this suit to recover damages for personal injuries received in a soccer game. Made defendants were Adrien Smith, a member of the opposing team who inflicted the injuries, and Smith's liability insurer, Allstate Insurance Company. The trial court rendered judgment in favor of plaintiff against both defendants and defendants have appealed. We affirm.

Both Smith and Allstate contend that the trial court erred: in not finding that Jones assumed the risk of injury by participating in the soccer game; and in failing to find that Jones was guilty of contributory negligence. Defendant Smith also contends that the trial court erred in finding him negligent. Allstate further contends that the trial court erred in finding coverage under its policy, which excludes injury intended or expected by the insured.

On June 9, 1974, Jones was playing goalie on a team sponsored by Boo Boo's Lounge. Smith was a member of the opposing team sponsored by Murray's Steak House and Lounge. According to Jones, who watched the first half of the game, the game was "a little bit rough," with players from both sides pulling on shirts, running into each other pretty hard, and elbowing; more of the rough conduct was initiated by the Murray's Steak House team, but Jones admitted that "I'm not going to say we weren't pushing back."

Jones began playing the position of goalie in the second half of the game; for the first five minutes of the second half, he was not involved in any play because the Boo Boo's Lounge team kept the ball in the opposing team's half of the field. Between five and ten minutes into the second half of the game, a Murray's Steak House player, whom Jones later learned was Smith, broke away with the ball and proceeded to run toward the goal Jones was defending; two of Jones's teammates were in close pursuit. To avoid the defenders, Smith was running and kicking the ball about 10 to 12 feet in front of himself. Smith last kicked the ball when he was seven or eight feet outside the penalty area boundary.The penalty area is an area marked on the field and extends about 18 yards in front of the goal. The goalie is the only player allowed to touch the ball with the hands, and only if the ball is within the penalty area; a ball controlled by a goalie's hands is considered "out of fair play" for all other players until the goalie releases the ball.

Jones came out of the goal box and into the penalty area to intercept. He waited for Smith to kick the ball one last time and then Jones advanced. When the ball crossed into the penalty area, Jones was about six feet inside the penalty area boundary line; he caught and was pulling the ball to his chest with both hands when he realized Smith was not stopping and was about to charge into him. Holding onto the ball, he turned and ran from Smith, a much bigger man, zigzagging in an effort to get away. Smith, unfortunately, was faster, grabbed Jones from behind in a classic American football tackle, and threw him to the ground, landing on top of him. Jones's neck was broken as a result, and he is now confined to a wheelchair. According to Smith's declaration, he "forgot" he was playing soccer, but in any case was only joking and did not mean to hurt Jones.

Pertinent to the trial court's decision was the following testimony:

Plaintiff Jones, age 22 at the time of trial, testified that he is 5′7″ tall. He knew there was a possibility of being slide-tackled, but as goalie had never imagined what actually happened, which he regarded as unbelievable under the circumstances.

John Gregory Laborde, a student at Tulane Law School, testified that he witnessed the incident from the sidelines and saw Smith turn and run directly toward Jones.

Smith did not attempt to decrease his speed and instead charged into the penalty zone, and seemed deliberately to tackle Jones.

Franz Lockerwood, soccer coach at Louisiana State University, testified as an expert witness that under the official FIFA rules of soccer, "Decision 4" says, "A tackle, which endangers the safety of an opponent, must be sanctioned as serious foul play." In such an instance, a player who tackled another player would be "shown the red card" and excluded from playing the rest of the game.

Steve Pressler, a teammate of Smith, testified that the game was suspended as a result, because the collision was a flagrant violation of the rules of the game and no one felt much like playing after Jones was taken by ambulance to the hospital.

Orthopedic surgeon Mike R. Wallace saw Jones following the accident and said the nature of the injury was consistent with someone being tackled, and characterized the injury as one that may have been common in football before the use of helmets and proper training in how to tackle.

While other testimony was presented, both cumulative and contradictory, the evidence summarized above provides a reasonable evidentiary basis for the trial court's conclusions.

There is no question that defendant Smith's conduct was the cause in fact of the harm to plaintiff Jones. Smith was under a duty to play soccer in the ordinary fashion without unsportsmanlike conduct or wanton injury to his fellow players. This duty was breached by Smith, whose behavior was, according to the evidence, substandard and negligent. Jones assumed the risk of being hit by a slide tackle. *Benedetto v. Travelers Insurance Company, 172 So. 2d 354 (La. App. 4 Cir. 1965)* writ denied *247 La. 872, 175 So. 2d 108; Richmond v. Employers' Fire Insurance Company, 298 So. 2d 118 (La. App. 1 Cir. 1974)* writ denied, *302 So. 2d 18.* As a goalie, Jones may also have assumed the risk of an injury resulting from being run into as he dove for the ball in the penalty area. However, Jones did not assume the risk of Smith going out of his way to tackle him. A participant in a game or sport assumes all of the risks incidental to that particular activity which are obvious and foreseeable. A participant does not assume the risk of injury from fellow players acting in an unexpected or unsportsmanlike way with a reckless lack of concern for others participating. *Hawayek v. Simmons, 91 So. 2d 49 (La. App. Orl. 1956); Carroll v. Aetna Casualty & Surety Company, 301 So. 2d 406 (La. App. 2 Cir. 1974); Rosenberger v. Central La. Dist. Livestock Show, Inc., 312 So. 2d 300 (La. 1975).* Assumption of risk is an affirmative defense which must be proven by a preponderance of the evidence, and the record here supports the trial court's conclusion that Jones did not assume the risk of Smith's negligent act.

There is no evidence in the record to indicate contributory negligence on the part of Jones.

Allstate contends on appeal that there is no coverage under its policy, because its insured, Smith, committed an intentional tort and should have expected injury to result.[1] However, while Smith's action was negligent and perhaps even constitutes

---

[1] The Allstate policy, exhibit D-1, provides an exclusion of coverage in the following language:

> This policy does not apply:
>
> . . . f. to bodily injury or property damage which is either expected or intended from the standpoint of the following Insured. (TR. 29).

wanton negligence, the evidence is that he did not intend the harm that resulted. The distinction between an intentional tort and one resulting from negligence is summarized in *Law of Torts*, 4th Ed., by William L. Prosser, at page 32, as follows: "... the mere knowledge and appreciation of a risk, short of substantial certainty, is not the equivalent of intent. The defendant who acts in the belief or consciousness that he is causing an appreciable risk of harm to another may be negligent, and if the risk is great his conduct may be characterized as reckless or wanton, but it is not classed as an intentional wrong." Smith was not motivated by a desire to injure Jones. Smith tried to regain the ball with a reckless disregard of the consequences to Jones. Smith's action was negligent but does not present a situation where the injury was expected or intended. There is coverage under Allstate's policy.

The trial court awarded plaintiff Jones $250,000 for his pain and suffering and $50,000 for his special damages. There is no dispute about the amount awarded. Jones's neck was broken and his spine severed. He will never be able to walk again, though luckily he retains use of his arms.

There is no manifest error in the trial court's conclusions which we summarize as follows: plaintiff Jones's injuries resulted from the negligence of defendant Smith; Jones was not guilty of contributory negligence and did not assume the risk of this particular accident; and defendant Allstate did not prove that coverage was excluded under the terms of its policy.

For the foregoing reasons, the judgment of the trial court is affirmed at the cost of defendants-appellants, Adrien Smith and Allstate Insurance Company.

Affirmed.

Holmes, J., dissents and assigns written reasons.

DISSENT:

Holmes, Judge, dissenting:

The majority affirms the lower court's judgment against the tortfeasor's liability insurer, concluding that the tortfeasor negligently injured the plaintiff. This writer strongly dissents, basing this disagreement on a finding that the majority opinion has wrongly characterized the tortfeasor's acts as negligent rather than intentional.

As correctly stated in the majority opinion, Smith admitted that he tackled Jones. As a result plaintiff received severe injuries, principally because of the difference in size between the two players; Smith was five feet, eleven inches tall and weighed two hundred ten pounds, while the plaintiff was five feet, seven inches tall and weighed one hundred forty pounds.

The majority opinion sets forth the distinction between an intentional tort and one resulting from negligence, as follows: "... the mere knowledge and appreciation of a risk, short of substantial certainty, is not the equivalent of intent."

In the present case the danger of Smith colliding with the plaintiff and causing him injury was more than a foreseeable risk which a reasonable man would avoid. The collision and resulting injury were a substantial certainty, particularly in view of the fact that Smith was larger than the plaintiff, was running in an upright position at full speed directly at the plaintiff, and intentionally tackled him in an impermissible effort to gain control over the ball. Even though Smith may not have intended to injure the plaintiff, he intended an impermissible contact with the plaintiff, and this constitutes an intentional tort,[1] for which the Allstate policy[2] excludes coverage.

CASE BRIEF

TITLE:

Jones *v.* Smith, Louisiana Appellate Court 1976

FACTS:

In a recreational game of soccer, π [or P] Jones was playing goalie. In an apparent attempt to regain control of the ball, Δ [or D] Smith ran full speed into Jones and tackled him. Jones was injured by the collision. A Tulane law student testified that Smith went out of his way to tackle Jones, and a soccer coach testified that acts such as Smith's are a flagrant violation of the rules of the game. Jones sued Smith and his liability insurer, Allstate, for damages.

PROCEDURAL HISTORY:

The trial court held: (1) Smith's negligence caused Jones's injuries; (2) Jones was not guilty of contributory negligence and did not assume the risk of this particular accident, and (3) Smith's insurance company was liable. Smith and Allstate appeal.

ISSUES:

(1) Was Smith negligent?
(2) Did Jones assume the risk of this particular accident, or was he contributorily negligent?
(3) Does Allstate have to pay because Smith intentionally injured Jones?

HOLDING:

Affirmed. (1) Smith was negligent, (2) Jones did not assume the risk, and (3) Allstate has to pay.

RATIONALE:

(1) Smith's conduct was negligent because he had a duty to play soccer in the ordinary fashion, the way a reasonably prudent player would, but instead used unsportsmanlike conduct that caused Jones's injury.
(2) Jones did not assume the risk of Smith's tackling him because Smith's conduct was unexpected and unsportsmanlike.
(3) Smith was reckless, but his actions were not motivated by a desire to injure Jones and the injury was unintentional. Therefore, because Allstate did not

[1] William L. Prosser, *Law of Torts*, § 9 (4th ed. 1971).
[2] See Footnote 1 of the majority opinion.

prove that the injury was intentional and that coverage was excluded, Allstate is obligated.

RULE:

(1) "A participant in a game or sport does not assume the risk of injury from fellow players acting in an unexpected or unsportsmanlike way with a reckless lack of concern for others participating." (2) An injury caused by a reckless lack of concern for others is not the same as an intended or expected sports injury with regard to a liability insurance policy's exclusionary clause.

DISSENT:

Judge Holmes dissents, arguing that Smith's act was intentional, not negligent, because even though Smith may not have intended to injure Jones, he intended the tackle and the resulting injury was a substantial certainty given the relative sizes of the parties.

OTHER THOUGHTS:

[These include your common-sense reactions to the case, and may well help you put the case in context, or provoke a good conversation in class.]

1. Was this really negligence, or in view of the dissent, could negligence be a "legal fiction" propounded by the court to ensure that Jones's injuries would be covered by the insurance policy?
2. What would happen if this became typical in recreational sports cases—wouldn't it discourage nonprofessional sports? Is this a typical case?
3. The case contains dicta in that the court mentions that Jones "assumed the risk of a slide tackle" and may also have "assumed the risk of an injury resulting from being run into as he dove for the ball," but none of these possible facts were present in the case. Would the court's decision have been different if Jones had been hit when he "dove for the ball"?

DISCUSSION NOTES

A. Introduction and U.S. common law as compared to civilian systems
   1. To what extent are judicial decisions binding in the legal system in which you were trained?
   2. What was your impression of U.S. common law? Why did you decide to study U.S. law?
   3. How much instruction or experience do you have in researching, analyzing, and writing about a client's legal problems?

B. As compared to Islamic traditions
   1. Does the Western view that law and morality are not always the same necessarily conflict with traditional Islamic law?
   2. Is the Western view good for society in that it encourages religious toleration, or does it tend to lead to amoral behavior?

C. As compared to Asian traditions
   1. How are the following types of private disputes usually resolved in your legal system: a) A breach of contract? b) An accident, leading to injury, and caused by someone's fault? c) An injury to a consumer caused by a manufacturer's defective product?
   2. How does U.S. civil trial procedure differ from what you are used to?

D. As compared to Marxist-Leninist theories
   1. Define rule of law, self-government, market economy, and limited government.
   2. How are post-socialist legal systems changing? Which of the concepts listed in question D.1 were most important to them in 1989? Has that changed since then? What ideas remain important from the socialist era?

E. Important terms in U.S. common law
   1. Define *stare decisis.*
   2. Why are scholarly treatises not law in the United States?
   3. What is the function of the jury in U.S. civil and criminal trials? What are some shortcomings of the jury trial system?
   4. Define *writ of certiorari* and *writ of habeas corpus.*
   5. What is the Socratic method? How does it help a student learn? What are some of its shortcomings?

EXERCISE

Read and brief the following case, which is reprinted in two columns, exactly as it appears in published form. Keep in mind that a case brief is a one-page summary that captures the most important points of the case, and try to strike a good balance between thoroughness and brevity.

Supreme Court of Wisconsin.*

Robert F. LESTINA, Plaintiff-Respondent,

v.

WEST BEND MUTUAL INSURANCE COMPANY and Leopold Jerger, Defendants-Appellants.

No. 91-3030.

Argued March 3, 1993.
Decided June 16, 1993.

Soccer player filed personal injury action against opposing team's player and homeowner's insurer seeking to recover for leg injuries suffered during game organized by adult recreational league. The Circuit Court, Waukesha County, Patrick L. Snyder, J., entered judgment in favor of injured player and opposing player appealed. On certification from the Court of Appeals, the Supreme Court, Shirley S. Abrahamson, J., held that negligence, rather than recklessness, was appropriate standard to govern cases involving injuries during recreational team contact sports.

Judgment affirmed.

Wilcox, J., filed dissenting opinion in which Steinmetz and Bablitch, JJ., joined.

Reprinted with permission from Westlaw from 501 N.W.2d 28 (Wis. 1993).

West Headnotes

[1] Theaters and Shows 🔑 6(1)
376k6(1) Most Cited Cases

Negligence, rather than recklessness, is appropriate standard to govern cases involving injuries during recreational team contact sports, in light of ability of negligence standard to subsume all factors and considerations presented by such sports depending on circumstances, and in light of sufficient flexibility of negligence standard to permit vigorous competition by players.

[2] Theaters and Shows 🔑 6(1)
376k6(1) Most Cited Cases

Determination of whether recreational team contact sport player's conduct is negligent, or contributorily negligent, should include consideration of material factors of sport involved, rules and regulations governing sport, generally accepted customs and practices of sport including types of contact and violence accepted, risks inherent in game and those outside realm of anticipation, presence of protective equipment or uniforms, and facts and circumstances of particular case including participants' ages, physical attributes, respective skills at game, and knowledge of rules and customs.

****28 *902** For the defendants-appellants there were briefs (in the Court of Appeals) by William J. Evans and Law Offices of James J. Pauly,****29** West Bend and oral argument by Mr. Evans.

For the plaintiff-respondent there was a brief (in the Court of Appeals) by Dean P. Laing and O'Neil, Cannon & Hollman, S.C., Milwaukee and oral argument by Mr. Laing.

***903** SHIRLEY S. ABRAHAMSON, Justice.

This is an appeal, from a judgment of the circuit court for Waukesha County, Patrick L. Snyder, Circuit Judge. The case comes to this court on certification by the court of appeals pursuant to sec. 809.61, Stats.1991-92. The sole question presented by the certification is "what is the standard of care in Wisconsin for a [recreational] sports player who is alleged to have caused injury to another player during and as part of the [recreational team contact sports] competition." The circuit court determined that negligence was the governing legal standard. For the reasons set out below, we conclude that the rules of negligence govern liability for injuries incurred during recreational team contact sports. Accordingly, we affirm the judgment of the circuit court.

I.

Robert F. Lestina, the plaintiff, filed this personal injury tort action against Leopold Jerger, the defendant, and Jerger's homeowner's insurer, West Bend Mutual Insurance Company, after the plaintiff was injured in a collision with the defendant. The collision occurred during a recreational soccer match organized by the Waukesha County Old Timers League, a recreational league for players over the age of 30.

The plaintiff (45 years of age) was playing an offensive position for his team and the defendant (57 years of age) was the goalkeeper for the opposing team on April 20, 1988, when the injury occurred. Shortly before the plaintiff was injured, he had scored the first goal of the game. After his goal the plaintiff regained possession of the ball and was about to attempt a second goal when the defendant apparently ran out of the goal area and collided with the plaintiff. The plaintiff asserted that the defendant "slide tackled" him in order to prevent him ***904** from scoring.[1] Although slide tackles are allowed under some soccer rules, this league's rules prohibit such maneuvers to minimize risk of injury. The defendant claimed that the collision occurred as he and the plaintiff simultaneously attempted to kick the soccer ball.

The plaintiff seriously injured his left knee and leg in the collision and commenced this action, alleging that the defendant's conduct was both negligent and reckless. The defendant moved

[1] A player "slide tackles" by sliding on his or her knee, with one foot forward, across the front of another player. The objective is to dispossess the opponent of the ball.

for summary judgment on the negligence issue, asserting that the plaintiff's allegations of negligence were insufficient as a matter of law to state a cause of action for injuries sustained during a recreational team contact sports competition. Relying on *Ceplina v. South Milwaukee School Board*, 73 Wis.2d 338, 243 N.W.2d 183 (1976), the circuit court denied the summary judgment motion.

Thereafter the parties agreed to limit the trial to the issue of negligence and to preserve the right to appeal regarding the appropriateness of the negligence standard. The parties also stipulated the amount of damages to be awarded the plaintiff on the basis of the jury determination of the defendant's negligence.

After the jury returned a unanimous verdict finding the defendant 100% causally negligent, the defendant filed motions raising, among other issues, the question whether negligence was the appropriate legal standard. The circuit court denied the post-verdict motions and entered judgment in favor of the plaintiff. The defendant appealed one issue to the court of appeals — whether negligence was the appropriate legal standard in this case. The court of appeals certified the cause to this court.

*905 II.

This case presents a single question of law: is negligence the standard governing ****30** the conduct of participants in recreational team contact sports? We review this question of law independently of the decision of the circuit court.

Relying on *Ceplina v. South Milwaukee School Board*, 73 Wis.2d 338, 243 N.W.2d 183 (1976), the circuit court held that negligence was the controlling standard. We do not view the *Ceplina* case as persuasive precedent. In *Ceplina*, two sixth grade students were on the same team in a playground softball game. The complainant was injured when her teammate unintentionally struck her in the face with a softball bat during the game. She brought an action in negligence against the batter, the school authorities, and the insurers. The batter moved for summary judgment, claiming that he owed no duty to the complainant to exercise care in swinging the bat because the danger of being struck under these circumstances was open and obvious to the complainant. The trial court declined to grant summary judgment, and this court affirmed the trial court's order.

The *Ceplina* court rejected the batter's absence of duty defense.[2] [C]omplainant had stated a cause of negligence which gave rise to a question for the jury "whether either or both of the actors were causally negligent." 73 Wis.2d at 344, 243 N.W.2d 183.

***906** While the *Ceplina* court considered the batter's duty and "open and obvious danger" argument within the context of the complainant's negligence claim and referred to this sport-related injury case as an ordinary negligence case, the opinion must be put in perspective. The court considered only whether the circuit court erred in refusing to grant summary judgment on the claim that the batter owed no duty because the danger of being struck by a bat was an open and obvious danger.

73 Wis.2d at 340-41, 243 N.W.2d 183. The *Ceplina* court was not asked to, and did not, evaluate the applicability of the negligence standard to a sports-related injury.[3] Whether negligence was the appropriate standard for gauging a teammate's conduct was not briefed or presented to the court for decision. Under these circumstances, *Ceplina* cannot be viewed as persuasive precedent on the issue in the case at bar. We therefore examine anew whether negligence is the appropriate standard in this case.

Courts in other jurisdictions have applied three divergent legal theories to uphold actions for sports-related injuries: 1) intentional torts,

---

[2] The court stated that the duty of any person is the obligation of due care to refrain from any act which will cause foreseeable harm to others. The court concluded that the complainant's appreciation of the dangers inherent in a swinging bat was, "under the circumstances of this 'ordinary negligence case'" properly accommodated by the principles of contributory negligence. 73 Wis.2d at 343, 243 N.W.2d 183.

[3] *See* vol. 3258 *Appendices and Briefs*, 73 Wis.2d 318-400.

2) willful or reckless misconduct, and 3) negligent conduct. See generally Raymond L. Yasser, *Liability for Sports Injuries*, in Law of Professional and Amateur Sports (Gary A. Uberstine ed., 1992) at sec. 14.01.

Courts have historically been reluctant to allow participants in contact sports to recover money damages for injuries, absent a deliberate attempt to injure. The intentional tort in a recreational team contact sport is assault and battery. A battery is the intentional, unprivileged, harmful or offensive touching of a person by another.[4] Both parties agree that a player in a recreational **31 team contact sport should be liable for an intentional *907 tort. Neither party urges us to hold that a player should be held liable only for intentional torts. The defendant asks the court to adopt the recklessness standard. The plaintiff urges that the negligence standard is appropriate.

Several courts have held that recklessness is the appropriate standard to apply in personal injury actions between participants in recreational team contact sports. From the various formulations courts have used to define reckless conduct, recklessness apparently falls somewhere on a continuum between an intentional act and an act of negligence. The Restatement (Second) of Torts (1965) describes recklessness as acting without intent to inflict the particular harm but in a manner which is so unreasonably dangerous that the person knows or should know that it is highly probable that harm will result.[5]

***908** *Nabozny v. Barnhill*, 31 Ill.App.3d 212, 334 N.E.2d 258, 261 (1975), is the lead case establishing that "a player is liable for injury in a tort action if his conduct is such that it is either deliberate, willful or with reckless disregard for the safety of the other player so as to cause injury to that player."[6]

---

[4] Restatement (Second) of Torts sec. 13 (1965). The *Restatement (Second) of Torts* (1965) addresses sports injuries only in the context of intentional torts and in the context of apparent consent to an intentional invasion. Comment b to sec. 50 describes the touching to which a player willingly submits by taking part in a game. The full text of the comment is as follows: *b. Taking part in a game.* Taking part in a game manifests a willingness to submit to such bodily contacts or restrictions of liberty as are permitted by its rules or usages. Participating in such a game does not manifest consent to contacts which are prohibited by rules and usages of the game if such rules and usages are designed to protect the participants and not merely to secure the better playing of the game as a test of skill. This is true although the player knows that those with or against whom he is playing are habitual violators of such rules.

[5] Section 500 of the Restatement states:
"The actor's conduct is in reckless disregard of the safety of another if he does an act or intentionally fails to do an act which it is his duty to the other to do, knowing or having reason to know of facts which would lead a reasonable man to realize not only that his conduct creates an unreasonable risk of physical harm to another, but also such risk is substantially greater than that which is necessary to make his conduct negligent."

[6] Commentators have observed that it is not clear from the *Nabozny* opinion exactly what legal standard the court intended to announce. Charles E. Spevacek, *Injuries Resulting from Nonintentional Acts in Organized Contact Sports: The Theories of Recovery Available to the Injured Athlete*, 12 Ind.L.Rev. 687, 701-02 (1979) (the *Nabozny* court "enunciated nothing more than an ordinary negligence standard of conduct, narrowly tailored to further the policy considerations unique to the activity to which it is applied."); Lynn A. Goldstein, *Participant's Liability for Injury to a Fellow Participant in an Organized Athletic Event*, 53 Chi.Kent L.Rev. 97, 105 (1976) ("it is unclear from the language used what standard of conduct should be applied. . . . One interpretation is that *Nabozny* enunciates an ordinary negligence standard of conduct.").

The claim pleaded in the *Nabozny* case was one of ordinary negligence. The court, moreover, considered whether the injured player had been contributorily negligent, a defense which would not have ordinarily been available in an action based on reckless conduct. 334 N.E.2d at 261.

Other commentators have viewed *Nabozny* as setting forth a recklessness standard. *See, e.g.*, Raymond L. Yasser, *Liability for Sports Injuries*, in Law of Professional and Amateur Sports (Gary A. Uberstine ed., 1992), at sec. 14.01[4], p. 14-5. Cases after *Nabozny*, including an Illinois case, have interpreted *Nabozny* as adopting a recklessness standard. *See, e.g.*, *Gauvin v. Clark*, 404 Mass. 450, 537 N.E.2d 94 (1989); *Dotzler v. Tuttle*, 234 Neb. 176, 449 N.W.2d 774 (1990); *Oswald v. Township High School District*, 84 Ill.App.3d 723, 40 Ill.Dec. 456, 406 N.E.2d 157 (1980); *Kabella v. Bouschelle*, 100 N.M. 461, 672 P.2d 290 (Ct.App.1983).

*909 Like the present case, *Nabozny* arose out of a soccer match where the litigants were members of opposing high school teams. The complainant, playing the goal position and having just captured the ball, was crouched in the goal area when the tortfeasor kicked him in the head. Witnesses testified at trial that the tortfeasor had an opportunity to turn away and avoid kicking the complainant and that the tortfeasor's action violated the rules under which the game was being played.

The *Nabozny* court adopted a recklessness standard, rather than a negligence standard, believing that recklessness strikes the proper balance between freeing active and vigorous participation in recreational team contact sports from the chilling effect of litigation and providing a right of redress to an athlete injured through the fault of another. On the one hand, wrote the court, care must be taken not to inhibit free and active participation in recreational team contact sports. Threatening participants with possible liability for injuries might make them reluctant to compete. On the other hand, the court also recognized that tort law condemns unreasonably dangerous behavior and that the playing field should not provide license to engage in unreasonably dangerous **32 behavior. Making the balance, the *Nabozny* court reasoned that public policy supported the application of the recklessness standard to organized athletics. "The court believes that the law should not place unreasonable burdens on the free and vigorous participation in sports by our youth. However, we also believe that organized, athletic competition does not exist in a vacuum. Rather, some of the restraints of civilization must accompany every athlete onto the playing field. One of the educational benefits of organized athletic competition to our *910 youth is the development of discipline and self control." 334 N.E.2d at 260.

The Massachusetts Supreme Judicial Court has similarly adopted the recklessness standard, explaining the policy considerations as follows: Allowing the imposition of liability in cases of reckless disregard of safety diminishes the need for players to seek retaliation during the game or future games. . . . Precluding the imposition of liability in cases of negligence without reckless misconduct furthers the policy that "[v]igorous and active participation in sporting events should not be chilled by threats of litigation." *Gauvin v. Clark*, 404 Mass. 450, 537 N.E.2d 94, 97 (1989) (citations omitted).

Several other courts have adopted the recklessness standard, often adopting the policy considerations expressed in *Nabozny.*[7] One commentator has discerned *911 a judicial trend toward holding sports-related injuries actionable only "if the aggrieved person demonstrates gross negligence or reckless disregard by the defendant." Mel Narol, *Sports Torts: Emerging Standards of Care*, Trial, June 1990, at 20.

The plaintiff asks this court to disregard these cases. He argues that these courts established a recklessness standard because they recognize

[7] *See, e.g., Gauvin v. Clark*, 404 Mass. 450, 537 N.E.2d 94 (1989) (applying reckless disregard of safety standard to injury arising in college hockey game); *Ross v. Clouser*, 637 S.W.2d 11 (Mo.1982) (applying "recklessness" standard to injury arising from church picnic softball game); *Dotzler v. Tuttle*, 234 Neb. 176, 449 N.W.2d 774 (1990) (applying willful or reckless disregard of safety standard to injury arising in a "pick-up" basketball game); *Marchetti v. Kalish*, 53 Ohio St.3d 95, 559 N.E.2d 699 (1990) (applying reckless standard to injury arising in "kick the can" game); *Oswald v. Township High School Dist. No. 214*, 84 Ill.App.3d 723, 40 Ill.Dec. 456, 406 N.E.2d 157 (1980) (applying *Nabozny* "deliberate, willful or reckless disregard" standard to injury in high school gym class basketball game); *Picou v. Hartford Ins. Co.*, 558 So.2d 787 (La.Ct.App.1990) (applying reckless standard to injury in softball game); *Crawn v. Campo*, 257 N.J.Super. 374, 608 A.2d 465 (1992) (applying reckless disregard of safety of others to injury in "pick-up" softball game); *Kabella v. Bouschelle*, 100 N.M. 461, 672 P.2d 290 (Ct.App.1983) (disallowing claim for negligence in injury in recreational football game, relying on *Hackbart v. Cincinnati Bengals, Inc.*, 601 F.2d 516 (10th Cir.1979), *cert. denied*, 444 U.S. 931, 100 S.Ct. 275, 62 L.Ed.2d 188 (1979), which disallowed claim for negligence and permitted claim for recklessness in injury in professional football game); *Connell v. Payne*, 814 S.W.2d 486 (Tex.App.1991) (applying reckless standard to injury in polo match).

the doctrine of assumption of risk. These cases do not apply in Wisconsin, urges the plaintiff, because the assumption of risk doctrine is not recognized in Wisconsin; conduct which was formerly denominated assumption of risk may constitute contributory negligence. *McConville v. State Farm Mut. Auto Ins. Co.*, 15 Wis.2d 374, 384, 113 N.W.2d 14 (1962). The plaintiff's analysis of the relationship between the recklessness standard and the assumption of the risk defense does not hold true for all the cases.[8] In any event we are not persuaded by these cases adopting the recklessness standard and dismissing claims based on negligence.

[1] A third basis for actions for sports-related injuries is negligence. Negligence consists of failing to use that ***912** degree of care which would be exercised by a reasonable person under the circumstances.[9]

****33** Few sports cases can be found which have allowed a complainant to recover on proof of negligence.[10] One commentator has concluded that this scarcity results from fear that the imposition of liability in such cases would discourage participation in sports-related activities. Cameron J. Rains, *Sports Violence: A Matter of Societal Concern*, 55 Notre Dame Lawyer 796, 799 (1980). We do not agree that the application of the negligence standard would have this effect. We believe that the negligence standard, properly understood and applied, accomplishes the objectives sought by the courts adopting the recklessness standard, objectives with which we agree.

***913** Because it requires only that a person exercise ordinary care under the circumstances, the negligence standard is adaptable to a wide range of situations. An act or omission that is negligent in some circumstances might not be negligent in others. Thus the negligence standard, properly understood and applied, is suitable for cases involving recreational team contact sports.

[2] The very fact that an injury is sustained during the course of a game in which the participants voluntarily engaged and in which the likelihood of bodily contact and injury could reasonably be foreseen materially affects the manner in which each player's conduct is to be evaluated under the negligence standard. To determine whether a player's conduct constitutes actionable negligence (or contributory negligence), the fact finder should consider such material factors as the sport involved; the rules and regulations governing the sport; the generally accepted customs and practices of the sport (including the types of contact and the level of violence generally accepted); the risks inherent in the game and those that are outside the realm of anticipation; the presence of protective equipment or uniforms; and the facts and circumstances of the particular case, including the ages and physical attributes of the participants, the participants' respective skills at the game, and the participants'

---

[8] *Kabella v. Bouschelle*, 100 N.M. 461, 672 P.2d 290, 292 (1983), *Picou v. Hartford Ins. Co.*, 558 So.2d 787 (La.App.1990) and *Connell v. Payne*, 814 S.W.2d 486 (Tex.App.1991), for example, applied the recklessness standard even though the defense of assumption of risk had been subsumed in those states by the defense of contributory negligence.

[9] *Osborne v. Montgomery*, 203 Wis. 223, 231, 242-43, 234 N.W. 372 (1931); *Schuster v. St. Vincent Hospital*, 45 Wis.2d 135, 140-141, 172 N.W.2d 421 (1969); Wis.J.I.Civil 1005.

[10] While several cases adopt the negligence standard, most of these cases do not involve contact team sports. *See, e.g., Babych v. McRae*, 41 Conn.Sup. 280, 567 A.2d 1269 (Super.Ct.1989) (applying negligence standard to injury in professional hockey game); *LaVine v. Clear Creek Skiing Corp.*, 557 F.2d 730 (10th Cir.1977) (applying negligence standard to injury in collision between snow skiers); *Gray v. Houlton*, 671 P.2d 443 (Colo.Ct.App.1983) (applying negligence standard to injury in collision between snow skiers); *Duke's GMC, Inc. v. Erskine*, 447 N.E.2d 1118 (Ind.Ct.App.1983) (applying negligence standard to golf injury); *Jones v. Smith*, 331 So.2d 40 (La.Ct.App.1976) (applying negligence standard to injury in softball game) (but see *Picou v. Hartford Ins. Co.*, 558 So.2d 787 (La.Ct.App.1990), adopting a reckless standard); *Jenks v. McGranaghan*, 32 A.D.2d 989, 299 N.Y.S.2d 228 (App.Div.1969) (applying negligence standard to golf injury); *Gordon v. Deer Park School District*, 71 Wash.2d 119, 426 P.2d 824 (1967) (applying negligence standard to softball spectator injured when struck on the head with a bat).

knowledge of the rules and customs. *Niemczyk v. Burleson*, 538 S.W.2d 737 (Mo.Ct.App.1976).

Depending as it does on all the surrounding circumstances, the negligence standard can subsume all the factors and considerations presented by recreational team contact sports and is sufficiently flexible to permit the ***914** 'vigorous competition' that the defendant urges.[11] We see no need for the court to adopt a recklessness standard for recreational team contact sports when the negligence standard, properly understood and applied, is sufficient.

[11] The plaintiff refers the court to sec. 895.525, Stats.1991-92, arguing that the legislature adopted a negligence standard for participants in recreational activities.

We do not address this issue. This statute was adopted after the date of injury in this case, and neither party argues the statute applies directly to this case. Furthermore the parties disagree whether recreational activity defined in sec. 895.525(2) includes team contact sports.

For the reasons set forth, we affirm the judgment of the circuit court.

The judgment of the circuit court is affirmed.

WILCOX, Justice (*dissenting*).

I dissent because I conclude that the unique nature of contact sports calls for ****34** the application of a standard of care other than ordinary negligence. I disagree with the majority's basic premise that ordinary negligence is flexible enough to be applied under any set of circumstances. I believe application of the ordinary negligence standard in personal injury actions arising out of participation in contact sports will discourage vigorous and active participation in sporting events. I agree with the majority of jurisdictions that have considered this issue and concluded that personal injury cases arising out of athletic events must be predicated on reckless disregard of safety; an allegation of negligence is not sufficient to state a cause of action. *See* cases cited in the majority opinion at footnote 7; an excellent analysis of many of the cases adopting ***915** the majority rule is provided in *Dotzler v. Tuttle*, 234 Neb. 176, 449 N.W.2d 774 (1990).

SUPPLEMENTARY EXERCISE

Read and brief ONE of the following cases and compare it to *Jones* and *Lestina*, considering how the law has changed since *Jones* or differs from state to state:

1. *Knight v. Jewett*, 834 P.2d 696 (Cal. 1992).
2. *Hemady v. Long Beach Unified Sch. Dist.*, 49 Cal. Rptr. 3d 464 (Ct. App. 2006).

BIBLIOGRAPHY

Comparative Law

Cappelletti, Mauro. *The Doctrine of Stare Decisis and the Civil Law: A Fundamental Difference—or No Difference at All? In Festschrift für Konrad Zweigert* (Herbert Bernstein, Ulrich Drobnig & Hein Kötz, eds.). 1981.

Daniow, Joseph, ed. *The Role of Judicial Decisions and Doctrine in Civil Law and Mixed Jurisdictions.* 1974.

Glendon, Mary Ann, Michael W. Gordon, & Christopher Osakwe. *Comparative Legal Traditions in a Nutshell.* West 1982.

Kötz, H. *The Role of the Judge in the Court-room: The Common Law and Civil Law Compared.* 1987 Tydskrif vir die Suid-Afrikaanse Reg (J.S. African L.) 35.

Merryman, John Henry, David S. Clark, & John O. Haley. *The Civil Law Tradition: Europe, Latin America, and East Asia.* Michie 1994.

Sauveplanne, J.G. *Codified and Judge Made Law: The Role of Courts and Legislators in Civil and Common Law Systems.* North Holland 1982.

Youngs, Raymond. *English, French, and German Comparative Law.* Cavendish 1998. Zweigert, K., & H. Kötz. *An Introduction to Comparative Law* (Tony Weir, trans.) 3d ed. Oxford University Press 1998.

Common Law History

Baker, J.H. *An Introduction to English Legal History.* 1990. Holdsworth, W.S. 1 *A History of English Law.* 1903.

Kempin, Jr., Frederick G. *An Historical Introduction to Anglo-American Law in a Nutshell.* 2d ed. West 1973.

Makdisi, John. *The Islamic Origins of the Common Law.* 77 N.C. L. Rev. 1635 (1999).

Milson, S.F.C. *Historical Foundations of the Common Law.* Butterworths 1969. Plucknett, Theodore F.T. *A Concise History of the Common Law.* 1956.

Pollock, Frederick, & Frederic William Maitland. 1 *The History of English Law: Before the Time of Edward I.* 2d ed. Little, Brown 1899.

Tubbs, J.W. *The Common Law Mind: Medieval and Early Modern Conceptions.* Johns Hopkins University Press 2002.

American Legal History

Johnson, William R. *Schooled Lawyers: A Study in the Clash of Professional Cultures.* New York University Press 1978.

LaPiana, William P. *Logic and Experience: The Origin of Modern American Legal Education.* Oxford University Press 1994.

Llewellyn, K.N. *The Bramble Bush of Our Law and Its Study.* Oceana 1985.

Sheppard, Steve. *An Introductory History of Law in the Lecture Hall.* In 1 *The History of Legal Education in the United States* (Steve Sheppard, ed.). Salem Press 1999.

American Law School

Burkhart, Ann M., & Robert A. Stein. *How to Study Law and Take Law Exams in a Nutshell.* West 1996.

Fischl, Richard Michael, & Jeremy Paul. *Getting to Maybe: How to Excel on Law School Exams.* Carolina Academic Press 1999.

Mermin, Samuel. *Law and the Legal System, an Introduction.* 2d ed. Little, Brown 1982.

Nygren, Carolyn J. *Starting Off Right in Law School.* Carolina Academic Press 1997.

CHAPTER 2

INTRODUCTION TO AMERICAN LEGAL RESEARCH AND THE FEDERAL SYSTEM

Most LL.M. programs have a substantial research and writing requirement, in recognition of the fact that one cannot fully understand how the United States legal system operates without having some knowledge of how to locate legal authority. Additionally, many LL.M. candidates hope to complete their studies in the United States with an internship in a U.S. law firm, or expect to be dealing with U.S. law and lawyers upon their return home. In the United States, it is primarily attorneys who conduct legal research. Although paralegals may do some of the research undertaken in a law firm, attorneys are responsible for the larger portion of the research, and are the ones who are liable under ethical rules if the research done does not reach professional standards. This chapter introduces the resources and skills used in researching U.S. legal authority.

I. UNITED STATES LEGAL RESOURCES

A. Types of Legal Resources

The United States has three types of legal resources: hard copy, commercial computer databases, and free noncommercial databases. *Hard copy*, meaning paper and books, is the traditional medium for legal research. The last two types are sometimes referred to as Computer-Assisted Legal Research or "CALR." Commercial databases have high-powered search tools that can significantly reduce research time, provided the researcher knows exactly what legal terms for which to search. Westlaw and LEXIS are the most prominent of the commercial databases, but a third database, Loislaw, is slowly gaining market share. Westlaw and LEXIS are famous for their sophistication, and many LL.M. candidates come to the United States in part to gain skill in using them; however, they are still prohibitively expensive for many attorneys outside the United States. Therefore, skill in using the commercial databases may be of little use once the LL.M. graduate returns home. The third source, free databases, includes search-engine sites and also sites sponsored by governments, universities, and other nonprofit organizations. Typically, the latter are under-publicized and underutilized in U.S. law schools because of the prominence of the commercial databases; however, practicing attorneys in mid-size and smaller firms find them extremely useful. Often the search capabilities of these sites are not as well developed as those of the commercial sites, but the free databases are often simpler and easier to master and navigate than the fee-based sites. That being said, however, CALR sources change very rapidly due to technological advances. For instance, Westlaw and Lexis-Nexis change the appearance of their Web sites and improve finding tools almost on a yearly basis. Non-fee databases are constantly changing as well. Consequently, although the descriptions of various CALR Web sites are accurate as of the time of this writing (2007), be aware that ease of use, finding tools, and price structures are constantly changing. Thus, by the time you read and study this text, some of the information about those sites may already be outdated—though the Web sites themselves will probably be recognizable and the techniques of using them will not have changed greatly. As a professional legal researcher, you should periodically check sites you have not recently used for changes and improvements and to keep your skills up to date.

B. Advantages and Disadvantages of Various Research Media

Some of the advantages of CALR are obvious: speed, "one-stop" researching from anywhere you can access the Internet, and continuous (and instant) updating of authorities. These advantages are especially seductive when combined with the free access to Westlaw and LEXIS given to law students in the United States. Unfortunately, there are also a number of disadvantages to CALR: the researcher must know exactly the right legal terms to use and must know what type of authority for which to search. This demands real skill, especially when you consider the multiplicity of sources of law in the United States: Law comes from statutes, cases, regulations, and constitutions that are separate for each of the 50 states in the United States, plus the U.S. federal government. Unless the researcher has a significant amount of skill and familiarity, researching on LEXIS and Westlaw, even with all the helpful finding tools they try to include, can be like looking for a needle in a haystack, when you don't even know what the needle you are searching for looks like.

Though they seem slow, cumbersome, and old-fashioned, traditional hard-copy sources have certain inherent advantages over CALR, particularly for researchers whose native language is not English or who are unfamiliar with U.S. legal terminology. *Finding tools*, such as tables of contents, outlines, and indexes, list terms and synonyms that make research much easier. Typically, a client presents himself to an attorney's office with a story and a legal problem. The attorney must categorize the legal problem and then research the applicable law. Unless she is thoroughly familiar with the area of law in question, the lawyer may not be aware of the correct terms. This difficulty can be amplified when the attorney's knowledge of English is limited. Tables of contents, indexes, and treatises can help her become aware of the appropriate legal terms, but these kinds of sources are often difficult to access on computer databases. They are much more readily available in hard copy. Thus, it often helps to gain an initial overview of the topic in a library, before going online.

Once the attorney knows the terms that apply to her client's problem, computer-based research becomes more efficient. The researcher formulates various searches using different combinations of those terms until she finds appropriate legal authority. Computer-based resources are also more efficient in terms of updating law: statutes are amended, new regulations are promulgated, and cases are vacated or overruled on a daily basis. Professionalism demands that legal research be up to date, but it takes time to print hard copy. It usually takes at least two weeks for hard copy to be updated and delivered to a law library, and then it is in the form of softbound materials or pocket parts slipped into the back of a hardbound book. Research with these materials is inefficient. In contrast, computer databases are updated within 24 hours, and can instantly alert a researcher to outdated material.

In addition to enabling an attorney to educate himself in a particular area of law, hard-copy research has another, subtler advantage: the materials he finds are in context. Once an attorney has located the appropriate authorities, hard-copy authority is more easily interpreted and accurately understood than online authority. The computer shows only one portion of a page at a time. It is easy to flip pages in a book, but difficult to refer back and forth to different portions of a statute or case when looking at them online. Consequently, a researcher who looks only at a computer screen can easily misunderstand, misinterpret, or read things out of context. It is much harder to gain an overview of the authority and how it fits together. In contrast, hard copy allows the researcher instantly to look back at things he read earlier, or to look forward for the conclusion. This makes it easier to absorb and completely understand the material. Therefore, it is typically best to begin and end research with hard copy, using computer research to locate and update authorities, but finishing by reading those authorities slowly and carefully in hard copy or a computer printout.

Computer and hard-copy research each have advantages and disadvantages. Optimally, LL.M. candidates should gain skill in researching U.S. law both in law libraries and online, and should learn the advantages and disadvantages of each. To that end, portions of the exercise at the end of this chapter are best done first in a law library and then on computer, using a commercial or noncommercial database. Because not all LL.M. candidates will have these resources at hand, research hints give advice on how best to proceed with each of the three resources for the exercises at the end of this chapter.

II. RESEARCH TECHNIQUES AND INTERPRETIVE SKILLS

Simply put, an attorney needs two research techniques and two interpretive skills to research U.S. legal resources.

Research techniques:

1. If given specific information about a written judicial opinion, statute, rule, treatise, or other legal authority, the researcher must be able to locate that authority.

2. If given a client problem, the researcher must be able to find the law that applies to that problem.

Interpretative skills:

1. Once having located applicable law, the researcher must understand what relative weight to accord to that authority (in other words, gauge how important the authority is).
2. The researcher must also understand how the authority applies to a given situation.

The first research technique (finding an authority given a citation or other locating information) is relatively easy to acquire, and is the subject of this section. This chapter then discusses how to judge the relative weight of authority, the first interpretive skill. It finishes with a short introductory discussion of the second research skill. Chapters 3, 5, 6, 7, and 10 further develop the remaining skills: how to research hypothetical client situations and how to interpret authority.

III. THE FIRST RESEARCH SKILL: LOCATING A GIVEN LEGAL AUTHORITY

Legal authority is subdivided into *primary authority* and *secondary authority.* Primary authority is itself law. In contrast, secondary authority helps a researcher understand law, but is not itself law. The United States has four generic sources of primary authority because each branch of the government makes law. Those sources include constitutions (the overarching law), statutes (passed by legislatures), regulations (promulgated by executive branches), and case law (developed by the judiciary). Treaties are a type of statutory law.

The previous paragraph used the plural in referring to constitutions, legislatures, and executive branches because of the dual-government system in the United States. The United States is a federal system, and the federal Constitution guarantees that every state "shall" have its own republican form of government.[1] State governments all have the same general structure as the federal government. Each of the 50 states not only has its own legislature, executive department, and judiciary, but also has its own constitution, case law,[2] statutes, and regulations.

Because the United States has so many primary and secondary legal sources, attorneys and judges are obsessive about identifying the exact source on which they

---

[1] U.S. Const. art. IV, § 4.

[2] Louisiana and Puerto Rico are mixed-civilian jurisdictions. Louisiana recognizes case law just as the common law states do, though it has no formal mechanism for doing so and has rejected any adoption of "the" common law. So far, Puerto Rico has maintained its civilian nature to a greater extent than has Louisiana, and does not formalize case law at the state level, though it does so in its federal courts.

are relying. All judicial opinions, briefs, legal memoranda, treatises, and articles in legal periodicals give a citation after every sentence that quotes, refers to, or relies on another source. The citations enable the reader to verify the author's assertions by checking the exact page of the authority referenced, and they enable the reader to measure the weight of the authority. Sometimes citations are included in the text of the work, and sometimes they are put into footnotes. For example, examine *Jones v. Smith* at page 27. The opinion contains citations in its discussion of assumption of risk, as well as in its discussion of negligence. The first citation is *Benedetto v. Travelers Insurance Co.*, 172 So. 2d 354 (La. App. 4 Cir. 1965). Similarly, *Lestina v. West End Mutual Insurance Co.* contains a number of citations on pages 33-36, both in the text and in footnotes. Admittedly, it is easier to read documents that put the citations into footnotes, but the tradition in the United States is to put them in the text immediately after the sentence that relies on the source.[3]

The rules of this citation system were originally set forth in *The Bluebook: A Uniform System of Citation*, compiled by student editors of the Columbia Law Review, Harvard Law Review, the University of Pennsylvania Law Review, and the Yale Law Journal. The Bluebook is now in its 18th edition. It is somewhat difficult to decipher, and perhaps needlessly complex. The Bluebook's competitor, the *ALWD Citation Manual* from the Association of Legal Writing Directors, was introduced in 2000, and is quickly gaining acceptance because of its simpler format.[4] This text recognizes that readers may work with either source.

To a novice, learning the many minor details of either system can be daunting and frustrating, especially when one is overwhelmed with learning other things that seem much more important. The least stressful way to learn either the Bluebook or the ALWD is to begin by studying the table of contents and familiarizing oneself with the structure of the manual. Next study the introductory material in the volume: Parts 1 and 2 of the ALWD or the introduction to the Bluebook. Then study particular chapters and sections of the citation manual as needed. The index in either manual is extremely useful whenever you have a question about a particular citation practice or portion of a citation.

Despite the existence of these two authoritative style manuals, the companies that publish legal authorities (notably West and LEXIS) also have developed and in some cases copyrighted their own symbols and abbreviations. These are not official citations and the researcher must translate them into Bluebook or ALWD form. To further complicate the issue, many courts promulgate their own variants. Therefore, when preparing a document to be filed with a court, an attorney must first translate a Westlaw or LEXIS citation into Bluebook or ALWD form and then adjust that citation to accord with that particular court's rules. This chapter will introduce standard Bluebook and ALWD forms; the complications can be learned gradually.

---

[3] The tradition dates from the time of typewriters, when it was very difficult to format footnotes. This is no longer true with modern word processing systems. Consequently, some legal writing stylists are now encouraging lawyers to put citations in footnotes, and the movement is gaining ground, as demonstrated by *Lestina*. *See* Bryan A. Garner, *The Winning Brief* (1999) (discussing the advantages of footnotes over citations inserted in the text).

[4] *See* Darby Dickerson, *ALWD Citation Manual* (3d ed., Aspen Law & Bus. 2006).

A. Primary Authority and Citation Forms

1. Constitutions

Citation example: U.S. Const. art. VI, cl. 2.
Explanation: U.S. Constitution article VI, clause 2
Generic sequence: Abbreviated locality name, the identifying abbreviation "Const.", article, and clause or section.

As discussed earlier, primary authority (law) comes from four sources: constitutions, legislatures, administrations, and the judiciary. Each source has its own form of citation, and it is relatively easy to decipher the abbreviations and find the source. The United States Constitution is the "[S]upreme Law of the Land."[5] Deciphering the abbreviations, the footnoted citation (U.S. Const. art. VI, cl. 2) indicates that the language quoted in the previous sentence is from the second clause (cl. 2) of Article VI (art. VI) of the United States Constitution. State constitutions are cited by substituting an abbreviation of the state's name for "U.S." Thus, "Conn. Const. art. XIII, § 1" translates into Article XIII, section one (§ 1) of the Connecticut Constitution. For abbreviations of state names, see the list in Figure 2-1.

2. Statutes

Citation example: 8 U.S.C. § 1101(a)(15)(F)(i) (2006).
Explanation: Title 8 of the United States Code, section 1101(a)(15)(F)(i) (published in 2001).
Generic sequence: title, abbreviated code name, section number (date of publication)

The United States Congress passes federal legislation using the process detailed in Article 1 of the Constitution. Initially given a public law number (abbreviated as *Pub. L. No.*), new statutes are then codified—organized by topic—in the *United States Code*, the "U.S.C." Each of 50 major topics is assigned a title number, in general alphabetical order, and each individual statute in that title is further organized by subtopic and given a section number. Most statutes are subdivided into subparts. Citations include the title number, the abbreviation U.S.C., the section and subpart numbers, and the year of publication of the statute (*not* necessarily the year in which the statute was passed). For example, 8 U.S.C. § 1101(a)(15)(F)(i) (2006) refers to title 8 of the *United States Code*, entitled "Aliens and Nationality," section 1101 ("Admissions of Nonimmigrants"), subpart (a)(15)(F)(i), published in 2001.[6] The *United States Code* is published in a series of volumes that look much like an encyclopedia, with title numbers printed on the spines. To locate this statute in hard copy, the researcher would look for the U.S.C. volume containing title 8 and then look up § 1101. On a computer, one could simply enter the citation as a search term.

[5] U.S. Const. art. VI, cl. 2.
[6] The date enclosed in parentheses indicates the date on the spine of the volume. *See* Bluebook rule 12.3.2 (18th ed. 2005). This is somewhat problematic, as most research is now done on computer.

FIGURE 2-1
UNITED STATES STATE AND TERRITORY ABBREVIATIONS

Alabama	Ala.	Nebraska	Neb.
Alaska	Alaska	Nevada	Nev.
American Samoa		New Hampshire	N.H.
Arizona	Ariz.	New Jersey	N.J.
Arkansas	Ark.	New Mexico	N.M.
California	Cal.	New York	N.Y.
Canal Zone		North Carolina	N.C.
Colorado	Colo.	North Dakota	N.D.
Connecticut	Conn.	Northern Mariana Islands	
Delaware	Del.	Ohio	Ohio
Florida	Fla.	Oklahoma	Okla.
Georgia	Ga.	Oregon	Or.
Guam		Pennsylvania	Pa.
Hawaii	Haw.	Puerto Rico	P.R.
Idaho	Idaho	Rhode Island	R.I.
Illinois	Ill.	South Carolina	S.C.
Indiana	Ind.	South Dakota	S.D.
Iowa	Iowa	Tennessee	Tenn.
Kansas	Kan.	Texas	Tex.
Kentucky	Ky.	Utah	Utah
Louisiana	La.	Vermont	Vt.
Maine	Me.	Virginia	Va.
Maryland	Md.	Virgin Islands	
Massachusetts	Mass.	Washington	Wash.
Michigan	Mich.	West Virginia	W. Va.
Minnesota	Minn.	Wisconsin	Wis.
Mississippi	Miss.	Wyoming	Wyo.
Missouri	Mo.	Washington, D.C.	D.C.
Montana	Mont.		

The outline sequence used in the U.S.C. to identify subparts is counterintuitive, so it is best simply to memorize it. The largest subdivisions are given a small letter identifier: *(a), (b), (c);* sub-subpoints are identified by numerals: *(1), (2), (3);* sub-sub-subpoints by capital letters: *(A), (B), (C);* and the smallest points by small roman numerals: *(i), (ii), (iii), (iv).* The sequence is easily visualized using the following diagram:

8 U.S.C. § 1101 (2006)

(a)

  (1)

    (A)

      i.

(b)

  (1)

    etc.

The U.S.C. is the official source of federal legislation. However, it is not the source most attorneys actually use, because it lacks efficient finding tools, does not provide keys to pertinent case law or cross-references to other authority, and is not as current as the commercial versions. For research purposes, most U.S. attorneys rely on either the LEXIS or the Westlaw version. The Westlaw version of the U.S.C. is titled the *United States Code Annotated*, abbreviated as *U.S.C.A.*; the LEXIS equivalent is titled the *United States Code Service*, or *U.S.C.S.* In hard copy, both of them are published in series of volumes that, like the U.S.C., look like encyclopedias. The exercise that follows this chapter provides an opportunity to compare the official version with a commercial one.

Treaties ratified by the United States Senate are law in the United States,[7] and are subject to interpretation in U.S. state and federal courts just as are any other federal laws. The United States Constitution gives treaty-making power to the president and the Senate:[8] The president has the sole power to make treaties, provided that two-thirds of the Senate subsequently ratifies the treaty.[9] States are prohibited from entering into treaties or alliances on their own.[10] Once accepted by the Senate, ratified treaties are then incorporated into the *United States Code* as an appendix. For example, the United Nations Convention on Contracts for the International Sale of Goods (CISG) is published in the appendix to title 15 of the *United States Code*. The official citation to a treaty includes the name of the treaty, the date it was signed, any subdivision being cited, and the official source in which it is published. Thus, the citation to Article 7 of the CISG would be:

> U.N. Convention on Contracts for the Int'l Sale of Goods, Apr. 11, 1980, art. 7, U.N. Doc.A/Conf 97/18 (1980).

To make it easier to find, often an unofficial source is added to the citation:

> U.N. Convention on Contracts for the Int'l Sale of Goods, Apr. 11, 1980, art. 7, U.N. Doc.A/Conf 97/18 (1980), *reprinted at* 15 U.S.C. App. 52 (2002).

As mentioned earlier, each state has its own statutes and publishes them, just as the federal government does. Each state in the United States codifies its statutes somewhat differently, often in more than one code, but the underlying format is quite consistent. The citation begins with an abbreviation of the state's name, an abbreviation of the code's name, the section number, and the year of publication: Ga. Code Ann. § 10-5-1 (1973) refers to section 10-5-1 of Georgia's Annotated Code. Similarly, Cal. Code Civ. Proc. § 410.10 (1973) refers to section 410.10 of the California Code of Civil Procedure.

Many states, rather parochially, adhere to citation styles or code abbreviations other than those promulgated in the authoritative style manuals. Some official

---

7 U.S. Const. art. VI, cl. 2.
8 U.S. Const. art. II, § 2, cl. 1.
9 *Id.*
10 U.S. Const. art. I, § 10, cl. 3.

codes go so far as to include a note to the effect of: "Cite as . . . ," giving the state-preferred abbreviation. You will often encounter these alternate forms in opinions issued by the courts of these states. However, while state courts may have special citation forms most U.S. law school courses want students to use the forms in the authoritative style manuals.

3. *Regulations*

Citation example: 8 C.F.R. § 214.1 (2007).
Explanation: Title 8 of the Code of Federal Regulations, section 214.1 (published in 2007).
Generic sequence: title, name of collection, section (publication date).

The administration, or executive branch, of the federal government is not by definition a law-making body. In specific instances, Congress grants it limited power to promulgate rules and regulations through enabling statutes. One such enabling statute is 8 U.S.C. § 1184(a)(1) (2006), wherein Congress gives the Attorney General the power to develop rules and regulations relating to the issuance of visas to nonimmigrants. Rules and regulations are first proposed and published in the *Federal Register*, and are then collected in final form in the *Code of Federal Regulations*, or C.F.R. The C.F.R. is organized using the same 50 titles as the U.S.C., and is similarly organized into numbered sections: 8 C.F.R. § 214.1 (2007) sets forth the requirements for admission of a nonimmigrant, in accord with the authority granted by Congress at 8 U.S.C. § 1184(a)(1) (2007).

Similarly, each state has its own administrative code comparable to the C.F.R. As one would expect, the citation includes the abbreviated name of the state, the abbreviated name of the code, the regulation, and the year. Like the C.F.R., it may also have a title number. Thus, "1 Va. Admin. Code § 30-120-90 (1999)" refers to title 1 of the Virginia Administrative Code, section 30-120-90, published in 1999.

4. *Case Law*

Citation example: *Lestina v. West Bend Mut. Ins. Co.*, 501 N.W.2d 28, 32 (Wis. 1993).
Explanation: Lestina versus West Bend Mutual Insurance Company, volume 501 of the *North Western Reporter*, Second Series, beginning on page 28, pinpoint page 32 (decided by the Wisconsin Supreme Court in 1993).
Generic sequence: case name, volume, reporter, beginning page, pinpoint page(s) (court, year).

In the United States, the judicial branch plays a very complex role. With very few exceptions, each case that is decided by a court becomes law not just for the parties themselves but also for other similar cases.[11] In addition to creating and shaping the

[11] Admittedly, because of a perceived overabundance of precedent, U.S. circuit courts now sometimes stipulate that certain cases should not be used as precedent. The constitutionality of this practice may be questionable but has not been tested.

common law through the doctrine of stare decisis, as discussed in Chapter 1, courts apply constitutions, statutes, and regulations to circumstances that may not have been foreseen when those laws were enacted.[12] The judicial interpretations are themselves law and are as important as the text of the provisions they interpret.

a. The Role of Judicial Review

Additionally, "[t]hrough the power of judicial review, originally asserted by Chief Justice Marshall in *Marbury v. Madison,*[13] the courts also determine the constitutionality of acts of the legislative and executive branches"[14]—leading to a consistent and persistent tension among all three branches of government in the United States. In short, U.S. courts make law when they interpret statutes and regulations, and they can also hold statutes and regulations unconstitutional or invalid. Furthermore, because both state and federal courts can review a statute for constitutionality, a decision ruling on the constitutionality of a statute or regulation or interpreting one is as much law as the original statute or regulation. Failure to consider and follow such decisions in researching and interpreting a statute or regulation constitutes legal malpractice.[15]

The tension among the three branches of government was demonstrated in *Dickerson v. United States,*[16] in which the Supreme Court invalidated as unconstitutional a federal statute, 18 U.S.C. § 3501 (2000), that had itself been intended by Congress to overturn a 1966 Supreme Court decision. In that earlier decision, *Miranda v. Arizona,* the Supreme Court held that the Fifth and Fourteenth Amendments to the Constitution require police to inform arrested suspects that (1) they have the right to remain silent; (2) everything they say can and will be used against them in a court of law; (3) they have the right to counsel; and (4) if they cannot afford counsel, counsel will be appointed for them.[17] The *Miranda* requirement was made famous in the television series *Dragnet* and has been recited in almost every segment of every United States TV police series since then. (I suppose we should be relieved to know that because of *Dickerson,* these shows are not outdated.)

Obviously, then, it is as important to be able to locate pertinent case law as it is to locate applicable statutes and regulations. Case citations are a bit more complex than statute and regulation citations, but still are not difficult to dissect. They begin with the case name (often underlined or italicized if it appears in text rather than a footnote) followed by a comma. After the comma is the volume number of the reporter in which the case is published, the abbreviated reporter name, and one or two page numbers. The first page number refers to the page on which the case begins; the second page number is the exact page of the case on which the cited language appears, called the *pinpoint* page. Finally, the citation ends with the abbreviation of the court name and the year of the decision in parentheses, so the reader can instantly assess whether the case is mandatory or persuasive authority and how current it is. For example, the citation to *Miranda*'s

[12] Morris L. Cohen & Kent C. Olson, *Legal Research in a Nutshell* § 1-2, at 3 (7th ed. 2000).
[13] 5 U.S. (1 Cranch) 137 (1803).
[14] *Id.*
[15] *Id.*
[16] 530 U.S. 428 (2000).
[17] 384 U.S. 436 (1966).

rule that accused suspects must be informed of their rights is as follows: *Miranda v. Arizona*, 384 U.S. 436, 467-68 (1966). The italicized portion identifies both parties to the case. The case is in volume 384 of the official *United States Reports* (abbreviated as U.S.), and it begins on page 436. The language in question can be found on pages 467 to 468, and the case was decided in 1966. No court identifier is needed because the *United States Reports* contains only United States Supreme Court cases.

b. Official and Unofficial Versions

Just as there are two commercial versions of the U.S. Code, so there are two commercial versions of the *U.S. Reports.* The Westlaw publication is titled the *Supreme Court Reporter* (abbreviated as S. Ct.), and the LEXIS equivalent is the *Lawyers' Edition* (L. Ed.). Just as with the Code, the commercial versions are more useful to the researcher than the official version, because they contain finding tools and other commentary. Most law firm libraries subscribe to either the S. Ct. or the L. Ed., but not the official *U.S. Reports.* Similarly, most law libraries will have West's U.S.C.A. or the LEXIS U.S.C.S., but not the U.S.C. On the Internet, Westlaw and LEXIS provide their respective commercial versions, with references to official page numbers.

c. Commercial Versions versus Official Versions

As mentioned earlier, most American attorneys, when researching hard copy, choose commercial reporters and codes because they contain helpful information above and beyond the language of the statute or opinion of the court. One note of caution, however, about commercial versions: it is easy at first to mistake commentary for law until one becomes familiar with the commercial format.

Similarly, with regard to case law, the opinion of the court is law. In all commercial versions, **the actual opinion begins after the name of the writing judge**. Anything after the caption and before the judge's name is added by the publisher and is not law. Examine *Lestina*, reprinted beginning on page 31. The caption indicates that the opinion is from the Supreme Court of Wisconsin, the case was between Robert F. Lestina, West Bend Mutual Insurance Company, and Leopold Jerger. The case was numbered 91-3030 by the Wisconsin Supreme Court's docket, and was decided on June 16, 1993. What follows, including the short summary of the case ("Soccer player filed personal injury action . . ."), up to and including headnotes 1 and 2 and the identification of attorneys for each side, is not law. The actual opinion begins after the name or names of the writing judge, in this case Justice Shirley S. Abrahamson. (Judges who sit on supreme courts are called *justices.*)

Headnotes are the short, numbered descriptions that appear before the actual text of the opinion. Although headnotes were described by Langdell's biographer as "the only useful part," this is overstated. Because they are not written by the deciding court, **headnotes are not law**. They are written by the editors of the reporter in which the opinion is published, and are designed to be a research tool to help the researcher locate a given legal principle rapidly. Furthermore, they can be inaccurate. Although the publisher submits them to the deciding court for review, headnotes are not always carefully checked, and occasionally contain errors. Use them only for research, but not as a source of language in a written work. Use the language of the court itself, or paraphrase that language yourself.

The numbers included by West at the beginning of each headnote serve several purposes. The bracketed number indicates where in the opinion the summarized legal point can be found. For example, in *Lestina*, headnotes [1] and [2] are on pages 36 and 37. The other numbers, the key icon, and the caption "Theaters and Shows" all refer to West's Digest system, which is a research system that catalogues legal points to help researchers identify cases dealing with those points. The points raised in *Lestina* and described in the headnotes are catalogued by West under Theaters and Shows 6(1), and listed under 376k6(1). By following these numbers, the researcher can find other similar cases. The Digest system is available both in hard copy and online, through Westlaw.

d. Federal Court Reporters

To reiterate, federal Supreme Court decisions are published in the *U.S. Reports*, West's S. Ct., and LEXIS's L. Ed. However, the federal court system, like most court systems in the United States, has three levels. Trial courts are called federal District Courts, and appellate courts are titled United States Circuit Courts of Appeal. The court of last resort that supervises them all is, naturally, the United States Supreme Court. In the United States, attorneys research federal appellate and trial court decisions as much or more than they do Supreme Court decisions. In contrast to Supreme Court opinions, however, not all district court or circuit court opinions are published. The lower courts submit only their more important cases for publication, though almost all decisions become part of the public record and can be researched at the court itself.

The official reporters for district court or circuit court opinions are both published by West. West publishes federal circuit court decisions in the *Federal Reporter* series. Each series includes up to 999 volumes, after which a new series starts. Currently, the *Federal Reporter* is in its third series, abbreviated as F.3d. The earlier series are, respectively, F. and F.2d. Thus, any citation listing F. or F.2d refers to a case decided before 1993. Similarly, federal District Court decisions are published by West in the *Federal Supplement* (F. Supp.), which is now in its second series.

Other reporters publish decisions of specialized federal courts. The federal reporters can be charted as follows:

Court	Official reporter, abbreviated	Unofficial reporter, abbreviated (publisher)	Unofficial reporter, abbreviated (publisher)
U.S. Supreme	U.S.	S. Ct. (West)	L. Ed. (LEXIS)
U.S. Circuit	F., F.2d, F.3d		
U.S. District	F. Supp., F. Supp. 2d		
U.S. Court of Federal Claims	Fed. Cl.		
U.S. Court of Int'l Trade	Ct. Int'l Trade	F. Supp., F. Supp. 2d	
U.S. Bankruptcy Courts	B.R.		

Court	Official reporter, abbreviated	Unofficial reporter, abbreviated (publisher)	Unofficial reporter, abbreviated (publisher)
U.S. Tax Court	T.C.		
U.S. Court of Appeals for Veterans Claims	Vet. App.		
U.S. Court of Appeals for the Armed Forces, Military Service Courts of Criminal Appeals	M.J.		

The federal appellate courts are divided into 11 circuit courts, each of which reviews cases from federal district courts in two or more states, plus the Court of Appeals for the Federal Circuit, and the Court of Claims (appellate jurisdiction). Figure 2-2 maps these circuits, showing which states are included in each circuit. Each circuit court reviews the cases from all United States District Courts (U.S. trial courts) in its circuit. It does not review cases from state courts, except through habeas corpus appeals. An example of a citation to a Second Circuit case is *Asch v. Phillips, Appel, & Walden, Inc.*, 867 F.2d 776, 780 (2d Cir. 1989). Notice that the court identifier is in parentheses. Because the case is published in the F.2d, the reader knows it is a U.S. Circuit court opinion, and from the court identifier, one knows that it was the United States Second Circuit Court of Appeals that issued the opinion. In addition to the 13 appellate courts, the federal court system has approximately 150 district courts. An example of a citation to a district court case is *Graham v. Hutto*, 437 F. Supp. 118, 125 (E.D. Va. 1977). The parenthetical information, together with the fact that the case was published in the F. Supp., indicates that this is a trial court decision from the United States District Court for the Eastern District of Virginia.

e. Regional Reporters

State court decisions are also published in reporters. Some states have official reporters, but most state case law research is done in West's regional reporters. The cases published in the regional reporters are all from state appellate or supreme courts (not state trial courts). Each regional reporter includes cases from several states. For example, the *Southern Reporter* contains cases from Louisiana, Mississippi, Alabama, and Florida. Figure 2-3 maps the regional reporters. The citation to the Louisiana case briefed in the introductory section is as follows: *Bourque v. Duplechin*, 331 So. 2d 40, 43 (La. Ct. App. 1976). This case is a 1976 decision of a Louisiana appellate court (La. Ct. App.), and it was published in volume 331, beginning at page 40, of the second series of the *Southern Reporter*. The language cited appears on page 43.

B. Secondary Sources

Citation example: 21 Charles Alan Wright & Kenneth A. Graham, Jr., *Federal Practice and Procedure* § 5023 (2d ed., West 1990).

FIGURE 2-2

THE 13 FEDERAL JUDICIAL CIRCUITS
(Adapted & reprinted with permission of Westlaw)

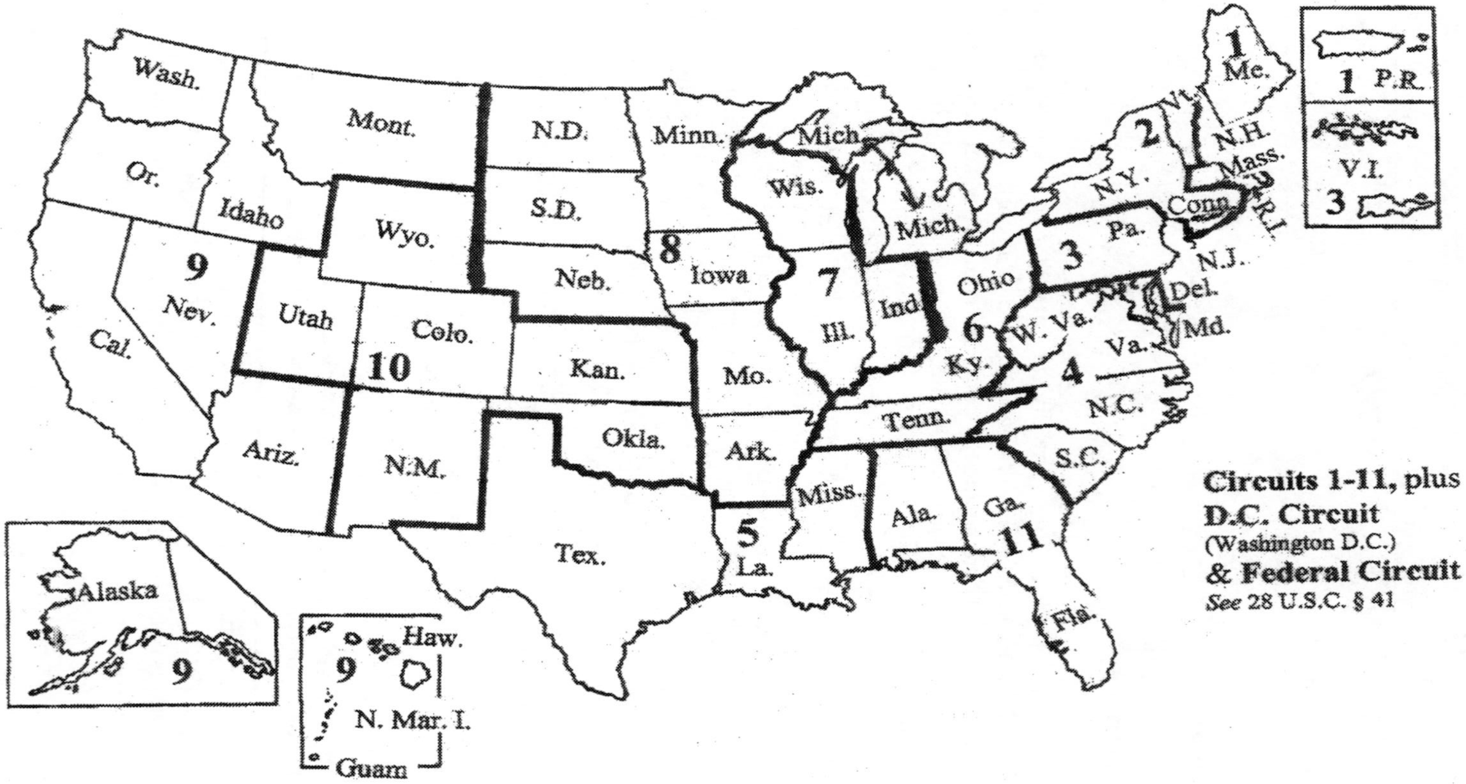

Circuits 1-11, plus
D.C. Circuit
(Washington D.C.)
& Federal Circuit
See 28 U.S.C. § 41

FIGURE 2-3
WEST'S REGIONAL REPORTER SYSTEM
(Reprinted with permission)

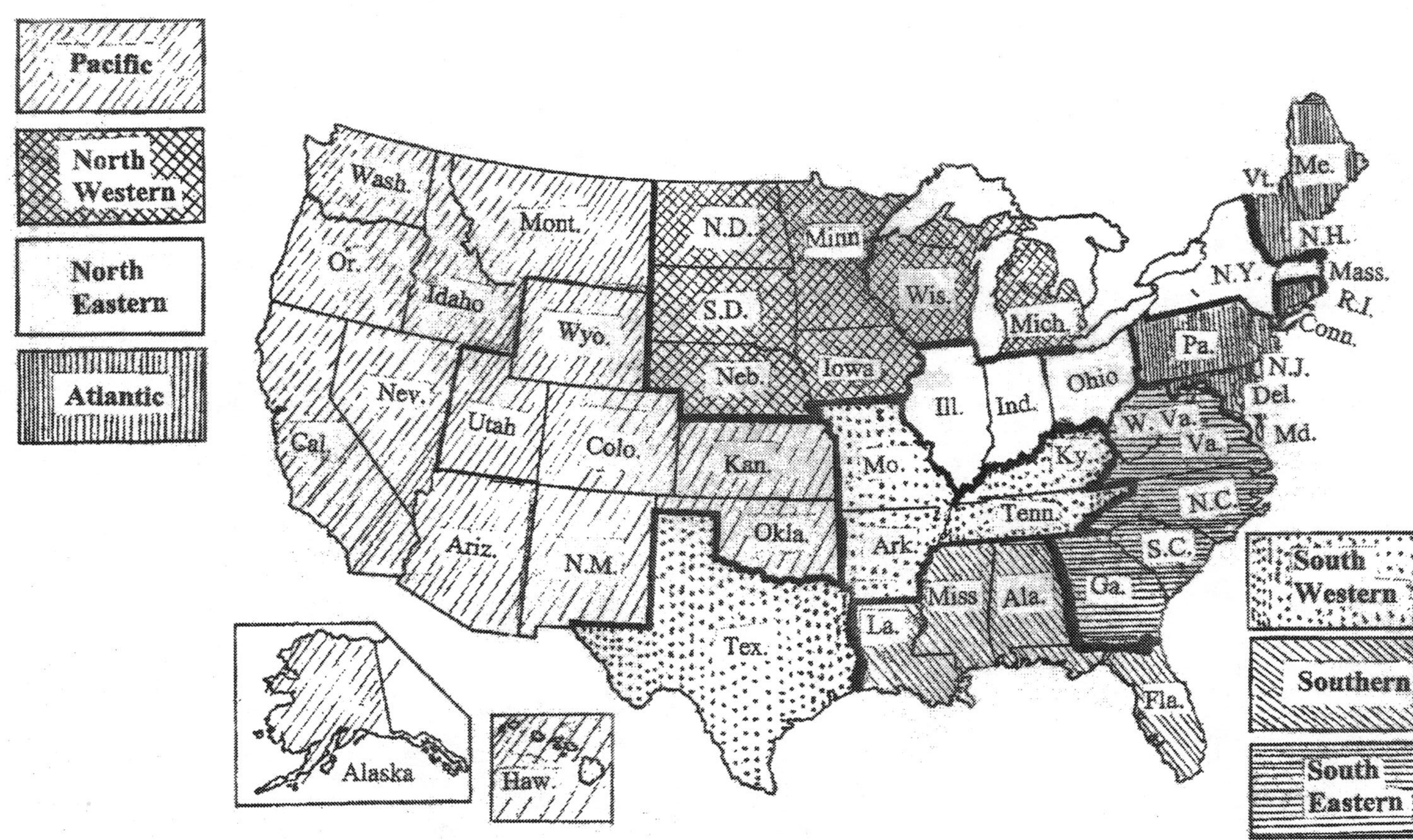

Generic sequence: Volume, author, title, page or section number (edition, publisher, year).

Eminent scholars in civilian jurisdictions have considerable influence on the interpretation of law through their written commentaries.[18] This influence is so strong that in a civilian jurisdiction, *la doctrine* is habitually taken into account by judges and legislators when they frame, interpret, or apply law.[19] For each civilian jurisdiction, the scholars who write commentary concentrate on the relatively manageable output of a single legislature and two sets of courts. Therefore, the interaction between legal institutions and the scholars who watch them in civilian jurisdictions tends to result in a more coherent and predictable body of national law than would otherwise be produced.[20]

This kind of thorough review of legal authority would be impossible in the United States, partially because of the federal system: A scholar would have to master the law of the entire federal system as well as of all 50 states. Furthermore, the common law tradition emphasizes practice, not theory. Therefore, in the United States, secondary authority is not law; however, it can become law if a court adopts it. The portion adopted by the court as discussed in the court's opinion is then law, but other portions not discussed in the opinion are not law, though they might be highly persuasive. Secondary authority includes Restatements, learned treatises, law review articles, American Law Reports, digests, and legal encyclopedias. In the United States, in contrast with civilian jurisdictions, eminent scholars' treatises and law review articles sometimes influence judges and regulators, but institutional authors tend to have much more influence. For example, the Restatements of Law, written under the auspices of the American Law Institute, are very influential.[21] Courts often adopt sections of a Restatement if those portions address the particular facts of the case before the court. That section then becomes law in that particular jurisdiction.

Although they are not law, and their influence may be somewhat less than in a civilian jurisdiction, secondary sources are still a vital source of information for an attorney researching U.S. law, and are particularly useful when the attorney must locate law applicable to a client's situation (the second research skill). Given a client's situation, the attorney must first decide what area (or areas) of law is at issue: contract, tort, corporations, state or federal law, and so on. Once the legal category is identified, if the attorney is completely unfamiliar with the area of law, the most efficient way to begin is to use a one-volume treatise on the subject to get a general sense of that area. Among other things, the attorney should determine whether there is likely to be an applicable statute or whether this particular issue is one of common law. Only after the researcher has secured some information from secondary sources does it become

[18] Carol Baudenbacher, *Some Remarks on the Method of Civil Law,* Tex Int'l L.J. 333, 354-55 (1999).
[19] Mary Ann Glendon, Michael W. Gordon, & Christopher Osakwe, *Comparative Legal Traditions in a Nutshell* 88 (West 1982).
[20] *Id.*
[21] For more information about the founding of the American Law Institute, go to *www.ali.org.*

productive to start searching primary sources. Failure to do adequate research in secondary sources is likely to lead to three unfortunate consequences:

1. The researcher will not identify the appropriate legal terminology and will find it difficult to research effectively.
2. The researcher will not be able to recognize primary, mandatory authority.
3. The researcher is likely to misinterpret primary authority even if he or she is able to find and identify it.

Citations of secondary authority follow the same general format as for primary authority. For books, first the volume number if there is more than one volume, and the authors' names are given, followed by a comma, then the title of the book and the page number or section number. Finally, the edition, publisher, and year of publication are included in parentheses: 21 Charles Alan Wright & Kenneth A. Graham, Jr., *Federal Practice and Procedure* § 5023 (2d ed., West 1990). The citation form for law review articles is similar. First the authors' names are given, followed by a comma; then the title of the article in italics, followed again by a comma; and then the abbreviated title of the journal preceded by the volume number and followed by the page number and pinpoint page number. The year of the journal is included in parentheses: Rieko Mashima, *Examination of the Interrelationship Among the Software Industry Structure, Keiretsu, and Japanese Intellectual Property Protection for Software*, 33 Int'l Law. 119, 121 (1999).

IV. THE FIRST INTERPRETIVE SKILL: RANKING OR WEIGHT OF AUTHORITY

In the United States, the relative weight accorded to legal sources differs.[22] Some materials are *primary authority*, meaning that they are themselves law. Primary law comes from four sources: constitutions, legislatures, administrations, and the judiciary. Because the United States is a federal system, we have primary authority from all 50 states (and Puerto Rico) as well as the federal government. Other legal sources are commonly referred to as *secondary sources*. Secondary sources are not themselves law, but can in certain instances be used to persuade a law-finding body. Examples of such secondary sources include Restatements of the law, legal periodicals, treatises, and hornbooks. The persuasive, authoritative value of these sources varies, depending on the source, the author, and the purpose for which the source is being used. In general, a Restatement, published by the American Law Institute, is very persuasive. American Law Report (A.L.R.) articles may also be quite persuasive because they are institutionally written. A major treatise is perhaps slightly less so, and periodicals even less authoritative, with commercially prepared law school

[22] Cohen & Olson, *supra* note 12, § 1-3b, at 6.

hornbooks and student-written articles at the bottom tier. However, even these latter sources can have substantial persuasive value, depending on the factors mentioned earlier. A subgroup of secondary sources includes books that are useful only as tools for finding other material but that are not themselves either primary or persuasive authority. For example, digests, legal encyclopedias, and various indexes have little or no authoritative value but are useful in locating both the law and authoritative information about the law.

A. Three-Tier Court System

As mentioned earlier, judicial systems in the United States generally have three tiers. In each judicial system, the decisions of a number of trial courts are reviewed (on request of one of the parties involved) by a lesser number of appellate courts. In turn, a court of last resort (usually known as a supreme court)[23] may, at its discretion, review the decisions of the appellate courts under its jurisdiction. Parties have a right to appeal to an appellate court, but when subsequently disappointed by that ruling, they do not have a right to review by the appropriate supreme court. They may only ask the court of last resort to review the appellate court decision. This request is presented in a document called a *writ of certiorari* or *cert.*, harking back to the original common law writ system, and the court of last resort may grant or deny the writ, at its discretion. If the court denies the writ, that simply means that the court refused to either affirm or reverse the decision. It adds little to the authority of the underlying appellate court decision. In contrast, if the court of last resort grants the writ, the appellate court decision may subsequently either be *affirmed* or *vacated and remanded.* If the appellate court decision is vacated and remanded, that means it has no authority and is no longer law. If the court of last resort affirms the lower court's decision, then it has more authority than it originally had—it carries more weight because now the holding has the imprimatur of the supreme court.

B. Mandatory versus Persuasive Authority

The rulings of a reviewing court are *binding precedent* or *mandatory authority* only on the courts under its jurisdiction and on itself. United States Supreme Court cases are, naturally, mandatory authority for all courts, whether state or federal, though there are times when the United States Supreme Court will refuse to decide a case, because it finds that the issue is one of state law rather than federal law. In these instances, the

---

[23] The terms *supreme court* and *court of last resort* are used interchangeably here, because courts of last resort are not always called *supreme courts.* For example, the court of last resort in New York is termed the New York Court of Appeals, while appellate and trial courts in that state are both termed "Supreme" courts. *See* Bluebook ______T1 New York 220-21 ______ (18th ed. 2005); ALWD ____________ (3d ed., Aspen Law & Bus. 2006).

Court declares that comity and respect for federalism compel it to defer to the decisions of state courts on issues of state law, reflecting its understanding that decisions of state courts are definitive pronouncements of the will of the states as sovereign entities.[24]

Determining whether a given case is mandatory authority is more complicated than simply looking to see whether it is a United States Supreme Court decision: a reviewing court has no power over courts that are outside its scope of authority, whether they rank above or below it. The rulings of the Michigan Supreme Court are binding over all appellate and trial courts in Michigan. However, the Supreme Court of Michigan has no power over a trial, appellate, or supreme court in Mississippi. Thus, a Michigan Supreme Court decision is not mandatory authority in Mississippi. The Mississippi trial court may, however, find that the Michigan decision is *persuasive*. Thus, *mandatory authority* is the law that a given court must follow. In contrast, *persuasive authority* may be law elsewhere, but is not law for that particular court (unless that court adopts it, in which case it becomes mandatory thereafter). Generally, state supreme court decisions have more persuasive authority (more *weight of authority*) than do appellate court decisions, and appellate decisions are stronger than trial court decisions. Nevertheless, a very well-reasoned opinion of lesser authority can sometimes persuade a higher court.

The same is true in the federal judiciary. Ninth Circuit case law is mandatory authority for all federal district courts in the Ninth Circuit (Arizona, California, Idaho, Nevada, Oregon, and Washington). It is not, however, mandatory authority for a federal district court in New York, because the New York court is in the Second Circuit, though the New York court may find a Ninth Circuit case persuasive. Things get even more complicated, though, when state and federal law interact.

C. Federalism, Subject Matter Jurisdiction, and the Preemption Doctrine

As mentioned earlier, Article VI of the United States Constitution provides that

> [t]his Constitution, and the Laws of the United States which shall be made in Pursuance thereof; and all Treaties made, or which shall be made under the Authority of the United States, shall be the supreme Law of the Land; and the Judges in every State shall be bound thereby, any Thing in the Constitution or Laws of any State to the Contrary notwithstanding.[25]

This section, commonly called the *Supremacy Clause*, leads one to expect that a federal decision will always be mandatory authority in a state court. In fact, this is by no means always so.

---

[24] *Bush v. Gore*, 531 U.S. 98, 112 (2000) (Rehnquist, Scalia, & Thomas, JJ., concurring).

[25] U.S. Const. art. VI, cl. 2.

In contrast to the Supremacy Clause, the Tenth Amendment to the United States Constitution provides that "[t]he powers not delegated to the United States by the Constitution, nor prohibited by it to the States, are reserved to the States respectively, or to the people." If these two provisions are interpreted together, one sees that the federal government was given certain enumerated powers, but that the states and the people retain all other law-making power, adding another dimension to the concept of a limited government. It is on this basis that the Supreme Court, and other federal courts, avoid issues of state law. Under the Supremacy Clause, if it is properly within the scope of an enumerated power, any law created by the federal government preempts contradictory state law. This is commonly referred to as the *preemption doctrine.* However, the state statute at issue usually does not directly contradict federal law, and may even fill a gap in federal law. Such state laws are left intact. There are many cases in which the major issue is whether a state statute is preempted by federal law.

This dichotomy between state and federal law is also seen in the limitations on the subject matter jurisdiction of federal courts. *Subject matter jurisdiction* is the power of a particular court to hear the type of case that is before it.[26] In keeping with the underlying U.S. norm of limited government, federal district courts are courts of limited jurisdiction, and by statute have the power to decide only a few kinds of cases:

- actions against foreign states[27]
- cases involving federal law[28]
- cases involving controversies between parties from diverse states or between a U.S. party and a foreign party (known as *diversity* cases)[29]
- admiralty cases[30]
- bankruptcy cases[31]

The second and third are the most common; cases involving federal law (known also as *federal question cases*) and diversity cases. As discussed earlier, in federal question cases, federal courts are not to tamper with a state law unless it directly contradicts a federal law—but things are further complicated in diversity cases. Federal courts sitting in diversity must apply the substantive state law of the state in which they sit. In diversity cases, state supreme court decisions are mandatory authority for a federal court. This is known as the *Erie* doctrine, stemming from *Erie Railroad v. Tompkins*, 304 U.S. 64 (1938). (Read the citation: which court decided *Erie*?)

Erie is a very famous case. In it, the U.S. Supreme Court established the now-ingrained principle that federal courts sitting in diversity apply the substantive law of the state in which they sit, thus demonstrating the Court's respect for the states as

---

[26] *Black's Law Dictionary* 870 (8th ed. 2004).
[27] 28 U.S.C. § 1330 (2000).
[28] *Id.* § 1331.
[29] *Id.* § 1332.
[30] *Id.* § 1333.
[31] *Id.* § 1224.

sovereign governments. Harry Tompkins, a citizen of Pennsylvania, was struck and injured by an open door on a passing Erie Railroad freight train.[32] Erie Railroad was a New York corporation and therefore a citizen of New York for purposes of diversity jurisdiction.[33] After recovering from his injuries, Tompkins's attorney chose to bring suit against the railroad in New York federal district court on a diversity basis so as to benefit from certain advantages of suing in federal rather than state court.[34] At trial, the parties argued about which law should apply.[35] The railroad wanted Pennsylvania negligence law (because it was pro-business and less plaintiff-friendly), and Tompkins wanted "general" common law, which was in his favor.[36] The trial court instructed the jury according to the latter, and Tompkins won at the trial-court level on the basis of general common law.[37] The Second Circuit affirmed the district court's decision, and the railroad was then granted a writ of certiorari by the United States Supreme Court.[38]

An earlier Supreme Court case had held that general common law could apply in the absence of statutory state law.[39] Recognizing that there had been a multiplicity of unanticipated political and social problems with the earlier doctrine, and also recognizing that no clause in the Constitution confers on federal courts the power to create such common law supplanting state common law, the Court overturned the earlier decision.[40] It ruled that there is no federal general common law, held that diversity cases should be decided on the basis of state law, and remanded the case to be decided on the basis of Pennsylvania law.[41]

While it may or may not be true that there is no federal common law, the *Erie* doctrine has grown and flourished since its inception in 1938. Occasionally, in diversity questions like that in *Erie*, a federal circuit court will be unsure about the applicable state law in the case before it. In these circumstances, the federal court will *certify* the question of state law to the state supreme court; in other words, it will ask the state supreme court for advice. In conclusion, although appellate decisions carry more weight of authority than do trial court decisions, and although state supreme court decisions carry more weight than do appellate decisions, except for United States Supreme Court cases, no one case will ever be mandatory authority for all courts, and there are times when a federal court must follow state law despite Article VI of the Federal Constitution. Therefore, when researching an issue, the attorney must always first consider whether the case law being considered is mandatory authority, and next—assuming it is only persuasive authority—consider how much weight it should be given. For a summary of relative authority, see Figure 2-4.

---

[32] *Erie RR. Co. v. Tompkins*, 304 U.S. 64, 69 (1938); *see also* Stephen C. Yeazell et al., *Civil Procedure* 222-27 (6th ed. 2004) (citing & quoting *Erie*, 304 U.S. at 64).
[33] *Erie*, 304 U.S. at 69-72, 78.
[34] *See id.* at 70.
[35] *Id.* at 70-71.
[36] *Id.*
[37] *Id. at* 70.
[38] *Erie*, 304 U.S. at 71.
[39] *Id.* (citing *Swift v. Tyson*, 10 L. Ed. 865 (1842).
[40] *Erie*, 304 U.S. at 73-78.
[41] *Id.* at 78-80.

FIGURE 2-4
WEIGHT OF AUTHORITY

Authority	Primary or Secondary	Mandatory	Persuasive
U.S. Constitution	Primary	Always mandatory	
U.S. Supreme Court case	Primary	Always mandatory	
U.S. Circuit Court case	Primary	Mandatory to circuit court itself and to federal district courts within deciding circuit	Very persuasive outside of deciding circuit
U.S. District Court case	Primary	Mandatory only to deciding court	Very persuasive within circuit, somewhat persuasive to other federal district courts
U.S. statute	Primary	Mandatory, preempts conflicting state statutes	
U.S. regulation	Primary	Mandatory if within scope of enabling statute	
State constitution	Primary	Mandatory in state	Persuasive in other states
State supreme court case	Primary	Mandatory in state and to federal district court sitting in diversity in that state	Reasonably persuasive in other states
State appellate and trial court cases	Primary	Mandatory only within appropriate state subdivision	Reasonably persuasive in comparable subdivisions
Restatements of Law	Secondary		Highly persuasive, often more so than persuasive case law
Treatises	Secondary		Can be very persuasive
Law review articles	Secondary		Can be quite persuasive, depending on author and topic match
ALRs, legal encyclopedias, etc.	Secondary		Very little persuasive value

D. Timeliness

Just as statutes are amended, making the original statute obsolete, cases can be vacated or overruled. When a case is *vacated*, the deciding court or its supervising court declares it null and void in its entirety; therefore, it lacks any authority and precedential value. A case that has been wholly or partially *overruled* is outdated because newer cases show that the law has changed since the overruled one was decided. Parts of the opinion may still be authoritative, but other parts may lack authority. For example, since *Bourque* was decided, a more recent Louisiana case has held that the doctrine of assumption of risk is outdated,[42] as it is in most states. However, although assumption of risk is gone, the case is otherwise still an authoritative and current discussion of liability for negligent behavior in recreational sports. Thus, an old, obsolete case, like an obsolete statute, may have very little legal authority on some points, but still be good or persuasive on others.

DISCUSSION NOTES

A. *Read and explain the following citations*

Constitutions

1. U.S. Const. art. IV, § 5(b).
2. Ala. Const. art. I, § 1.
3. Conn. Const. art III, § 13.
4. Mich. Const. art. IV, § 2.
5. N.M. Const. art. I, § 2.

Statutes

1. 18 U.S.C. § 922(b)(1) (2007).
2. La. Civ. Code § 1983 (West 2007).
3. N.Y. Envtl. Conserv. Law § 11-0101 (McKinney 2007).
4. Del. Code Ann. tit. 4, § 1201 (2007).
5. Wyo. Stat. Ann. § 6-3-502 (Michie 2007).

Regulations

1. 8 C.F.R. § 214.1 (2007).
2. Wis. Admin. Code F.D. § 1.01 (2007).
3. Mont. Admin. R. 1.2.205 (2007).
4. Mass. Regs. Code tit. 105, § 530.001 (2007).
5. Ariz. Admin. Code R12-4-407 (2007).

Cases

1. *Dickerson v. United States*, 120 S. Ct. 2326, 2336 (2000).
2. *Lestina v. West Bend Mut. Ins. Co.*, 501 N.W.2d 28, 32 (Wis. 1993).

---

[42] *Picou v. Hartford Ins. Co.*, 558 So. 2d 787, 789 (La. Ct. App. 1990).

3. *McGraw v. Holland*, 257 F.3d 513, 515 (6th Cir. 2001).
4. *Auckenthaler v. Grundmeyer*, 877 P.2d 1039 (Nev. 1994).
5. *Roe v. Wade*, 410 U.S. 959, 93 S. Ct. 1409, 35 L. Ed. 2d 694 (1973).
6. *Picou v. Hartford Ins. Co.*, 558 So. 2d 787 (La. Ct. App. 1990).
7. *Films by Jove, Inc. v. Berov*, 250 F. Supp. 2d 156 (E.D.N.Y. 2003).

Secondary Authority

1. 1 E. Allen Farnsworth, *Farnsworth on Contracts* 1 § 2.2 (2d ed. 1998).
2. *Restatement (Second) of Contracts* § 90 (1979).
3. Konrad Zweigert & Hein Kötz, *An Introduction to Comparative Law* 162 (Tony Weir trans., Oxford Univ. Press 1998).
4. Lawrence R. Helfer & Anne-Marie Slaughter, *Toward a Theory of Effective Supranatural Adjudication*, 107 Yale L.J. 273, 276, 280, 282 (1997).
5. Roscoe Pound, *The Development of American Law and Its Deviation from English Law*, 67 Law Q. Rev. 49, 59 (1951).

B. *Explain whether the following sources are primary or secondary*

1. *Roe v. Wade*, 410 U.S. 959 (1973).
2. 1 E. Allen Farnsworth, *Farnsworth on Contracts* § 2.2 (2d ed. 1998).
3. 8 C.F.R. § 214.1 (2000).
4. *Auckenthaler v. Grundmeyer*, 877 P.2d 1039 (Nev. 1994).
5. Roscoe Pound, *The Development of American Law and Its Deviation from English Law*, 67 Law Q. Rev. 49, 59 (1951).

C. *Explain whether the following are mandatory or persuasive*

1. *Roe v. Wade*, 410 U.S. 959 (1973), in a Florida state trial court?
2. *McGraw v. Holland*, 257 F.3d 513, 515 (6th Cir. 2001), in a Texas federal district court? In the Eleventh Circuit? In a federal district court sitting in Ohio? In an Ohio state court?
3. *Lestina v. West Bend Mut. Ins. Co.*, 501 N.W.2d 28, 32 (Wis. 1993), in a Wisconsin state trial court? In a federal district court sitting in Wisconsin?
4. *Auckenthaler v. Grundmeyer*, 877 P.2d 1039 (Nev. 1994), in the Nevada supreme court? In a California trial court?

EXERCISE *Locating Legal Authority Given Identifying Information*

A. *Locating authority, separating law from commentary, comparing official to commercial versions*

Using hard copy, find the authority, then answer the questions.

1. Find the following statutes and summarize their content:
   a. 28 U.S.C. § 1331
   b. 28 U.S.C. § 1332
   c. 28 U.S.C. § 1333

2. When was each of the following statutes first passed? When was each last amended?
   a. 28 U.S.C. § 1331
   b. 28 U.S.C. § 1332
   c. 28 U.S.C. § 1333
3. If you wanted to find a case discussing the constitutionality of § 1331 or the amount in controversy § 1332, (from question 2), where in the U.S.C.A. or U.S.C.S. would you look?
4. What are the first and last phrases of the following statutes?
   a. 11 U.S.C. § 524
   b. 18 U.S.C. § 924
5. Find *Miranda v. Arizona*, 384 U.S. 436, 86 S. Ct. 1602, 16 L. Ed. 2d 694 (1966), in an unofficial reporter.
   a. What is the first sentence of the opinion?
   b. Quote the first sentence of the portion of the opinion associated with headnotes 25-28 (S. Ct.) or 24-25 (L. Ed. 2d).
   c. On what page of the official U.S. reporter would this language be found?
   d. If both unofficial reporters are available, which do you prefer? Why?
6. Find *Roe v. Wade*, 410 U.S. 113, 93 S. Ct. 705, 35 L. Ed. 2d 147 (1973), in an unofficial reporter.
   a. What is the first sentence of the opinion?
   b. Quote the first sentence of the portion of the opinion associated with headnote 10 (S. Ct.) or 18 (L. Ed. 2d).
   c. On what page of the official U.S. reporter would this language be found?
   d. If both unofficial reporters are available, which do you prefer? Why?

B. Locating federal case law when given partial information

Given the case name, court, and year of decision, find the following cases and complete the citation. If you are using hard copy, use the appropriate Table of Cases volume in the Federal Digest 4th to do this.

1. *Klump v. Duffus*, _______ F.3d _______ (7th Cir. 1995).
2. *Bensusan Rest. Corp. v. King*, _______ F.3d _______ (2d Cir. 1997).

C. Locating state authorities

1. Summarize the content of the following statutes:
   a. 735 Ill. Comp. Stat. 5/2-209 (2001).
   b. N.Y. C.P.L.R. 302 (McKinney 2001).
2. Locate the following cases and summarize the main issue:
   a. *Malone v. Equitas Reinsurance*, 101 Cal. Rptr. 2d 524 (Ct. App. 2000).
   b. *Banco Colpatria Cayman, Inc. v. Illial Int'l, S.A.*, 758 So. 2d 1288 (Fla. 2000).

D. Ranking weight of authority: Distinguish between primary and secondary, mandatory and persuasive authority, given each court

1. Florida appellate court:
   a. a Kansas Supreme Court case
   b. a Florida statute

   c. a federal statute
   d. the Restatement (Second) of Contracts
   e. an Eleventh Circuit case
2. The United States Seventh Circuit:
   a. a Second Circuit case
   b. a Wisconsin case
   c. an Illinois statute
   d. a treatise
   e. the Vienna Convention on Sales

E. Using secondary authority to help with coursework

Although Socratic dialogue leads to active knowledge of a subject, students may still be somewhat confused or want more detail. In these instances, hornbooks (one-volume treatises) are often very helpful. Locate one of the following well-known hornbooks, look up one of the following topics using the table of contents or index, and give a short one-paragraph description of the applicable principle:

1. Torts: negligence in recreational sports.
2. Federal Civil Procedure: Foreign Sovereign Immunities Act.
3. Contracts: promissory estoppel.

EXERCISE HINTS FOR VARIOUS MEDIA

On hard copy

Exercise B: Use the Tables of Case Names volumes in the Federal Digest 4th Edition.

Exercise E: Hard copy is vastly superior to computer for research in secondary authority.

On Westlaw

Exercise A: Use "Find" and enter the numerical portion of the citation. Results will give the U.S.C.A. and the S. Ct. annotated versions of authority.

Exercise B: choose "allfeds" database, then enter one or more parties' names in a title search. For example: ti(Bensusan)

Exercise C: use "Find" and enter the numerical portion of the citation.

On LEXIS

Exercise A: Choose the "Get a Document" and then "By citation" tabs, then enter the numerical portion of the citation. Results will give the U.S.C.S. and L. Ed. annotated versions.

Exercise B: Choose the "Get a Document" and then "by party name" tabs, then choose the appropriate database. Results will give the LEXIS version and headnotes.

Exercise C.2: Follow the directions for Exercise B.

On No-Fee Databases

Exercise A.1, 2, 3, 4 (U.S. Code): Use *www.law.cornell.edu/uscode* or *www.findlaw.com*; then, under "U.S. federal resources," choose "legislative" and enter the numeric portion of the statute citation.

Exercise A.5: (Supreme Court cases): Use *www.law.cornell.edu/supct*, then choose "archive of decisions," and look up the case name, or findlaw.com. Because these are noncommercial sources, there will be no headnotes.

Exercise B: The text of the opinion can be found by following links from *www.law.cornell.edu* and using the case names in a search, but there will be no citation information for F.3d, and no headnotes.

Exercise C:

1. State statutes: follow links from *www.findlaw.com* to the appropriate state, and from there to the appropriate statute.
2. State cases: more difficult, but some case laws are made available through links from *www.law.cornell.edu* to official state Web sites.

CHAPTER 3

LEGAL REASONING AND OBJECTIVE LEGAL WRITING

INTRODUCTION

All legal writing has one of three goals:

1. to predict the legal consequences of an action;
2. to persuade someone; or
3. to create legal obligations or prevent certain acts or conflicts.

The first type of writing is called *objective* or *predictive writing*; the second is referred to as *persuasive writing*; and the third is termed *preventive writing*. Objective or predictive writing is usually in the form of a law firm memorandum or a scholarly article. Law firm memoranda contain a concise objective analysis of a narrow area of the law and then use that analysis to predict how a court will decide a particular client's legal problem. Most scholarly articles analyze a narrow area of the law objectively, explaining how and why courts have decided the way they did and commenting on that analysis. Persuasive writing is usually intended to persuade a court that it should decide in favor of a client, and includes documents such as motion memoranda and appellate briefs. The third type of writing, preventive writing, is used in drafting contracts aimed at preventing legal problems or resolving them in advance. This chapter focuses on predictive writing and the underlying common law legal reasoning it requires, but it also gives a short description of the other two types of legal writing, which are more fully developed in Chapters 11 and 12.

The success of a predictive memo depends on whether the writer researched the law effectively, interpreted that research correctly, and logically connected that interpretation to the client's particular action (legal reasoning). The success of a persuasive document builds on these same research and interpretive skills, but also incorporates skillful presentation of and emphasis on legal arguments that are in the client's favor and careful rebuttal of opposing arguments. The third type of legal writing requires skill in creating legal rules and relationships in such a way as to prevent legal problems, as with drafting contracts, wills, and legislation.

The interoffice memo, which is the standard predictive document, explains how a court is likely to decide a given legal issue. It explains how a particular court has dealt with similar situations in the past and how it is likely to deal with a client's specific situation in the future. Based on this type of legal memo, an attorney is then able to give a client accurate advice about how to proceed in a particular case. Because of the multiplicity of legal authorities in the United States, being able to predict how a court is likely to decide a client's particular legal issue requires an understanding of how attorneys in the United States approach law. To this end, this chapter begins by introducing and explaining deductive and analogical legal reasoning as used in the United States; explaining IRAC (Issue, Rule, Application, Conclusion) reasoning; and showing how it is used in the interoffice memo. IRAC reasoning is an organizational tool used in most, if not all, legal writing in the United States, including law school exams, motion memoranda, appellate briefs, and court opinions as well as law office briefs. When you use it to organize legal reasoning, IRAC analysis helps you further develop that reasoning.

Furthermore, LL.M. graduates who become associate attorneys or interns employed in U.S. firms can expect that many, if not most, of their assignments will be to research and write interoffice memos. Developing skill in IRAC reasoning and being able to write a well-reasoned and well-written law firm memo are important parts of learning and understanding how the legal system of the United States works.

I. DEDUCTIVE REASONING AND THE SYLLOGISM

In the United States, deductive reasoning provides the underlying organizational framework for most legal analysis. Analogical reasoning then supplements and supports the deductive framework. The classic expression of deductive reasoning, the syllogism, was first stated by the ancient Greek philosopher Aristotle and consists of three simple statements, as in the following:

1. All men are mortal.
2. Socrates is a man.
3. Therefore, Socrates is mortal.

Socrates was an ancient Greek philosopher who founded the tradition of teaching followers by asking them series of questions. He was forced by the elders of his city, Athens, to commit suicide because they believed he was corrupting the youth of the city. Nevertheless, his thinking and teaching style have become important both to the Western philosophical tradition and to American-style law school teaching. Socrates taught Plato, who in turn taught Aristotle, who wrote this famous syllogism.

The syllogism consists of (1) a major premise, (2) a minor premise containing a subgroup of the major premise, and (3) a conclusion that must follow if points 1 and 2 are true. The syllogism is also known as the transitivity principle in mathematics, with which you may be more familiar: (1) A = C, (2) B = A, (3) therefore B = C. The syllogism is highly persuasive, partially because its logic is inexorable and partially because it is very easy to follow. For a syllogism to be valid, both premises must be true, and the terms used must match. For example, compare the first syllogism to this one:

1. All men are mortal.
2. Socrates is a cat.
3. Therefore, Socrates is mortal.

This syllogism fails for two reasons. First, the premise in point 2 is untrue, because Socrates was a man, not a cat. Second, the terms do not match (the first premise contains the term *men*, while the second makes no mention of that term and instead uses *cat*). As a result, whether man or cat, Socrates may still be mortal, but the syllogism has not proven him so.

In a legal argument, the major premise is a legal rule, the minor premise applies the specific facts of the situation to the requirements of the rule, and the conclusion is the legal result, as in the following example drawn from *Lestina*:

1. Players of recreational sports who flagrantly violate the rules of the game and thereby cause injury to other players are liable for negligence.
2. Jerger, by slide-tackling, flagrantly violated his league's soccer rules and caused injury to Lestina.
3. Therefore, Jerger is liable for negligence.

However, unlike the Socrates example, the truth of the premises in a legal argument is not usually so straightforward and obvious. The attorney must demonstrate the truth of both premises, and must show that the terms match, if the deductive logic of her argument is to be convincing. The process of proving both premises and the resulting conclusion is called IRAC reasoning.

II. IRAC AND CRAC REASONING

IRAC, and its variant *CRAC*, are acronyms widely used by U.S. attorneys and law schools to refer to a standard way of developing syllogistic arguments in both objective and persuasive documents. IRAC stands for Issue, Rule, Application, and Conclusion, in that order. The variation CRAC (pronounced see-rak) substitutes Conclusion for the Issue, so that the conclusion is stated twice. IRAC/CRAC analysis is used in law school exams, objective law-firm memos, persuasive documents filed with courts, and court opinions themselves. Different legal writing instructors may prefer one or the other, and one or the other may be more appropriate in a given situation. For example, the author recommends IRAC for law school exams and objective legal memos, and CRAC for persuasive documents. Using IRAC analysis, when an attorney is called upon to address a legal question, he:

1. identifies the legal question or *issue* to be addressed,
2. states and explains the applicable legal *rule* (the first premise),

3. *applies* that legal authority to the specific facts of his client's situation (the second premise), and
4. *concludes* by answering the question asked in step 1.

The syllogistic core of IRAC analysis can be seen in the following pattern.

> Given a particular situation and a stated legal **Issue** (IRAC) or **Conclusion** (CRAC), the attorney explains:

1. The first premise: the legal **rule**
2. The second premise: **application** of the rule to the specific facts of the particular situation
3. His **conclusion**

Looking at the preceding *Lestina* syllogism, the first premise is a statement of the general rule about liability in recreational sports cases; the second applies that rule to the particular facts of the case; the third statement concludes that because the requirements of the rule are fulfilled, the defendant is liable. The syllogism example is fine as far as it goes, but would not be regarded as persuasive to an American attorney because it does not explain or prove either premise: The syllogism does not explain how the definition of negligence is derived, nor does it explain how each element of that definition applies to Jerger's acts. IRAC analysis allows for expansion and proof of both the major and minor premises in a legal syllogism. The amount of expansion and proof needed varies, depending on the purpose of the proof and the complexity of the legal issue.

Exam answers to hypothetical questions are the simplest and most concise, usually consisting of a string of IRAC paragraphs. Each paragraph identifies a different issue, states the appropriate legal rule, explains with particularity how the rule applies to the facts of the hypothetical, and concludes, stating that one party or the other either is or is not likely to be liable.[1] In contrast, interoffice law firm memos and persuasive documents may discuss only one or two issues, and have a whole section, called the "Discussion" section, devoted to IRAC analysis. In such documents, after the **issue** is identified, several paragraphs or pages may explain the applicable legal **rule**; then several paragraphs or pages explain how the rule **applies** to the specific situation, including arguments on both sides where applicable; and then the **conclusion**, stated in a final paragraph, explains which arguments are most persuasive.

Usually, after researching the law and locating the most relevant authorities, the attorney prewrites or sketches out the discussion section, working through the rule and application and reaching a conclusion. The analysis consists of five interrelated steps:

1. Identifying the legal issue
2. Dissecting the components of the rule
3. Analyzing how previous cases define or explain these components, in light of the facts in those cases

[1] See II.B. in Appendix A, on writing exam answers.

4. Comparing the facts of the present case to the facts of the precedents to analyze whether each component or the rule has been met or established
5. Concluding whether the rule applies

As mentioned earlier, common law reasoning incorporates both deductive and analogical reasoning. IRAC organization is an expansion of syllogistic, deductive reasoning. Analogical reasoning is incorporated into the fourth step when the attorney compares the facts of his case to the facts of previous cases to see if he can draw an analogy. If his case is like previous cases because the facts are similar, then the result should also be similar, under the principle of stare decisis. Although it may require some adjustment to master IRAC organization, the major difference in reasoning between civilian and U.S. common law legal reasoning is the use of analogy and focus on particular facts. The next section illustrates the steps in this IRAC analysis, explaining in greater detail how facts and analogies are developed. The final section of the chapter explains how this analysis is used in an interoffice memo.

A. I: Identification of an Issue

Learning how to spot and state a legal issue is a complex task. A client generally enters the attorney's office with either a specific legal question or a story of something that happened. In either instance, the client may believe that the question or problem is simple, but upon examination, the attorney may discover that it implicates a number of different areas of law, each of which must be carefully researched and analyzed before the client can be advised. In the context of a U.S. law school exam, professors look to see if a student is skilled at "issue spotting": Can the student spot a practical example of a potential legal issue pertaining to one or more components of a legal rule that was taught in the course? Gaining skill at spotting issues on law school exams helps law students gain skill at identifying clients' legal problems.

In the context of legal research and writing and IRAC analysis, the associate attorney who is assigned the task of writing an in-house memo is usually given a legal question, and therefore may not need to identify the issue. Some legal questions seem to be fairly straightforward. The area of law is identified, and the question relates to one small component of that area. However, even here the legal question can be phrased in a number of different ways, but only one or two phrasings may be productive for research, appropriate for the situation, or appropriate in a particular court, because different jurisdictions use different terms and even different rules. Thus, part of the attorney's task is to phrase the issue as accurately and precisely as possible. Generally, one begins with a tentative question and then changes that question as research and analysis develop. The question is eventually focused on one or more components of a legal rule. Formulating the issue requires that one identify and analyze the appropriate legal rule, then break it down into its components, and finally decide exactly how to phrase the question. Therefore, although *issue* is the first word in IRAC, as a practical matter an attorney must usually understand the applicable rule first, before refining her understanding of exactly how to phrase the client's issue.

B. R: Analysis of a Legal Rule

The rule component of IRAC analysis is the accurate statement and explanation of a legal rule or principle. In general, it consists of two steps. First, the rule is dissected to determine its component parts and how they relate to each other. Then, each component is analyzed using reference to appropriate authority. For example, in analyzing a statute, one considers not only the language of the statute itself but also how courts have interpreted various parts of that statute. In explaining how courts have interpreted statutes, common law reasoning often requires that the specific facts of the cases be discussed, as well as the courts' reasoning, so that one can see what kinds of facts are likely to elicit what kinds of decisions. This reference to factual context is later developed into the analogical thinking that underlies the application portion of common law legal reasoning.

1. Types of Legal Rules

The various parts of a rule can relate to each other in a few different ways: conjunctively, disjunctively, as exceptions, as factors, as balancing tests, and as totality-of-the-circumstances tests.[2] Each type is discussed in turn here.

a. Elemental or Conjunctive Rules

Some rules are composed of several different elements, all of which must be present. These are called *conjunctive* ("and") rules. Negligence is one such conjunctive rule: a person is liable for negligence if he had a duty to do something, he breached that duty, *and* the plaintiff was harmed *and* the defendant's breach of that duty caused the plaintiff's harm. In other words, negligence requires four elements: duty *and* breach *and* causation *and* damages.

One variation of the conjunctive rule is termed a "prong" test. Usually there are at most two or three prongs. All of the requirements of all prongs must be met in order for the rule to apply, so these rules are in essence conjunctive. For example, the Fourth Amendment of the U.S. Constitution requires a warrant before a suspect's property can be searched for contraband. To secure a search warrant, police must submit an affidavit (a sworn, written statement) to a court showing probable cause to search. Sometimes the affidavit is based on information obtained from an unidentified informant. This kind of affidavit must satisfy a two-prong test to qualify as "probable cause" for the search. The first prong requires that the affidavit show the basis of the informant's knowledge about the location of the contraband. The second prong requires that the affidavit include information that led the police to conclude that the informant was credible or reliable.[3]

b. Disjunctive Rules

Rules can also be *disjunctive* ("or" rules) or can be a combination of conjunctive and disjunctive. For example, under the common law rules of negligence, a duty can be

[2] Linda H. Edwards, *Legal Writing: Process, Analysis, and Organization* (3d ed. 2002).
[3] *Illinois v. Gates*, 462 U.S. 213 (1983).

a duty either to do *or* not to do something. Turning from tort to criminal law, because of the strict requirements of the Constitution that crimes be clearly delineated by statute, most (if not all) criminal statutes are conjunctive or disjunctive rules. An example used later in this chapter focuses on the following statute: It is a separate crime, punishable by a term of imprisonment for up to five years, for a defendant to use or carry a firearm in connection with a drug-trafficking crime.[4] What elements are required under this statute? Where is the disjunction?

c. Exceptions

Many rules have exceptions, and a correct statement of the rule requires that both the general rule and the exception(s) be stated. For example, if a witness lies to a grand jury, she can be convicted of the crime of perjury, *except* if she admits that she lied before her lie became generally known and the lie caused no harm to the proceeding.[5] Does this example consist solely of a rule and an exception, or is it itself a combination of rule types, like the previous example?

d. Factors and Balancing Tests

A number of rules are composed of flexible factors that must be present to a lesser or greater extent. For example, for a court to grant a motion to dismiss for *forum non conveniens*, the moving party must establish (1) that there is an adequate alternative forum, and (2) that public- and private-interest factors favor dismissal.[6] Private-interest factors include the "relative ease of access to sources of proof; availability of compulsory process for attendance of unwilling, and the cost of obtaining attendance of willing, witnesses; possibility of view of premises . . . and all other practical problems that make trial of a case easy, expeditious and inexpensive."[7] Public-interest factors include "administrative difficulties flowing from court congestion; the local interest in having localized controversies decided at home; . . . the avoidance of unnecessary problems in conflict of laws, or in the application of foreign law; and the unfairness of burdening citizens in an unrelated forum with jury duty."[8] This is a combination of a conjunctive rule and a factors rule. Notice also that this factor test, like most, includes a nonexclusive list of factors: There may be other aspects of public or private interest like these that the trial court may consider as well. It was under this test that the United States District Court for the Southern District of New York made the controversial decision to dismiss the Bhopal–Union Carbide case in favor of trial in India.[9]

Like the factors test, a balancing test consists of several factors. Instead of merely considering them, though, a court is required to balance them, weighing the quality or strength of the arguments for each. Thus, a balancing test weighs competing factors,

---

[4] 18 U.S.C. § 924(c)(1).

[5] *United States v. Scrimgeour*, 636 F.2d 1019 (5th Cir. 1981) (discussing 18 U.S.C. § 1623), considered *infra* in Chapter 7.

[6] *Piper Aircraft Co. v. Reyno*, 454 U.S. 235, 257 (1981).

[7] *Id.* at 241 n.6 (citation and quotation omitted).

[8] *Id.*

[9] *In re Union Carbide Corp. Gas Plant Disaster at Bhopal, India in Dec., 1984*, 634 F. Supp. 842, 866-67 (S.D.N.Y. 1986).

rather than similar factors as listed in the *forum non conveniens* test, and the factors listed are generally exclusive. Courts weigh not only the number of factors that support one party but also the strength of the argument that supports each factor balanced. However, if one factor weighs very strongly in favor of one party, even if the other factors weigh in favor of the opposing party, then the first party may still prevail. For example, four factors must be balanced when a criminal defendant claims a violation of the right to a speedy trial granted by the Sixth Amendment: (1) the length of the delay, (2) the reason for the delay, (3) the defendant's assertion of his right to a speedy trial, and (4) prejudice that the defendant suffered because of the delay. All four factors must be weighed to determine the outcome of the case.

e. Totality-of-the-Circumstances Rules

A totality-of-the-circumstances test is like the factors test, except that specific factors are not delineated. Furthermore, unlike a balancing test, which has a set number of considerations, a totality-of-the-circumstances test requires the court to consider all the circumstances of a case—a process that, on appeal, can mean an exhaustingly detailed review of all the evidence presented at trial. For example, it is unlawful for an employer to refuse to hire, to fire, or to discriminate against an employee on the basis of the employee's race, color, religion, sex, or national origin.[10] One form of unlawful harassment under this statute is that of a hostile environment, in which an employee is consistently and severely abused on the basis of his or her race, sex, or ethnicity.[11] A totality-of-the-circumstances test is used to determine what constitutes a hostile environment: To determine whether an environment is sufficiently hostile or abusive to be actionable, a court should look "*at all the circumstances*, including the frequency of the discriminatory conduct; its severity; whether it is physically threatening or humiliating, or a mere offensive utterance; and whether it unreasonably interferes with an employee's work performance."[12] A reviewing court will go through the entire trial record, examining each and every instance of discriminatory conduct and its severity.

2. Difficulties in Stating Common Law Rules

Not all cases state the applicable common law rule directly, completely, or accurately. Therefore, developing skill in dealing with common law demands that one learn to spot the best phrasing of the rule in a case; compare that phrasing to other, similar cases; and test the accuracy of any particular phrasing of the rule by comparing it to the result in other cases. Because of the nature of stare decisis, a case is built on the reasoning and language of those that came before, and thus newer cases generally state any given rule more accurately and more completely than do older cases.

For example, *Jones v. Smith* discusses negligence in only one cryptic passage, stating: "There is no question that defendant Smith's conduct was the cause in fact of the harm to plaintiff Jones. Smith was under a duty to play soccer in the ordinary

---

[10] 21 U.S.C. § 2000e-2(a)(1).

[11] *Meritor Sav. Bank, FSB v. Vinson*, 477 U.S. 57, 67 (1986).

[12] *Faragher v. Boca Raton*, 524 U.S. 775, 787 (1998).

fashion without unsportsmanlike conduct or wanton injury to his fellow players. This duty was breached by Smith, whose behavior was, according to the evidence, substandard and negligent."[13] Although this paragraph touches on the elements of duty, breach, causation, and damages, it does not explain any of those concepts, nor does it discuss any other sports. It would be difficult to formulate a general rule about negligence in recreational sports from this one case, or even get a good understanding of the negligence standard and how it operates in various situations. At the time the fictional *Jones v. Smith* case was allegedly decided (1976), there were very few recreational sports cases.

In contrast, *Lestina*, a real case written almost 20 years later, in 1993, exhaustively discusses the negligence standard and how it should be used (in Wisconsin) in the context of recreational sports. It mentions and cites a number of different sports cases in a long footnote. When it comes to a statement of the applicable legal rule, *Lestina* defines negligence as a "failure to use that degree of care which should be exercised by a reasonable person under the circumstances."[14] This is a fairly standard, modern definition of negligence, and is quite comparable to the *bon père de famille* standard used in French and other civilian jurisdictions to determine when someone is at fault and therefore liable for a tort. Furthermore, in the context of a recreational sport, *Lestina* states that "to determine whether a player's conduct constitutes actionable negligence . . . the fact finder should consider such material factors as the sport involved; the rules and regulations governing the sport; the generally accepted customs and practices of the sport . . . ; the risks inherent in the game and those that are outside the realm of anticipation . . . ."[15] *Jones* gave a rule limited to the facts of the soccer game at issue, but *Lestina* more directly states a rule applicable to many recreational sports — one that can be applied in other, similar cases.[16]

Thus, in addition to being of different types, rules can be stated in different manners. Technically speaking, the rule of a case is limited to the facts that caused the court to decide the way it did. Thus, a rule may be stated as narrowly as the holding of the case. *Jones*'s rule could be stated as it was in the case: *A soccer player has a duty to play soccer in a sportsmanlike manner. If he breaches that duty by blatantly breaking the rules and his breach causes serious damage to another player, then he is liable for negligence.* However, such narrow statements are of very little use when an attorney needs to predict what a court will do with a similar issue in a different case. Over time, courts look to series of cases and often reinterpret them to help decide new cases. These reinterpretations are often phrased as generalizations from earlier cases, and sometimes courts speculate on what they would have decided had they been given different facts. *Jones v. Smith* makes such a speculation when it mentions that the plaintiff might have assumed the risk of being slide-tackled or run into, but the fact was that he was not hit this way.[17]

[13] *See Bourque v. Duplechin*, 331 So. 2d 40 (La. Ct. App. 1976) (the softball case from which the hypothetical case *Jones v. Smith* is taken).
[14] *Lestina v. West Bend Mut. Ins. Co.*, 501 N.W.2d 28, 32 (1993).
[15] *Id.* at 33.
[16] Louisiana and Wisconsin both use a negligence standard in recreational sports injury cases, but most other states use "recklessness" instead in these types of cases.
[17] 331 So. 2d at 42.

Technically these generalizations and speculations are *dicta* and not law, because they exceed the scope of the decision made by the court, but they are nevertheless very useful in predicting future cases because they express the court's inclinations. Generalizations are often repeated in case after case, and therefore develop the force of law.

Sometimes one can find a rule accurately stated in a later case or an authoritative treatise, but sometimes one has to synthesize a rule by combining cases. Different cases may elaborate on the nature or definition of different elements, as did *Lestina*, and it may be necessary to consider the facts, holdings, and rationales of several cases to construct an accurate rule.

3. *Incorporating Case Law into the Rule Analysis*

In the context of a law firm memo or other professional-caliber legal document, getting a complete statement of the applicable rule and understanding its components and how they relate to each other is just the beginning of legal analysis. Because the law of each case is limited to the facts that led to the decision, the next step in being able to predict how a court will decide is to examine both the holdings and the material or operative facts of applicable case law and determine what types of fact patterns are needed for each element, factor, or balance. *Material* or *operative facts* are those facts that led a court to make a particular decision. The attorney considers which fact is related to which component of the rule, and analyzes the component in the light of the facts and how they led to the court's decision. For example, the fact that Smith flagrantly violated the rules of soccer was material to the court's decision. The court found that he had a duty to play by the rules, and that he breached that duty by going out of his way to run into Jones. The fact that Jerger, the *Lestina* defendant, violated the rules of his soccer league by slide-tackling was similarly material to the Wisconsin court's decision for the same reason: The court found that he had a duty to play by his league's rules and that he breached that duty when he slide-tackled Lestina. By synthesizing these two cases, one can develop a rule statement that encompasses both: Players in team sports have a duty to obey the rules of their sport or league. If they breach that duty by violating a rule, and the breach causes injury to another player, then they may be found negligent.

4. *Incorporating Policy Concerns*

To fully understand the reasoning of a particular legal principle, the attorney should also consider the underlying policy concerns that led to the court's decision, or that may have affected the court's decision. Policy concerns are often mentioned in the body of an opinion, and become key issues in dissents. For example, in *Jones*, the dissent questioned the intentionality of Smith's act. Had the court found the act intentional, the insurance company would not have had to pay for Jones's injury. The dissent felt that it was obvious that the act was intentional and that the insurance company should not pay for it. The majority's decision to regard the act as unintentional demonstrates both a concern for the perceived weaker party and a desire to distribute the cost of tort injuries through insurance. These cases demonstrate that policy concerns of tort law involve protecting weaker parties and distributing the cost of injuries; however, in sports law cases, courts are further concerned that holding players and their teams' insurance companies liable will discourage recreational sports. Thus, although the *Lestina* court held Jerger's insurance company liable, another court might not have done so, because slide-tackling is acceptable in most leagues and not as egregious a violation of the rules. Furthermore, if you were representing a client who had slide-tackled another player in a soccer game, but (1) the game was not in Wisconsin, (2) slide-tackles were ostensibly against the rules, but that rule had never been enforced, and (3) recreational sports clubs were having trouble paying insurance premiums, then you might acknowledge that *Lestina* is still good law, but predict that it is unlikely that the court would follow it in your case because the policy concerns underlying *Lestina* were not present here. Knowing what policy concerns underlie a court's decision helps a lawyer substantially in predicting what a court will do in another case.

Fact-and-policy-focused legal reasoning is the essence of common law thinking, and is perhaps the most difficult to grasp at first because it forces you not only to read a case but also to dissect it and relate it back to the underlying legal rule. The two skills— analysis of the rule and consideration of how different factual situations are treated by the courts—are intertwined in common law thinking: One cannot completely understand a rule until one understands how it applies to a particular set of facts. Generally, in discussing case law in a rule section, one should include the facts, the holding, and the court's reasoning or rationale. When handling a number of cases, it is often best to begin by charting them, so as to master the facts of each case and specify which elements of the rule each case addresses. A chart allows the attorney to see at a glance how the various cases compare; an example is given in subsection III.D of this chapter. Once you become proficient in analyzing case law, you may no longer need to chart cases, but you will always need to find some way to organize them and fix that organization into your understanding of the applicable area of law.

Once the cases are charted, construction of the rule analysis is quite systematic. After stating the applicable rule and explaining any underlying policy considerations, address each component of that rule in turn, using facts, holdings, and reasoning from the cases to illustrate what kinds of facts will either establish or fail to establish that particular component. Generally, the only way to get a complete understanding of a legal principle is to consider both positive and negative fact patterns: cases in which the rule was held to apply, as well as cases in which the court held that the rule did not apply, and the reasons therefor.

5. *Considering Relative Weight of Authority*

In explaining a rule in light of interpretive case law, one must also consider the relative weight of authority. Generally, when working on the rule section of an objective memo, it is best to consider and present mandatory authority first, because the impatient reader will want to know exactly what the court *must* follow first, before any discussion of what the court *might* follow. However, if the full statement of the applicable rule is made only in secondary authority, then the secondary authority should be presented first, with mandatory or persuasive authority then used to demonstrate how the rule operates in specific factual situations. As you read court opinions, examine how their authors organize the discussion of prior authority. Generally a court discusses Supreme Court authority first, if there is any, then its own prior decisions, and then persuasive authority. Some authorities are more persuasive than others. For example, courts whose standing is as high or higher than that of the deciding court are more persuasive than lower courts, but cases with extremely similar facts may be persuasive even though they come from a lower court. An example from a Restatement or prominent secondary authority may be more persuasive than mandatory authority from the same court, especially if the facts of the mandatory case are very dissimilar from those of your case.

C. A and C: Application and Conclusion

Once each and every component of the rule has been thoroughly explained, the attorney then turns to the application portion of IRAC. For civilian-trained attorneys, this is the most difficult part of IRAC analysis. Civilian analysis often ends with identification of the applicable rule and a simple conclusion that it applies. In contrast, common law analysis begins a statement of the rule and then an explanation of it, but the most important part is the explanation of how prior case law compares and then how the rule applies to the given facts. Nevertheless, if the rule section is thorough and well-explained, the application section will be relatively simple to construct. Address each element of the rule, and show how it is or is not established by the facts of the situation. It is at this point that analogy is particularly relevant. The facts of the cases discussed in the rule section are compared to the facts of the given situation, and the appropriate legal implications are linked back to each element of the rule. The effect of policy concerns is also considered. This process is more easily explained through illustration, and will be dealt with at more length in the following section. Nevertheless, if the facts are substantially similar to the preceding case law, each element of the rule can be established through comparison to prior cases, and the same policy concerns apply, then the attorney can predict that a court will treat her client's problem similarly. In contrast, if the client's factual situation is entirely different from those in the case law, not all elements of the rule can be established, and policy implications do not follow, then the rule should not apply. This is termed "distinguishing the case on its facts," and it is a very widely used premise for argument, providing another reason for considering both positive and negative cases in the rule analysis.

III. EXAMPLE OF IRAC ANALYSIS: THE GUN-IN-THE-BOOT PROBLEM

To demonstrate how rule-and-application analysis works, we will begin with the following hypothetical problem, which is taken from a real case.

A. Facts and Basic Rule Analysis

James Harris (not his real name) was arrested in Galveston, Texas, when he sold two kilograms of cocaine to an undercover policeman. When the arresting officer asked him if he was "packing" (a slang term), Harris admitted that he had a firearm in his boot, but did not explain why he had the gun. He was searched, and a .22 caliber pistol was found in his right boot. He pleaded guilty to the cocaine charge. The issue now is whether he is guilty of a second crime stemming from the same circumstances: 18 U.S.C. § 924(c)(1) states in pertinent part that "[w]hoever, during and in relation to any . . . drug trafficking crime . . . uses or carries a firearm, shall in addition to the punishment provided for such . . . drug trafficking crime, be sentenced to imprisonment for five years." Harris argues that he did not "use" the gun, as required by the statute, and therefore is not guilty of a § 924(c)(1) violation.

Analysis of the rule shows that it combines the following elements:

1. a predicate drug-trafficking crime
2. a gun
3. that is
   a. "used" or
   b. "carried"
4. in connection with the drug-trafficking crime.

B. Case Law

Because Galveston is in the Southern District of Texas, Fifth Circuit authority (as well as U.S. Supreme Court authority) is mandatory. Research discloses the following four authorities, in addition to the statute itself:

1. *United States v. Bailey*, 516 U.S. 144, 148 (1995). In *Bailey*, the United States Supreme Court held that with respect to "use" under § 924(c)(1), a conviction requires evidence sufficient to "show active employment of the firearm" by the defendant, and defined *use* as including "brandishing, displaying, bartering, striking with, and most obviously, firing or attempting to fire, a firearm."
2. *United States v. Ramos-Rodriguez*, 136 F.3d 465, 468 (5th Cir. 1998). In *Ramos-Rodriguez*, the Fifth Circuit held that a § 924(c)(1) conviction can rely on either the "use" or the "carry" prong of the statute. It defined *carry*, for purposes of the statute, as involving some dominion or control more than mere possession, and requiring a showing that the firearm was in reach during the commission of and in relation to the predicate offense. Although he did not use the gun, Ramos-Rodriguez's conviction was upheld because he expressly admitted that he carried the firearm "in order to protect and guard the heroin and cocaine" he was dealing from his residence, and he admitted that he carried the firearm while dealing drugs.

3. *United States v. Pigrum*, 922 F.2d 249, 251 (5th Cir. 1991). The issue in this case was the wording of a § 924(c)(1) indictment, rather than the meaning of the statute itself. Nevertheless, codefendant Allen's conviction was upheld. The operative facts were these: Several agents of the Mississippi sheriff's office and federal Customs agents arrived at Allen's house late one evening to execute a search warrant. When they entered the house, Allen was seated at the kitchen table, on which was an array of drug paraphernalia, including a mirror, razor blade, knife, and set of scales that was subsequently found to contain cocaine. Cocaine was found in Allen's pants pocket, and he was sitting on a .22 caliber revolver, loaded with three bullets. Though he seemed to be trying to reach for the gun, he never actually touched it. Instead, he raised his hands and stood up when ordered to do so.
4. In addition to these three cases, *Muscarello v. United States*, 524 U.S. 125, 128-38 (1998), indicates that a § 924(c) violation occurs even when the gun was locked in the glove compartment of the defendant's truck while the defendant was transporting marijuana for sale, because he knew that he had the gun, and even admitted that he had it for protection. *Id.* at 127, 138. Furthermore, the violation is established even when the defendant does not specifically admit that he had the gun for protection, if circumstances indicate that the defendant purposefully carried the gun in connection with the drug crime. *See id.* at 127, 138. In the second case considered in *Muscarello*, the Court affirmed the § 924(c) conviction of defendants who had "placed several guns in a bag, put the bag in the trunk of a car, and then traveled by car to a proposed drug-sale point, where they intended to steal drugs from the sellers." *Id.* at 127. The Court reasoned that *carry* should be defined broadly, for purposes of this statute, as implying "personal agency and some degree of possession," and that the term is further limited by the requirements that the firearm be carried *both* during *and* in relation to the drug-trafficking crime. *Id.* at 134, 137. However, the statute does not require that the gun be immediately accessible. *Id.* at 137.

C. Issue Identification

Before charting these cases, it is helpful to verify whether the issue they discuss is the same as the issue in Harris's case. Harris argues that he is not guilty of a § 924(c)(1) violation because he never actually used the gun. He is not arguing that he did not have a gun, or that he was not trading drugs, or that his possession of a gun was unrelated to his dealing drugs. The only element at issue is whether he used or carried the gun. The statute requires "using or carrying," and at first reading is disjunctive: one commits a § 924(c)(1) violation by either using *or* carrying a gun in connection with a drug-trafficking crime. *Ramos-Rodriguez* confirms that this element is read in the disjunctive. *Bailey* defines "use," while *Ramos-Rodriguez, Pigrum*, and *Muscarello* all define "carrying." All four cases are concerned with the meaning of this one element of the crime, which is the same element that Harris is questioning. Therefore, because the issue in Harris's case matches almost exactly the issue discussed in the other cases, the cases are *on point*, as further demonstrated by the chart in subsection D. (Saying a case is on point is a way of saying that the opinion is important to the legal question at hand because the material facts and legal issues are very similar.)

D. Example of a Case Law Chart

Element	*Bailey* (S. Ct.)	*Ramost-Rodriguez* (5th Cir.)	*Pigrum* (5th Cir.)	*Muscarello*	*Harris*
Firearm	Yes	Yes	Yes	Yes	Yes
Predicate drug crime	Yes	Yes	Yes	Yes	Yes
Use of firearm	No, but defines *use*	No	No	No	No
Carrying of firearm	Not at issue	**Yes**. Holds that the statute is disjunctive: use **or** carrying, and defines *carrying* as "more than mere possession."	**Yes**. Demonstrates carrying: **sitting on gun.**	**Yes**. *Carry* requires personal agency and some degree of possession, as well as relation to drug crime. Placement in locked compartment can still be "carrying," even though no specific admission.	**?** Did not admit that he carried gun to protect drugs, but did admit to having **gun in boot.**
In connection with	Not at issue	**Yes.** Admitted carrying gun to protect drugs.	**Yes**; no mention of whether admitted to carrying gun to protect drugs.	**Yes**, in both cases.	**Facts like *Pigrum*.**
Holding:	Not guilty	**Guilty**	**Guilty**	**Guilty**	**Guilty?**
Ranking	S. Ct.: Mandatory, highest rank	5th Circuit: Mandatory, somewhat dissimilar facts	5th Circuit: Mandatory, very similar facts, but older case	S. Ct., newest: Mandatory, somewhat dissimilar facts, highest rank	5th Circuit and S. Ct.: Mandatory.

E. Factual Comparisons to the Harris Problem

With the help of the rule chart, it is easy to see that all the other elements of the crime have been established, and the only possible issue as to Harris's guilt is whether he was "carrying" the firearm. The case law demonstrates that carrying requires control over and possession of the gun. Having a gun locked in one's home while dealing drugs two kilometers away would not be carrying, because no connection can be shown between the dealing and the gun. But sitting on a gun while dealing drugs demonstrates the requisite control, as does admitting that you keep a gun handy in order to protect your drugs. In between is a large gray area. For example, it is unclear what a court would rule if the gun were locked in the glove compartment of the car while the defendant was dealing drugs some distance away. Would there still be dealing "in relation to" the gun if the gun were 1,000 meters away, 50 meters, 5 meters? Luckily, these questions do not matter, as they do not correspond to Harris's case. However, it is helpful to consider them before addressing the facts at issue in your case.

In applying this analysis to Harris's case, one must remember that, unlike Ramos-Rodriguez, he did not admit that he had the gun specifically to protect his drugs, nor did he use the gun. However, *Pigrum* and *Muscarello* make the admission unnecessary if the facts show that the gun was in the defendant's reach, such as if he were sitting on it. The only remaining question is whether Harris's having a gun in his boot is like the *Pigrum* defendant's sitting on one. If you have watched American cowboy or spy movies, you will know that it is apparently quite easy to reach a gun tucked in your boot, almost as easy as reaching one you are sitting on; therefore, one could conclude that Harris had "control and dominion" over the gun (using the Fifth Circuit's language). Using the language of the Supreme Court, he demonstrated "personal agency and possession" — no one else could have put the gun in his boot, nor could he have been unaware of its being there.

F. Policy Analysis

On researching the policy considerations of the statute, one becomes aware that Congress passed this law because drug traffickers who carry guns to protect their trade are often involved in violent crimes. Congress hoped that the statute would discourage drug dealers' use or carrying of guns to protect their trade. Harris never admitted that he was carrying the gun to protect his trafficking, but that is the logical implication of his keeping the gun in his boot. Thus, the statute was aimed at people in his exact situation, and applying it to him is in keeping with underlying policy concerns. Because he pleaded guilty to the predicate drug-trafficking crime that he committed at the same time, and because he was carrying a firearm during and in relation to that drug-trafficking crime, Harris is very likely to be convicted of a § 924(c)(1) violation.

G. Summary

With the analysis of a rule chart (subsection D above) or informal prewriting analysis demonstrated in subsections E and F, the legal question is fairly well answered in the attorney's mind. What remains is for the attorney to explain that answer to her law firm in the form of an interoffice memo. The purpose of an interoffice memo is to advise a law firm about a client's particular situation. Thus, it must convince the reader that (1) the writer understands the applicable law, and (2) she understands how that law applies to the facts of the question.

Please be aware that this example was chosen because it is very clear and straightforward. Because it begins with a statute, the preliminary rule analysis is quite simple, and the clear and determinative case law makes factual comparisons easy. With luck, you, as a student, should be able to focus more on the analysis and drafting methods, rather than struggling with the legal concepts at issue or with ranking of authority. Given the clarity and force of the case law in this area, it would be very unusual for a defendant to make this kind of argument, as a court could find it frivolous and therefore sanctionable (punishable). The actual case was tried in 1997, before *Muscarello,* when there was more room for these kinds of arguments. In the original case, the defendant was found guilty of a § 924(c)(1) violation after a bench trial, and the conviction was affirmed on appeal.

Normally, the answer to a client's legal question will not be as clear as in the Harris example. An objective analysis of the situation in light of current case law will usually show that arguments can be made on both sides. The objective memo must consider and develop all such arguments and weigh their relative strength before predicting an answer. Consequently, very often the most accurate short answer is "maybe," not "yes" or "no."

IV. THE INTEROFFICE MEMO

CHECKLIST FOR DRAFTING INTEROFFICE MEMOS

- ☐ 1. Identify the applicable rule.
- ☐ 2. Dissect the rule.
- ☐ 3. Brief all cases.
- ☐ 4. Prewrite or chart the rule and application as interpreted by cases; check completeness of research.
- ☐ 5. Draft discussion section (indicate citation placement and content); recheck research.
- ☐ 6. Draft fact section, incorporating all facts used in discussion section plus additional information as needed.
- ☐ 7. Draft introduction, issue, short answer, and conclusion sections.
- ☐ 8. Revise, checking language, sentence structure, tone, grammar, and spelling.
- ☐ 9. Put citations in proper form.

The interoffice memo is a document designed to be used in a law firm. It is usually used to help the firm decide how best to advise the client or how to approach litigation, and is never disclosed to the opposing party. As such, it is a completely objective analysis of what the results of litigation are likely to be, and to that end considers both the strengths and the weaknesses of the client's position in an even-handed manner. Subsequently, it may be used in preparing an advocatory document, such as a memorandum in support of the client's case, but when it is so used it will be recast so as to stress the strength of the client's position and minimize any weaknesses. It may also be used as a reference in future cases, and therefore is written so that a person who is completely unfamiliar with the case will have no trouble following it. Consequently, its content is very repetitive.

A. The Assignment: Interviewing the Employer

Too often, when a law firm partner gives an associate or intern an assignment to write a memo, the dialogue goes something like this:

> MS. PARTNER (in a hurry, and thinking about a number of different cases): "Ms. Smith, I'd like you to draft a memo concerning our client X who did Y. Please have it ready by Friday."
>
> MS. SMITH (wanting very much to impress the partner both with the quality of her work and her competency): "Certainly, Ms. Partner, I'll have it ready for you by Friday morning."

Ms. Smith goes back to her carrel or office, and realizes, in a panic, that she does not know what jurisdiction client X is in, knows nothing about that area of law, and does not know whether the partner wants an in-depth law review article on the subject, or whether it should just be a quick, short memo covering only the most important points. She then either (1) guesses what is wanted, taking a chance on turning in the wrong thing; (2) tries to elicit advice from her coworkers, who likely do not know the answers to her questions; or (3) goes back to ask the partner, who by now has turned to another project and might not welcome the interruption.

Rather than flailing about aimlessly, it is better to interview the partner about the project at the time the assignment is given, while she is still thinking about it and is most likely to be both willing and able to give complete answers. Some appropriate questions might be:

1. What jurisdiction is this in? Have we filed suit yet? Are there other issues about which I should be concerned?
2. About how long should the memo be? Do you want a very in-depth memo, or just the quick-and-dirty? (i.e., what is the client willing and able to pay for?)
3. Do you have an example of a similar memo that I can see?
4. Do you know this area of law? What would be a good source for me to start my research with?

In general, it is a far better strategy to get the needed information early on, rather than either turning in an unusable document or having to repeatedly interrupt the partner with more questions.

B. Interoffice Memo Form

Although there is some variation with regard to the sequence used, and different law firms have different preferences with regard to headings and font, the interoffice memo form is fairly standard. The top of the first page has a heading or title identifying the type of document and stating to whom it is addressed, who it is from, concerning what subject, and the date. Most firms have a standard heading that they want all memos to follow, and which can be downloaded from a macro, template, or other similar pattern document. Following the heading are usually three to five centered subheadings, which are often capitalized: ISSUE or ISSUES, SHORT ANSWER, FACTS, DISCUSSION, and CONCLUSION. The three-subheading version includes FACTS, DISCUSSION, and CONCLUSION. This text uses the five-heading version but that can easily be converted into a three-heading memo, if desired. Typeface is usually required to be 12 point, double spaced (to allow editing); the preferred fonts are usually Times New Roman or Ariel, and each page after the first one is numbered at the bottom center. Often the text is justified on both margins to give a neat, professional format. Memos that do not follow the standard form are likely to be rejected. More explicitly, and in more detail, a memo is as follows.

MEMORANDUM

TO: Marla Marples

FROM: Joseph Green, summer intern

RE: *United States v. Harris*, 18 U.S.C. § 924(c)(1): use or carrying of a gun in connection with a drug-trafficking crime

DATE: February 22, 2002

Notes on the heading: Center the title, and tab over twice after each colon so that the TO/FROM/RE/ and DATE entries line up neatly, as in the example. Do not abbreviate the date. Give a neat finish to the heading by running a continuous underline one line under the "Date" entry.

Following the heading, there may be a short introduction to the memorandum, especially if the case or the law implicated is complicated, or if it would help the reading partner refresh his mind about the case or assist another reader who is completely unfamiliar with the case.

ISSUE

Is Mr. Harris's conduct sufficient to constitute "the use or carrying of a firearm in connection with a drug-trafficking crime," as defined by 18 U.S.C. § 924(c)(1) because he had a gun in his boot while he was selling cocaine?

Notes on the statement of the issue or issues: The issue is the question (or questions) that the writer was asked to answer. As phrased, the issue example here is very specific. It employs the operative facts of Mr. Harris's situation, and it incorporates the language of the applicable rule, which in this case is a statute. Sometimes, however, law firms plan to use the same memorandum for a number of cases, and want issue statements to be phrased generally: "Is a client who had a firearm hidden on his person while dealing drugs guilty of the use or carrying of a firearm in connection with a drug-trafficking crime?" You may need to determine which kind of issue statement your law firm will want, but it should be formulated so that the answer will be yes, no, or maybe. If you have more than one issue, number and list them:

1. Is Acme Motors, Inc. liable under strict products liability for a manufacturing defect . . . ?
2. Alternatively, is Acme liable for a design defect . . . ?

SHORT ANSWER

Beginning with "Yes," "No," or "Maybe," answer the question or questions posed by your statement of the issue in one or two sentences, incorporating language from the applicable rule as well as specific facts of the case. If you have more than one issue, number and list the answers exactly as they were listed in the issue section.

FACTS

This is a short, objective statement of the facts of the case. The parties are introduced, and then the story of what happened to bring them to conflict is told in chronological order. Every legally relevant detail should be included, as well as any other details necessary for the reader to get a clear sense of the parties and their interactions. Assume that the reader knows or remembers little, if anything, about the case. Avoid emotional language: The purpose of a law firm memo is to analyze the client's position objectively and predict, as accurately as possible, what a court is likely to decide.

DISCUSSION

The discussion section consists of a full explanation of the rule and how it has been interpreted in various cases, followed by a full explanation of how that rule applies to the facts of the problem case, including fact-to-fact comparisons with the case law explained previously. (Because this is the most important part of the memo, subsection C gives a more complete explanation.)

CONCLUSION

The conclusion section is usually quite short, at most a paragraph for each issue. It reiterates the rule and its application in a bit more detail than do the issue and short answer statements. Furthermore, it may mention side issues or points that the writer feels the reader may not have considered, but that may be important to the case.

C. Discussion Section

DISCUSSION SECTION CHECKLIST/OUTLINE

1. Rule Section (major premise)
   a. Statement of rule and identification of major components
   b. Explanation, supported by authority, of components not at issue
   c. Explanation of components at issue
      i. Case 1: component, facts, holding, rationale
      ii. Case 2: component, facts, holding, rationale
2. Application Section (minor premise)
   a. Fact-to-fact comparison of problem facts to Case 2 facts; conclusion about whether Case 2 component and results apply and why
   b. Fact-to-fact comparison of problem facts to Case 1 facts; conclusion about whether Case 1 component and results apply and why
   c. Explanation of how other components of rule apply
3. Concluding sentence, incorporating facts and all major components of rule

As indicated in the section on IRAC analysis, the discussion section is the most important part of the memo. Its purpose is to explain the law, and how the law applies to the particular case, in a clear, concise, and convincing manner. For purposes of clarity, the explanation of the rule is referred to as a *rule section*, and the explanation of how that rule applies to the problem is referred to as an *application section*, but in the final memo there is no delineation or demarcation between the two portions of the discussion section, other than a normal paragraph break.

1. Two-Issue Discussion Sections

The rule section includes a dissection of the rule as well as an explanation of case law and how case law has interpreted that rule. If there is more than one issue, identify each with a heading, just as in the issue section, and then address each issue with its own IRAC analysis.

a. Rule Section (major premise)

Begin the discussion of the rule by stating the applicable rule and identifying its components. Each component is then defined or explained in light of relevant mandatory or secondary authority, with more explanation being given to the component or components that are at issue in the case. This usually completes the first paragraph.

Once the rule is dissected, case law is used to describe how a component has been interpreted. Each such case law paragraph begins with a transitional sentence identifying the component at issue and explaining how the case interpreted that component. Subsequently, the facts, issue, holding, and rationale of the case should be described so that the reader can see the specific facts of the case and how they led to the court's decision. This substantiates the interpretation given in the first sentence of the paragraph. Each important case is similarly treated in its own paragraph. Important cases are those that either are mandatory, or have fact patterns similar to that of the problem. Often it is best to include full discussion of a case in which the component at issue is not established, as well as one in which it is, so that the reader will gain a complete understanding of how the component operates in different situations.

The credibility of a rule section depends on clear, complete, and well-reasoned explanation of all mandatory authority plus relevant secondary authority. Four common errors made in rule sections include:

1. Failure to fully explain the facts, holding, and rationale of an important case
2. Failure to cite sources fully
3. Mixing rule and application by referring to the client's problem in the rule section
4. Listing cases in laundry-list fashion without analysis of their importance.

Failing to fully explain important case law leaves the reader confused and unconvinced that the writer understands the law. Similarly, failing to cite authority leads the reader to question whether the writer fully researched and analyzed authority. To prove to the reader that the legal arguments presented are not new and the rule section is well founded in legal authority, a citation *must* be given after every sentence in the rule section, giving the source and exact page on which the statement, fact, or reasoning referred to is presented. Mixing rule and application, like failure to fully explain, also confuses the reader. The client's situation should not be discussed or even referenced in the rule section, because it distracts the reader from a clear analysis and comprehension of applicable law.

The final common error in a rule section is to list cases one after another, giving facts, holdings, and rationales without explaining how the cases relate to the rule or why they are being discussed; this is often referred to as a "laundry list" of cases. The laundry-list approach is ineffective because it fails to explain to the reader why a case is important or what it has to do with the rule. The way to avoid this is to begin by identifying the rule component that the case illustrates and summarize what the case says about that component, before explaining the facts, holding, and rationale of the case.

b. Application Section (minor premise)

The application section is the most important part of the discussion section. It incorporates everything in the fact and rule sections, so one way to check the effectiveness of an application section is to verify that it analyzes every fact given in the fact section in light of each component and case discussed in the rule section. The heart of an application section, however, is fact-to-fact comparison. To effectively show that a case does or does not apply to the facts of the problem, the application section must compare the *specific* material facts of the relevant case law with the *specific* material facts of the case at hand (i.e., the client's problem) and draw the logical legal implications from that comparison. For example, the sample memo in section V analogizes the facts of the *Harris* case to the most important facts of the most similar precedent:

> The facts of Harris's case are very similar to those in *Pigrum* because putting the gun under one's body is similar to putting the gun in an article of clothing. In both cases, the gun was easily available to the defendant. Therefore it is likely the court would hold the gun was under Harris's control and dominion.

The component at issue here was whether Harris was carrying the gun, when case law defined *carrying a gun* as having the gun under one's dominion and control. These three sentences compare Harris's having the gun in his boot to the *Pigrum* defendant's sitting on one, and draw the logical conclusion that if sitting on a gun is carrying, so is having a gun in one's boot. Fact-to-fact comparison is, at first, often difficult to understand, and certainly one can find examples of memoranda that fail to do it. However, it is the single best way to fully convince the reader that your analysis and conclusions are accurate.

2. *Concluding Sentence*

After making all the necessary fact-to-fact comparisons, and explaining how each component of the rule applies to the case at hand, the reader needs a short summation of how those components add up, in terms of the major premise, before moving to the more fully developed reiteration in the conclusion section. Granted, the memorandum form is quite repetitive, because the same material is repeated in the short answer, concluding sentence, and conclusion sections, but this is one of the elements that makes it reader-friendly and effective. The reader should be able to read a memo once through and understand it fully, without having to refer back to previous parts.

D. Other Information about the Interoffice Memo

1. *Tone and Style*

The tone should be professional and formal. It should be written for someone who is intelligent and educated, but not familiar with either the facts of the case or the law at issue. The goal of an interoffice memo is to be as reader-friendly as possible. The reader should understand what you are saying without having to read anything a second time. Therefore, aim for clear, simple English and straightforward sentences. Use signposts, transitions, and linking words so that the reader understands exactly where you are and where you are going at every point. Do not make the reader refer back to anything said or cited previously. Paragraphs should be between five and seven sentences long. Each paragraph should begin with a topic sentence and end with a conclusion. Paragraphs should be connected with transitional phrases or sentences. Avoid the first person (no *I* or *we*), all legalese terms (words such as *hitherto, to wit, aforementioned, inter alia*), all contractions (use *cannot,* not *can't*), and all colloquialisms (courts *find* facts and *hold* rulings, they do not *lay down* a rule). Avoid, as well, the passive voice: *The court held,* not *It was held by the court.*

2. *Citations*

As mentioned earlier, the convention is to have a **citation after every sentence that refers to or mentions anything from an authority**. The purpose of such obsessive citation practice is to establish your credibility by demonstrating that your arguments are not original and that they are soundly based on established law, policy, or other authority, as well as to convey to the reader the exact weight of that authority. To be effective, a citation must enable the reader to locate the exact authority on which you are relying and the exact page to which you are referring, quickly and easily. Do not be misled: readers can and do verify those citations for a number of reasons, so if they are missing, incomplete, or inaccurate, your credibility as a legal writer is weakened or destroyed. The first time an authority is cited, the citation should be a full, formal citation. Thereafter, you may use a shorter form, as long as it is clear to the reader what source is being referred to, and exactly which page. Both the ALWD and Bluebook manuals list correct short citation forms for various sources.

Traditionally, citations are included in the text, immediately after the textual sentence to which they refer, because there was no other simple solution before word processors. Only professional publishers could format footnotes properly. Unfortunately, this can make the text difficult to read, because the eye must skip over the citation after every sentence in order to follow the train of the argument. Although textual citations remain the rule in both in-house and court documents (not law review articles), the rule is gradually changing. Some firms and some courts either allow or encourage citations to be placed in footnotes, so that the text is easier to read. This textbook asks that you use textual citations in the interoffice memoranda and advocacy documents, but footnotes in scholarly articles. However, you should determine which your instructor wants and honor that preference, just as you would with a law firm employer.

When drafting documents that require citations, it is tempting to leave the citations until last, after the document has been drafted and revised. This is a serious mistake. Usually, the writer finds that he cannot identify the source of certain language and wastes hours of precious time re-locating the citation. Of course, it can also be frustrating to use correct full and short citation forms from the first draft, because the cutting and pasting that are a normal part of revision will force continual changes and revisions of citation form. The best approach, therefore, is to note the exact page of the source in the initial draft using a personal shorthand indicator of the source, and maintain that informal citation throughout the drafting and revising process. For example, "Les12" could refer to page 12 of *Lestina.* One of the last steps, then, is to correct citation form.

3. *Plagiarism*

Meticulous citation is important because (1) it establishes your credibility as a legal writer, and (2) it enables you to avoid any charge of plagiarism. United States law schools have very strict rules about what constitutes plagiarism, and how it will be punished. These rules are set forth in the school's honor code. Unfortunately, LL.M. students are often punished for honor code violations because they either failed to read the honor code or failed to fully understand it, especially as it may differ substantially from what they are used to in their home country. The sanctions can include a lower grade on an assignment, failing an assignment, failing a course, or even being forced to leave an LL.M. program.

Plagiarism is taking and using someone else's thoughts or writings and passing them off as one's own. In a law firm, documents are very often "shared"—one lawyer will use another's document as a pattern, changing language only where needed, and no one will object because the policy saves work for the firm and money for the clients. An applicable U.S. expression is "Why reinvent the wheel?" However, in law school, your grade is a reflection of your own work, not the work of your law firm. Therefore, when you turn in an assignment, you are certifying to the professor that you, and you alone, wrote the entire paper, except where you cite authority; and that you have not borrowed language or thoughts from anyone else, including your classmates, without acknowledgment. Most people understand that copying another student's paper and claiming it as your own is plagiarism, and therefore sanctionable. Likewise, taking the thoughts, facts, or language of a court opinion or any other source and not citing the exact page on which they were found constitutes plagiarism, as is copying someone else's footnotes and not checking the sources yourself.

What many LL.M. students have difficulty with, however, is that most honor codes punish both the student who copies another student's work *and* the student who intentionally gives her work to the copying student—whether or not she subjectively knew that the receiving student was going to copy that work. The reason behind sanctioning both relates to some of the ethical concerns underlying the practice of law in the United States.

A lawyer has dual duties to both the client and the court.[18] He must represent his client diligently and zealously.[19] He may not help his client commit a crime, nor may he knowingly allow his client to lie to the court, and he must obey all rules and regulations.[20] Without these ethical limitations on attorneys, the rule of law and the legal system would fail. An attorney is responsible for upholding the legal system by obeying its rules and preventing others from breaking them if possible. Knowingly allowing another student to break honor code rules indicates to law school administrations that neither student is committed to supporting a legal system, and therefore both may be ethically unqualified to be attorneys.

[18] Model Rules of Prof'l Conduct R. 3.3 (5th ed. 2003).
[19] Model Rules of Prof'l Conduct R. 1.3 (5th ed. 2003); Model Code of Prof'l Responsibility Canon 7 (1981).
[20] Model Rules of Prof'l Conduct R. 3.3, 3.4 (5th ed. 2003).

It is normal to want to help your friends. The honor code does not preclude that, but avoid anything that might facilitate plagiarism. Do not post your written work in a class computer forum where anyone might download it. Do not share files or USB flash drives, or leave the latter lying around, and do not show your friends what you wrote in answer to a question. Instead, if the teacher allows it, you might discuss the question with your friend if she asks for advice, or refer her to the best source for advice and help—the instructor. Professors in the United States are, for the most part, immensely approachable. They are usually pleased when a student brings them a question because it shows that the student is interested in learning. Furthermore, students' questions give professors some idea of where their students are having trouble—as long as you do not wait until the last minute before the exam or paper is due to ask the question.

It may sound highly unlikely that you would ever experience an honor code problem, and it is easy to assume that the rules you followed even without thinking at your home university apply in the United States as well. Unfortunately, this can be a very costly mistake. One semester, the author sanctioned no fewer than 8 students out of the 65 in her legal research and writing class for plagiarism. Most of the sanctions were quite minor. The students involved received failing grades on any assignment that showed clear plagiarism. In two instances, however, the assignments plagiarized were the most important assignments in the class, and the students failed the entire course as a result. Because the course was required as part of the LL.M. program, they were forced to make it up by taking a second legal research and writing course—a needless waste of their precious LL.M. time because both students were fully capable of doing professional-quality work on their own.

Incidentally, in case you are under the impression that perhaps the author is a particularly harsh instructor, and detects plagiarism even where none is present, be warned that it quite simple to detect. When an entire class has the same assignment, logically some answers are wrong and some are correct. Correct answers contain the same general content, and may even be organized in a similar fashion. This is entirely different in the case of plagiarism, which is apparent when answers are verbatim (the same) down to the same exact organization, the same exact paragraph and sentence structure, and even the same typographical and syntactical mistakes. Legal writing instructors are very sensitive to how language is used, even with large classes, and develop elaborate systems to check and recheck the fairness of their grading systems. Be warned and be careful: do your own work, protect it, and cite your sources meticulously.

4. *Revising*

Good writing style is short, clear, and to the point. It comes only from revising. Check the overall organization and analysis for logical flow and coherence. In the discussion section, verify that you have committed none of the errors described earlier. Be sure you can identify the underlying syllogistic structure: identify the major premise (rule) and minor premise (application), and make sure that you have proven both and that the terms in each match. Verify that the fact section flows smoothly and is easy to follow, and that the issue and short answers are accurately stated. Check paragraph length and structure. Look at each sentence, revising it until it says exactly what you want it to say and is clear and easy to understand. Grammar check and spell check are good programs but will miss certain types of word errors; therefore, you will need to read at least one hard-copy version before finalizing the memo. Check every citation, and check for missing citations. Once you think you have finished all your revisions, put the memo away for at least 24 hours so that you can look at it objectively when you return to it. If you have been working hard for a number of hours, days, or weeks on a project, it is easy to see in it what you want to see rather than what is actually there. After some time away from it, you will be more able to spot remaining errors. (See Chapter 8 for more detail on rewriting and revising.)

V. SAMPLE INTEROFFICE MEMO

The following is a sample memo, using the gun-in-the-boot example.

MEMORANDUM

TO: Marla Marples

FROM: Joseph Green

RE: *United States v. Harris*, 18 U.S.C. § 924(c)(1): use or carrying of a gun in connection with a drug-trafficking crime

DATE: July 4, 2003

James Harris, our client, argues that his conduct does not constitute the use or carrying of a firearm during the course of a drug-trafficking crime, as defined by 18 U.S.C. § 924(c)(1). Section 924(c)(1) provides in pertinent part that "[w]hoever, during and in relation to any . . . drug trafficking crime . . . uses or carries a firearm, shall in addition to the punishment provided for such . . . -drug trafficking crime, be sentenced to imprisonment for five years."

ISSUE

Does Mr. Harris's conduct constitute the use or carrying of a firearm in connection with a drug-trafficking crime because he admitted he had a gun in his boot while he was selling cocaine, though he did not actually use the firearm?

SHORT ANSWER

Yes. Harris's conduct constitutes a § 924(c)(1) violation because having the gun in his boot shows that he had dominion and control over the gun during and in connection with the cocaine sale, to which he pleaded guilty.

FACTS

Harris was apprehended when he sold two kilograms of cocaine to an undercover agent. When the arresting officer asked him if he was "packing," Harris admitted that he had a firearm in his boot, but did not say that he was carrying the gun in order to protect his cocaine. He was searched, and a .22 caliber pistol was found in his right boot. Harris pleaded guilty to the resulting cocaine charge, but objects to the § 924(c)(1) charge, arguing that because he was not using the firearm at the time he committed the drug-trafficking crime, he should not be convicted of a § 924(c)(1) offense.

DISCUSSION

A § 924(c)(1) violation is established when a defendant uses *or* carries a firearm in connection with a drug-trafficking crime. 18 U.S.C. § 924(c)(1) (1998). Three elements must be proven: (1) the use or carrying of the gun, (2) a predicate drug-trafficking crime, and (3) a connection between the two. The Supreme Court has held that with respect to "use" under § 924(c)(1), a conviction requires evidence sufficient to "show active employment of the firearm" by the defendant. *Bailey v. United States*, 516 U.S. 137, 144 (1995). The Court defined "use" narrowly as including "brandishing, displaying, bartering, striking with, and most obviously, firing or attempting to fire, a firearm." *Id.* at 148.

If the firearm is not actually used, the Fifth Circuit and the Supreme Court have both held that a § 924(c)(1) violation is still established if the gun was "carried" during and in connection with a drug-trafficking crime. *United States v. Ramos-Rodriguez*, 136 F.3d 465, 468 (5th Cir. 1998); *see also Muscarello v. United States*, 524 U.S. 125, 136 (1998) (affirming two "carrying" convictions). Although "use" should be interpreted narrowly, the statute uses "carry" in the ordinary sense, meaning that the gun need not be on the person or immediately accessible — it can be locked in the glove compartment of a truck while the defendant uses the truck to transport marijuana for sale. *Muscarello*, 524 U.S. at 129, 135. "Carry" involves some personal agency, dominion, or control over the firearm, whether or not the defendant actually admits to having the gun, as long as the facts show that the gun was carried during and in connection with the drug-trafficking crime. *Id.* at 133, 137; *Ramos-Rodriguez*, 136 F.3d at 468 (citations omitted). In *Muscarello*, one defendant admitting having the gun; the others did not, but all three convictions were upheld. *Muscarello*, 524 U.S. at 127, 138. In *United States v. Pigrum*, 922 F.2d 249, 251 (5th Cir. 1991), the Fifth Circuit affirmed a § 924(c)(1) conviction under the carrying prong because the defendant was found to be sitting on the firearm in question at the time of his arrest for dealing cocaine, even though he neither used the gun nor admitted having it.

The facts of Harris's case are very similar to those in *Pigrum* because putting the gun under one's body is similar to putting it in an article of clothing. In both instances, the gun was easily available to the defendant. Because of this similarity, a court would likely hold that Harris's gun was under his dominion and control.

The fact that he admitted having the gun further demonstrates personal agency and intentional possession of the gun, but he would probably be convicted even had he not admitted to having the gun. He carried the gun in his boot while he was trafficking in cocaine—in other words, "during and in connection with" the drug-trafficking crime—and he was convicted of the cocaine charge. Therefore, because all the elements of a § 924(c)(1) crime are established, Harris is likely to be convicted on this charge as well, if the issue comes to trial.

CONCLUSION

Harris's argument that he did not use the gun and should therefore not be convicted under 18 U.S.C. § 924(c)(1) is not viable. Both the Supreme Court and the Fifth Circuit have held that a § 924(c)(1) conviction can stand on the carrying prong of the statute, provided the facts show that the defendant had control over and possession of a firearm during and in connection with the predicate drug-trafficking crime. Harris had the gun in his boot while he sold two kilograms of cocaine. He pleaded guilty to the cocaine charge, and even admitted that he had the gun on his person during the crime. Therefore, he will likely be convicted of this second charge. He should be encouraged to negotiate a guilty plea on this count as well.

VI. THE OPEN RESEARCH MEMO

A. Definition of an Open Research Memo

It is unlikely that you will be assigned an open memo project until after completing Chapter 8 of this text, but knowing the difference between an open memo and a closed memo is helpful even at this early stage. A law firm memo is the document used in law firms to evaluate a client's problem objectively. In U.S. law schools, it is known as an *open research memo* or simply *open memo*. In this assignment, the student is given a hypothetical client situation, and must both research and write an objective memo just as she might do in a law firm. The *closed universe memo*, or simply *closed memo*, is a similar assignment, except that the student is also given the legal authorities upon which she must base the memo; she is not to do any additional research. The purpose of the closed memo is to enable a student to learn how to write a memo without having to tackle learning how to research at the same time. Typically, the closed memo is assigned first, and the open memo is assigned only after the student has developed knowledge of U.S. legal research, legal reasoning, and legal writing.

B. Similarities and Differences between Closed and Open Memos

The writing of an open memo follows exactly the same process as a closed memo, and the final format is exactly the same. The only difference is that in the closed memo the student is given the authorities upon which he must rely, whereas for the open memo, the student also researches the underlying legal problem.

Typically, LL.M. candidates find that writing and rewriting the closed memo helps them tremendously in learning IRAC analysis and U.S.-style objective legal writing. However, the closed research memo has inherent drawbacks. It is an unrealistic assignment given only in U.S. legal research and writing courses. The open memo is much more like a real-world project, because it requires the student first to research and then to write about a specific legal problem. Because it is a synthetic assignment, the closed research memo creates some further underlying frustrations and limitations. The student is given authoritative sources and is typically prohibited from doing further research, under honor code rules. Thus, there may be better sources, but the student is prohibited from finding or using them in the analysis. Furthermore, the student must analyze the authorities without much (if any) helpful secondary material, and is therefore at a fairly great risk of misinterpreting the law. Instructors understand this, and therefore sometimes guide students' interpretation of the law in a closed memo. These frustrations are not inherent in an open-memo assignment. Because the writer is free to do as much research as time limits allow.

The open memo involves its own perils, though. Generally, those perils lie in the most difficult parts of the process: misinterpretation of the law, incomplete analysis, and conclusional application. The first danger, misinterpretation of the law, is usually a result of failing to do enough research. As discussed in the next chapter, after verifying that (1) the applicable rule has been identified, (2) each component of that rule has been researched, and (3) all authorities have been updated, the researcher knows he has found the best sources and fully researched the area when further research turns up only the same sources, again and again.

Incomplete analysis is caused by inadequate prewriting; therefore, be sure to outline and re-outline the rule section of an open memo before writing, so that both the outline and the memo are well organized and coherent. The prewriting techniques described in Chapter 9, on scholarly writing, will also work for open memos on complicated subjects. The application section of an open memo depends first on adequate research, next on careful analysis of the law, and finally on careful thought about how the authorities found apply to the specific facts of the problem. It should be organized in the same way as the application section of a closed memo. Just as with the closed memo, an open memo must use fact-to-fact analogy where appropriate, explain how each component of the rule applies to the facts of the client problem, and reach sensible conclusions based on accurate interpretation of the law.

C. Checklist: Researching and Writing the Open Memo

The process of researching and writing an open memo is a synthesis of the techniques shown in this and the next four chapters. The following chart summarizes, on a general level, those steps.

OPEN MEMO CHECKLIST

Research

- ☐ 1. Stage 1: Interviewing employer, background research and preparation
- ☐ 2. Stage 2: Researching mandatory and persuasive authority
- ☐ 3. Stage 3: Updating research and prewriting

Writing

- ☐ 1. First draft
- ☐ 2. Rewriting
- ☐ 3. Editing
- ☐ 4. Polishing

DISCUSSION NOTES

A. Rule dissection

Explain whether the following rules are conjunctive, disjunctive, prong, factors, balancing, or a combination of two or more types. It might help to diagram the components of the rule. Furthermore, identify which terms are open to interpretation and are therefore likely to generate case law, as with the statute in the Harris example.

1. "The district courts shall have original jurisdiction of all civil actions where the matter in controversy exceeds the sum or value of $75,000, exclusive of interest and costs, and is between (1) citizens of different States; (2) citizens of a State and citizens or subjects of a foreign state; (3) citizens of different States and in which citizens or subjects of a foreign state are additional parties; and (4) a foreign state . . . as plaintiff and citizens of a State or of different States." 28 U.S.C. § 1332.
2. Judicial review of a U.S. government agency's interpretation of a statute that it administers involves a two-step process. *Chevron*, 467 U.S. at 842-43 (as cited in *Mississippi Poultry Ass'n Inc. v. Madigan*, 992 F.2d 1359, 1363 (5th Cir. 1993). The threshold inquiry is whether Congress clearly expressed its intent in the plain language of the statute. *Id.* If it did, that is the end of the matter. *Id.* If, however, and only if the language of the statute is determined to be either ambiguous or silent on the particular issue, then the reviewing court is to determine whether the agency's interpretation is based on a permissible construction of the statute. *Id.* As long as the agency's interpretation is reasonable, the court should defer to that interpretation and not impose its own construction on the statute. *Id.*

3. To state an actionable claim for securities fraud under 17 C.F.R. § 240.10b-5 (Rule 10b-5), a plaintiff must allege "(1) the defendant made an untrue statement of material fact or failed to state a material fact; (2) the defendant made the misrepresentation in connection with the purchase or sale of a security; (3) the defendant made the misrepresentation with scienter; and (4) the plaintiff relied on the misrepresentation and sustained damages as a proximate result of the misrepresentation." *United Int'l Holdings, Inc. v. Wharf (Holdings) Ltd.*, 210 F.3d 1207, 1220 (10th Cir. 2000).

B. *Rule synthesis*[21]

Synthesize a rule from the following authorities:

1. N.H. Rev. Stat. Ann. § 265-A:2 (2007)
DRIVING UNDER INFLUENCE OF DRUGS OR LIQUOR; DRIVING WITH EXCESS ALCOHOL CONCENTRATION

I. No person shall drive or attempt to drive a vehicle upon any way:

(a) While such person is under the influence of intoxicating liquor or any controlled drug or any combination of intoxicating liquor and controlled drugs; or

(b) While such person has an alcohol concentration of 0.08 or more or in the case of a person under the age of 21, 0.02 or more.

II. [Repealed.]

*2. **State v. Willard,*** **660 A.2d 1086 (N.H. 1995)** (June).
Facts: A police officer approached a vehicle in a parking lot. The vehicle's engine was idling, and the defendant was asleep in the driver's seat. The officer woke the defendant, determined that he was intoxicated, and arrested him for driving while intoxicated.
Procedural History: The trial court dismissed the driving-while-intoxicated (DWI) charge, and the state appealed.
Issue: Was defendant "driving" and showing actual physical control of the vehicle?
Rule: "Driving" for purposes of RSA 265:82 means operating or having actual physical control of the vehicle.
Holding: Reversed and remanded. If the defendant had started his car before falling asleep — if so, then he was in actual physical control while awake and in the driver's seat. The court says that the word "drive" does not necessarily mean "operate."
Reasoning: The court notes that the law used to be that the arresting officer had to see the defendant actually driving and a previous case supported that. But the statute has recently been amended, and the legislature now defines "drive" as "operate or have actual physical control" — actual physical control is different

[21] From an exercise developed by Sophie Sparrow, "Using Active Learning Techniques in the Legal Writing Classroom," presented at the Legal Writing Institute Biennial Conference, Knoxville, Tennessee, June 1, 2002.

from operation under a plain meaning analysis, and as defined by *Webster's Dictionary*. The court says that if the occupant of the car is totally passive and has not actively tried to control or is not imminently going to control the car, then that occupant should not be penalized by the law.

3. ***State v. Holloran*, 669 A.2d 800 (N.H. 1995)** (December).
Facts: A police officer approached a parked pickup truck when he saw the defendant sitting alone behind the wheel. Although the engine was not running, the keys to the truck were in the ignition. The defendant seemed drunk: He was unsteady on his feet, his eyes were glassy and bloodshot, and he appeared disheveled. The defendant stated that he was waiting for a call from his wife to pick her up from a party in another town. He had been driving, but parked to wait for his wife's call. Although he claimed that he had not been drinking, he failed three field sobriety tests, and was arrested for DUI.
Procedural History: The trial court found the defendant guilty of DUI, and the defendant appealed.
Issue: Was defendant "driving" and showing actual physical control of the vehicle?
Rule: "Driving" for purposes of RSA 265:82 means actual physical control of the vehicle. "Actual physical control" varies according to the facts of the case, but when it is reasonable to assume that the defendant will be imminently operating a vehicle rather than using the vehicle for stationary shelter, the defendant will be found to be in actual physical control.
Holding: Affirmed. The defendant was driving and in actual physical control of his vehicle when found sitting behind the wheel, with keys in the ignition, the vehicle parked, and engine and lights off.
Reasoning: The court looks at all the evidence and notes that the standard for driving has to be applied in the context of all the facts and circumstances, not in isolation. Because the defendant said he was waiting for a call from his wife, who needed to be picked up in another town, and because the keys were in the ignition, the defendant was found to be about to drive, not merely using the car for shelter. The court reasons that a defendant has actual physical control when it is reasonable to assume that he or she is about to jeopardize public safety.

C. *Issue statement*

Draft a preliminary issue statement or statements based on the following client situation: This morning, Martha Marples, a partner in your law firm, had an initial consultation with Robin Shymite, M.D., a fourth-year resident in Emergency Room medicine at Stanford, New Hampshire's Memorial Hospital. Dr. Shymite gave the following story. Yesterday, because it was a Saturday, the emergency room of Memorial Hospital was extremely busy. Memorial Hospital, because it is publicly funded, is required to treat all patients who ask for help, whether or not they have private medical insurance. Other hospitals, those that are privately funded, are required only to stabilize uninsured patients before transferring them to Memorial. Furthermore, because Memorial has the best-equipped trauma center in the city, it has become known as a "knife and gun club," full of patients with life-threatening emergencies, and is therefore an excellent place for a young doctor like Shymite to receive training and experience.

Unfortunately, yesterday was a very difficult one for Shymite. After 47 hours of almost continuous work, one of Shymite's patients, a young child, died despite all his efforts. Shymite was distraught about the child's death, and felt that he should have handled the case differently. In an effort to cheer him up, his colleagues invited him to have a drink with them at a local bar after work, something he has never done before. He had two or three beers, and then decided to drive home. Before moving the car, he realized that he was too tired to drive. He turned off the engine. However, he left the keys in the ignition so that he could listen to the radio while resting. Approximately a half hour later, a policeman woke him up by knocking on the window. The policeman insisted that he take a blood-alcohol test, then told Shymite that he had failed the test and put him in jail. Shymite's friend arranged for his release this morning, and Shymite then went directly to Ms. Marples's office, but forgot to bring the papers the police gave him. He is worried that he will lose his medical license if convicted of driving under the influence of alcohol.

D. *Development of arguments on both sides*

Chart the case law from subsection B so that you master the facts of the various cases and then develop arguments for both Dr. Shymite and his potential prosecution on charges of driving under the influence (DUI). Which arguments do you believe are stronger?

EXERCISE

Closed Memo Assignment: Draft a closed universe memo according to your instructor's assignment. (For a closed universe memo, you are not to research any authorities, and must use only the materials supplied by the instructor.)

CHAPTER 4

The Legal Process

INTRODUCTION TO CIVIL AND ADMINISTRATIVE PROCEDURE

Chapter 1 introduced some of the differences between U.S. common law and other legal systems. Some of the normative differences include the focus on the separation of law and morality (U.S. law as compared to Shar'ia law), the use of adversarial process as an acceptable means of resolving private disputes (U.S. law as compared to Confucian tradition), and the legal and political focus on market economy, limited government, the rule of law, and individuality (U.S. law as compared to Marxist/Leninist theories).

In addition to focusing on normative differences, Chapter 1 focused on the development of common law legal systems and their emphasis on court opinions as a source of law, as opposed to the civilian tradition, which downplays court opinions. Thus, substantive common law subjects such as torts, contracts, and property developed very differently from their civilian counterparts. However, there has been a lot of *convergence*[1] between these two related legal systems: The common law concept of *consideration* is markedly similar to the civilian *cause*, the standard of negligence in both systems focuses on the behavior of a reasonably prudent person (or *bon père de famille*). Furthermore, even where common and civilian law have not converged, and substantive legal differences remain, the result in any particular case will often be the same or similar. The reason for both the convergence and the similarity in result may be an underlying normative agreement between the two systems: for instance, both legal traditions grant private parties the right to sue other private parties, and the private causes of action that have developed as a result recognize values such as freedom of contract and a societal desire to discourage negligent behavior and provide private remedy for those who were harmed by such negligence. This similarity may also reflect

[1] Convergence means that the law on some topic is the same in two different legal systems, even though there is no negotiation or treaty in place.

the demands made by a global market economy for law and policy recognizing the importance of property rights and the centrality of contracts.

The greatest gap between common law and the civilian tradition, therefore, may lie not in substantive legal topics such as contracts and torts, but in procedural differences. As mentioned in Chapter 1, things that shock or surprise civilian attorneys about U.S. law are generally procedural concerns, such as the right to a jury in a civil trial, an attorney's power to demand production of evidence from an opposing party, contingency fees, and the fact that a common law trial takes place in one sitting rather than over a period of time. Furthermore, as you may have seen from working on the closed memo in Chapter 3, the adversarial, one-sitting nature of common law procedure means that attorneys must not only prepare arguments for their own client's case but also anticipate what the other side will argue — merely rebutting those arguments once they are made in court is insufficient. This chapter, therefore, will focus on providing an introduction to both civil and administrative procedure so that you can gain a further understanding of how the U.S. legal system works.

I. CIVIL TRIAL SEQUENCE

A. Summary of Civil Trial Sequence

Figure 4-1 provides a simplified outline of a civil trial sequence. A civil lawsuit begins when the plaintiff files a *complaint* in a court of his choosing. Once the defendant receives proper notice that a suit has been filed against him, he has a limited period of time in which to file a *responsive pleading.* After these initial filings have been made, the court meets with the parties to discuss scheduling. During this pretrial phase, the parties conduct *discovery* (collect evidence), and the court hears any pretrial motions on discovery issues or on pretrial motions to dismiss. The vast majority of lawsuits settle or are dismissed sometime in this period. Assuming the lawsuit is neither

FIGURE 4-1

OUTLINE OF CIVIL TRIAL SEQUENCE

1. Complaint filed, defendant served
2. Defendant files response
3. Scheduling conference
4. Pretrial motions and discovery
5. Trial
   a. Voir dire, jury seated
   b. Opening remarks, plaintiff then defendant
   c. Case-in-chief, plaintiff then defendant
   d. Closing remarks
   e. Jury charge by court
   f. Jury verdict
6. Judgment
7. Motion for Judgment as a Matter of Law, or for New Trial
8. Appeal filed

settled nor dismissed, if the lawsuit is such that a jury can hear it, either party can demand a jury trial, or they can both elect to have the case heard by a judge alone (this is called a *bench trial*). Bench trials tend to be shorter and less expensive to conduct, but the damages awarded may also be less.

In a jury trial, the first order of business after all pretrial preparation is concluded is to choose a jury. A pool of jurors (citizens called to jury duty) is brought into the courtroom, and either the attorneys or the judge conducts *voir dire*: they question the potential jurors to eliminate any who have an interest in the matter or who otherwise could not make a fair decision. Then, once the jury is seated, first the plaintiff's attorney and then the defendant's each make their opening remarks, explaining their theory of the case to the judge or jury. After opening remarks, the plaintiff presents his case-in-chief by having a series of witnesses testify. After each witness testifies, the defendant can *cross-examine* the witness (i.e., ask his own questions). Then, once the plaintiff rests his case, the defendant presents her case-in-chief, with the testimony of her own witnesses (followed by the plaintiff's cross-examination). Once both parties have presented their cases, the parties each make their closing remarks, and the judge instructs the jury on the law they are to apply in reaching their decision. During the trial, if either party believes that the other side cannot prove his or her case, the party can again ask that the case be dismissed.

The jury then retires to the jury room, where they discuss the case among themselves and reach a verdict. Unlike criminal trials, the jury verdict in a civil trial need not always be unanimous. After trial, the losing party can ask the court that the verdict be set aside, or ask for a new trial. Assuming the judge denies both of these requests (motions), and issues a final judgment, the losing party has a right to file an appeal within a certain period of time.

B. Documents and Details of Civil Trials

Most legal research and writing courses require students to learn to draft not only objective memoranda designed to advise another attorney about the strength of a client's position, but also persuasive documents that will be filed as part of that client's case. In fact, Chapter 11 explains such documents in detail in the anticipation that you will be asked to draft such a document as part of your legal writing course. In addition to explaining the civil trial sequence in greater detail, this section will introduce the various documents used in that sequence. As you learn a bit more about civil procedure, bear in mind that the vast majority of civil lawsuits settle before trial, or are decided before they reach a full trial when the court realizes that one or the other party will be unable to prove his case. When you read appellate opinions, note whether the appeal arose after a full trial in the court below, or whether it arose after the appealing party's case was dismissed before trial. For an in-depth, detailed view, see the flow chart in Figure 4-2 below.

FIGURE 4-2
CIVIL TRIAL SEQUENCE

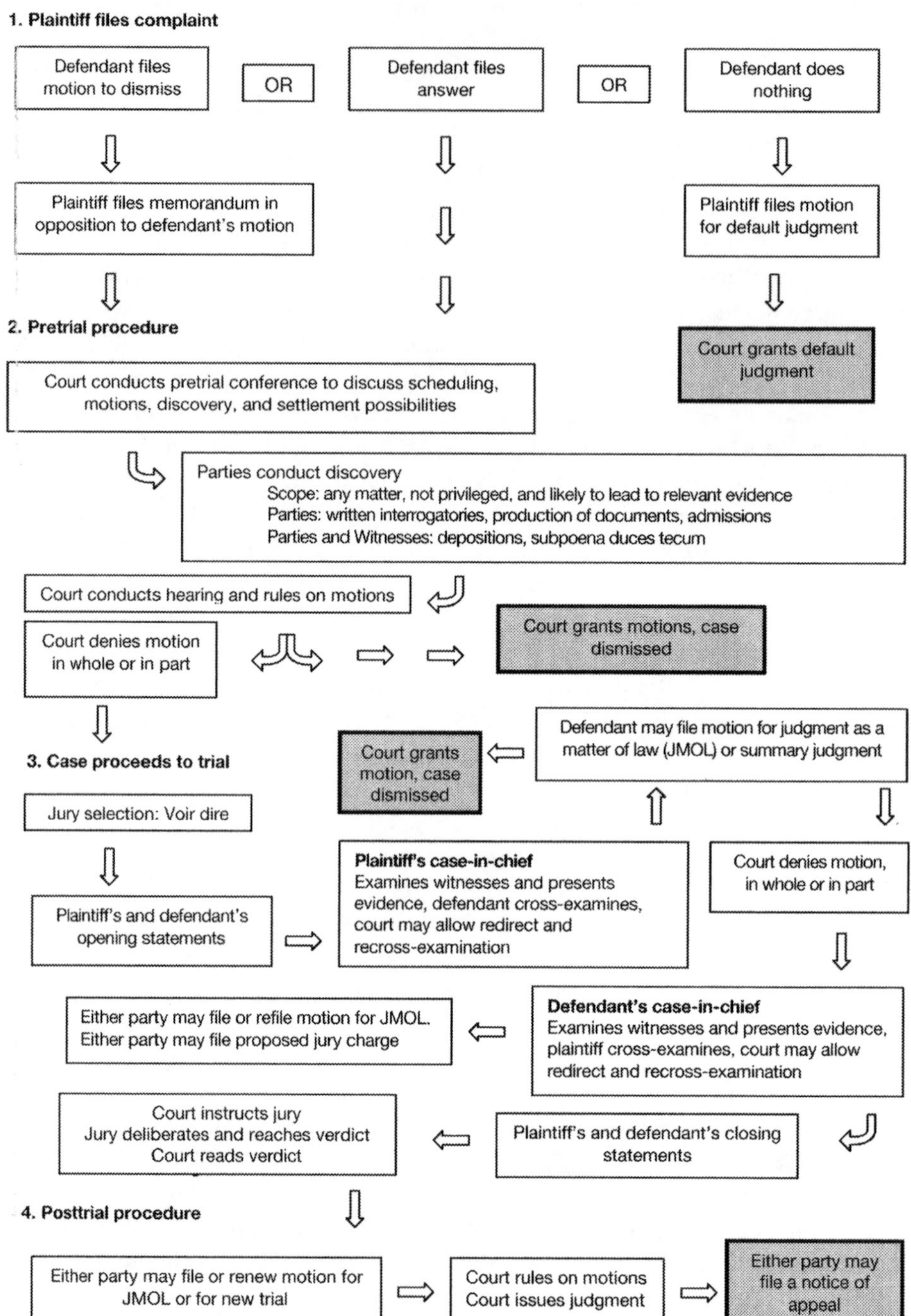

A. Pretrial Procedure and Documents

1. Preliminary Documents

Under the Federal Rules of Civil Procedure, litigation begins when the plaintiff files a *complaint* and a draft *summons* notifying the defendant of the lawsuit and requiring his response. The court then signs and sends the *summons* and the plaintiff sees that the complaint and summons are delivered to the defendant.[2] This is called *service of process*. All pleadings, motions, or other papers filed with the court must be both signed by the attorney or party filing them and *served* upon the other parties to the lawsuit.[3] The signature constitutes a certificate that the signer has read the filing, that it is being filed in good faith and after reasonable inquiry, and that it is not being filed for an improper purpose such as to harass or cause unnecessary delay to the lawsuit.[4] The party serving the document must establish that service has been accomplished according to the appropriate rules of civil procedure by providing a *certificate of service* identifying the fact and manner of service.[5]

After the complaint is filed, the defendant has a limited time to file a *responsive pleading*.[6] If the defendant does nothing to respond to the service of process, after 20 days (for federal district courts) the plaintiff can file a *motion for default judgment*. When the court enters a default judgment, the allegations presented in the complaint are taken as true, and the court may grant the plaintiff the requested relief.[7] The defendant will then have a difficult time if he chooses to litigate the resulting default judgment. The defendant's proper response is to file either a *motion to dismiss*, if he feels the suit was improperly brought, or an *answer*, if he has one or more affirmative defenses, or the two combined into one document.[8]

In a motion to dismiss, the defendant argues in effect that even if what the plaintiff alleges is true, the plaintiff still has no grounds to sue, for one or more reasons. These reasons may include that the court lacks personal or subject matter jurisdiction, that the applicable statute of limitations has run or lapsed, or that the plaintiff has failed to state a cause of action upon which relief could be granted.[9] The defendant could also argue that the suit was improperly served, or that the venue is improper or inconvenient for both the court and one or more parties (i.e., *forum non conveniens*). In filing any motion, the defendant actually files four documents: the motion itself, a notice to the opposing side indicating when the motion is scheduled for hearing, a memorandum in support of the motion, and a certificate of service. The motion is a very short

---

[2] Fed. R. Civ. P. 4 (effective Dec 1, 2007) The language of the Federal Rules of Civil Procedure was amended in 2007 in an effort to make them more easily understood. The changes were intended to be stylistic only. Committee Note, Fed. R. Civ. P. 1 2007 U.S. Order 30.

[3] Fed. R. Civ. P. 5, 11(a) (2007).

[4] Fed. R. Civ. P. 11(b) (2007).

[5] Fed. R. Civ. P. 5(d) (2007).

[6] *See* Fed. R. Civ. P. 12(a)(1)(A)(i) (2007) (generally 20 days from being served with summons and complaint).

[7] Fed. R. Civ. P. 55(a)(b) (2007).

[8] Fed. R. Civ. P. 12(a)(1)(A), (a)(4), (b) (2007).

[9] Fed. R. Civ. P. 12(b) (2007).

document describing the relief requested and the legal basis for the request; the notice and the certificate of service are similarly short, often less than a page in length. A memorandum in support, which is generally much longer, presents and explains the defendant's arguments about why the motion should be granted. In rebuttal, the plaintiff will file a memorandum in opposition to the defendant's motion explaining the legal reasons why the defendant's motion should be denied.

In contrast to a *motion to dismiss*, which raises pretrial issues, in an *answer* the defendant sets forth affirmative defenses. For example, the defendant to a battery suit might deny that the incident ever happened or assert that though it happened, he was acting in self-defense, or both. In a contract suit, the defendant could argue that the alleged contract at issue was unenforceable for one or more reasons, or that she did not breach the contract.

If the defendant has her own claims to make against the original plaintiff, she includes a *counterclaim* in her answer.[10] The plaintiff must then file a *reply* in answer to the counterclaim. Sometimes a party has a claim against a co-party that arises out of the same transaction or subject matter of the original action; if so, he files a *cross-claim* against that co-party.[11] If an interested person not named in the lawsuit wants to participate, she can file an *intervention* seeking a court order to allow her to enter the suit as an *intervenor.*[12] An intervenor is often the trustee of a large sum of money who is obligated to disburse the sum, but cannot do so until a court determines to whom the money should go. Furthermore, if the defendant feels that she is not at fault, but a third party not named in the lawsuit is, then she can add that person as a *third-party defendant.*

After the initial filings, once the parties and initial claims are sorted out, the judge will confer with the parties' attorneys at a *scheduling conference* long before the trial date.[13] At this conference, the judge and the attorneys prepare a schedule setting out when discovery should be completed, when pretrial motions will be heard, and when the trial will take place. At some point, the parties also exchange witness lists, and the judge may order settlement conferences as part of the pretrial process — though the judge cannot force parties to settle, many judges' dockets are overloaded and therefore they are strongly motivated to encourage parties to settle their own disputes.

2. Discovery

Once the parties to a suit have been identified and served, the process of discovery, or fact gathering, begins. American discovery rules differ markedly from those in civilian jurisdictions. Indeed, non-common law jurisdictions often find American attorneys' broad powers of discovery shocking, more like the power given to judges in other legal systems. The Hague Convention,[14] which entered into force for the United States on October 7, 1972, sets forth discovery guidance for international litigation, but if the

[10] Fed. R. Civ. P. 13 (2007).
[11] Fed. R. Civ. P. 13(g) (2007).
[12] Fed. R. Civ. P. 24(a)(2) (2007).
[13] Fed. R. Civ. P. 16(b)(1) (2007).
[14] *See* Multilateral Convention on Taking Evidence Abroad Adopted at the Eleventh Session of the Hague Convention July 27, 1970, 23 U.S.T. 2555.

suit is set in the United States, U.S. courts may impose the discovery rules they usually use,[15] rather than the methods provided in the Convention.

a. Policy Reasons for Broad Powers of Discovery

The more information attorneys have about both sides' positions, the more likely they are to persuade their clients to settle before trial, because they know the strengths and weaknesses of each other's cases. Furthermore, under the adversarial system, it is thought that the truth is more easily and reliably determined when parties zealously attack each other's positions. To do this, they must each be aware of all factual information, and therefore there should be no surprises for either party's attorney at a civil trial. As mentioned previously, the trial takes place at one sitting: first the plaintiff and then the defendant presents its *case-in-chief.* In other words, each party presents all of its admissible evidence and attempts to minimize or explain away the opponent's evidence. To do this, each side needs to be fully aware of all evidence the other party intends to present at trial before the trial occurs. To accomplish this, they have full power of discovery, backed by the power of the court. Failure or refusal to produce evidence requested by the other side may lead a court to sanction (i.e., punish) the attorney at fault. Nevertheless, such battles are common in cases involving a lot of money, and can become heated. If the battles become too acrimonious, the court may sanction an attorney for vexatious, abusive discovery requests. Particularly combative parties sometimes significantly delay the trial process with protracted battles over discovery in the form of *motions to compel* or *to limit discovery.* The court may intervene if these battles become abusive, but the parties themselves may also limit their attorney's discovery battles: Because each party pays for its own attorneys' costs, the parties themselves can pressure attorneys into resolving discovery disputes by objecting to the cost of such battles.

b. Types of Discovery

The Federal Rules of Civil Procedure provide different times at which evidence must be disclosed and four methods of discovery. Within 14 days of their initial conference, and without being asked, parties must make certain required initial disclosures of their potential witnesses, documents, damage computations, and any applicable insurance agreements.[16] Later (at least 90 days before trial), they must disclose any expert witnesses they plan to use, and they must provide a final witness list at least 30 days before trial.[17] The four methods of discovery include *written interrogatories, requests for admission, oral deposition,* and *requests for document production. Written*

---

[15] Article 1 of the Convention states that:

> In civil or commercial matters a judicial authority of a Contracting State may, in accordance with the provisions of the law of that State, request the competent authority of another Contracting State, by means of a Letter of Request, to obtain evidence, or to perform some other judicial act.

The United States Supreme Court has interpreted this language to mean that the Hague Convention is not the exclusive means for a party to a suit in the United States to obtain discovery from parties and witnesses located abroad. *Societé Nationale Industrielle Aerospatiale v. United States Dist. Court,* 482 U.S. 522 (1987).

[16] Fed. R. Civ. P. 26(a) (2007).

[17] Fed. R. Civ. P. 26(a)(2), (a)(3) (2007).

interrogatories are a series of questions, not to exceed 25 in number, designed to elicit basic information about the opposing party.[18] They are usually used to determine the parties' exact names and titles, their proper addresses, and other basic, non-sensitive information. Counsel can also request *production of documents* and other evidence. To simplify issues of fact for trial, parties may request *admissions* and thereby admit certain agreed-upon facts in writing, so that they are not issues at trial.[19] Such admissions save time at trial so that more pressing issues can be litigated. Furthermore, an admission may benefit one of the parties strategically if litigating the issue would not only be futile but also would emphasize a fact that party wants to de-emphasize.

Of the four methods of discovery, the most powerful and most controversial American discovery tool is the *oral deposition*:[20] An attorney can *subpoena* the opposing party or any of its witnesses to demand that person to meet with him and give deposition,[21] usually at the attorney's law offices. At that meeting, the attorney may ask any question that might lead to relevant evidence, as long as the question does not violate an established *privilege* (for example, communications between attorney and client are privileged).[22] A *subpoena duces tecum* requires the *deponent* to bring with him any relevant documents. Once he arrives at the attorney's office, the deponent is sworn in, just as in court, and is required to tell the truth under threat of perjury. Counsel from both sides attend a deposition, and witnesses may bring their own attorneys. Depositions may last for several hours or longer.

The Federal Rules of Civil Procedure require that oral depositions be recorded, though this can be done by various methods.[23] Usually, a court reporter, herself an officer of the court, is hired for the occasion and both administers the witness's oath and records his testimony. Sometimes the deposition is recorded on videotape. Depositions can even be taken by means of teleconferencing, especially when the deponent is out of the country.[24] Rule 28 of the Federal Rules of Civil Procedure provides that depositions may be taken in a foreign country pursuant to any applicable treaty or convention before a person authorized to administer oaths in the locale where the examination is held or before a person so commissioned by the court.[25] Usually the deposition is recorded by a court reporter and then reduced to a transcript, which the deponent signs, attesting that he or she in fact said everything in the transcript and that everything said was true, to his knowledge. As you may have surmised, depositions can be very expensive.

More often than not, the discovery process reveals that one or the other party's position is weak, or that the litigation is likely to cost much more than originally contemplated, and the parties decide to settle. The vast majority of all cases settle before trial. However, even if the parties do not settle, and a pretrial motion to dismiss

---

[18] Fed. R. Civ. P. 33 (2007).
[19] Fed. R. Civ. P. 36 (2007).
[20] Fed. R. Civ. P. 30 (2007).
[21] Fed. R. Civ. P. 30(b)(1) (2007); see Fed. R. Civ. P. 45 (2007).
[22] Fed. R. Civ. P. 30(d) (2007).
[23] Fed. R. Civ. P. 30(b)(2) (2007).
[24] Fed. R. Civ. P. 30(b)(3) (2007).
[25] Fed. R. Civ. P. 28(b) (2007).

has already been heard and denied, one or the other may file a *motion for summary judgment* if he believes that discovery has shown that the other side cannot prove its case.[26] Many of the cases published in the reporters are summary judgment opinions, and not the result of a full trial. If there are no material issues of fact, then the only thing that must be determined is the applicable law, and no trial is necessary. A summary judgment motion may be filed by either party, can relate to the entire case, or can be partial, relating only to some issues or causes of action and not the entire case or controversy. If a motion for summary judgment relating to the entire case is granted, then the case is over, the moving party wins, and the court issues a judgment and opinion in the moving party's favor. (As a technical point, any pretrial motion for dismissal becomes a motion for summary judgment if discovery is required before the court can decide the issue.)

If the case is transnational, and foreign law is involved, then foreign law is itself discoverable. The party who intends to raise an issue concerning the law of a foreign country must give notice, and then produce evidence of the law at issue. The court, in determining foreign law, may consider any relevant material or source, including testimony, "whether or not submitted by a party or admissible under the Federal Rules of Evidence."[27]

B. The Trial

If there is to be a jury, either the judge (federal court) or the attorneys (state court) will question the jury pool to eliminate jurors who may know a party or cannot for other reasons decide fairly.[28] As mentioned earlier, this questioning is called *voir dire.* Once the jury is chosen and seated, the trial begins with counsel giving their opening remarks: first plaintiff's, then defendant's counsel. Each side then presents its case-in-chief. The plaintiff presents its first witness, has him sworn in, and asks questions of that witness, introducing documentary evidence as needed along the way. The questioning of a party's own witness is called *direct examination.* After direct examination, the witness is subject to *cross-examination* by opposing counsel. After cross-examination of a witness, plaintiff's counsel may have an opportunity for *redirect examination,* and the defendant may have an opportunity for *recross.* Then the plaintiff's next witness is introduced and subjected to the same process. Once the plaintiff has presented his entire case, the defendant does the same with her case. Finally, both sides give their closing remarks. At the end of either party's case-in-chief, or at the end of trial, either party can file a *motion for a judgment as a matter of law,* asserting that the evidence is insufficient for a reasonable jury to find for the opposing party.[29] This motion may be made at the end of trial and renewed after the verdict is rendered, but is rarely granted (the reasoning is that if there was enough evidence for an entire trial,

[26] Fed. R. Civ. P. 56 (2007).
[27] Fed. R. Civ. P. 44.1 (2007).
[28] *See* Fed. R. Civ. P. 47 (2007).
[29] Fed. R. Civ. P. 50 (2007).

then it is unlikely that one or the other side's arguments lack *any* basis in fact). If such a motion is made after the verdict is rendered, it may be combined with a *motion for a new trial*, which is also very rarely granted.[30]

Before the jury retires to deliberate, the judge gives the jury instructions on the law that the jury will need in reaching its findings of fact and its verdict.[31] This is known as a *jury charge*. Prior to this time, each party submits its own proposed instructions for the judge's consideration. The judge may choose either side's proposal, or may use a different charge. The choice of a jury charge can itself be a contentious process, and appeals have been won when a reviewing court found that the charge was reversibly inaccurate or inadequate, or unconstitutional.[32]

In addition to, or instead of, a *motion for judgment as a matter of law*, a party dissatisfied with a trial court's decision may file a *notice of appeal* within 30 days after entry of a judgment.[33] The notice of appeal must indicate the errors that the party contends were made by the trial court.[34] The party appealing (the *appellant*) then files an *appellate brief* explaining the case and the errors made, and the opposition (now the *appellee*) must file a brief in response within a certain period of time.[35] Although a party has a right to an appeal, the appellate court will not hear witnesses or retry factual issues; therefore, appellate decisions are made either on the paper only (the trial record and the parties' briefs) or after oral argument by counsel from each side.

Finally, a party dissatisfied with an appellate court decision may file a petition for rehearing, asking that the appellate court reconsider its decision, or a petition for a *writ of certiorari* with the United States Supreme Court (if in federal court), or with the state supreme court (if in state court). Occasionally on appeal, but more often after a grant of cert., a third party will want to advise that court, because it believes that it may be strongly affected by the outcome of the litigation; if so, it will file an *amicus curiae* (friend of the court) *brief*,[36] even though it cannot be a party to the suit. The court, whether state or federal, will then consider the amicus briefs along with the parties' briefs in making its decision.

C. Levels of Proof and Standards of Review

1. *Level of Proof at Trial*

Most people who watch American movies or television series about legal issues (such as *Law and Order*) are aware that the level of proof required to convict someone of a crime in the United States is *beyond a reasonable doubt*. Reasonable doubt refers to doubt such that it "prevents one from being firmly convinced of a defendant's guilt, or

[30] Fed. R. Civ. P. 59 (2007).
[31] Fed. R. Civ. P. 51 (2007).
[32] *See Sandstrom v. Montana*, 442 U.S. 510, 524 (1979) (unconstitutional); Wilson v. Des Moines, 442 F.3d 637, 644 (8th Cir. 2006) (discussing reversible errors in jury instructions).
[33] Fed. R. App. P. 4 (2002).
[34] Fed. R. App. P. 3(c) (2002).
[35] Fed. R. App. P. 28(a), (b) (2002).
[36] Fed. R. App. P. 29 (2002).

the belief that there is a real possibility that a defendant is not guilty."[37] In a civil trial, however, the plaintiff's burden of proof is much lower. Usually, he need only prove his case to a *preponderance of the evidence.* He is required to provide evidence that is sufficient to incline a fair and impartial mind to one side of the issue rather than the other. The evidence need not be sufficient to free the mind wholly from all reasonable doubt.[38] The jury is instructed to find for the party that, on the whole, has the stronger evidence, however slight the edge may be.[39] For example, O.J. Simpson was found not guilty of murdering his ex-wife and her friend at his murder trial, but he was found liable for their wrongful deaths at the subsequent civil trial brought by the murder victims' families. In other words, although the government had not proven him guilty of murder beyond a reasonable doubt, the plaintiffs proved, by a preponderance of the evidence, that he had probably killed them. (He was ordered to pay the families $33.5 million, which he has not yet paid[40]). *Clear and convincing evidence* is a standard of proof sometimes used in civil trials that is higher than *preponderence of the evidence*, but lower than *beyond a reasonable doubt.*

2. *Standards of Review*

The standard of review is a concept used in appellate courts that serves a function similar to the level of proof used at the trial level. It is the test applied by a reviewing court in deciding whether to interfere with a decision of a lower court or tribunal. Because it cannot see the witnesses itself and assess their credibility, an appellate court reviews the lower court's findings of fact only for *clear error.* This means that in reviewing the evidence of record, the court will not overturn the lower court's factual findings unless it has a definite and firm conviction that the trial court mistook the facts. This standard defers to the trial court's findings, overturning them only occasionally. In contrast, an appellate court will review a lower court's holdings of law thoroughly (*de novo*).

Another commonly used standard of review is that used in reviewing the grant of a summary judgment. In these cases, the reviewing court uses the same standard the lower court used in granting the summary judgment in the first place: did the movant demonstrate that there were no issues of material fact, and that he or she should be granted summary judgment as a matter of law. In such cases, the reviewing court looks to see if there were any disagreements as to material facts, and reviews the lower court's legal reasoning de novo. As the U.S. Supreme Court described it: Summary judgment must be granted

> against a party who fails to make a showing sufficient to establish the existence of an element essential to that party's case, and on which that party will bear the burden of proof at trial. In such a situation, there can be "no genuine issue as to any material fact," since a complete failure of proof concerning an essential element of the

[37] Black's Law Dictionary 1293 (Bryan Garner ed., 8th ed. 2004) (defining *reasonable doubt*).
[38] *Id.* at 1220 (defining *preponderance of the evidence*).
[39] *Id.*
[40] Steve Gorman, Exclusive: O.J. Simpson Signed Off on Book: Ghost Writer (Reuters, Can., Aug. 3, 2007), *available at* http://ca.today.reuters.com/news/newsArticle.aspx?type=entertainmentNews&storyID=2007-08-03T184839Z_01_N02454477_RTRIDST_0_ENTERTAINMENT-SIMPSON-BOOK-COL.XML.

> nonmoving party's case necessarily renders all other facts immaterial. The moving party is "entitled to a judgment as a matter of law" because the nonmoving party has failed to make a sufficient showing on an essential element of her case with respect to which she has the burden of proof.[41]

This standard of review for a summary judgment is approximately the same as that given to the grant of a judgment as a matter of law (also known as a judgment notwithstanding the verdict).[42]

The most deferential standard of review is that used in reviewing those rulings that a trial court makes in order to keep a case moving forward through its docket: Decisions such as whether or not to admit a particular witness, or grant a party extra time, or the like. Such decisions are reviewed only for *abuse of discretion*: Only decisions that are grossly unsound, unreasonable, illegal, or unsupported by the evidence will be overturned. Often, this is the same standard of review that courts use in reviewing the decisions of administrative agencies, as discussed in the next section.

II. ADMINISTRATIVE PROCESS

For good or for ill, in the United States, as in many countries, the administrative state has become increasingly important, possibly more important and more powerful than the legislative state. A number of writers noted the rise of administrative agencies and bureaucracy by the end of the 19th century and often satirized their inefficiencies, including writers such as John Stuart Mill,[43] Charles Dickens,[44] and Nikolai Gogol.[45] German sociologist Max Weber may have been the first to classify it as a novel and distinctive mode of governance.[46] Weber defined administrative government as a rational, legal regime in which groups of full-time, salaried officials, chosen on the basis of their credentials and placed within hierarchical organizations, conduct official

---

[41] *Celotex Corp. v. Catrett*, 477 U.S. 317, 322-23 (1986).

[42] *Id.*

[43] *See* John Stuart Mill, *Utilitarianism, on Liberty, Considerations on Representative Government* 360-64 (Geraint Williams ed., 1993), *cited in* Edward Rubin, *It's Time to Make the Administrative Procedure Act Administrative*, 89 Cornell L. Rev. 95 n.10 (2003) [hereinafter Rubin].

[44] *See* Charles Dickens, *Little Dorrit* 104-23 (1992 [sic]), *cited in* Rubin, *supra* note 42, at n.11, and noting that Dickens names his archetypical agency the Circumlocution Office; staffs it with a number of officials from the Barnacle family, and develops a motto for it "How Not to Do It.

[45] *See, e.g.*, Nikolai Gogol, *Dead Souls* 49-61 (George Gibian ed., 1985) (a swindler buys title to serfs who have died but are still listed as alive on the public tax registry); Nikolai Gogol, *The Government Inspector* (M. Beresford ed., 1996) (a lowly clerk is mistaken for a government inspector by a small town's officials); Nikolai Gogol, *The Nose*, in *The Overcoat and Other Tales of Good and Evil* 203 (David Magarshak trans., 1957) (a civil servant of the eighth rank finds his nose traveling around town as a civil servant of the fifth rank); Nikolai Gogol, *The Overcoat, in The Overcoat and Other Tales of Good and Evil* 233, 261-64 (a poor clerk whose overcoat is stolen is viciously abused when he complains to the Very Important Person about police inefficiency in retrieving it), *all cited* in Rubin, *supra* note 42, at n.12.

[46] 1, 2 Max Weber, *Economy and Society* 217-26, 956-1003 (Guenther Roth & Claus Wittich eds., Ephraim Fischoff et al. trans., 1978); *see also* 2 Weber, *id.* at 1393-1405.

business according to established rules within a defined jurisdiction and for defined instrumental purposes.[47]

This definition may still work today, but unlike the Federal Rules of Civil Procedure, which set forth a unitary procedure followed by all U.S. district courts, the Administrative Procedure Act (APA)[48] allows federal agencies a great deal of freedom with regard to decision-making. The justification for this is that each agency has its own governmental purpose and must be allowed to develop its own rules and procedures. Those rules and procedures must be within the scope of the powers granted to it by Congress and in keeping with the due process requirements of the United States Constitution's Fifth Amendment, which provides that no person shall "be deprived of life, liberty, or property, without due process of law." Thus, the study of "administrative law" in the United States refers to the study of the complex processes by which governmental agencies such as the Social Security Administration, the Environmental Protection Agency, the Securities and Exchange Commission, and the Federal Trade Commission reach decisions.[49]

Under the APA, administrative procedures are classified according to two broad distinctions: (1) the distinction between rulemaking and adjudication, and (2) the distinction between formal (or trial-like) and informal; thus there are formal and informal rulemaking procedures, formal and informal adjudication procedures.[50] Rulemaking is a determination of general applicability and predominantly prospective effect, such as setting out the number of copies that must be included in an application.[51] It is comparable to legislative activity.[52] In contrast, adjudication is a determination of individual rights or duties.[53] It is the decision-making process for applying preexisting standards to individual circumstances, and is trial-like in that it is the resolution of an individual controversy or question.[54]

A. Rulemaking Processes

In general, the APA requires transparency. Agencies must notify interested persons of proposed rules and allow them to participate in the rulemaking process.[55] Thus, it requires codification and publication of agency-made rules of conduct and further provides that if a rule or regulation[56] is of the sort required to be published, and if it is not so published, then the agency cannot use that rule adversely against anyone.[57] Generally, a proposed regulation begins as a petition brought by the private sector

[47] 2 Weber, *supra* note 45, at 956-63., *discussed at length in Rubin, supra* note 42.
[48] 5 U.S.C. §§ 551-559 (2000).
[49] Charles H. Koch, Jr., *Administrative Law as a Legal Discipline*, 1 Admin. L. & Prac. § 1.2 (2006); Alfred C. Aman, Jr. & William T. Mayton, *Administrative Law* 1(West 1993).
[50] Koch, *supra* note 49, § 2.10.
[51] *Id.* § 2.11.
[52] *Id.*
[53] *Id.*
[54] *Id.*
[55] 5 U.S.C. § 553(c).
[56] For the purposes of this chapter, *rule* and *regulation* will be used interchangeably.
[57] 5 U.S.C. § 553(c).

or from within the agency asking that a rule be issued, amended, or repealed.[58] If the agency determines that a rule is in order, then a proposed rule is drafted and submitted to the notice and comment process of Section 553. Notice of the substance of proposed rules is published in the *Federal Register*, and interested parties are given an opportunity to submit their views on the proposal. Published by the Office of the Federal Register, National Archives and Records Administration (NARA), the *Federal Register* is the official daily publication for rules, proposed rules, and notices of federal agencies and organizations, as well as executive orders and other presidential documents. Agencies are required to respond to significant comments,[59] and must keep records of decisional processes sufficient to show rationality to a reviewing court.[60] Regulations that are eventually adopted are formally incorporated into the *Code of Federal Regulations* (CFR). However, the APA exempts some types of rules from this process: matters relating to agency management, personnel, public property, or military or foreign affairs functions are exempted.[61] Even where the type of rule is not specifically exempted under the APA, notice and comment may not be needed for interpretive rules and statements of policy or for "good cause."[62]

B. Adjudication Processes

As indicated above, adjudication is a determination of individual rights or duties. It can be as formal as a trial conducted in front of an Administrative Law Judge (ALJ), or as informal as a "no action" letter. Section 554 of the APA requires formal trial-type procedures "in every case of adjudication required by statute to be determined on the record after opportunity for a hearing. . . ." This includes a wide variety of agency actions, for example, government grants, licensing decisions, contract determinations, and the various kinds of high-volume cases associated with programs such as social security, workers' compensation, welfare, or veterans' benefits.[63] A procedural adjudicative system that replicates a trial is called "formal" in administrative law, meaning that it provides for (1) timely and adequate notice, (2) opportunity to participate in the decision-making, (3) effective opportunity to defend by confronting any adverse witnesses and rebutting other information, (4) representation by counsel; (5) a record of the proceedings and some form of reasons for the decision; and (6) an impartial decision-maker.[64] Nevertheless, as compared to civil trials, formal adjudicative processes still maintain a high level of procedural flexibility and variety.[65] This flexibility is limited by due process requirements. Where there is a formal procedure, review is

58 Aman & Mayton, *supra* note 49, § 2.1.1.
59 *Id.* § 2.1.4.
60 *Id.* § 2.1.5.
61 5 U.S.C. § 553(a).
62 5 U.S.C. § 553(d).
63 Aman & Mayton, *supra* note 48, § 9.2.
64 Koch, *supra* note 48, § 2.13 (citation omitted).
65 *Id.*

generally available either from a separate reviewing body or in federal court or both. For example, asylum requests are decided by Immigration Judges. If asylum is denied, then appeal can be made to the Board of Immigration Appeals. The Board of Immigration Appeals (BIA or Board) is the highest administrative body for interpreting and applying immigration laws. If the BIA denies asylum, then appeal can be made to a federal court.[66]

Under Supreme Court interpretive case law, a court reviewing agency decisions for constitutionality must determine two things: first, whether there was a deprivation of a protected interest (life, liberty, or property), and second, whether the procedures provided were adequate.[67] Even where the adjudication does not involve a full trial-like proceeding, if there is a written application, petition, or other request, Section 555(e) requires prompt notice of the denial and a brief statement of the grounds on which that denial was based.[68] The underlying purposes of this section are to ensure the overall fairness of agency proceedings, provide a basis for judicial review, to keep the agency within proper authority and discretion, to avoid or prevent arbitrary, discriminatory, or irrational action by the agency, and to inform the aggrieved person of the grounds of the administrative action so he can decide his course of action.[69]

Informal agency actions constitute the everyday business of an administrative agency's substantive agenda and are the "lifeblood of the administrative process."[70] They fall outside both the rulemaking and adjudicatory provisions of the APA. Many agencies have processes for considering requests for exceptions, waivers, and exemptions to existing agency rules. Some agencies provide opportunities for modifications, waivers, no-action letters, variances, or rulings, and all of these provide a mechanism for relief from general rules for individual applicants. All of these represent attempts by individuals to have an agency review their own individual circumstances and are therefore adjudications. Agencies generally provide explanations for their various informal adjudicative mechanisms on their Web sites. Agencies provide for equitable adjustments and rulings with varying degrees of informality. For example, the least formal may be an interpretation of a rule or order over the telephone — a private party may simply speak with agency staff and receive an interpretation of agency law over the telephone. In fact, in helping corporate clients with customs compliance questions, the author regularly sought advice from customs officials via telephone or e-mail. Usually an agency is not bound by the advice of its staff and such advice is not judicially reviewable, but many agencies agree to be bound by the informal advice and as a practical matter, informal staff rulings are illustrative of what the agency is likely to do.[71]

---

[66] *See* www.usdoj.gov/eoir/biainfo.htm.
[67] Koch, *supra* note 49, § 2.20.
[68] Aman & Mayton, *supra* note 48, § 9.3.
[69] *Id.*
[70] *Id.* § 9.1.
[71] *Id.* § 9.4.2.

C. Judicial Review of Agency Decisions and the *Chevron* Standard of Review

As indicated above, not all agency decisions are reviewable by a court. The question of whether or when a court will review an agency action can be reasonably complicated, depending on the doctrine of separation of powers as well as a sensible division of work between courts and agencies. Questions about the availability of judicial review can involve matters of jurisdiction, standing, and sovereign immunity. The availability of review can also include questions raised by the Administrative Procedure Act, the extent to which Congress has precluded review or so committed a matter to agency discretion that it is beyond review. Timing of review may also be dependent on whether the private party has exhausted all administrative remedies.[72]

Administrative agencies are created by Congress to carry out certain statutorily defined duties, goals, and functions. A primary purpose of judicial review is to ensure that an agency does not go beyond its statutory powers in carrying out its tasks. Thus, despite the limitations described above, judicial review of agency decisions serves as an important check on the legality of the action that agencies may undertake. Section 706(2)(C) of the APA gives courts the power to focus on what agencies actually do and to set aside agency action found to be "in excess of statutory jurisdiction, authority, or limitations, or short of statutory right." The section also allows a court to "compel action unlawfully withheld or unreasonably delayed," and it provides juridical review of the processes used by agencies. Nevertheless, the standard of review a court uses in reviewing an agency decision is often more deferential than a review of a lower court decision, whether reviewing agency determinations of fact, law, or policy. Furthermore, there are instances where courts are precluded by statute from reviewing agency determinations such as with asylum determinations.[73]

One such deferential standard of review with respect to a determination of law instead of a finding of fact is that set forth in *Chevron, U.S.A. v. NRDC*, 467 U.S. 837 (1984), applying to agency actions that involve questions of law. *Chevron* involved a challenge to EPA rulings defining the meaning of a statute in the Clean Air Act.[74] The Supreme Court set forth a two-step approach to the review of an agency's interpretation of a statute, an approach that at first seems counterintuitive, but which seems to make sense in light of the fact that a court must recognize and respect the lawful exercise of power by both the legislature and the administrative agency. Under the *Chevron* test, the reviewing court must determine whether the text of the statute at issue is clear or not. If the text of the statute is, in the court's view, clear, and the agency's interpretation is at odds with the court's, the court will then freely disregard what it considers to be an erroneous agency view. On the other hand, if the statute is silent or ambiguous with respect to the specific issue, then second, "the question for the court is whether the agency's answer is based on a permissible construction of

---

72 *Id.* § 12.

73 8 U.S.C. § 1252(a)(2)(A)(iii).

74 42 U.S.C. § 7409.

the statute."[75] If the agency's construction is a permissable one, then the court must defer to it.

DISCUSSION NOTES

1. **Civil Procedure**
   a. You represent Aerospatiale, a French Airplane Manufacturer. It has just been sued in Louisiana by Mr. Jobe, who owns a small commuter airline flying between New Orleans, Louisiana, and Jackson, Mississippi. Jobe claims that Aerospatiale had intentionally negotiated in bad faith with him for two years concerning the promised sale of six small commercial commuter jets, eventually refusing to sell him the airplanes, selling 50 planes to his competitor (Continental Airlines) instead and divulging information about his company to Continental, information Aerospatiale had promised to keep confidential. Assume that "intentional bad faith negotiations" and "detrimental reliance" are tort claims under Louisiana law, and that tort claims have a one-year prescriptive period (statute of limitations) under Louisiana law. You notice that Jobe's complaint alleges that your client's bad act took place three years ago. What argument would you like to make to the court in response to the complaint, and what will you ask the court to do?
   b. Assume the same facts as in question a, however this time Mr. Jobe filed suit in Mississippi (not Louisiana), and Mississippi has a four-year statute of limitations. However, your client told you that all its dealings with Mr. Jobe took place at his office in Metairie, Louisiana, not Jackson, Mississippi. If this is true, then under the Mississippi Long-Arm Statute and the U.S. Constitution, the Mississippi court does not have any power over your client—it lacks personal jurisdiction. Though you do not address the merits of Mr. Jobe's claim, the court allows you to conduct discovery solely to determine whether or not Mr. Jobe's primary office is in Metairie (a written interrogatory), and to get his phone records to see from where he telephoned your client (a subpoena). Determining that Mr. Jobe's own records indicate that all his dealings with your client took place in Louisiana, you file what kind of motion, attaching the results of your discovery as exhibits in support of that motion?
   c. Assume the facts given in question a—Mr. Jobe filed suit in Louisiana, and assume as well that he files within the one-year prescriptive period. However, as discovery continues, his attorney learns that it will be difficult or impossible to prove that Aerospatiale intentionally negotiated in bad faith, and Mr. Jobe eventually drops that claim, so the only remaining issue for trial is whether he can prove his detrimental reliance claim. A cause of action for detrimental reliance under Louisiana Civil Code art. 1967 is defined as follows: A party may be

[75] *Chevron*, 467 U.S. at 843.

obligated by a promise when he knew or should have known that the promise would induce the other party to rely on it to his detriment and the other party was reasonable in so relying. This is substantively the same concept as *promissory estoppel* used by common law states. In addition to damages, Mr. Jobe wants to get an injunction to stop Aerospatiale from giving away any more of his company's confidential information. Mr. Jobe can get a jury trial on the promissory estoppel issue and on the amount of damages he is due, but can the jury decide on the injunction as well?

d. Under detrimental reliance as defined in question c, Mr. Jobe has to prove three things: (1) that Aerospatiale made a promise (to sell him the airplanes), (2) that he was reasonable in relying on that promise, and (3) that he was damaged as a result of his reliance. At trial, during the presentation of the plaintiff's case, Mr. Jobe admits on cross-examination that he knew Aerospatiale was probably not going to sell him the airplanes because the sales agent for Aerospatiale kept telling him that his company was having manufacturing problems and was hesitant to agree to deliver the planes. You quickly realize that this means that either Aerospatiale never promised to sell him the planes, or if they did, it was unreasonable for him to rely on that promise. So, what can you file with the court to cut the trial short?

2. Administrative Procedure

a. Are you likely to find the organizational structure of any particular federal agency in the Federal Register?

b. You work with an association of doctors who have seen patients made ill by nutritional supplements containing an unregulated substance, *guafanaco.* The doctors believe that, at the very least, such supplements should carry cautionary warnings on them. In very general terms, how would you (or someone working in the appropriate federal agency) go about promulgating an appropriate regulation?

c. Your client, who is disabled due to an accident, was just denied Social Security Disability benefits (unfortunately, this is a fairly common occurrence—so common that there are attorneys in the U.S. who specialize in pursuing SSD claims). You believe that the decision was unjustified and want to argue her case. Do you expect that the review process will be formal or informal? If formal, what types of due process safeguards should be in place?

d. You represent a company that has a question concerning customs requirements for a piece of complicated machinery that it will be taking into international waters. A search of the CFR fails to reveal any regulation that is directly applicable. Where else could you go to look for advice on what your client should do?

CHAPTER 5

THE RESEARCH PROCESS

INTRODUCTION

Chapter 2 described two research skills: (1) finding an authority when given a citation or other specific locating information, and (2) locating authority when given a client problem or situation. It also described two interpretive skills: (1) understanding relative weight of authority, and (2) understanding how to interpret authority and apply it to a given problem or situation.[1] Chapter 2 then explained the first research skill and the first interpretive skill. Chapter 3 explained the second interpretive skill: how to interpret or synthesize authority and apply it to any given situation. At this point, you should be able to locate an authority when given a citation or even a partial citation, and you should have some understanding of how to combine various sources of authority, interpret them, and apply them to a particular problem.

After an explanation of the ethical and practical demands faced by attorneys doing legal research in the United States, this chapter begins development of the remaining research skill: locating authority when given a situation or problem. First it describes the process of legal research, and then it divides situational research into three stages. Stage 1 research, which consists of background research into secondary sources, is also covered in this chapter, and a Stage 1 checklist is given. The chapter also includes several advisory discussions, including a comparison of research media, hints on how to avoid tangents, and methods for planning research projects. Stages 2 and 3, how to research and update primary authority, are covered in Chapters 6 and 7. The three chapters combined will help you develop your skills in researching U.S. law given a specific client problem or situation.

---

[1] Chapter 2, § II.

I. ETHICAL AND PRACTICAL DEMANDS

Each of the 50 United States sets standards of ethical behavior for attorneys, and most of them have enacted some version of the American Bar Association's Model Rules of Professional Conduct. Failure to follow these rules can lead to disbarment, as well as civil liability for malpractice. One of the most important of these rules is that a lawyer shall represent clients *competently*, which is defined as having the "legal knowledge, skill, thoroughness, and preparation reasonably necessary for the representation."[2] In the United States, an attorney can be sued if he or she fails to know "those plain and elementary principles of law which are commonly known by well-informed attorneys," or fails to discover additional rules that "although not commonly known, may readily be found by standard research techniques."[3] Thus, legal research is part and parcel of an American lawyer's skill.

For a given client's problem, the lawyer must find the necessary mandatory authority, helpful and persuasive primary authority, and useful secondary authority. However, researching law in that sequence—mandatory, primary, secondary—is usually difficult, if not impossible. It is better to plan on researching secondary authority first, then mandatory, followed by persuasive authority. To be thorough, the researcher may have to backtrack more than once: One is much more able to locate authority that is exactly on point, whether primary or secondary, when one is familiar with the specific area of law at issue.

Often, law students idealistically expect that the law firm that eventually employs them will have them work only on problems in their area of specialization, or at least on problems involving areas of law they have studied. Students who specialize in intellectual property, for example, expect that their employer will give them only problems involving intellectual property. In fact, because of business needs, most law firms must accept the cases that are presented to them, regardless of the area of law at issue (though there are some areas, such as family practice, that may require specialization). The partner responsible for the case then delegates research to the associate who has the most time available, regardless of the associate's area of particular interest and specialization. Occasionally, as a reward for work well done, a partner will take an associate's interests into consideration and assign the associate a case in his or her area of interest. However, most partners are unable to do this on a regular basis. The result is that the vast majority of recent law school graduates usually find themselves researching problems in areas of the law they never studied in law school. Consequently, it is important to develop skill and confidence in researching areas of law that are new to you.

---

[2] Model Rules of Prof'l Conduct R. 1.1 (1983). *See* Dates of Adoption of the Model Rules of Professional Conduct, Center for Professional Responsibility, at www.abanet.org/cpr/mrpc/alpha_html (listing state adoption dates).

[3] *Smith v. Lewis*, 530 P.2d 589 (Cal. 1975).

II. THE RESEARCH PROCESS

In researching a client's situation, the goal is to locate all applicable mandatory authority, as well as the best persuasive and secondary authority, as efficiently as possible. Research is a process, however, and cannot be reduced to a simple methodology. It is inherently inefficient and a researcher can easily be led in any number of tangential directions. Therefore, the researcher must maintain control over the process, constantly focusing on obtaining the best match between law and fact. Maintaining control means that the researcher must be systematic, methodical, and a good record-keeper. An easy and systematic way to maintain control is to divide the process into three stages. The first stage involves analyzing the problem, obtaining background information, and planning the research. The second stage involves researching primary authority; the final, third stage includes updating the authority found, reorganizing the research, and filling in any research gaps that appear following the reorganization. As the flowchart on the next page shows, however, research rarely flows smoothly from one step into the next. The researcher should expect to zigzag back and forth somewhat among steps. This is normal and appropriate. What is most important, however, is that the researcher know at all times where she is, where she has been, and where she is going.

III. RESEARCH ADVICE

A. Media Choices

Before we address the various components of Stage 1 research individually, an in-depth discussion of media choices will be helpful. Media available may include hard copy, Internet sources, and possibly CD-ROM or microforms. Many LL.M. candidates come to the United States eager to focus on what is perceived to be an extremely sophisticated Internet-based legal research system, and this book is written with exactly that focus in mind. However, efficient researching means taking best advantage of the available media choices. Different media have different advantages and disadvantages, even when they cover the same source.

For example, the *United States Code* is the same, whether in hard copy, on Westlaw, on LEXIS-NEXIS, on Loislaw, or a U.S. government agency's Web site. However, researching any particular statute of the U.S.C. may be easier or harder, depending on which form of media you are using. At times, searching for an authority is faster on a computer; however, often it is easier for the researcher to absorb information from an authority by flipping pages back and forth in a book or reading a hard-copy printout than by scrolling down a computer page. Computer formats also often put footnotes in the middle of the page, making the authority difficult to read. Furthermore, computer databases may be incomplete. It is sometimes difficult for their sponsors to include material published long before the inception of the database,

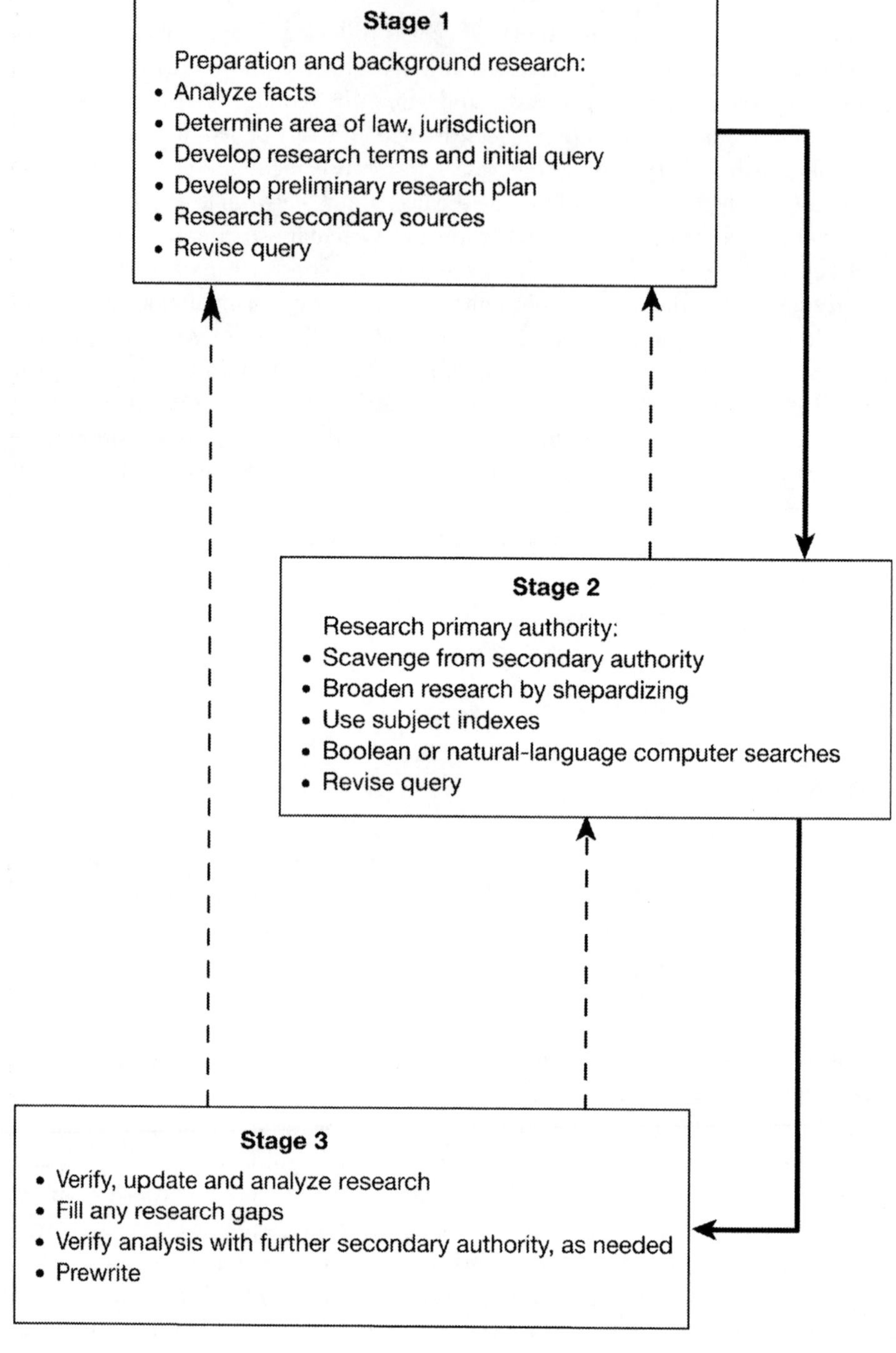
RESEARCH FLOWCHART
Stage 1
Preparation and background research:
• Analyze facts
• Determine area of law, jurisdiction
• Develop research terms and initial query
• Develop preliminary research plan
• Research secondary sources
• Revise query
Stage 2
Research primary authority:
• Scavenge from secondary authority
• Broaden research by shepardizing
• Use subject indexes
• Boolean or natural-language computer searches
• Revise query
Stage 3
• Verify, update and analyze research
• Fill any research gaps
• Verify analysis with further secondary authority, as needed
• Prewrite

unless it is considered vitally important. For example, although both Westlaw and LEXIS include U.S. Supreme Court opinions dating from the inception of the Court, the law review databases on both commercial providers date only from approximately 1984. Law review articles from before that date must be researched in hard copy or perhaps on HeinOnline.org if it is available. Therefore, it is important to be aware of and consider the comparative advantages and disadvantages of various media when developing a research plan. There are times when hard-copy research is most efficient, and times when computer research has inherent advantages.

In addition to having various research advantages and disadvantages, certain media may have practical or financial advantages and disadvantages that non-American attorneys should consider in deciding which resources they want to learn to use efficiently. For example, Westlaw and LEXIS are the most widely used commercial legal databases in the United States. However, if it is unlikely that you will have access to them upon completing your LL.M. degree, you might want to focus on developing stronger research skills using noncommercial databases, while still taking advantage of Westlaw and LEXIS while they are available to you free of charge. Some of the search skills you will develop with the commercial databases can be used on the noncommercial sites, but the noncommercial sites will not have as many or as sophisticated search capabilities (*finding tools*) as do the commercial ones.

1. Comparison of Fee-Based Computer Databases

> There are two full-text online legal information systems that will be central elements in your legal education. Westlaw and Lexis are great shimmering cyberspace libraries of legal information. Each contains the full text of judicial opinions, statutes, administrative rules and more related legal information than any three dimensional library could ever hope to house. . . . You will get home access, in-person training, a blizzard of manuals, crib sheets and even an 800 number to call for research help. Westlaw and Lexis are engaged in the equivalent of a World Wide Wrestling Federation Texas Death Match for market share. They want you to love them so that when you leave law school you will want to use (and pay them full price for) their product. This makes life good for law students.[4]

The two most widely used computer databases are Westlaw.com and Lexis.com. Westlaw and LEXIS are quite similar. Loislaw, a newcomer, is trying to develop in a slightly different direction. Westlaw and LEXIS used to offer similarly complicated pricing structures, and the overall cost of using Westlaw or LEXIS can still be unaffordable for a small firm or for one not based in the United States.[5] Perhaps as a result

---

[4] Robert C. Berring & Elizabeth A. Edinger, *Legal Research Survival Manual* 9 (2002) (this concise, informal little book is very helpful).

[5] Westlaw describes its pricing structure at http://west.thomson.com/westlaw/subscriptions (visited October 16, 2007; LEXIS describes pricing at http//law.lexisnexis.com (visited October 16, 2007). Westlaw indicates that large firms may find a broad selection of databases most cost effective, and that

of competition from Loislaw, however, both of the mega companies are now offering "fixed-rate" plans, though you can purchase smaller increments. These fixed-rate plans allow unlimited research in a specified package of databases for a specific amount of time. However, even with the fixed-rate plans, Westlaw and LEXIS may levy additional charges for updating authority, printing, or transferring to a different database to check an associated authority. Thus, it can be difficult for a firm to control costs with either company. For this reason, even though Westlaw and LEXIS are becoming increasingly affordable, law firms that use one or the other still sometimes limit associates' access to them, which provides students with a strong incentive to learn how to use these tools as efficiently as possible while they have free access.

Loislaw, though it offers a much smaller range of databases and fewer search methods, prides itself on its simple pricing structure and a guaranteed monthly or annual flat rate. The law firm pays one price for researching (one) state's primary law and all federal law, a different fee for primary national law, and supplementary fees if you want to add one or more treatise libraries.[6] Both of their plans include a citating tool, GlobalCite. This simple pricing structure may allow Loislaw to quickly gain market share, especially among small firms whose research needs are limited, in an otherwise highly competitive market. The others are quickly developing similar packages. LEXIS recently converted LexisOne.com, its formerly free database, to one for small firms, with a much simpler and less expensive fee structure: In 2007, their Web site indicated that the per-day cost for their services would range from $37 (for cite checking) to $227 (for full access to the legal library). Although this service may lack the sophisticated finding tools of the full Lexis.com Web site, it may still be very useful for small firms with strict budgetary limitations. Though not as widely publicized, many American law schools pay to offer Loislaw free of charge to their students, just as they do Westlaw and LEXIS. You can ask your law school's librarian if this option is available to you, depending on what you anticipate your post-graduation needs will be.

In addition to pricing differences, the three computerized legal research companies offer different substantive advantages and disadvantages. LEXIS-NEXIS traditionally has prided itself on having a very broad range of databases that allows one to research many professional fields other than law, as well as a well-developed international law database. Therefore, if you, as an attorney, were working on a problem concerning a field other than law, or were researching international law, you would be able to research that field through LEXIS-NEXIS. However, since the Thomson Corporation, a multinational provider of information, purchased West Group, Westlaw has legal databases on International law and international news as well. Loislaw, now owned by Aspen Publishers, a Wolters Kluwer Company (the publisher of this textbook), limits itself to United States law.

Cost and breadth of information are two characteristics of online commercial databases that an attorney will want to consider, but there is one more as well: ease

---

smaller firms should look at WestlawPRO, which offers monthly rates for groups of databases by jurisdiction or category. LEXIS similarly offers different pricing structures for full-service firms, specialized firms, and small firms.

[6] As indicated by Product Information at http://www.loislaw.com (visited on October 16, 2007).

of use. Research takes a significant amount of valuable time and effort, and eyestrain from too many hours in front of a computer can become a serious problem. When deciding to focus on one or another of the commercial legal databases, consider as well which provides the format that is easiest for you to read. This is basically a matter of personal opinion, but the concern is that you maximize efficiency. If one company provides a format that makes it easier for you to assimilate information quickly, that is a strong argument in its favor.

2. Noncommercial, Non-Fee Computer Databases

Noncommercial and non-fee computer databases constantly improve, and their numbers constantly increase. However, the majority of them do not have the sophisticated search tools that Westlaw and LEXIS have. Most noncommercial databases use simple Boolean search tools comparable to those of Google, Ask.com, AltaVista, and other Internet crawlers with which you may be familiar. They do not have the natural-language or expanded Boolean search capabilities that Westlaw and LEXIS have, and their databases may be limited by time as well as breadth. They may include only cases back to a certain date. For example, Wisconsin's state Web site has its appellate and supreme court case law online only back to 1996, and the case law database can be searched only by case name or docket number. A number of other state government Web sites are similarly limited. Most noncommercial databases are complete enough for simple research problems, but if your problem is state law rather than federal, sophisticated, or historically based, or if you need secondary sources, a commercial database or hard copy may well be the only efficient choice. When choosing a computer database, whether commercial or noncommercial, be aware also of content limitations that may affect the accuracy and completeness of your research.

With regard to federal statutory law, some noncommercial databases are often easier to search than the commercial databases because they have well-tailored subject lists (tables of contents). This is especially true with federal agency Web sites (i.e., federal administrative law). One systematic approach is to start with an agency Web site to locate the applicable statutes and regulations, and then move to a commercial Web site to expand research and locate interpretive case law. The greatest shortcoming of the noncommercial databases is probably that they lack secondary sources. However, a number of law firms publish useful articles on their Web sites, and the ABA Web site has a wide range of resources that one can research. Two of the best non-fee Web sites are *www.law.cornell.edu* and *www.firstgov.gov*. A longer list of noncommercial, non-fee Web sites is provided in Chapter 10.

3. CD-ROM and Microforms

Not too long ago, West Group was marketing CD-ROM libraries to small law firms. The law firm would subscribe to "Lawdesk" and be given compact disks on which were read-only memory files containing volumes of reporters, depending on the library or libraries to which the law firm subscribed. For updates, the firm would have to go online. At the time, it was more cost effective than the hourly or transaction-based charges; however, the difficulty was that updating was costly. Therefore, West Group replaced its CD-ROM system with WestlawPRO fixed-rate online plans.

Microforms are an entirely different medium. They were developed many years ago as a way of preserving paper materials in a small space, and are found only in hard-copy libraries. Essentially, a document is photographed on clear plastic, and reduced in size. A special machine is then used to display and enlarge the photographed document. Microforms are used primarily for old copies of newspapers, some government documents, and other time-sensitive material, so it is unlikely that you will be using them unless you work on a project involving legal history. If you find that you need to use them, a reference librarian can quickly show you how to locate the documents you want on microfilm and then how to load and operate the machinery.

B. Finding Tools

Finding tools are the means by which legal researchers can locate legal authority. They include topic lists, indexes, numbering systems, and the like. The usefulness of any source or medium depends on the quality and quantity of its finding tools. For example, although it is authoritative, the official *United States Code* is almost useless for research because it has very few and limited finding tools. Furthermore, neither it nor the official Supreme Court reporter *U.S. Reports* is updated nearly as frequently as the computer databases (daily) or even commercial hard copy (monthly). *U.S. Reports* has no finding tools. It merely gives the text of opinions, one followed by another, in chronological order based on the dates of the opinions. The U.S.C. has tables of contents and popular name tables, but they are incomplete and unsophisticated as compared to the wealth of finding tools included in the hard copies of the U.S.C.A. (Westlaw's version of the Code) and the U.S.C.S. (LEXIS's version). These tools include volumes of indexes, lists of amendments, related statutes, secondary sources discussing the topic, and extensive lists of cases that have interpreted various aspects of each statute. The online versions of the U.S.C.A. and the U.S.C.S. have exactly the same finding tools as do their respective hard copy. Though administrative law can be researched on Westlaw and LEXIS as well, often the best first source is the agency Web site, because of its easy access.

When it comes to searching for case law, students are quickly intrigued by the high-powered term (Boolean) and natural-language searches possible on Westlaw and LEXIS. They are often the first search techniques introduced by the commercial database representatives. However, these are the most inefficient searches, and should be used only when the researcher has become very familiar with the field and has exhausted all other search methods. If you are unfamiliar with the field, it is difficult or impossible to use the correct, precise language needed in formulating either term or natural-language search queries — the result is that your search results are worthless and you waste a vast amount of time. Computer experts refer to this kind of human error as "garbage in, garbage out."

Whichever legal research Web sites you choose to focus on, be sure to familiarize yourself well with their finding tools. It is best to limit yourself to one or two Web sites until you become proficient with them. If you have access to free instruction offered by one or more commercial sites, take advantage of any and all of that instruction, but be aware that one hour of instruction per Web site will not be enough. You will need to work with the service on your own for several hours at least to obtain some amount of mastery, especially with Westlaw and LEXIS.

C. Keeping on Track, Saving Citations

At any step in the research process, the researcher must guard against becoming distracted by authority that is not completely pertinent to the problem. The only way to avoid such tangents is to **constantly compare the facts of the problem to the authority found.** Keep comparing the problem's factual details with the types of facts demanded by or contained in each authority found. Then read each authority only enough to determine if it is *on point*—if the legal issue matches the one in your problem. You might think of this as scanning an authority. A computer scans authorities and finds those that contain certain words chosen by the researcher. The researcher's task then is to scan the authorities containing those words and pick out only those that apply to the research problem. When you find that a particular authority is not on point, discard it quickly and move on. If it is partially on point, you might want to note or mark it for reference, so that you can return to it if necessary. **If it is fully on point, keep it and its citation.** Print it out if possible, or download it into a research file you have created for the project.

As you work through your research strategy, keep track of which media you have used and which sources you have checked. Furthermore, if you are trying different queries on computer, keep track of which terms are working, and cross out the search terms that do not yield appropriate or efficient results. That way, if you have to stop your research temporarily, or find subsequently that you need to do more research, you can quite quickly re-create successful searches and methodologies, and you can effectively change research methods that are not working. Some of the commercial computer databases will keep an automatic "research trail" that you can access. However, the automatic trail will not indicate which searches were successful. You will need to be aware of what is working and what is not. A simple handwritten list on notepaper can be enough for this purpose. Separate your research strategy and research term list from your list of research results.

D. Preserving Research Results

It is vital to keep track of useful research results. The more useful the result seems to be, the more of it you will need to preserve. For authorities that seem to be somewhat on point, simply note the citation and a word or two about the content of the authority, so that you can check it later if necessary. However, sometimes you can see that a research result is exactly on point, and therefore worthy of more thorough study. The best way to preserve these good research results is to print out a hard copy of part or all of the authority and note on the front of that hard copy why it is important. Alternatively, especially if your paper supply is limited, you could download the authority into a CD, flash drive, or research file on your hard drive, again being careful to note why the authority is important. Similarly, one might cut and paste portions of the authority into a file. The danger of this last approach, however, is that the portion taken will be out of context and therefore subject to subsequent misinterpretation. Furthermore, it is very easy to omit needed portions of the citation information when you are cutting and pasting, leading to a waste of hours or even days of precious time as you try to re-create your research or write your memo. This is why the word **citation** was bolded in the previous section.

E. Reading for Research

Keeping notes of authorities does not necessitate an immediate close reading of those authorities. During the research stage, skim authorities, reading only enough to determine that (1) the source is on point, (2) you have isolated the most applicable portion of the source, and (3) you have checked the source to see if it cites other authorities that should be checked. The time for careful reading occurs after the bulk of the research has been done, during the prewriting stage. That is when you will read (or reread) the best authorities slowly, carefully, and in context, so that you can verify that you have found and understand *all* of the applicable law, not just pieces of it.

As you proceed with your research strategy, note as well (on paper or in a computer file) which sources you checked, which were productive, and which were not. Keep rethinking your strategy, considering which sources or methods might work better, and considering whether you might have missed an important source. If you are stuck, a great deal of help is available. Westlaw's and LEXIS's 24/7 hotlines, law school libraries' research librarians, and research instructors will all be happy to help you.

If, despite your best efforts to stay focused on the assigned problem, you find that you spent hours researching and developing a line of research that later proves to be irrelevant, discard it. Do not be tempted to use it merely because it took time to develop.

F. Planning Project Time

Most attorneys in the United States use computer-based calendars to help them plan out time for researching and writing projects. The amount of time for a project is often dictated by court dates and clients' requirements. Thus, an attorney will work backward from the due date, while considering other projects, and plan out the amount of time he or she feels will be necessary for research and writing. Generally, research and prewriting should occupy approximately two-thirds of the allotted time. Most people cannot write competently until they have researched thoroughly and carefully thought through a project. The exact amount of time needed, however, is a very personal matter. Speed and efficiency of research develop with experience, and different people approach projects differently. The most important principle, however, is to avoid procrastination, especially with large projects or new tasks, because they will usually take much more time than you anticipate. When assigned a project, sit down and plan out when you will research, the date on which you will begin writing, and a date when you want to have the project all but polished. As time passes, adjust your internal deadlines as needed.

G. Determining When Research Is Complete

An old quip says that research ends when the researcher runs out of time. This is very often true, because more research is almost always better than less. However, there are two or three guidelines you can use to decide how much research is enough. Research and writing are all part of the same process. If you keep a research log, you will find that notations of facts, search terms, and search queries gradually give way to citations of sources and eventually identification of the applicable rule. Once the applicable rule is identified, the rest of the research usually goes fairly smoothly, requiring only systematic researching of authorities on each component of the rule. Then, once you have researched each component of the rule, start to chart or prewrite a rule analysis, encompassing pertinent case law as you did with the closed memo. If you cannot explain the applicable rule easily, without too much struggle, then more research is probably needed. Furthermore, difficulties in explaining how the components of the rule apply to different factual situations will reveal gaps in research. In contrast, if your research keeps disclosing the same authorities, which you have already checked, your research is probably complete and you are ready to start prewriting. In other words, your research is probably done when you have already found all "new" sources through earlier searches. Bear in mind, however, that even though you have apparently exhausted all the pertinent sources, when you start writing you may discover new gaps that will require further research. As noted in the previous subsection, generally, research and prewriting should occupy approximately two-thirds of the allotted time. Writing, gap-filling research, and rewriting occupy the last third.

IV. STAGE 1: BACKGROUND RESEARCH AND PREPARATION

STAGE 1 CHECKLIST

- ☐ A. Facts
- ☐ B. Jurisdiction, area of law, and issue or search terms
- ☐ C. Research media choice
- ☐ D. Initial research plan
- ☐ E. Research in secondary sources
  - ☐ 1. Get an overview of area of law and underlying policy considerations
  - ☐ 2. Identify probable source or sources of law — case law, statutes, or regulations
  - ☐ 3. Revise list of search terms or issue statement
  - ☐ 4. Locate applicable legal principle, if possible
  - ☐ 5. Scavenge secondary sources for citations to mandatory authority
- ☐ F. Issue statement refinement
- ☐ G. Research plan refinement

Researching in U.S. sources can be very much like looking for the proverbial needle in a haystack. The best way to begin researching a specific client's problem is to assess the problem and then develop a research strategy using a research log to maintain control of the process. Start by analyzing the facts of the situation and determine what area or areas of law are implicated: tort, contract, civil procedure, securities regulation, antitrust law, immigration, or others. Once you have identified the appropriate area(s) of law, assess what media you have available: Usually hard copy and commercial and noncommercial Internet sites are the most appropriate sources, though other media may be available as well. Then tentatively plan which media and which sources you will use, and in which sequence. Once you have assessed your media choices, use secondary authority to research the area and develop search terms and a preliminary issue or research query. If the assignment includes a legal term, the process is simplified. Look up the term in a legal dictionary or thesaurus, and identify synonyms or related terms. From there, research the topic in one or more in-depth secondary sources: treatises, Restatements, legal periodicals, *American Law Report* annotations (ALRs), or legal encyclopedias.

Begin by preparing a research log in a format that is portable and easy for you to access at a moment's notice. For this purpose, a simple legal-size or 8½-by-11-inch notepad of lined paper is a very good tool: It is easily carried from library to computer, is large enough to deliver a substantial amount of information at one glance (unlike index cards), and can be read without the help of any electronic device. Put headings on separate pages. The first page could be labeled *facts*, the second *issue*, the third *media*, and the fourth *research plan*.

A. Facts: Who, What, When, Where, Why, and How

Assume that you have been assigned a particular client's legal problem, and have interviewed your supervisor concerning the assignment as described in Chapter 3. The first step is to analyze the facts of the situation and record that analysis in a form that you can reference quickly. Identify the parties involved and the appropriate jurisdiction. Note the subject matter of the problem, which could be a contract, someone's misbehavior, or an item of property (intellectual or otherwise). Examine the relationships among the parties, and any factual details that might have legal significance. One useful factual analytical technique is to use traditional series of questions used by journalists: who, what, when, where, why, and how. *Who* are the parties, and *where* are they from? (This information is needed for jurisdictional reasons.) *What* happened? *When* and *where* did it happen? *Why* did it happen? *How* did it happen?

Unless you are familiar with the law at issue, it may be difficult to anticipate what factual details will be legally significant. Furthermore, attorneys new to common law analysis tend to err by omitting needed factual detail. Because of this, if you are unsure about whether a fact is legally significant, it is better to include it than to omit it from your research log. The researcher's factual analysis should be instantly accessible during research, so that the researcher can continually compare the facts to the law found during the research process. Therefore, write an outline or list of the facts on the first page of your research log and keep it immediately at hand while you do your research. Refer to it often as you do your research to help you stay focused on pertinent authority and not be distracted by tangents.

B. Jurisdiction, Area of Law, and Issue or Search Terms

From the factual answers to the who, what, and where questions, you should gain some idea of which jurisdictions are pertinent. The assignment may or may not identify the pertinent area of law or applicable legal theory. If it includes a legal theory, look the theory up in a legal dictionary or thesaurus. This serves two purposes. First, it will give you terms with which you may not have been familiar. Furthermore, it will give you an accurate understanding of the terms already included in the assignment. When consulting the dictionary, take advantage of its easy access by examining various phrases that include the subject terms and looking up new terms as they appear. If a dictionary entry is particularly useful, note the source and the citation. For example, the definition of *implied contract* can be found in *Black's Law Dictionary* 345 (8th ed. 2004) under *contract.*

However, if the assignment does not identify the area of law or applicable legal theory, then the researcher has to develop one or more possible *theories of the case* (i.e., legal claims or defenses). The researcher does this by categorizing the problem first into general and then into increasingly specific subject areas. Begin by identifying the major, overarching area of law at issue: Is the problem one of civil or criminal law? Is it likely to be one of contract, tort, securities regulation, environmental law, intellectual property, or a combination of two or more subjects? Once you have the general area, next consider possible legal theories, using any background knowledge of law that you have. Consider as well any possible defenses, and what relief is likely to be sought. On the notepad, after the outline of facts, jot down any preliminary legal terms, causes of action, defenses, or relief that may occur to you, and check their meanings with a legal dictionary or thesaurus just as you would if the assignment had included a legal issue. Formulate a preliminary issue statement, if possible.

C. Research Media Choice

Once you have some preliminary idea about the nature of the problem and the likely area of law, you can formulate a preliminary issue statement (or theory of the case), and can begin to decide which media, resources, and authorities are most likely to be helpful. Will you have access to a full law library, the Internet, and one or more of the commercial databases, or will you be limited? If you have more than one form of media available, which is likely to be most useful? Which would be best to use first?

Consider as well how the jurisdiction will affect your choice of media and authority. For example, if the case concerns tort or contract, then state law is likely to be authoritative, and you will want to use state law databases (computer) or digests and codes (hard copy). In contrast, a bankruptcy or constitutional question will involve federal statutory and case law, and you would use federal databases and Web sites (computer) or the federal digest and annotated codes (hard copy). Because of federal diversity jurisdiction, a problem concerning parties from two different states or a party from outside the United States is likely to involve both state and federal interpretations of state law. Note on your research plan the types of media you plan to use, and in what general order.

D. Initial Research Plan

Canvass your resources and, on a new page of the notepad, list the sources you plan to check, in the sequence you plan to use. For example, first list the appropriate hard-copy secondary sources you plan to check, then perhaps the computer databases (commercial and noncommercial). As you work through them, cross off the ones that proved unhelpful, and add any new sources you think of, when you think of them. In other words, if you think of a new source while doing something else, immediately jot it down in your research plan before you forget it, even if you are involved in doing something else. The research plan will change and develop as you learn more about the appropriate area of law.

E. Research in Secondary Sources

Research in secondary sources has five separate goals. Keep them (as well as the facts of your problem) in mind as you research secondary authority, to minimize being distracted by tangential information. Sometimes a particular secondary source will not fulfill all five goals, but any information it gives may be extremely helpful in both finding the law and interpreting it.

1. Get an Overview of Area of Law and Underlying Policy Considerations

Understanding the overall shape of a particular area of law, as well as its underlying policy considerations, is key to a correct interpretation of any particular case or statute. It is also instrumental in predicting what a court is likely to do in a particular situation.

2. Identify Probable Source or Sources of Law

Determine whether the law applicable to your situation is likely to be case law, statutory law, administrative law, or constitutional law. This will further determine which primary sources and media you will search.

3. Revise List of Search Terms or Issue Statement

The development of search terms and an issue statement begins with a dictionary or thesaurus, but continues throughout the research process. Secondary authority is extremely helpful in this regard, as it will identify similar legal principles and terms, many of which will have to be either eliminated or taken into account as you continue to research. For example, the common law concepts of *unjust enrichment* and *promissory estoppel* are different, but can both apply to the same situation, and are terms you would consider in conjunction with an *implied contract* theory. If you were familiar with one term but not the others, a secondary source such as a treatise or the *Restatement (Second) of Contracts* would help to explain the similarities and differences, and when one or the other would apply.

4. *Locate Applicable Legal Principle*

Ideally, a secondary source will give you the exact legal principle that applies to the research situation. Even if it does not, it quite possibly will come close enough that you will be able to recognize the applicable rule when researching mandatory authority. As a result, you will be better able to search mandatory authority and will be better able to interpret that authority when you find it.

5. *Scavenge Secondary Sources for Citations to Mandatory Authority*

Secondary sources are exactly what they purport to be: secondary discussions and explanations of primary authority. As such, they must be based on primary authority and must cite it to establish their credibility. These citations, given in footnotes and other indexes, should be noted in the research log and searched, as they are a valuable way of locating mandatory authority and helpful primary persuasive authority.

F. Issue Statement Refinement

Once the researcher has canvassed secondary sources enough to become familiar with the applicable field or fields of law, it is time to update the issue statement again and add appropriate terms to the search query, in light of the knowledge gained from secondary sources.

G. Research Plan Refinement

In addition to modifying the issue statement and search terms, the researcher should update the original research plan in accord with the information given in secondary sources. New sources of authority may be suggested, as well as new methods of searching them. The researcher may well want to start by investigating the citations to primary authority that he or she finds in secondary literature.

H. Sample Research Log

The following is a sample research log, based on the Dr. Shymite problem in Chapter 3. Each chart is intended to represent a separate page of a legal pad.

1. FACTS

Who: Robin Shymite, M.D., E.R. resident at Memorial Hospital
What: poss. driving while intoxicated charge & loss of M.D. license
When: Saturday (get exact date)
Where: parking lot of hospital? Outside of a bar? Which? Stanford, New Hampshire
Why: Arrested last night on DWI or DUI charges, spent night in jail
How: upset over loss of child after 48-hour shift, invited by colleagues for (2–3?) beers. Left bar, got into car to drive home but realized too tired to drive. Turned off engine but left keys in so could listen to radio. Woke up 1/2 hr. later when policeman knocked on window, administered a blood-alcohol test, and arrested. Spent night in jail, brought no documentation.

2. JURISDICTION, AREA OF LAW, ISSUE, OR TERMS

Jurisdiction: Stanford, New Hampshire & criminal law, therefore probably state law.
Area of Law: (1) Criminal law, therefore statutory plus case law, (2) New Hampshire Medical Association regulations
Issue: probably 2: (1) driving while intoxicated or driving under the influence, and (2) Could Shymite lose his M.D. license if convicted of DUI?

3. RESEARCH MEDIA

Secondary Sources: hard copy in library, A.L.R. online?
Mandatory: (1) New Hampshire Criminal Code Annotated, online
(2) Call N.H. Medical Association for info. on regulations?

4. RESEARCH PLAN

Secondary sources: A.L.R., legal encyclopedia., crim. treatise, law reviews?

Primary sources:

(1) N.H. Criminal Code Annotated, then check annotations, then use statute to find case law online, then Shepardize cases, then develop term search using jurisdiction & language from appropriate statute.

(2) Depending on results of phone call, could search state gov't database or N.H. Medical Association Web site.

5. SECONDARY SOURCES

(1) A.L.R.:
(2) Legal encyclopedia:
(3) Treatise:
(4) Law reviews:

V. THE PURPOSE AND IMPORTANCE OF SECONDARY RESEARCH

Unless you are very familiar with the area of law at issue, researching mandatory authority without first checking secondary authority can either be frustrating or lead to serious interpretational mistakes. To prove that it can be frustrating, pretend that you are working on a problem concerning a recreational softball game in Wisconsin. From hindsight, you know that you need to find *Lestina*—but if you did not know that was the case you needed, how would you find it? If you have already been introduced to term searches on Westlaw or LEXIS, you would have to guess about terms that might occur in the opinion within the parameters you set. The words you might use could include *softball* and *negligence*, but you would have to guess whether they occur together or apart in the opinion, and how far apart. Wisconsin might not have a softball case, so you might need to omit that term, substitute *recreational sports*, and extrapolate a rule from the recreational sports cases it does have—in this example, that would be soccer rather than softball. Furthermore, legal terms can vary from jurisdiction to jurisdiction and case to case. Suppose your softball problem was played in Iowa instead of Wisconsin. Many states do not use a negligence standard in the context of recreational sports, and you would need to use *recklessness* instead, or *assumption of risk*, in Iowa.[7] How would you know which legal term to use? You might eventually find mandatory authority, but it could take a great number of random term searches before you do.

In addition to wasting time, lack of research into secondary authority can also lead to serious interpretational mistakes. There is an old parable about several blind mice examining an elephant. One mouse climbs on the elephant's trunk, and decides that the elephant is long, thin, and pliable, like a snake. Another climbs on the ear, and decides that the elephant is thin, wide, and floppy. A third mouse, on the elephant's back, decides that an elephant goes on in all directions forever, and is hard, lumpy, and somewhat hairy. Each mouse assesses a portion of the elephant, but none of them has any idea of what the entire animal is like, so they all reach absurd conclusions about elephants. Research into primary sources without a preliminary assessment of secondary authority can lead to the same piecemeal mistakes: you might miss an important case or the fact that a statute is controlling, and you can easily misinterpret primary authority even if you happen to find it. Secondary sources give an overview of an area of law, so that you can properly fit various primary sources together.

To review, initial research into secondary authority has five very specific goals:

1. To give the researcher an overview of the area, and especially its underlying policy concerns
2. To determine whether mandatory authority is likely to be primarily case law, statutory law, regulatory law, or a combination
3. To generate a list of search terms and sub-issues that may have to be researched
4. To locate an approximation of the applicable legal rule
5. To locate mandatory authority, which may be cited or listed in footnotes.

[7] *Leonard ex rel. Meyer v. Behrens*, 601 N.W.2d 76 (Iowa 1999).

A. Secondary Sources: Hard Copy or Online?

Hard copy is usually far superior to computer searches for an initial foray into secondary authority. The researcher's first need is to get an overview of the subject and to identify appropriate legal terminology and principles, and there can be a number of synonyms or related concepts, all of which must be understood. Therefore, what is most helpful at the initial stage is a well-organized treatise or hornbook, complete with a table of contents or other finding tool, which will help the researcher identify and sort through the various topics in a specific area of law. (A *hornbook* is a one-volume treatise, usually intended for law students. Although not as detailed as multivolume treatises, hornbooks are often most helpful in the initial stages of research because they are easily and quickly searched.) Generally, one can quickly locate the table of contents or other finding tool in a hard-copy treatise and then easily identify those topics that are likely to have some bearing on the problem being researched. Policy concerns are usually discussed early on. One can turn from topic to topic, flip back and forth in the book quickly, and easily scan footnotes for sources of mandatory authority.

In contrast, computers never show more than a screen's worth of material at one time, making it difficult and sometimes impossible to get an overview of a subject. Additionally, computer databases include very few secondary sources, and they are usually somewhat difficult to access. The databases that include some secondary authorities are almost always commercial, and sometimes expensive. Even when secondary sources are online, it can be difficult to access their tables of contents— though this is changing. Westlaw and LEXIS now include a "Table of Contents" feature for some authorities. Furthermore, if you input relatively appropriate terms, West's "Results Plus" and other tools provide hyperlinks to other helpful secondary sources, as well as hyperlinks to the primary sources cited therein. One area of secondary authority where both Westlaw and LEXIS excel is legal periodicals. As shall be seen, this is one of the most useful areas of secondary authority, but you need to have generated at least some search terms before you can access periodicals efficiently.

Most secondary authority (such as treatises and Restatements) is unavailable on noncommercial databases, because it is copyrighted. Occasionally, one can find useful secondary authority by using a Web crawler to search articles put on the Web by law firms. If a hard-copy library is available, though, it is most efficient to search its treatises first, then find legal periodicals through Westlaw or LEXIS, and then possibly finalize your secondary source research with a quick Web crawl. Remember as well that on-line services change rapidly and the advice and directions given here concerning on-line research tools may have changed since this text was written.

B. Types of Secondary Sources

There are six commonly used types of secondary sources:

1. Restatements
2. Treatises and hornbooks
3. Legal periodicals

4. American Law Reports
5. Legal encyclopedias
6. Digests

Each is discussed in turn here.

1. Restatements

The immense geographical and industrial growth of the United States in the mid-19th century generated a proportionate increase in litigation and case law. Legal scholars such as Langdell, known as the "rationalists," were concerned about inconsistencies in the flood of decisions, which left the law irrational and unpredictable.[8] Harvard Law School Dean Christopher Columbus Langdell's attempt to bring order to the common law, by training future lawyers using casebooks, was echoed in the 1920s by a group of prominent professors, judges, and lawyers who created the American Law Institute (ALI).[9] Consistent with natural-law aims, the ALI hoped to reduce U.S. common law to a consistent, organized, and scientific system. Their aim was to reduce the complexity and uncertainty of American common law by reforming common law principles into one authoritative, rule-like source known as a Restatement for each area of common law. Although not primary law, the Restatements of Law that the ALI has produced are a very important source of secondary authority in the United States, and are very often cited in court opinions. When a court uses a section of a Restatement to reach a decision in a case, the language used becomes primary authority for that jurisdiction. Although the Restatement itself is still not primary authority, the court's use of Restatement language makes that portion primary authority, and other parts of the same Restatement section may be highly persuasive as a result.

The first series of Restatements took more than 20 years to finish and focused on making precise statements of principles of common law. The drafters of the first series did not take into account "what the law ought to be," but focused only on majority opinions. Subsequently, the ALI became concerned that a Restatement's de facto codification of a majority rule could retard the growth of minority rules and so inhibit the natural evolution of common law doctrine. Therefore, in 1966, the ALI changed its policies to allow the reporters who write Restatements to choose, among multiple formulations of principles, those they feel are the most accurate and up to date.[10] Consequently, the newer Restatements may predict or reveal a trend toward which the law is changing. For example, the *Restatement (Second) of Contracts* § 90 defines "promissory estoppel" as "(1) A promise which the promisor should reasonably expect to induce action or forbearance on the part of the promisee or a third person and which does induce such action or forbearance is binding if injustice can be avoided only by enforcement of the promise." The treatise *Corbin on Contracts* discusses this formulation in detail, pointing out the inconsistencies in interpretation across the

[8] Christina Kunz et al., *The Process of Legal Research* 97 (4th ed. 1996).
[9] David S. Clark, "The Sources of Law," in *Introduction to the Law of the United States* 49 (2d ed. 2002).
[10] Herbert Wechsler, *Restatements and Legal Change: Problems of Policy in the Restatement Work of the American Law Institute,* 13 St. Louis U. L.J. 185 (1968).

United States, and explaining that the formulation in § 90 is predictive rather than descriptive in many of the 50 states.[11]

The drafting of each Restatement is supervised by an eminent scholar known as a *Reporter*. The Reporter prepares a draft with the help of assistants. Then a committee of advisers, themselves experts in the field, reviews and revises the draft. The Reporter then submits the revised draft to the ALI Council (a group of approximately 50 ALI members) for review. Once the Council approves a draft, they submit it to the annual meeting of the ALI members, who again discuss and may further revise it. While in process, a piece may have several names: "preliminary draft," "Council draft," "tentative draft," or "proposed final draft." Once a final draft is approved by both the Council and the ALI membership, it is published in final form.

The Restatements have been so successful that the number of subjects covered has increased through what is now a third series. Subjects include contracts, property, torts, judgments, agency, conflict of laws, restitution, security, trusts, foreign relations law, unfair competition, suretyship, and guaranty. Each Restatement is organized by chapter, each chapter is divided into topics, and each topic is divided into numbered sections. Each section begins with a Restatement rule, printed in boldface, followed by comments and then illustrations. The comments explain the Restatement rule and may offer insights into the rationale underlying it. The illustrations use examples to further explain the rule and the comments. Most of the examples are based on real cases, which are cited. In the second and third series, the illustrations may be followed by "Reporter's Notes," which typically explain the history of the rule, note cases, identify primary authorities, and provide other useful references. Appendices to the Restatements are published regularly and list cases that have cited Restatement sections.

The Restatements are extremely useful and one of the most authoritative secondary sources. Their tables of contents and indexes are good finding tools, the rules are well stated, and the comments and illustrations add greatly to the researcher's understanding. Furthermore, although they are not primary authority, parts of them are often adopted by courts.[12] To reiterate, when part of a Restatement is adopted by a court, the adopted language (but not the Restatement itself) then becomes primary authority in that jurisdiction. When a court has no mandatory law on a particular point, it often finds a Restatement section more persuasive than primary authority from another jurisdiction. Courts rely on the comments and illustrations, as well as the sections themselves. Thus, advocates often use Restatements in conjunction with primary authority to support arguments when no mandatory authority exists in a particular jurisdiction. Furthermore, they may use sections of a Restatement to persuade a court to reject adverse primary authority. The only shortcomings are that the Restatements cover only a limited number of subjects; also, because of the length of the drafting process, they can become outdated before a new series is issued. Furthermore, because of the ALI's current policy to allow adoption of desirable law, commentators occasionally object that a particular Restatement is biased, rather than being a dispassionate and accurate record of existing common law.

---

[11] Eric Mills Holmes, 3 *Corbin on Contract* § 8.11 (1996).

[12] Kunz et al., *supra* note 8, at 96.

To use a Restatement, begin by determining whether your research problem is in an area covered by one of the Restatements. Next, determine which series on that subject is useful in your research. Unless your problem has an historical aspect, or you have a citation from a mandatory authority to an older series, the newest, most current series is the one you should choose. Once you have determined the appropriate subject and series, familiarize yourself with the particular Restatement at issue. How many volumes does it contain? What are its finding tools, and where are they located? Most Restatement volumes have a table of contents of the entire subject in that series; for a few subjects, though, the table of contents may cover only topics found in that particular volume. Similarly, most Restatements have an index for the entire series in the last non-appendix volume of the set, but some have an index in the back of each volume indexing only sections located in that volume.

Once you have a general idea of how the Restatement is organized, locate one or more sections that seem applicable by using either a table of contents or an index. Usually, if you are unfamiliar with the language of the topic at issue, it is best to scan most of the table of contents first, and look for possible search terms. Then read each such term or principle carefully, including comments and illustrations, to see if it applies to your problem. Find the one section that best fits your problem, and record both its citation and its contents, either in your research log or (preferably) by photocopying it. Next, scan the index for entries you might have missed, looking up the terms you found useful in your search of the table of contents. Finally, note references to cases, and check for updated citations in the appendix volumes. Look for citations to mandatory authority, as well as the most powerful persuasive authority listed—either a jurisdiction that has the strongest persuasive power possible, or a case with facts very similar to yours. Record those citations in your research log.

One last note on Restatements: When West publishes the Restatements, it adds cross-references to the American Law Reports (A.L.R.), which can further help in researching a particular legal issue. Researching the referenced A.L.R. annotations may further help you find and interpret mandatory authority.

a. Media Choices

In making media choices with regard to the Restatements, hard copy is probably best, for the reasons discussed earlier: It is easiest to absorb the structure and use the amenities on hard copy, and easiest to gain an overview of the subject when one can flip through pages quickly. However, hard copy is not the only choice. West has most of the Restatements online, as does LEXIS. Thus, one can read the same material that appears in hard copy online, and theoretically do research online. Locating the table of contents for some of the Restatements is easier on LEXIS than on Westlaw, but Westlaw's "Results Plus" feature, discussed previously, is very helpful. In fact, some researchers prefer it to hard copy. Loislaw does not have any of the Restatements online.

b. How to Cite Restatements

Citation of a Restatement is quite simple. For the first citation, cite the entire name, then the section symbol and number, and the year of the Restatement publication. Comments are abbreviated as "cmt.," and illustrations as "illus." Include any modifying information, such as Tentative Draft, in parentheses along with the date. Example: Restatement (Second) of Contracts § 2 cmt. d, illus. 1 (Tent. Draft No. 1, 1964).

c. *Updating Restatements and Scavenging for Primary Authority*

As mentioned earlier, the process of revising a Restatement is long and convoluted, and therefore they are not revised as frequently as would be optimal. However, appendices are frequently published. The appendices list and describe courts' use of Restatement sections. Furthermore, a researcher can enter a Restatement section as a search term of an online database, or check a citation database to determine whether a particular jurisdiction has discussed or used that section, or to determine whether that section has been widely adopted in a variety of jurisdictions.

2. *Treatises and Hornbooks*

Treatises are works written by one or more legal scholars, practitioners, or publishers' staffs. They cover a specific area of law in great detail. They provide a very high level of analysis and detail and give extensive references to primary and related sources in footnotes and appendices. Some treatises are multivolume works, such as Wright and Miller's *Federal Practice and Procedure*,[13] which is a highly informative source of detailed information on federal civil procedure. Often, if the author is an eminent scholar, his or her name is included in the title: for example, *Farnsworth on Contracts*.[14] Treatises are used by judges, lawyers, and legal scholars. Although they are not as authoritative as Restatements, they too can be highly persuasive authority, depending on their authors' eminence in the field of law or jurisdiction at issue.

In contrast, *hornbooks* are legal texts written expressly for law students, by law professors, using plain language. They condense an area of law into a single volume and give a clear overview of the evolution of the law, a discussion of current interpretation, and an explanation of underlying policy as well as current application. Though there is no clear line between a hornbook and a treatise, hornbooks are generally not as detailed and provide fewer references to other sources. West's one-volume, green-bound series of treatises, though entitled "hornbooks," actually fall somewhere between hornbooks and treatises, and can occasionally be cited as persuasive authority. In general, however, hornbooks are less authoritative than treatises. Hornbooks can be extremely helpful to law students who might need further information about a course topic, but though an attorney might use a hornbook to gain some background understanding of a new field of law, he or she might choose to cite a more authoritative source in formal legal writing. The books in West's "Nutshell" series provide less detail and fewer references than those in the hornbook series. Nevertheless, some of the Nutshell series are extremely well written by prominent authorities in their respective fields and very helpful. Others are not. Other hornbooks include West Group's "Black Letter" series, Aspen's "Examples and Explanations" series, and LEXIS's "Understanding the Law"

---

[13] Charles Alan Wright & Arthur R. Miller, *Federal Practice and Procedure* (3d ed. 2002).

[14] E. Allan Farnsworth, *Farnsworth on Contracts* (2d ed. 1998) (Professor Farnsworth is the Alfred McCormack Professor of Law at Columbia University).

series. These latter series provide fewer references and should never be cited. When looking for a hornbook to help you in a particularly difficult course, it is always best to ask the professor for a recommendation. For research purposes, you might begin with a hornbook to gain background in a new area of law, but then move on to a more formal treatise.

A treatise typically contains at least three parts: (1) the scholarly text, with footnote citations to primary authority; (2) finding aids, such as a table of contents, an index, and other tables; and (3) other features, such as a preface and appendices that might include the text of important statutes or other authorities. A treatise may also have a supplement or pocket part to help with updating.

A treatise can be extremely useful when beginning a research project. It can help the researcher familiarize himself with the vocabulary, issues, arguments, and policies underlying the research problem; help the researcher develop an issue statement; and guide the researcher to the appropriate legal principle or principles. Footnotes and citations may provide mandatory or at least primary authority, and background information can give insight into related issues that may or may not be important.

To locate a treatise or treatises in a law library, look up the topic in the library's catalog and identify those treatises that seem both pertinent and up to date. While locating them on the shelves, browse the area and see if there are others you might have missed, or which might be more helpful. Often a law library will keep the most popular (and therefore most authoritative) treatises in a reserved area, and it might be helpful to ask a librarian, professor, or colleague knowledgeable about that area of law to recommend a treatise.

a. Research Methods for Treatises

As with Restatements, the most useful finding tool for a researcher new to the topic is the table of contents. One can scan it quickly, locating topics that might be appropriate and developing vocabulary. However, there are other finding tools that can be helpful. If you have the name of a leading case, use the treatise's *table of cases* to ascertain how important the case is and why, to find other cases, and to get a scholar's understanding of the leading case. If the case is not listed in a table of cases, or if you have a specific term or legal topic, use the index.

b. Media Choices

As with Restatements, the best way to search a treatise is in hard copy, either bound volumes or *loose-leafs* (meaning they are issued in two- or three-ring binders so that pages can easily be replaced). If hard copy is unavailable, however, Westlaw, LEXIS, and Loislaw have some treatises online. Some treatises are available in CD-ROM format as well. Once you have some familiarity with the topic, it is easy to broaden research into secondary sources on line with Westlaw or LEXIS.

c. How to Cite Treatises

The citation of a treatise begins with the author's or authors' names, the volume number and title of the treatise, the page or section number, and (in parentheses) the edition and publication year: Richard A. Lord, 1 *Williston on Contracts* § 1:4 (4th ed. 1990).

d. Updating Treatises

Be sure to update the information provided in a hard-copy treatise by using the treatise's *pocket part, supplement,* or *loose-leaf* pages to get the most current information. Treatises vary in terms of how and how often they are updated. Some are updated infrequently, but are supplemented or contain pocket parts. Others, especially loose-leaf services, are updated weekly. Although loose-leaf services may be up-to-the-minute, compare the information given to that in a more established treatise: the former may discuss the most recent cases, but the latter may contain better-digested material. Like Restatements, one can also do a term search on a commercial service to see whether or how often a particular treatise is cited. A work that is cited more is generally considered more authoritative than one that is rarely if ever cited.

3. Legal Periodicals

As with treatises and hornbooks, the persuasive value of legal periodicals varies. Law reviews published by ABA-accredited law schools are often the most persuasive. Articles in state bar journals and legal newspapers, like hornbooks, often lack citations, and are therefore much less persuasive. A state bar journal's primary purpose is to inform the membership of that association's activities, to comment on pending and recent legislation, and to review local court decisions. Bar journal articles emphasize the practical aspects of the law and advise members on how different matters might best be handled. Though they might help guide the researcher and can give an indication of subjects that are of current interest to practitioners, they should never be cited as authoritative secondary sources.

In contrast to law *journal* articles, law *review* articles can be invaluable as a secondary source, because (1) they analyze a narrow area of law in great depth; (2) they contain a tremendous number of footnote references to both primary and secondary authorities in that particular area; and (3) they consider the most current law. In fact, a recent study has shown that law review articles are more frequently cited by the United States Supreme Court than treatises.[15] The persuasive value of a law review article depends partly on the prominence of its author, partly on the prestige of the law school that publishes the law review, and partly on the quality of the article itself.

Generally, articles written by prominent scholars and published in prominent law reviews are more persuasive than the casenotes and comments written by law students, but an especially well-written or on-point student-written work may be persuasive as well. Usually the only students invited to write casenotes or comments are the top 10 percent of a given law school class, and even then only the best one or two casenotes or comments submitted are published. (A *casenote* is an in-depth discussion of a single case, whereas a *comment* is a thorough discussion of a very narrow area of law.) Although most law reviews are student-edited, a few are faculty-edited. There seems to be little difference in persuasive value between the two, though particular scholars may respect a specific faculty-edited review more than a specific student-edited one. Being asked to join a law school's name law review is more prestigious than joining a

---

[15] William H. Mang, *Citations in Supreme Court Opinion and Bricks: A Comparative Study*, 94 Law Libr. J., 267, 276 (2002).

specialty law review, but either position is coveted, as it adds to a U.S. law student's résumé and adds greatly to his or her attractiveness to law firms. Some periodicals have opportunities for LL.M. students to contribute articles; because LL.M. candidates attend U.S. law schools for only one year, though, they are usually unable to become law review editors, the positions that carry the most prestige.

Most law schools publish their name periodical (e.g., the *Harvard Law Review*, the *Northwestern Law Review*) as well as one or more specialty topic periodicals. Typically, a law school periodical is published quarterly, subsidized by its institution, and sold at a modest cost primarily to law libraries, alumni, and local practitioners. Student-edited reviews, whether name periodicals or specialty periodicals, usually have two sections. The first section consists of "lead articles" on various topics, usually written by prominent law professors or practitioners. These articles are usually lengthy, scholarly in nature, and the most likely to have a substantial impact in changing the law. The second section typically contains scholarly book reviews and student-written articles. The book reviews are of scholarly books, written by academics, and require a certain amount of research and citation. The student-written works consist of casenotes (*notes*) and comments. Comments are usually written by more advanced students who are members of the law review, and casenotes by students who have just recently been admitted to the law review.

a. Finding an Appropriate Article

There are several ways to locate law review articles. On hard copy, one can use either the *Index to Legal Periodicals and Books* (I.L.P.) or the *Current Law Index* (C.L.I.). Both are indexes to law review articles published in the United States. Each volume of the I.L.P. is divided into four categories: "Subject and Author Index," "Table of Cases," "Table of Statutes," and "Index of Book Reviews." C.L.I. similarly contains four categories: the subject division, a table of cases, a table of statutes, and an author/title division. The most useful in either series is probably the subject division, which lists subject headings in alphabetical order, using subject divisions used in most law library catalogs. If you have an author's name, you can locate his or her articles in either series. The table of cases and table of statutes enable you to find articles on a particular case or statute. Both series are published 12 times a year, with a final hard-bound annual accumulation. The disadvantage of this method is that the researcher must often check several years' worth of volumes to locate articles that may—or may not—be pertinent.

A more efficient way of researching legal periodicals is on *LegalTrac*, a CD-ROM form of the C.L.I. index that many law libraries maintain. In addition to a subject-guide search, which will locate several articles on a given subject, *LegalTrac* offers a keyword search, which finds articles that contain a specific search term or terms in the title or subject heading. Similarly, the I.L.P. has a CD-ROM version on *Wilsondisc. LegalTrac* and *Wilsondisc* are an improvement on the hard-copy indexes, but not as efficient as searching on Westlaw's JLR or LEXIS's LAWREV databases using either term or natural-language searches. Because the term-search connectors are more sophisticated, one can compose a more accurate search with the commercial databases. One can then scan the retrieved documents and quickly choose the most pertinent ones. However, bear in mind that neither database extends to articles written before approximately 1984, so for earlier articles the CD-ROM versions are probably best. HeinOnline.org includes earlier articles in its database, so if your school or employer subscribes to it, it may be very helpful.

b. Citing Law Review Articles

The full citation of a law review article includes the author's name, the title of the article (in italics), the volume number and abbreviated title of the journal, the beginning and pinpoint page numbers, and the year of publication: Darryl K. Brown, *Jury Nullification Within the Rule of Law*, 81 Minn. L. Rev. 1149, 1151 (1997).

c. Updating Law Review Articles

Shepard's Law Review Citations, either hard copy or on LEXIS, can be used to verify how influential the article has been since it was published or to locate other similar articles. One could also use portions of the title or author's name in a term search to see if the article has been cited in a particular jurisdiction, using Westlaw. However, generally one can tell by how recently the article was published whether or not it will be useful and encompasses comparatively up-to-date information.

4. American Law Reports

The American Law Reports (A.L.R.) is a multivolume and multiseries collection of annotations and case discussions widely used by practitioners. It was originally published by Lawyer's Cooperative Publishing, which became part of West Group in 1996, and is now published under the West Group name. The annotations focus on controversial legal issues or controversial cases. They are written by the publisher's staff attorneys or by attorneys hired by the publisher specifically to write particular selections. Since 1969, the series has been separated into two: the numbered series, beginning with A.L.R.3d, deals only with state law issues, whereas the A.L.R. Fed. covers federal law. (The current state law series is A.L.R.5th.)

A relevant A.L.R. annotation can be very helpful. Annotations are comparable to the casenotes published in law reviews, but are more concise and to the point. They begin with discussion of a particularly controversial or important case on a particular issue, and then discuss a number of related cases. The attorney writing an annotation researches the entire area of the law covered by that topic, collects a number of cases from a wide variety of jurisdictions, and then presents general principles deduced from the cases, giving their exceptions, qualifications, and applications. A.L.R. annotations can be a good source for locating primary authority, as well as for finding potential arguments and defenses. However, they are not as authoritative as Restatements or treatises and usually should not be cited, though of course the primary authority on which they are based can be used.

a. How to Find A.L.R. Annotations

In hard copy, one can locate A.L.R. annotations through the multivolume A.L.R. Index, which indexes all annotations in both federal and state A.L.R. series, with the exception of the First series. One can also use the one-volume Quick Index for state law, again for all series after the First. The A.L.R. Index is kept current by annual pocket-part supplements, and subjects can be located in alphabetical order. Furthermore, there are a number of cross-references to A.L.R. annotations in West's various series of primary law; annotations are listed in Shepard's Citations; and relevant annotations are also listed in the Supreme Court L. Ed. reporters (another series put out by Lawyer's Cooperative Publishing).

Online, A.L.R. annotations can be found in LEXIS-NEXIS's ALR library, and in West's ALR database, through both Boolean and natural-language searches.

b. Updating A.L.R. Annotations

In hard copy, A.L.R. annotations can be updated — checked to see if they have been superseded or supplemented — by checking the citation in the appropriate A.L.R. update volume or by using the Annotation History Table located in the T–Z volume of the A.L.R. Index. That table gives the history of annotations in all of the A.L.R. series, and indicates whether any given annotation has been supplemented or superseded.

Online, one can check A.L.R. annotations with LEXIS-NEXIS's Auto-Cite, as well as with West's Key Cite.

c. Citing A.L.R. Annotations

In the unlikely event that you want to cite an A.L.R. annotation, the form parallels that of a law review article. The citation starts with the author's name, the word *Annotation,* the title of the annotation in italics, the volume number and series abbreviations, first and pinpoint page numbers, and the year in italics: William B. Johnson, Annotation, *Use of Plea Bargain or Grant of Immunity as Improper Vouching for Credibility of Witness in Federal Cases,* 76 A.L.R. Fed. 409 (1986).

5. *Legal Encyclopedias*

Legal encyclopedias, like other encyclopedias, are multivolume series organized alphabetically by topic. Unlike other reference encyclopedias, however, they include footnote references to cases on point and are updated with supplements or pocket pamphlets. They can be helpful to researchers who lack any knowledge of the topic or who want a review of a broad topic, and are cross-indexed in a number of other sources. However, legal analysis therein, especially as compared with that of a law review article or A.L.R. annotation, is minimal. Therefore, they lack authority and should not be cited. Use their tables of contents and indexes to locate and reference likely topics, and then check primary authorities referenced in their footnotes. The two major encyclopedias are *Corpus Juris Secundum* (C.J.S.) and *American Jurisprudence 2d* (Am. Jur. 2d). West publishes the C.J.S. Although Am. Jur. 2d is still published under the Lawyer's Cooperative Publishing imprint, both companies are part of Thomson.

6. *Digests*

West's Digests are very useful research tools for locating primary authority, primarily case law, and are widely used. They include both a subject index and a topical outline of case law from various jurisdictions. In each series, legal principles espoused in reported cases are organized numerically according to subject. Like the A.L.R. series, there are two primary series, one for federal and one for state law. West's Digests, whether in hard copy or online (the online version is known as the "key search" system). The Federal Digest is now in its fourth series, and the collected state law digest is in its eleventh series, entitled the *Eleventh Decennial Digest.* West also publishes a Regional Digest for each regional reporter as well as Digests for some individual states. The regional and individual state Digests are easier to use than the Decennial series.

Each Digest series is based on an extensive topic index. Each volume contains one or two main topics, indicated on the spine of the volume. Each main topic is then divided into subtopics and sub-subtopics. Each topic, subtopic, and sub-subtopic is assigned a "key number." Additionally, the Digests have finding tools located in separate volumes. For example, if you know the name of a case, you can locate the citation through a Digest's "Table of Cases" volumes. Other volumes index cases by "Words and Phrases" or "Descriptive Words." The series are updated monthly in softbound volumes. (LEXIS similarly has a topic index, though its online Research System does not use numbers).

When a court sends an opinion to West for publication, West's attorneys read the opinion and analyze it according to West's topic index. They then draft headnotes using the key numbers. Thus, theoretically, cases discussing the same legal issue can be identified because they will have headnotes with the same key numbers, and summaries of them will appear in the same place in the Digest. This method often works to group similar cases similarly, but sometimes the categorizations are not what one would expect. For example, one headnote in the case *Bourque v. Duplechin*, 331 So. 2d 40 (La. Ct. App. 1976), discussed in Chapter 1, is assigned key number 376k6(19), among others. *Lestina v. West Bend Mutual Insurance*, the slide-tackle soccer case, similarly has a headnote with the same key number. However, that key number is categorized under *Theaters and Shows*. Most attorneys looking for cases involving negligence in the context of recreational sports would not think to look under *Theaters and Shows*, and would not find these two cases. Thus, the list of subjects can be somewhat quirky, as can the assignment of cases under any particular topic. In general, however, the Digest system works and will help you find some, but not all, cases on a particular topic. LEXIS's system is also based on an extensive topic index, but is a bit more generalized and was more recently developed. It does not usually have the quirkiness that West's system does. The two systems will lead to some, but not all, of the same cases, and each will lead to cases not listed in the other system. Therefore, if you have access to both systems, you might as well use both to try to ensure the most efficient search.

DISCUSSION NOTES

1. Is the U.S. requirement that an attorney provide competent research substantively any different from the ethical demands of your home jurisdiction?
2. What media are available in your home jurisdiction?
3. If you have developed a strategy for research in your home jurisdiction, how does it differ from the one described in this chapter?
4. If you have used a variety of computer databases, which do you prefer? Why?
5. Which databases will you focus on most in this course? Why?
6. How do you normally plan your project time?
7. Research Dr. Shymite's problem in some secondary sources. Which sources are best?
8. Which secondary sources would work best for which kinds of problem?

EXERCISE

Following the research checklist, develop a research log for the following hypothetical problems. Then research the problems in secondary authorities: Restatements, treatises, law reviews, ALRs, and legal encyclopedias. Document your research log and cite the best result in each secondary source that proves to be productive. If one or more secondary sources cite mandatory authority or highly persuasive primary authority from the same general jurisdiction, provide the citation to the mandatory authority as well and give a short (one-paragraph) informal answer to the research question.

1. Ms. McMahan has come to your law office to find out if she can sue on behalf of her son, Geoffrey, whose eyesight was permanently damaged in a paintball game. Geoffrey and his friend Chumley Braindead, both 12 years old, went to Pete's Paintball Palace to play. The purpose of paintball is to hit players on the opposing side with gelatin capsules filled with colored vegetable oil, which are intended to break on contact. Pete's Paintball Palace is decorated to resemble a darkened, abandoned factory, and is lit softly and eerily with black light. Each team's goal is to gain control over the factory. Players at Pete's Paintball Palace are given padded vests with luminous targets printed on them and air-powered guns loaded with the capsules. Players are instructed to wear both goggles and vests during the games. Geoffrey and Chumley were assigned to opposing teams. Unfortunately, Geoffrey's goggles, which Chumley had loaned to him, had a tendency to fog over. Chumley knew about this problem, but did not warn Geoffrey. During game play, the goggles fogged over, and Geoffrey removed them from his eyes, resting them on his head instead. While the goggles were up, Geoffrey was shot in the eye with a paintball apparently fired by Chumley. Chumley was unaware that Geoffrey had removed his goggles, but one of Pete's referees had seen Geoffrey with his goggles off and said nothing. Ms. McMahan wants to know if she can sue Chumley's parents, Pete's Paintball Palace, or both for Geoffrey's injury.

Geoffrey's accident took place in Iowa. Assume further that your preliminary research into a legal dictionary gave you the following terms: reckless, disregard of safety, negligence, sports, and athletics.

2. Mrs. Brown and her husband recently visited their favorite McDonald's for a post-bowling dinner in Cleveland, Ohio. Like many Americans, Mrs. Brown is concerned about her weight and cholesterol levels, and decided to order a McLean Deluxe sandwich instead of her usual Big Mac. A Big Mac has 560 calories, of which 280 are from saturated fat. In comparison, a McLean Deluxe (without mayonnaise) has 390 calories, of which 60 are from fat. Shortly after her meal, Ms. Brown developed a rash, difficulty breathing, blue lips, and hives. Mr. Brown drove her to the hospital emergency room, where the doctor treated her immediately, keeping her there for five hours to make certain she was all right. The doctor said that she was allergic, probably to something she had eaten, and was going into anaphylactic shock. He also said that she might have died if Mr. Brown had not gotten her to the hospital right away.

Mrs. Brown has known for a long time that she is severely allergic to fish, seafood, and even seaweed. Only after looking up the ingredients of the McLean burger did the

Browns learn it has the food additive carrageenan in it, and that carrageenan is a seaweed derivative. The emergency room doctor said that very few people are allergic to carrageenan and Mrs. Brown must be unusually susceptible. Mrs. Brown's allergist, however, says that an allergy to it is not so uncommon. Carrageenan is a seaweed extract that is commonly used in processed foods as a thickener or stabilizing agent. Foods that often contain carrageenan include prepared pudding, yogurt, condensed milk, and soymilk products. Carrageenan sometimes causes gastric distress, and may be linked to stomach and breast cancer. Your partner wants to know if the Browns can sue McDonald's for strict products liability, under a failure-to-warn theory.

3. John Elton recently came to your supervising partner's office (in New York City) for legal advice. Five years ago, he and his "partner" George, who had lived together for several years in New York City, were married under the Massachusetts Same Sex Marriage statute. After their marriage, they resumed living in John's multi-million dollar condominium in Trump Towers, and he purchased a ski chalet in Aspen, Colorado, in George's name as a gift. Unfortunately, their relationship fell apart, and they decided to separate.

In September of 2005 John's attorney drafted a "separation agreement" (the "Agreement"), which both parties signed. The Agreement recites in relevant part that "the parties desire to confirm their separation and make arrangements in connection therewith, including the settlement of their property rights, and other rights and obligations growing out of the marriage relation. . . . Now, therefore, in consideration of the premises and of the mutual promises hereinafter contained, the parties agree as follows: . . . ." Among other things, the Agreement provides for division of the real and personal property accumulated by the parties during their time together; it also provides for a one-time payment by John to George of the sum of $780,000, described as "the only support, maintenance, or other form of payment by either party hereto to the other." George was to return the ski chalet to John's ownership. The Agreement, which contains mutual releases, was fully performed upon its execution by the parties, respectively, on September 21 and September 22, 2005: i.e., John paid the $780,000, and George returned the ski chalet.

On January 10, 2006, George sued John for a divorce, demanding alimony. John is now angry and wants to know if he can get the $780,000 back. Your supervising partner wants to know if the marriage was valid under New York law. If it was not, then he wants to know if the Agreement itself is enforceable in and of itself as a contract. He advises you that common law contracts require *mutual assent* (consisting of offer and acceptance) and especially *consideration* (which means *bargained-for exchange*, not the civilian concept *cause*, which refers to a person's motive).

CHAPTER 6

Researching and Updating Case Law

INTRODUCTION

Chapter 5 explained Stage 1 background research in secondary sources. At this point in the research process, the researcher may have a fairly well-developed idea of (1) the area of law at issue in his client's problem; (2) its policy concerns; (3) its primary sources (constitutional, statutory, or case law); (4) the terms used; and (5) an issue statement, though he will undoubtedly continue to refine the issue statement throughout the research and writing process. Do not expect to fully understand the law after completing all Stage 1 research steps — that is possible only after Stages 2 and 3 have been completed. Chapters 6 and 7 provide strategies for Stages 2 and 3: locating primary authority, both mandatory and persuasive, and verifying it. Verifying law includes both updating and analyzing authorities. This chapter assumes that the client problem is in an area of law dominated by case law. Although a statute may be involved, the main focus of the problem is on case law. Chapter 6 discusses how to find, verify, and cite case law.

I. FINDING AND VERIFYING CASE LAW

CASE LAW RESEARCH CHECKLIST

- ☐ A. Scavenge from secondary sources.
- ☐ B. Use a citator to verify, update, and broaden research.
- ☐ C. Use subject indexes.
- ☐ D. Use term and full-sentence searches online.

Essentially, there are four methods of researching case law: scavenging them from secondary sources, using citators, using subject indexes, and using term (Boolean) and full-sentence searches online. All four methods are computer-compatible, and it is best to alternate between methods as your knowledge and understanding of the area gradually increase.

A. Scavenging from Secondary Sources

Chapter 5 explained that often research into secondary authority will yield primary or even mandatory authority. Once the researcher has located the applicable legal principle in secondary authority, it is easy to check the sources upon which that secondary authority is relying by reading the footnoted citations. If the citations are to cases, the researcher can determine whether a case is mandatory or persuasive authority by examining the court identification in the citation. If a case cited in a secondary source is mandatory authority, the researcher has a major advantage and can easily transition to Stage 2 research by reading the case cited in the secondary source. All of the exercises in Chapter 5 led to secondary sources that cited mandatory case law.

Even if a secondary authority does not cite cases that are mandatory authority for the client problem, it may be worthwhile looking into citations to persuasive authority. Sometimes a case discussed in a secondary source, though it is not mandatory authority, will have facts so similar to your client's problem that it is highly persuasive. For example, suppose your client, a sea captain in Maine, is complaining that a company that agreed to buy all his lobster catch at a specific price later refused to buy it at the agreed-upon price, frustrated all his attempts to make a profit from the contract, and even tried to extort money from him. A law review article discussing a case in which a New Jersey company abused its contract to buy clams from a sea captain would be highly persuasive to a Maine court.[1] Thus, if the key facts are substantially similar to the facts of the client problem, it may be worthwhile to scavenge even a persuasive case from a secondary authority.

Furthermore, if you are somewhat unsure about whether the principle you are looking at in a secondary source applies to your problem, scanning one of the cases cited to see if the legal principle at issue is on point may help you decide whether your research is headed in the right direction. Just be careful not to waste valuable research time needlessly researching useless cases. In sum, one way to find case law is to scavenge it from citations given in secondary sources, looking for (1) mandatory authority, (2) highly persuasive authority, or (3) reassurance that your research is well directed.

B. Using Citators to Verify, Update, and Broaden Research

Typically, Stage 1 research into secondary authority will give the researcher both the applicable rule and at least one case that clearly illustrates the rule. Once a researcher has found this proverbial *one good case*, research becomes much, much easier, because that case will easily lead to others through the citation system. Check the cases cited in your

---

[1] *Sons of Thunder, Inc. v. Borden, Inc.*, 690 A.2d 575 (N.J. 1996) (holding against Borden in suit for breach of contract and breach of the duty of good faith and fair dealing).

good case, and check the cases that have cited your good case since it was decided. This both updates the case and constitutes an extremely productive method of case law research.

1. Scavenging Cases from Citations Given in a Case

Just as one can scavenge case law from cases cited in secondary sources, one can scavenge case law from the citations given in the one good case. If you examine any opinion, you will notice that it contains a number of citations to other cases. One of the easiest ways to broaden case law research is to selectively check the cases cited in an opinion. Look for citations to cases that purportedly support legal principles that apply to your situation, and read those cases. If a case is cited more than once in an opinion, or is discussed in depth, or is cited in support of a point you want to make, it is likely to be an important case for your purposes, and should be read. Additionally, if a cited case is mandatory authority for your situation, you should examine it carefully. Such cited cases may be better for your purposes than the one you first found.

2. Citators

Once a case has been decided by an upper-level court, under the principle of stare decisis that opinion becomes binding precedent for similar cases in the same court and in the lower courts it supervises. Lower courts will cite that case when they rely on it, and also when they distinguish it. Furthermore, that opinion may persuade other courts to adopt its reasoning, and when they do, they will cite the case as well. Over the course of time, important, influential cases are cited more often. The converse is true as well: A higher court may *reverse* or *vacate* a lower court's opinion, and after it does, the lower opinion will rarely if ever be cited. Occasionally a court will vacate its own opinion. In any of these instances, it is as if the opinion had never been written — at least insofar as concerns the points that caused the case to be reversed or vacated. Sometimes the law changes, and a case that was once good law becomes outdated or is overruled. Cases that are overruled, reversed, vacated, or simply outdated are rarely cited.

To learn whether this has happened to a particular case, lawyers use citators. *Citators* are tools that monitor the life of a case and keep track of each time it is cited in another legal authority. The two most prominent citators are Shepard's and KeyCite.

For 120 years, Shepard's citators had no competition. Attorneys "Shepardized" all their cases by hand, painstakingly looking up each and every case on which they were relying in Shepard's volumes of books to make sure it had not been vacated or reversed, and also to see whether it had been cited by other courts. Shepard's volumes are simply lists: the researcher looks up the citation of the case she is checking, which will be printed in bold, and then reads the small-print list of citations that follow it.

With computerization, both West Group and LEXIS contracted with Shepard's and put its material online. Then, in 1997, Shepard's was bought by LEXIS. (One commentator compared this to the thought of Switzerland joining either NATO or the Warsaw Pact during the Cold War.[2]) LEXIS soon announced that it would not

[2] Robert C. Berring & Elizabeth A. Edinger, *Legal Research Survival Manual* 63 (2002).

renew Westlaw's licensing agreement. Westlaw countered by introducing KeyCite, which has been fully accepted by the market.

Shepard's and KeyCite's online coverage extends from cases back into the 1700s and up to opinions issued yesterday. In fact, both systems update on a daily basis, so that cases are incorporated as both cited and citing references within 24 to 48 hours after they are received. Coverage includes both published cases (cases that courts indicate should be published) and unpublished opinions (cases that courts indicate should not be either published or cited).[3] Loislaw also has a citator, though it is purposefully less detailed than the other two.

3. *Using Citators to Verify Case Law*

Usually, the first thing an attorney wants to do is verify whether a case is still *good law*: He wants to make sure that it has not been vacated, reversed, overruled, or otherwise outdated by changing legal principles. Therefore, Shepard's and KeyCite make this information immediately available. In fact, they attempt to indicate whether a case is still good even before you go to the citator (i.e., before you push the Shepard's or KeyCite button) by putting red, yellow, and green signals on the computer screen, along with the first page of any case. Do not overvalue red and yellow signals!

A red signal merely means that the *editors* of LEXIS or Westlaw have decided there *is* some sort of negative history, and a yellow means there *may* be some. These assessments by Shepard's and KeyCite can be misleading. A red signal could mean that the case has *negative direct history*— in other words, it has been vacated or reversed by its supervising court and should not be used. It is as if the opinion had never been written. However, a red signal could also mean that one or more principles at issue in the case were overruled in a later opinion, and that the law has changed since then. In this situation, the case cannot be used to support the point of law that was overruled, but there might be other points in the case that are still valid. When one or more points of a case are overruled by a later case, KeyCite refers to the later case as *negative indirect history*. You could still use the prior case, as long as your point is still valid and your citation indicates that the case was overruled. Thus, if KeyCite or Shepard's gives a case a red signal, you will need to verify whether the case is still good law. A yellow signal is weaker than a red one but indicates that the citator found one or more cases that seem to disagree with the one cited, or that some of the concepts in the cited case are no longer as accepted as they once were.

For example, KeyCite gives *Bourque v. Duplechin*[4] (the softball case on which *Jones v. Smith* was modeled) a red flag, whereas Shepard's gives it a yellow signal. If you check the case that they feel is negative indirect history, *Picou v. Hartford Insurance*,[5] you will find that *Picou* says *Bourque* is outdated because Louisiana no longer uses *assumption of risk*. In some other states, however, assumption of risk is still

[3] A few courts, concerned about the vast volume of cases being published, designate that some opinions should not be published and should not be relied upon for purposes of stare decisis, even though they give the text of those opinions to Westlaw or LEXIS. This practice has become a bit controversial, but at this juncture, there is little reason for courts not to continue doing so.
[4] 331 So. 2d 40 (La. Ct. App. 1976).
[5] 558 So. 2d 787 (La. Ct. App. 1990).

used. *Bourque* is still good law with regard to everything else it covers, and certainly can still be cited, but you should not use it to support an assumption-of-risk argument. Loislaw uses no signals in its citator, believing that they are confusing and that the researcher is capable of determining for herself whether a case is still good law.

Generally, if there is an error in KeyCite or Shepard's signals, it will be a false negative, not a false positive. In other words, a researcher can usually trust a green signal as some indication that the case has been neither vacated nor overruled. But even this is not enough. To see whether a case has been influential or whether it simply "died" over time, check the case history (Shepard's) or direct history (KeyCite). If a case has been cited often, by a variety of jurisdictions, and recently, then it is still influential. In contrast, if the case has not been cited in the last 20 years, you might want to find out why. Does it mean that the case is outdated, or does it simply mean that it stands for an obscure point (yours)? If the latter, the case is still good law.

In addition to listing all the times a case is cited, Westlaw and LEXIS classify those citations. Hard-copy Shepard's volumes use letters to indicate what effect a citing case has on the case being cited, and lists citing cases according to the importance of their effect on the case being cited. Citing cases that vacated or reversed the cited case are listed before cases that merely distinguished it or mentioned it. With computerization, however, Shepard's has improved upon this. It still uses classifications like "distinguished," but it also arranges citations by court: Decisions from the same jurisdiction as the cited case are listed first, with decisions from higher courts coming before lower court decisions. Citations are then separated by reporter and listed chronologically, much as they were in the hardbound Shepard's volumes. However, the computer allows the user to manipulate those arrangements to show immediately whether a court in any particular jurisdiction has cited the case at issue.

In creating KeyCite, Westlaw decided to do things a bit differently. Westlaw ranks citations by depth of discussion. In addition to indicating negative direct or indirect history, Westlaw uses a star system: more green stars mean more extensive treatment of the cited case; no stars means the case was merely mentioned in passing. Cases are arranged by the amount of discussion, and sorted according to whether the mention was positive or negative. If you click on the hyperlink to the citing case, either Westlaw or LEXIS will take you directly to the page of that case containing the citation to the case you are checking, so you can examine for yourself what is being said about it.

4. *Using Citators to Locate Case Law and Secondary Authority*

Because of these hyperlinks, once a researcher has the *one good case* described earlier, it is easy to search through citing cases using either KeyCite or Shepard's, both to expand research and to see how the law has developed since the cited case was decided. For example, the author of this textbook located all the recreational sports cases used in this textbook by checking cases that cited *Bourque v. Duplechin* and then checking cases that cited those cases. This is one of the easiest and most efficient ways of locating other cases dealing with the same topic. If a case has been cited 10,000 or more times, both Shepard's and KeyCite provide the researcher with methods to limit results. Shepard's makes it particularly easy to limit results to one particular jurisdiction. KeyCite's green-star system can be similarly useful in searching for other good cases that focus on the same issue as the cited case.

In addition to listing citing cases, if the researcher scrolls all the way down to the bottom of the citation list, both services include citations from other sources. Therefore, if the cited case was discussed in an A.L.R. annotation, law review, or treatise, the researcher can quickly see what that secondary source said about the cited case. Some cases, particularly Supreme Court cases, are long and convoluted and it is difficult to understand what they stand for. Secondary authority can provide the researcher with a great deal of assistance in digesting such complicated cases.

A word of warning: Logically one would think that a case either is or is not cited in another authority, and that (computers being the efficient machines they are) the result of a citator search should be exactly the same list of authorities, regardless of which citator is used: Shepard's, KeyCite, or Loislaw. This is not, in fact, what happens. You may find some cases on Shepard's that are not listed on a KeyCite search, and vice versa. Citations sometimes seem to get misplaced in cyberspace. Therefore, it is worth using both citators to locate the greatest number of references.

5. The Importance of Citators

As indicated in Chapter 5,[6] an attorney in the United States who fails to make sure that the legal authority she is relying on is still current subjects herself to possible punishment by the court, as well as to possible liability for malpractice. An attorney who carelessly misinterprets authority by failing to verify that she has interpreted it accurately may also be subject to punishment. Standard, careful research and interpretation skills can help an attorney avoid careless misinterpretations. Updating case law, however, requires use of a citator, whether computerized or in hard copy. Noncommercial case law databases, especially state-run databases, often are incapable of even simple Boolean searches. Often such databases contain cases only from the last five to ten years, and can be searched only by case name or docket number. A database that is capable of a Boolean search can be used as a rudimentary citator if one can use the name of the cited case as a search term, but this is no guarantee that one will be able to locate a vacating or reversing case. The easiest and best way to verify that a case is still good law is to use a commercial online citator. Even small firms that cannot support much other commercial online research will often pay for access to a citator. Furthermore, citators vastly increase the researcher's efficiency in locating other cases that discuss the same or similar issues.

C. Locating Case Law Using Subject Indexes

If the researcher did not find a good case from a preliminary search of secondary sources, or if the researcher still needs more research terms, or if he simply wants to make sure that he has not missed a good case, the next method of researching case law he will use is the subject index method. This is the type of system provided by West's Digest and KeySearch systems, as well as others. Each subject index breaks down the law into a series of basic, easily understood categories. Each category is then itself

[6] *See* Chapter 5, § I.

broken into subcategories, then sub-subcategories, and so on. The researcher begins with a basic category and then gradually narrows down the search by working through the sub- and sub-subcategories. With this method, one must continually compare and recompare the client problem to the category to verify that the category, subcategory, or sub-subcategory chosen is the most appropriate for the particular problem. You can expect to make some wrong turns before choosing the right sub-subcategory, but try to keep the detours short.

West's Digest system breaks down legal principles into an organized series of outlines, and then assigns each outlined principle a Key Number. The computer-based KeySearch system on Westlaw is based on the same categories as the original hardcopy Digest system. The topic divisions on which the KeySearch and Key Number system are based date back quite a long way. Because of this, many U.S. attorneys have shaped their thinking around these categories. Paradoxically, the opposite can also be true. As mentioned in Chapter 5, some attorneys occasionally find that categorizations are outdated and anti-intuitive, and find LEXIS's similar Search Advisor system easier to follow because the categories are newer. Thus, you may find that one system's categorizations match your thinking better and are therefore easier for you to use. If you have access to both systems, however, it might be best to alternate between them; as with citators, results will vary somewhat from system to system.

In addition to Westlaw and LEXIS, other legal databases use subject indexes as finding tools, and they can be very handy devices. For example, U.S. government agency Web sites often have subject indexes that are easier to find and follow than those in commercial databases or other resources.[7]

D. Term and Full-Sentence Searches on Internet Databases

Today, most law students, whether LL.M. or J.D. candidates, arrive at school having some familiarity with Internet searches. Internet browsers and services like Yahoo, Microsoft Explorer, and AOL all allow the user to use a simple term search: the search system allows one to search using one, two, or more terms. Westlaw and LEXIS have expanded on this, but both systems use basically the same methods, and both allow a choice of two types of searches: Boolean (joining specific words) and Natural Language (Westlaw) or Freestyle (LEXIS) in which one simply types a full or partial sentence into the search box and lets the computer does the rest. Each method has advantages and disadvantages.

1. Choosing the Appropriate Database

When using Westlaw and LEXIS term searches, you first choose the database you will be searching. A database is like a specific and limited library. Westlaw and LEXIS divide their information into hundreds of databases, each assigned a specific abbreviation. One can search all states' case law, all federal case law, or a particular state, or

[7] *See infra* Chapter 10 for list and discussion of noncommercial and nonfee computer-assisted legal research Web sites.

a particular federal circuit, merely by choosing the appropriate database. In the early 1990s, Westlaw and LEXIS issued hard-copy lists of the various databases. Now, however, both systems provide an automated method to help one choose the correct database. This method is another variant of the index search described earlier: major categories — federal law, state law, law reviews, news, and so on — devolve to smaller and smaller categories. Usually, the best database to choose is the smallest one necessary for the task. For instance, it is best not to choose a database that includes cases from all 50 states when one is interested only in Michigan case law.

2. *Choosing between Boolean and Full-Sentence Searches*

Once she has chosen the database, the researcher then chooses the type of search she wants: Boolean or full-sentence form. Students new to Westlaw and LEXIS instinctively like the idea of a sentence-form search because they do not have to learn how to use specialized connectors. One merely types in a question, hits the Enter key, and *voilà!* — the computer compiles a bunch of cases. This is even more attractive to attorneys whose first language is not English: It is difficult enough to formulate a sentence, let alone have to decide exactly what word to use and figure out the seemingly complicated system of connectors. However, uninformed use of sentence-form searches is even more likely to yield inaccurate results than is a Boolean search, for several reasons. In a Boolean search, you deliberately choose the terms you want to have in your document, and you control how those terms relate to one other. You do not have this kind of control in a sentence-form search. With a sentence-form search, the computer decides how to connect the terms. When you type in a sentence-form query, the computer first identifies terms, and then ranks them by how often they appear in normal language. The computer then decides how those terms should be connected and automatically converts your sentence into a Boolean search. The resulting search query may or may not include all the terms you thought were important. If you happened to use the same words in a manner similar to that in the kinds of cases you want, then your search is likely to be successful. Often, though, the computer's choice of how to construct the search yields cases that have absolutely nothing to do with the legal issue you have in mind.

To make things worse, the computer may rank results in twenties, giving you the first 20 cases that include the most discussion of the terms it decided you wanted, then the next 20 and so on. The case you want may be buried somewhere in a number of cases that have nothing to do with the legal issue you are researching, and you will have a hard time identifying and finding it. In other words, sentence-form searches can be even more inaccurate than Boolean searches, because you have less control over how the terms are connected. Therefore, it is probably best to work with a Boolean search first, gain some idea of which terms are likely to yield results, and then switch to a sentence-form search. Frustration with one method can be dealt with by switching back and forth between the two types of searches, trying various combinations of likely terms.

3. *Avoid Boolean and Full-Sentence Searches until You Have Used Other Methods*

With either Boolean or full-sentence searches, the aim is to design a search query that will yield the best documents for the research problem. The training that LEXIS and Westlaw give tends to make this seem easy, but it is not. It is easy to design search queries that are underinclusive (bring back too few cases), overinclusive (bring back too many), or inaccurate (bring back the wrong cases). As you may already have experienced, simply guessing the terms that should be in a relevant case is guaranteed to yield the most inaccurate results. For this reason, you should do preliminary research in secondary sources, citation searches, and subject index searches first, before attempting either Boolean or sentence-form searches. Once you have used these other methods, you will have a good idea of the terms that are likely to be found in an appropriate document. Furthermore, with regard to cases, you will probably have already found the most relevant cases; by the time you begin a computer search, you are merely checking to see if there were any you missed.

4. Tailoring Boolean Searches for Accuracy

The choices of connectors and limiting terms are easily accessed on Westlaw and LEXIS, so there is no reason to explain them here. With use, the researcher will become familiar with them quite quickly. As mentioned earlier, in addition to difficulties in choosing the appropriate terms, you may encounter difficulty in avoiding underinclusive and overinclusive searches with Boolean searches. However, there are a couple of strategies that work to help resolve these last two problems. If your search was underinclusive, and your result was that no documents were found, then you eliminate terms, use more flexible forms of terms, or adjust connectors so that the terms are further apart. For example, if your original search asked for cases that included the words *negligent* and *softball* within five words of each other, you could do the following:

- Use a variable ending for the stem "negligen" so that the computer will search for *negligent*, *negligence*, and *negligently*.
- Substitute the phrase "recreational sports" for the term *softball*.
- Ask that the two terms be within a paragraph of each other, instead of only five words.

If the contrary was true and your search yielded hundreds of documents, then you might do the following:

- Narrow your choice of database.
- Add terms.
- Ask that terms be closer together.
- Ask only for cases issued in the last five years.

II. CITING CASES

As explained in Chapter 2, a full and correct citation to a case contains: (1) the case name; (2) reporter information, including volume and page numbers; and (3) court and year:

Lestina v. West Bend Mut. Ins. Co., 501 N.W.2d 28, 32 (Wis. 1993).

1 2 3

Although the Bluebook and the ALWD Citation Manual diverge slightly on minor sequencing and abbreviation issues, they agree far more than they disagree. This text cannot give detailed or precise instructions on citation rules, which are best learned by studying either primary source, but it will endeavor to present some of the most important general rules in a clear and simple fashion. The exercises that follow will require the use of one of the two citation-style manuals.

A. The Case Name

The rules for formulating a case name are given in Rule 10.2 of the Bluebook or Rule 12.2 of the ALWD, and there is very little difference between the two systems. The purpose of both systems of rules is to simplify the formal name of the case so that the resulting citation is as short as possible while remaining accurate. Three types of entities can be parties to a case: real people, organizations (businesses and nonprofit organizations), and governments. Generally, if formulating a case name for a citation in which both parties are people, use only their last names: *Mary Brown versus John Smith* becomes *Brown v. Smith.* If one of the parties is an organization, abbreviate the name according to the abbreviation rules of the citation manual: *Toyota Motor Sales, U.S.A., Incorporated* becomes *Toyota Motor Sales, U.S.A., Inc.* With governmental entities, omit phrases such as *State of* or *Commonwealth of,* and you may sometimes abbreviate the geographic name: *Commonwealth of Massachusetts* becomes *Massachusetts* or *Mass.* However, if the case was decided by a court of that same state, the state name is omitted and *Commonwealth* or *State* is retained. For example, if the Massachusetts Supreme Court decided a case in which the Commonwealth of Massachusetts was a party, the party name would be *Commonwealth,* not *Mass.*: *Commonwealth v. Therrien,* 703 N.E.2d 1175 (Mass. 1998).[8]

1. Short-Form Case Names

Very often a legal writing will discuss or cite a case previously cited. It would become repetitive to use the full case name each time the case is mentioned, so usually only the first party's name is used. *Brown v. Smith* becomes *Brown.* If referring to the case by the first party only would be confusing, then use the last party's name. For example, when the subject of the writing is federal criminal law, it would be very confusing to refer to a case as *United States* because the plaintiff in a federal criminal case is always the United States. Therefore, use the defendant's name. *United States v. Roberts* becomes *Roberts.* When referring to a shortened case name in a sentence, italicize the name. If you want to refer to the party rather than the case, do not italicize it. Thus, *Brown* refers to the case, but "Brown" refers to Mary Brown, the plaintiff.

[8] ALWD at 62; *see also* Bluebook at 60.

Often organizations have long names. To indicate how you are abbreviating a long name, put the shortened form in parentheses immediately after the full name: "The Teamsters Brewery & Soft Drink Workers Local Union 896 (Local 896) argues that the collective bargaining agreement with Anheuser-Busch, Inc. is unfair." Thereafter, use the short form consistently. Some stylists prefer to add quotation marks to indicate a short form: Teamsters Brewery & Soft Drink Workers Local Union 896 ("Teamsters"). If formulating a short-form case name from a long party name, put the italicized short form in brackets after the entire citation, and add *hereinafter*: Teamsters Brewery & Soft Drink Workers Local Union 896 v. Anheuser-Busch, Inc., 587 N.E.2d 997 (Ill. 1968) [hereinafter *Teamsters*].[9]

B. Reporter Information, Volume and Page Numbers

ALWD and the Bluebook use the same sequence for formulating the central part of a case citation: volume number (space) abbreviated name of the reporter (space) beginning page number (comma, space) and pinpoint page number. The easiest way to locate the proper abbreviation of a reporter's name is to use Table 1 of the Bluebook (the first table in the blue pages) or Appendix 1 in the ALWD and look up the appropriate jurisdiction. Looking up Alabama in either source will indicate that Alabama cases can be found in the Southern Reporter, which is currently in its second series: So. 2d (the ALWD and the Bluebook disagree on whether there should be a space between "So." and "2d"; use the one your instructor or employer prefers).

1. *Parallel Citations*

Some case citations cite to more than one reporter in the central section of the citation: *Roe v. Wade*, 410 U.S. 959, 93 S. Ct. 1409, 35 L. Ed. 2d 694 (1973). These are termed *parallel citations* because although they cite different reporters, they all refer to exactly the same opinion. The official reporter is always cited first, followed by the unofficial. Parallel citations must be used only when the document will be filed with a state court (Bluebook rule P.3) or is required by local court rules (*id.*; ALWD 12.4(c)(2)) and the case being cited was decided by that court or its immediate supervising court. If parallel citations are used, the official reporter is always cited first, and all citations must include both beginning and pinpoint page numbers. Thus, if the document is to be filed in a New York state court, a citation to a New York state court decision would be as follows: *People v. Taylor*, 73 N.Y.2d 683, 690, 541 N.E.2d 386, 389, 543 N.Y.S.2d 357, 360 (1989).

Because of all of the internal commas, parallel citations are difficult to read. They are even more difficult to formulate than they are to read, because they require the writer to meticulously locate and cite the exact same language in more than one source. At one time, they were helpful and even necessary because court and law firm libraries usually had only one or another series, and it would have been difficult to verify a citation if only one source were cited. Thus, even though it was not required by the

[9] Bluebook rule 4.2(b).

Bluebook, for a long time it was standard practice to cite to all three U.S. Supreme Court reporters in all documents, not just filings. Parallel citations are becoming less needed with computerization.

2. Pinpoint Citations

Pinpoint citations are absolutely required part of a case citation[10] because they give credibility to the writer's text. The writer is saying: "Mr. Reader, *Brown* says X, and to prove it, you will find X on page 6 of the case." Readers, including law clerks, judges, supervising attorneys, and researchers, check citations for many reasons; therefore, pinpoint citations must be accurate. The only time a pinpoint citation is not needed is when nothing specific about the case is discussed.

a. Locating Page Numbers

When formulating pinpoint numbers, page numbers are easiest to locate in the original hard-copy reporter: one simply looks in the upper or lower corner of the page. If the reporter is an unofficial one, page numbers for the official reporter will be indicated in small print at the appropriate spot in the text. Similarly, online commercial databases indicate page numbers for various official and unofficial reporters within the text by prefacing them with a series of asterisks.

b. Citing Multiple Pages

Suppose the language cited or referred to in a case appears on more than one page, or continues across several pages? The pinpoint citation should reflect this as well. If you are referring to specific pages, simply list them separated by commas. Similarly, a spread or range of pages can be referred to by using a hyphen: *Lestina v. West Bend Mut. Ins. Co.*, 501 N.W.2d 28, 32, 34 (Wis. 1993); or *Lestina v. West Bend Mut. Ins. Co.*, 501 N.W.2d 28, 32-34 (Wis. 1993).

C. Court and Year

A properly cited case includes the abbreviated name of the court that wrote the opinion, plus the year, in parentheses. The court identifier is not needed if it is otherwise apparent from the rest of the citation. For example, no court identifier is needed in a citation to *U.S. Reports* because the only decisions therein are from the United States Supreme Court. To locate the correct way to abbreviate a court name, look up the jurisdiction in Table 1 of the Bluebook or Appendix 1 of the ALWD.

D. Subsequent History

As mentioned earlier, if a subsequent decision has significantly changed the precedential value of a case, this should be indicated. The citation information for

---

[10] ALWD 5.2(b)(1), (2); *see also* Bluebook rule 3.3.

the subsequent decision is added at the end of the first full citation; the two are separated by commas and an italicized abbreviation indicating how the subsequent case affected the original. For example, *Central Ill. Pub. Serv. Co. v. Westervelt*, 342 N.E.2d 463 (Ill. App. Ct. 1976), *aff'd*, 367 N.E.2d 661 (Ill. 1977),[11] indicates that the Illinois Supreme Court affirmed the appellate court's opinion.

Rules for when subsequent history should be included, as well as abbreviations for the procedural phrases, are given in ALWD rule 12.8 and Bluebook rule 10.7. Generally, subsequent history is needed when a case is affirmed, enforced (by a court after an administrative decision), reversed, overruled, or vacated. Contrary to what you might expect, a denial of certiorari is usually not needed, because it affects precedential value only slightly. The vast majority of petitions for a writ of certiorari are denied. A denial means only that the court did not feel that the case was important enough for it to examine or did not feel that the mistakes made by the court below were serious enough to mandate correction. Therefore, unless the denial of certiorari was decided within the last two years or is particularly important to the discussion, it should be omitted.[12] A grant of a writ of certiorari, however, has some effect on the precedential value of an opinion, and should be included as subsequent history until the supreme court issues a decision affirming or reversing the original.

E. Short Citation Forms

The purpose of a short citation form is to avoid unnecessary duplication of information while still making it easy for the reader to locate the authority being cited accurately and quickly. There are three (and only three) short forms for citations to case law:

1. short name, volume and reporter, at pinpoint: *Lestina*, 501 N.W.2d at 34
2. volume and reporter, at pinpoint: 501 N.W.2d at 34
3. *id.* or *id.* at pinpoint, if a different page is being cited: *id.* at 34

Because the purpose of a citation is to enable the reader to locate authority easily and accurately, the correct short form in any particular instance is the one that fulfills both goals. Start with the most complete short form, and then move to the less complete ones if the reader does not need the additional information. For example, if the case has not been cited for a while, and other authorities have been cited in the interim, form 1 is appropriate because it gives the reader the necessary information and prevents confusion. This short form is always appropriate. Use the second form only if the short-form name of the case was given in the textual sentence and the reader will not be confused about which case is being cited:

> *Lestina* involves a soccer game. 501 N.W.2d at 34.

The third form, *id.*, should be used only if the reader cannot possibly be confused, because the immediately preceding source was the same. If any other source intervenes between the two citations, then the second citation must follow **Form 1**.

---

[11] Bluebook rule 10.7.

[12] Bluebook rule 10.7; ALWD 12.8(7).

DISCUSSION NOTES OR EXERCISES: FINDING AND CITING CASE LAW

A. *Scavenging from secondary sources*

1. Look for an Iowa case involving a paintball accident much like Chumley's (from the exercises in Chapter 5) in the following secondary sources and give the correct citation to that case:
   a. Restatement (Second) of Torts
   b. Am. Jur. Proof of Facts
   c. A.L.R.5th
2. Look for an Ohio case involving an allergy attack caused by a McDonald's McLean Deluxe burger much like Mrs. Brown's (from the exercises in Chapter 5) in the following secondary sources and give the correct citation to that case:
   a. *Madden & Owens on Products Liability*
   b. Am. Jur. 2d

B. *Using citators*

1. *Broadening research with citators*

KeyCite or Shepardize each of the following cases and locate the indicated citing authority. Give the correct citation for the citing authority.

a. *Hanlon v. Lane*, 648 N.E.2d 26 (Ohio Ct. App. 1994); look for a 1999 Ohio case involving McDonald's.
b. *Bourque v. Duplechin*, 331 So. 2d 40 (La. Ct. App. 1976); look for a 1987 Ohio case.
c. *Lestina v. West Bend Mut. Ins. Co.*, 501 N.W.2d 28 (Wis. 1993); look for a Wisconsin law review article discussing it at length.

2. *Locating and understanding subsequent authority*

KeyCite or Shepardize each of the following cases and explain whether the case is still good law. Explain as well any subsequent authority and give a full citation to the case, including the citation to appropriate subsequent authority.

a. *Husain v. Olympic Airways*, 316 F.3d 829 (9th Cir. 2002).
b. *Marathon Oil Co. v. Ruhrgas, A.G.*, 115 F.3d 315 (5th Cir. 1997).

3. *Using citators to measure the importance and timeliness of a case*

Look up *Hoffman v. Red Owl Stores, Inc.*, 133 N.W.2d 267 (Wis. 1965). Skim through the opinion quickly so that you know generally what happened and what the issues were, and then check the case with a citator. Is this case still good law? How do you know?

4. *Using subject indexes*

a. You are in Michigan. Your client, an 11-year-old, hurt his knee when his soccer coach fell on it during a scrimmage. Using subject lists, locate mandatory authority.
   (1) Cite the case.
   (2) What subject or Key Number worked?

b. You are in Wisconsin. Your client's knee was injured in a recreational soccer game when a member of the opposing team slide-tackled him.
   (1) Cite the case.
   (2) What subject or Key Number worked?

c. Were the subjects you used to find these cases the same? If not, what does that tell you about the indexing system?

5. *Using term searches to locate case law*

You are in Nevada. Your client was riding a horse in a hunting-dog training exercise when she was kicked and injured by another rider's horse. Using either Boolean or natural-language searches, or both, find mandatory authority.

a. Cite the case.

b. Would either subject or Key Number used in exercise 4 have worked? Why or why not?

CHAPTER 7

Researching and Interpreting Constitutions, Statutes, Regulations, and International Law

This chapter explains how to find and research constitutions, statutes, and regulations and how they are interpreted in the United States. It also gives guidance on researching international and arbitration law, fields that are of growing importance in the United States. Experience shows that although attorneys in other countries use some of the same interpretive methods, the U.S. focus on legislative history and other methods of interpretation is unusual.

I. STATUTE, REGULATION, OR CASE LAW: WHICH IS IT?

Although this text focused first on case law and how to find it, in the United States, as in most countries, the amount of statutory law has increased to the extent that most court decisions involve the application or interpretation of statutes.[1] Thus, as one advisor explains, "[w]hen you venture into the real world it is much more likely that you will be researching a statute rather than a case."[2] The researcher's first concern, therefore, is to determine whether the client's problem is controlled by statutory or case law. Research into secondary authorities will often indicate that a statute is involved. However, before you begin research in secondary sources, it helps to have some generic understanding of which areas of U.S. law tend to be statute-driven, which run by regulations, and which are more likely to be driven by case law.

Traditional areas of common law include contracts, torts, and property law. Furthermore, these are also traditional areas of state, as opposed to federal, law.

[1] Louisiana rejected Article 2 of the UCC, on Sales of Goods (because of its mixed-civilian tradition), but amended its Civil Code to minimize friction with the other 49 states. It has otherwise adopted most of the UCC.

[2] *See* Guido Calabresi, *A Common Law for the Age of Statutes* (Harvard Univ. Press 1982) (discussing the impact this growth of legislation has had on courts).

State statutes affect these areas when there has been friction with commerce or public policy. For example, to facilitate interstate commerce, all 50 states in the United States have enacted their own versions of the Uniform Commercial Code (UCC) to deal with sales contracts.[3] Tort law is based largely on case law, except with regard to strict products liability and an increasing number of tort reform statutes that limit damages in some way. Property law has come to be dominated by statute in the process of developing systems to efficiently record the sale, mortgage, or other encumbrance of real (immovable) property.[4] Family and inheritance law, like contracts, torts, and property law, are largely regulated by state, as opposed to federal, government. However, because of public policy concerns, they, like property law, are largely dependent upon statutes.

In a number of fields, one should look first for statutes and then for cases that have interpreted those statutes. Whether state or federal, civil procedure is code-based, as are business law and securities regulation (Securities and Exchange Commission law is purely federal). Bankruptcy law is based primarily on a federal code. Federal and state criminal and tax law must, under constitutional principles, be based on statutes. The latter two areas of law developed the way they did because of the history of the United States War of Independence (1776). Several of the strictures in the first ten Amendments to the Constitution were designed to prevent what the founders saw as excessive prosecutorial powers. Furthermore, the famous revolutionary rallying cry was "No taxation without representation!"

When statutes result in the creation of agencies, the regulations created by those agencies are also law. For example, immigration law is driven by both statutes and regulations, as is environmental law. (Immigration law is solely the power of the federal government, whereas both states and the federal government enact environmental law.) Social security law is regulatory in nature. The Internal Revenue Service (IRS) and the Securities and Exchange Commission (SEC) have both created a large body of regulations, as well as "opinion" letters, which are quasi-statutory or quasi-regulatory in nature. As explained in Chapter 4, regulations issued by an executive agency must be within the scope of the rule-making mandate delegated to that agency by the legislature. They must also comport with the notice and an opportunity to be heard stricture of the U.S. Constitution's Fifth Amendment.

In sum, once the researcher has determined which area of law applies, she will already have some idea of whether the applicable law will be statute-, regulation-, or case-law-based. The nature of the problem will often determine whether the researcher should look for state law, federal law, or both. Additionally, research into secondary authority will indicate whether a particular legal issue is governed by statute, regulation, case law, or an amalgam.

Remember that even if a statute controls, under stare decisis, all cases interpreting that statute are also primary authority and must be both researched and interpreted.

[3] Robert C. Berring & Elizabeth A. Edinger, *Legal Research Survival Manual* 79 (West Group 2002).

[4] For an interesting comparative study of the effect of property law on various countries' economic situations, see Hernando de Soto, *The Mystery of Capital: Why Capitalism Triumphs in the West and Fails Everywhere Else* (Basic Books 2000).

II. RESEARCHING CONSTITUTIONS

The United States Constitution is the supreme law of the land.[5] It establishes the framework of the U.S. federal government; divides power between the federal government and the states, as well as among the three branches of the federal government; and announces principles that bind the federal government, the states, local governments, and private individuals. It also is a pattern for state constitutions. The text of the U.S. Constitution can be found in any number of places: encyclopedias, various versions of the U.S. Code, at the front of most state codes, in separately published pamphlets, on the Internet, on CD-ROM products, and on the various commercial databases. Westlaw and LEXIS often distribute free and convenient "pocket constitutions" to students in U.S. law schools.

A substantial amount of commentary is also available. Both the *United States Code Annotated* (U.S.C.A.) and the *United States Code Service* (U.S.C.S.) provide clause-by-clause commentary on the U.S. Constitution, listing cross-references, providing research guides, and listing interpretive notes and decisions. Another source of constitutional commentary is the *Constitution of the United States of America: Analysis and Interpretation*, published by the Government Printing Office. The commentary it contains is more in-depth than that provided by the annotated codes. Finally, there are a number of good treatises on the U.S. Constitution.

State constitutions are also primary authority. Furthermore, they are the supreme law of the state in which they are enacted. Like the U.S. Constitution, a state's constitution creates that state's government, divides power among the three branches of that government, and binds both the government and the people of that state to the legal principles it announces. A state constitution is allowed to provide more protection (more rights) to the people of its state, but not less than the federal Constitution. Furthermore, because the U.S. Constitution guarantees all states a republican form of government,[6] all state constitutions must establish a republic.

The easiest place to find a copy of a particular state's constitution is in the statutory code for that state. Many state codes are annotated, and the state's constitution is likely to be annotated on a clause-by-clause basis, just as the U.S.C.S. and U.S.C.A. do for the federal constitution. Furthermore, each state usually includes its constitution on its state government Web site, which can be located easily either with a generic search or through the links provided by Cornell, Findlaw, or other Internet legal crawlers.

To find mandatory and persuasive case law interpreting a constitution, use the same methods described in § III of this chapter for statutory law. Be aware, however, that case law interpreting U.S. constitutions, especially case law involving individual rights, can be voluminous, seemingly contradictory, and particularly difficult to interpret; therefore, seek additional help with interpretation from secondary sources.

[5] U.S. Const. art. VI, cl. 2.
[6] U.S. Const. art. IV, § 4.

III. RESEARCHING STATUTES

A. Locating Statutes

1. *Scavenge from Secondary Sources*

If Stage 1 research into secondary sources indicated that a statute is controlling law for the client's problem, it is also likely that the same secondary source gave the citation to that statute. Even if reading the statute given by the secondary source shows that it is not the correct one, the correct statute may be in the same section of the code, and it is therefore well worth examining not only the cited statute but also associated statutes. Among the various secondary sources, A.L.R. annotations often prove to be particularly useful in leading the researcher to the appropriate statute, but treatises, law review articles, and other secondary sources can also be helpful.

CHECKLIST FOR STATUTORY RESEARCH

- ☐ 1. Scavenge from secondary sources.
- ☐ 2. Use subject indexes to locate controlling statute.
- ☐ 3. Analyze associated statutes.
- ☐ 4. Locate and analyze noted cases in annotations.
- ☐ 5. Use citators to update and broaden case research.
- ☐ 6. Use term and sentence-form searches.
- ☐ 7. Research legislative history if needed.

2. *Use Subject Indexes to Locate Controlling Statute*

Although neither the U.S. federal government nor any of the individual states (except for Louisiana and Puerto Rico) uses a "Civil Code" in the traditional sense, all statutes are organized into various codes. Looking for statutes in a code is quite straightforward. If research into secondary sources did not yield the controlling statute, then break up the issue into relevant terms and phrases, just as for any legal issue, and (on hard copy) research those terms either in the appropriate code's table of contents, the index, or both. In the *United States Code*, first locate the appropriate title, and then use the table of contents for that title, or work with the index. If given a choice, use an annotated version. Alternatively, if you have the popular name of an act, you might look up that phrase in the popular name index of a hard-copy version. An example of a popular name might be "white-slave laws."

In commercial computerized research systems, the same subject index methods used to locate cases will work for statutes, though not the same mechanisms. West's Key Search system works only for case law. To search a code, use the "Table of

Contents" feature to locate the appropriate legal source. Continuous clicking of the small box symbols to the left of the list selectively expands sections of the table. For example, to locate federal crimes involving firearms, first choose federal, as opposed to state, international, or secondary sources. Then choose the U.S.C.A, then Title 18, and then chapter 14 (on firearms offenses). On LEXIS, if one ignores the term-search option and instead clicks the circled + signs, the process is the same. Once you have located the controlling statute through either Westlaw or LEXIS, you will find that the annotations are exactly the same as in the hard-copy versions of their respective annotated codes. The codes' tables of contents are often more useful than the commercial subject indexes. If hard copy is unavailable, the noncommercial and government databases might be a better first choice than one of the commercial ones, because the subject indexes are more easily accessed and simpler to read.

If searching secondary sources and subject indexes fails to produce the controlling statute, try locating it through case law research using some of the methods given in Chapter 6. Cases that interpret statutes must, of necessity, cite those statutes; and any statute that has been on the books at least one year is likely to have interpretive case law.

3. *Analyze Associated Statutes*

Once you identify the controlling statute, be sure to locate and read associated statutes. Generally, any one statute or section is only one of several interrelated statutes — each given a different section number, but all of which must be read together. For example, in the U.S. Code, often the first statute on a particular topic describes the purpose of the original act. The next section is frequently a list of definitions that apply to the topic. To interpret the controlling statute, you may need both purposive and definitional statutes, as well as any others that relate to the controlling statute.

After locating all related statutes, and before proceeding to look for interpretive case law, analyze the statutory scheme, thinking through how the statutes were designed to work together. Thus, if you are researching 18 U.S.C. § 924(c)(1), on the use or carrying of a firearm in connection with a drug-trafficking crime, look for statutes defining each term in the crime, what penalties are possible, the statute of limitations, and any other statutes necessary to make sense of that specific statutory section. Sometimes a statute will contain internal references to other statutes, which should also be researched. Furthermore, annotations may cross-reference still more statutes that should be researched. Collecting, analyzing, and organizing all necessary statutes before turning to interpretive case law and returning to secondary sources helps to prevent confusion and helps the researcher update and reorganize the research plan efficiently.

4. *Locate and Analyze Noted Cases in Annotations*

After analyzing the statutory scheme, skim through the noted cases in the annotations of the controlling statute. Note which portions of the statute have been litigated, check what the issues have been, and look for mandatory and highly persuasive case law. If the statute has been interpreted by a large number of cases, there might be a table of contents that simplifies the process by organizing the noted cases. If this is so, look up only the cases that involve issues relevant to your understanding of the statute or the client's problem.

5. *Use Citators to Update and Broaden Case Research*

The citators on Westlaw and LEXIS update statutes, as well as list sources citing them. Updating statutes in commercial computer databases is particularly simple because amendments are posted immediately, and a note is attached to the heading of the affected statute to show that an amendment is pending. Thus, citators are not as crucial for updating statutes as they are for updating cases. However, citators can be convenient and effective research tools for locating interpretive case law.

6. *Use Term and Sentence-Form Searches*

Researching annotations and citations yields some of the cases interpreting a statute. However, those results may still be incomplete. Thus, it is still sensible to perform some term or sentence-form searches to verify that you have found all informative and important cases interpreting a statute. One can use the statute citation as a search term, or key words from the statute, or both.

7. *Research Legislative History If Needed*

When a statute is new, there will be very little interpretive case law on it, so courts must look to other sources for interpretation. One source is the body of documents generated during the time the bill was being considered for passage. Documents generated during that time are termed *legislative history*, and are discussed, along with other principles of interpretation, in § V of this chapter.

B. Congressional Powers and the Legislative Process

1. *Structure and Functions of Congress*

The United States Congress, like the legislatures of most (if not all) of the 50 states, is a bicameral institution created by the United States Constitution. It is composed of the Senate and the House of Representatives. The House of Representatives is the lower house. It was designed to be more representative of the people: The number of representatives is based on the population of each state, so more populous states have more representatives. Each representative serves a two-year term, with reelection possible for an infinite number of terms.[7] As delineated by the Constitution, the House has some exclusive powers. For example, it has the sole power to initiate an impeachment of the president and other federal officials,[8] and it alone can initiate legislation that spends federal money.[9] With regard to other legislation, however, either the House or the Senate can initiate new laws, but any proposed bill must be passed by both houses before it can become law.[10]

---

[7] U.S. Const. art. I, § 2, cl. 1.
[8] U.S. Const. art. I, § 2, cl. 5.
[9] U.S. Const. art. I, § 7, cl. 1.
[10] U.S. Const. art. I, § 7, cl. 2.

The Senate is the higher house and purportedly representative of the states, as opposed to the people. Each state elects two senators.[11] Senators serve terms of six years, with the possibility of reelection. The Senate has certain powers that the House does not. For example, although the House must initiate an impeachment, only the Senate can try the impeached official.[12] Furthermore, the Senate ratifies treaties and confirms major presidential appointees.[13]

2. How a Bill Becomes Law

The Constitution does not provide much detail on how a bill is made into a law. It provides only that "[e]very Bill which shall have passed the House of Representatives and the Senate, shall, before it become a Law, be presented to the President of the United States."[14] If the President approves of the bill, it becomes law once he signs it. If he does not approve, then he returns it to Congress, along with his objections. After reconsideration, Congress may then make it law if the bill passes both chambers with a two-thirds majority.[15] The process is graphically plotted in Figure 6-1.

As mentioned earlier, a member of either chamber of Congress can initiate a bill. Once a bill is introduced, it is usually referred to an appropriate committee, and from there to the appropriate subcommittee. The committee or subcommittee considers the bill, collects information about the problem the proposed law will address, hears testimony from various parties both for and against the bill, and modifies the language of the bill in accord with its findings. If the committee feels that the proposed bill is still not passable, then it lets the bill die. However, if the committee votes to recommend the bill, it then submits the bill along with a report of its recommendations to the entire chamber.

In the House of Representatives, once they leave the committee, controversial bills go to the Rules Committee so that it can schedule debate, amendment, and voting (known as *floor action*) by the full House. Some bills are "privileged" and go directly to the floor. Other procedures exist for routine bills. The process is more streamlined in the Senate.

After the bill passes one chamber of Congress, it is then submitted to the other, and goes through the same process once again. Sometimes, a bill is introduced into both houses of Congress at the same time. If both houses pass the bill in the exact same form, it is then submitted to the President for signature, and becomes law once signed. If the Senate's version of the bill differs in any way from the House's, it is sent to a joint committee where a compromise bill is drafted; the changed bill must be voted upon before being submitted to the President.

This lengthy and complicated process was originally designed to minimize the amount of legislation passed, as well as to ensure that both the people as a whole and

---

[11] U.S. Const. art. I, § 3, cl. 1.

[12] U.S. Const. art. I, § 3, cl. 6.

[13] U.S. Const. art. II, § 2, cl. 2.

[14] U.S. Const art. I, § 7, cl. 2.

[15] *Id.* The President can either accept or reject the bill in total; he cannot revise it. Though a line-item veto power passed Congress once, it was rejected by the Supreme Court as unconstitutional. *See Clinton v. New York City*, 524 U.S. 417 (1998).

FIGURE 7-1
HOW A BILL BECOMES A LAW*

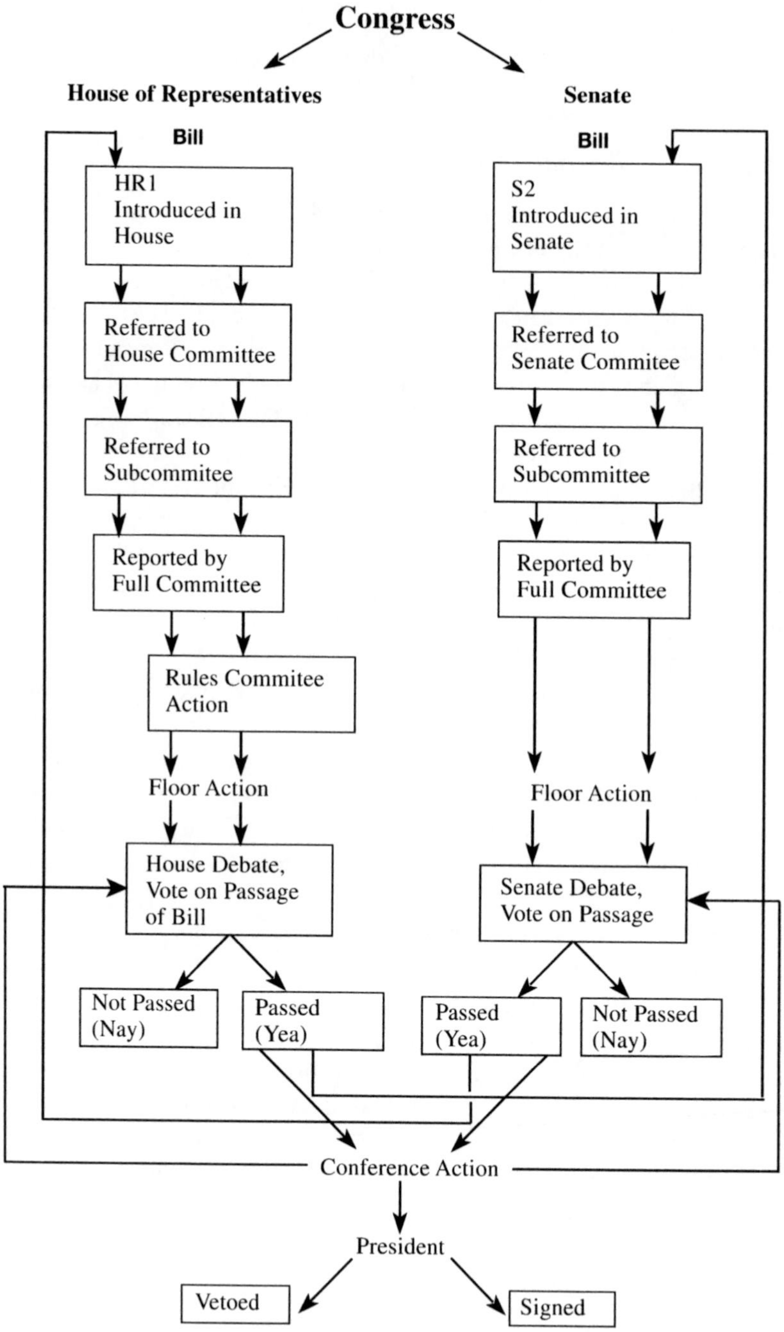

* Adapted from *How a Bill Becomes Law*, Congressional Quarterly Guide to Congress, App. 92-A (4th ed. 1991).

the states have significant input into any federal legislation.[16] Two aspects of the process periodically draw attention and controversy. First, there is no law about what a bill might contain, and some of the bills passed contain material completely unrelated to the ostensible original purpose of the bill — in other words, they contain a wide variety of new laws, only some of which conform to the original intent of the bill as introduced. Many such statutes show the effect of lobbying by various special interests. Furthermore, the President can either accept or reject the entire bill. He does not have a line-item veto and cannot accept some portions of a bill while rejecting others.[17] If he decides to reject a bill, his veto can be overridden only by a two-thirds vote of both houses.

3. *Researching New Statutes*

A new law is first published in "slip" form, a separately issued pamphlet that contains the text of a single legislative act. Each new law is given a Public Law number, consisting of the number of the Congress that passed it, then a hyphen, and then a number. Thus, Public Law 99-610 (abbreviated as Pub. L. No. 99-610) was the 610th statute passed by the 99th Congress. Once a particular legislative session has been completed, all of the laws it passed, termed *session laws*, are compiled and published in chronological order. Federal session laws are published in the *United States Statutes at Large*. Finally, the new laws are separated into individual statutes and added to the appropriate titles of the *United States Code*. Amendments to existing statutes follow exactly the same process, from bill to slip law to session law to code.

"Slip laws" can be found at the end of the government publication *Statutes at Large*; in the advance sheets for the U.S.C., U.S.C.A., and U.S.C.S.; and in the advance sheets for the *United States Code Congressional and Administrative News* (U.S.C.C.A.N.). However, all of these paper copies take several days to a few weeks to be distributed. Thus, the first place a new law is posted is on an electronic bulletin board accessible through the Internet. The federal government and a number of states post new legislative acts, in slip-law form, on the Internet. However, most states do not distribute hard-copy slip laws very widely.

Rather than reading every slip law issued, either in hard copy or on an electronic bulletin board, which would be inefficient and a waste of time, a researcher needs to be able to locate recent amendments to the statute she is researching. As you undoubtedly have already discovered, any amendments are indicated in both the official and annotated versions of the *United States Code*, immediately after the most current form, and it is usually a fairly simple process to see when and how a statute has been modified.

The careful researcher's concern, however, is to determine whether there has been a recent amendment, either in slip or session form, since the publication of the codified

[16] *See The Federalist* No. 58 (James Madison); *see also* Federalist No. 62 (discussing the role of Senate in comparison to the role of House of Representatives); *see also* correspondence between Jefferson and Madison representing Senate as saucer to cool off hot coffee of House. 3 Max Farrand, ed., *The Records of The Federal Convention of 1787*, 359 at CCXLIX (1911).

[17] *Clinton v. New York City*, 524 U.S. 417 (1998) (holding line-item veto unconstitutional).

version of the statute she has found. Updating hard-copy annotated statutes is somewhat tedious, but can be done and is accurate to within a few months. Many of the annotated codes have places for pocket parts—supplements to the bound volume that slide into the back and are replaced every few months. If there is a pocket part, then simply check the statute's listing for any amendments. If there is no pocket part, then the series is probably updated by softbound volumes and pamphlets filed at the end of the series. One may have to check several such volumes. Online, the commercial databases usually indicate an amendment within 24 hours of its passage, by putting a flag warning at the top of the statute. Clicking on the flag hyperlinks to the amended version.

IV. RESEARCHING AND UPDATING ADMINISTRATIVE REGULATIONS

Researching administrative rules and regulations is done with many of the same techniques as researching statutes, thus the same Checklist would apply. If you have located the general regulatory area, you can turn to Westlaw's RegulationsPlus, a tool much like its ResultsPlus. This excellent finding tool includes a table of contents feature, an index, and a section outline to help locate a controlling regulation as well as analyze associated regulations. It also lists noted cases, agency opinions, and decisions, and gives references to secondary sources and the *Federal Register.* So, for example, assume that you want to learn about how one might seek asylum in the United States. Using the C.F.R. database, a term search of *asylum /s immigration* yielded 67 documents, of which 8 C.F.R. § 208.1 described requirements for seeking asylum (it was the fourth listed document at the time of the author's search). Linking to that document showed its text on the right-hand side of the computer screen, and RegulationsPlus on the left. Another way to locate information about a regulatory area is to locate the appropriate statute in Westlaw or LEXIS and follow the links to associated regulations. Thus, pulling up 8 U.S.C.A. § 1101(a) (the applicable definitional statute for asylum) and then using "locate" to find references to asylum or refugee status led to the applicable C.F.R. regulations. LEXIS provides similar tools.

Although the commercial databases are very helpful, research into regulations must include a search of the applicable federal agency's official database. Using the previous asylum example, one could begin by going to *firstgov.gov* and following links to immigration. You would need to be aware that the appropriate agency is the United States Citizenship and Immigration Services (USCIS) and is part of Homeland Security. Once at the USCIS Web site, clicking the Laws and Regulations tab showed the availability not only of the appropriate statutes and C.F.R. sections, but also agency interpretations, BIA decisions, handbooks and manuals, and policy memoranda.

Finally, in researching administrative rules and regulations, review the information provided in Chapter 4 with regard to administrative law, due process, and enabling statutes.

V. INTERPRETING STATUTES

Generally, finding statutes and regulations in the United States is not as difficult as reading and interpreting them. Although there are a number of excellent drafting institutes, statutes in the United States are often long, difficult to navigate, and poorly worded, especially when compared to the simple eloquence of some other countries' Civil Codes. This may be one reason why common law jurisdictions regard legislation with disdain, in addition to a traditional avoidance of legislating unless absolutely necessary.[18] Navigating a statute in the United States often requires a meticulous analysis of its phrasing.

Chapter 3, in explaining how to synthesize cases, also showed one way in which U.S. courts approach the interpretation of a statute. The Harris "use or carrying of a firearm" problem synthesized several cases that interpreted the statute at issue. As you may have surmised, the first thing a court does is to read the statute in context. After ascertaining what seems to be the plain meaning of the statute, the court then looks for cases (mandatory and persuasive) that interpret the statute. A court will look for such cases regardless of whether the meaning of the statute is "plain," because both the statute and case law interpreting the statute are primary authority. If the court finds mandatory precedent and the question of law at issue is answered, then the inquiry goes no further. This was what happened with the Harris problem: Mandatory Supreme Court and Fifth Circuit cases interpreted every pertinent term of the statute. Therefore, no other authority was needed.

However, sometimes case law is only mildly persuasive, or does not explain the statutory language at issue, or is in some other way lacking. Courts then turn to other methods of statutory interpretation. United States courts combine three interpretive methods. They look to:

1. The language of the statute (the textual approach)
2. The purpose of the statute (the purposive approach)
3. Other policy considerations

---

[18] *See, e.g.*, the following comparison of British and French attitudes to biomedical legislation and regulation:

> There is in human nature a scale of different possible reactions to the slogan: from ethics to law. At one extreme is the temperament which feels, if it's wrong, we must legislate at once. Let us forbid it in the Penal Code, or at least write it into the Civil Code, and if we can't do either of those, then let us outlaw it in some other code or body of law, such as the Public Health code. The British think that is the French way.
>
> At the other extreme is the temperament which feels: if it's wrong, let us educate everybody to know that it is wrong, and that will surely solve the problem. At the very most, let us hope the professionals will regulate it in their own codes of practice; medical nursing and so on. Above all, *no new law*. The French think that is the British way.

Sev S. Fluss, "An International Overview of Developments in Certain Areas, 1984-1994," in *A Legal Framework for Bioethics* 13 (Cosimo Marco Mazzoni ed., Kluwer Law Int'l 1998) (emphasis added).

A. Plain Language

Justice Frankfurter once admonished his law students that the way to interpret is to "read the statute, read the statute, read the statute."[19] Using this method, jurists see if the meaning of the statute is "plain." If it is, then once case law has been examined to see how the statute has been interpreted in different factual situations, generally no further interpretation is needed. The underlying premise is that in a democracy, the legislature is omniscient and judges should refrain from interfering with the legislative will: "A court is not empowered to substitute its judgment for that of the legislature on matters of policy, nor to strike down a statute which is not manifestly unconstitutional even though the court may consider it unwise."[20] Thus, when faced with an unwise statute, a judge must still apply it, though he or she will do his very best to interpret it in as sensible a way as possible: "If my fellow citizens want to go to hell, I shall help them. That is my job."[21]

In theory, courts have the power to overturn an absurd statute as unconstitutional if it violates the Equal Protection Clause in the Fifth and Fourteenth Amendments to the United States Constitution: "nor shall any State . . . deny to any person within its jurisdiction the equal protection of the laws." This clause guarantees that similar individuals will be dealt with in a similar manner by both state and federal government.[22] If a statute is unfair because it treats people who are similarly situated in a dissimilar manner, it may be reviewed for constitutionality.[23] Statutes so reviewed are usually examined only to verify that the classification bears a "rational relationship to a legitimate state interest."[24] However, the Court has repeatedly said that this rational-basis review "is not a license for courts to judge the wisdom, fairness, or logic of legislative choices."[25] A statute so reviewed "must be upheld against equal protection challenge if there is *any reasonably conceivable state of facts that could provide a rational basis* for the classification."[26] In other words, a statute that is absurd, but based on a conceivably rational classification, will still be upheld as constitutional. Thus, because of separation-of-power concerns, statutes reviewed under this standard are only very rarely held to be unconstitutional. Statutes that classify people according to sex or gender are reviewed under a somewhat higher standard, and therefore are somewhat more likely to be overturned,[27] whereas statutes that discriminate on the basis of race or ethnicity are subject to "strict scrutiny" and will be ruled unconstitutional unless the government shows that they are justified by a "compelling" government interest.[28]

---

[19] R. Perry Sentell, Jr., *The Canons of Construction in Georgia: "Anachronisms" in Action*, 25 Ga. L. Rev. 365, 366 (1991) (quoting Frankfurter).

[20] Norman J. Singer, *Statutes and Statutory Construction* § 2.01, at 15-16 (4th ed. 1985).

[21] Attributed to Justice Oliver Wendell Holmes. R. Perry Sentell, Jr., *The Canons of Construction in Georgia: "Anachronisms" in Action*, 25 Ga. L. Rev. 365, 336 (1991).

[22] John E. Nowak & Ronald D. Rotunda, *Constitutional Law* 634 (6th ed., West Group 2000).

[23] *Id.* at 635.

[24] *Pennell v. City of San Jose*, 485 U.S. 1 (1988).

[25] *Heller v. Doe*, 509 U.S. 312, 319 (1993) (citations omitted).

[26] *Id.* (emphasis added).

[27] *Nguyen v. INS*, 533 U.S. 53, 60 (2001) (describing intermediate scrutiny as requiring that the challenged gender-based classification serve "important governmental objectives and the discriminatory means employed are substantially related to the achievement of those objectives.").

[28] *City of Richmond v. J.A. Croson Co.*, 488 U.S. 469, 493 (1989).

In practice, courts will do their best to interpret a statute in such a way that it will make sense and remain in keeping with its purpose, and they avoid constitutional issues if a decision can be made on any other basis. In doing so, U.S. courts occasionally reach beyond what courts in other countries would do. However, such "judicial legislation" is limited by a court's natural desire that its opinions not be overturned on review by a higher court.

Unfortunately, U.S. legislatures, including Congress, are not known for well-drafted legislation. Some statutes are easy to read, even if the case law that interprets them is vast, as with 28 U.S.C. § 1331: "The district courts shall have jurisdiction of all civil actions arising under the Constitution, laws, or treaties of the United States." Other statutes, however, are poorly constructed. Some are extremely long, badly organized, and difficult to untangle and analyze. They may list exceptions before giving the general rule, have a number of interdependent clauses, and include obscure terms and legalese. For example, examine the following statute:

> (c)(1)(A) Except to the extent that a greater minimum sentence is otherwise provided by this subsection or by any other provision of law, any person who, during and in relation to any crime of violence or drug trafficking crime (including a crime of violence or drug trafficking crime that provides for an enhanced punishment if committed by the use of a deadly or dangerous weapon or device) for which the person may be prosecuted in a court of the United States, uses or carries a firearm, or who, in furtherance of any such crime, possesses a firearm, shall, in addition to the punishment provided for such crime of violence or drug-trafficking crime—
>
> (i) be sentenced to a term of imprisonment of not less than 5 years;
>
> (ii) if the firearm is brandished, be sentenced to a term of imprisonment of not less than 7 years; and
>
> (iii) if the firearm is discharged, be sentenced to a term of imprisonment of not less than 10 years.
>
> (B) If the firearm possessed by a person convicted of a violation of this subsection—
>
> (i) is a short-barreled rifle, short-barreled shotgun, or semiautomatic assault weapon, the person shall be sentenced to a term of imprisonment of not less than 10 years; or
>
> (ii) is a machinegun or a destructive device, or is equipped with a firearm silencer or firearm muffler, the person shall be sentenced to a term of imprisonment of not less than 30 years.
>
> (C) In the case of a second or subsequent conviction under this subsection, the person shall—
>
> (i) be sentenced to a term of imprisonment of not less than 25 years; and
>
> (ii) if the firearm involved is a machinegun or a destructive device, or is equipped with a firearm silencer or firearm muffler, be sentenced to imprisonment for life.

(D) Notwithstanding any other provision of law—

(i) a court shall not place on probation any person convicted of a violation of this subsection; and

(ii) no term of imprisonment imposed on a person under this subsection shall run concurrently with any other term of imprisonment imposed on the person, including any term of imprisonment imposed for the crime of violence or drug trafficking crime during which the firearm was used, carried, or possessed.

(2) For purposes of this subsection, the term "drug trafficking crime" means any felony punishable under the Controlled Substances Act (21 U.S.C. 801 et seq.), the Controlled Substances Import and Export Act (21 U.S.C. 951 et seq.), or the Maritime Drug Law Enforcement Act (46 U.S.C. App. 1901 et seq.).

(3) For purposes of this subsection the term "crime of violence" means an offense that is a felony and—

(A) has as an element the use, attempted use, or threatened use of physical force against the person or property of another, or

(B) that by its nature, involves a substantial risk that physical force against the person or property of another may be used in the course of committing the offense.

(4) For purposes of this subsection, the term "brandish" means, with respect to a firearm, to display all or part of the firearm, or otherwise make the presence of the firearm known to another person, in order to intimidate that person, regardless of whether the firearm is directly visible to that person.

18 U.S.C. § 924(c) (2001). This is the same firearm crime discussed in so much detail in Chapter 3 but is almost unrecognizable in its original form. The excerpt itself is only a portion of § 924: the full statute contained complicated (a), (b), and (d) sections as well as (c), all dealing with penalties for various gun-related crimes. It is no wonder that one U.S. court complained: "All we can say is that in a world of silk purses and pigs' ears, [28 U.S.C. § 2264[29]] is not a silk purse of the art of statutory drafting."[30] Often, the best way to read a difficult statute is to read it three times and diagram it, going a bit beyond Justice Frankfurter's instructions, and then to look to the statutes referenced and put the one at issue in context.

B. Textualist Approach

After reading a statute carefully, and researching case law, if you find that the terms of the statute are still unclear, then you may wish to try the traditional textualist approach, which is to employ one or more of the canons of interpretation. One such canon is that

[29] § 2264. Scope of Federal review; district court adjudications.
[30] *Lindh v. Murphy*, 521 U.S. 320, 336 (1997).

"every word of a statute must be given significance; nothing in the statute can be treated as surplusage"; or "repeals by implication are not favored"; or "statutes in derogation of the common law will not be extended by construction." However, the canons of interpretation have themselves been strongly criticized in the United States as being ambiguous and susceptible to manipulation by judges desirous of a certain interpretation.

This criticism of the canons was made famous in the United States by a law review article written in 1960 by the legal scholar and professor (i.e., *jurist* in the classical sense) Karl Llewellyn, famous for drafting the Uniform Commercial Code. Llewellyn argued that to every canon there is an equal and opposite canon, and included a list that beautifully illustrated his argument (a portion of which is excerpted in Figure 7-2:[31]

FIGURE 7-2

Thrust	But	Parry
1. A statute cannot go beyond its text.		To effect its purpose, a statute may be implemented beyond its text.
2. Statutes in derogation of the common law will not be extended by construction.		Such acts will be liberally construed if their nature is remedial.
6. Statutes *in pari materia* must be construed together.		A statute is not *in pari materia* if its scope and aim are distinct or where a legislative design to depart from the general purpose or policy of previous enactments may be apparent.
12. If language is plain and unambiguous, it must be given effect.		Not when literal interpretation would lead to absurd or mischievous consequences or thwart manifest purpose.
16. Every word and clause must be given effect.		If inadvertently inserted or if repugnant to the rest of the statute, they may be rejected as surplusage.

Llewellyn argued that because of this inherent ambiguity, a court can manipulate the canons in any way it pleases to interpret a statute, and that interpretation may have very little to do with what the legislature originally intended.[32] Therefore, he concluded that a reliable statutory construction can be achieved only by using "the good sense of the situation and a *simple* construction of the available language to achieve that sense, *by tenable means, out of the statutory language*."[33] This criticism continues and is well

[31] Karl N. Llewellyn, *Remarks on the Theory of Appellate Decision and the Rules or Canons about How Statutes Are to Be Construed*, 3 Vand. L. Rev. 395, 399-406 (1950); *see also* Karl N. Llewellyn, *The Common Law Tradition* 521-35 (1960).

[32] Llewellyn, *Remarks*, 3 Vand. L. Rev. at 400.

[33] *Id.* at 401 (emphasis in original).

enough known in the legal literature to have made many judges hesitant to rely to any great extent on the canons, or at least hesitant to rely solely on them.[34]

C. Purposive Interpretation

In employing the purposive method, courts look to the purpose of the statute by researching *legislative history,* meaning documents that were generated while the law was making its way through the legislative process. Researchers look through those documents for information that indicates what the legislature's intent was in passing this law.

1. Documents Generated During the Legislative Process

Documents generated by Congress itself are published in the *Congressional Record* (abbreviated as C.R.). Some of these include the text of bills, floor debate transcripts and statements, and votes. When a bill is first introduced, it is given a number that indicates the house in which the bill was introduced (S. for Senate, H.R. for House of Representatives), the chronological number of the bill, the number of the Congress (each Congress lasts two years), the session (each Congress has two sessions), and the year. For example, S. 933, 101st Cong., 1st Sess. § 1 (1990), refers to section 1 of Senate Bill 933, introduced in the first session of the 101st Congress, in 1990. Numbers are consecutive for each session of Congress: Any bill not passed during a particular session dies and must be given a new number if it is reconsidered during the next session.

Documents are also generated when the bill is in committee. Committees generate hearing transcripts, committee prints, and committee reports. Hearing transcripts include the exact testimony of witnesses, as well as any documents the witnesses presented to the committee. Committee prints are written by committee research staffs, the Library of Congress, or independent consultants. They provide the committee with information such as statistics, scientific studies, historical data, bibliographies, bill comparisons, and other documents. Committee reports contain the committee's findings and recommendations. These documents are published, separate from the *Congressional Record,* in a number of different publications, and kept in government-document collections and libraries. Except for committee reports, which are available on the House and Senate Committee Web sites, Thomas, and Westlaw and LEXIS, one would probably need the help of a specialized government documents librarian to find these types of preparatory legislative documents.

2. Weight of Authority in Legislative History

The purpose of legislative history is to help determine what the legislature's purpose was in drafting a particular statute. Some of the documents generated along the way are more useful than others. For example, among the most useful are joint committee reports, because they often fully reflect the intentions of both houses

[34] *See* Richard A. Posner, Statutory Interpretation — *In the Classroom and In the Courtroom,* 50 U. Chi. L. Rev. 800, 805 (1983).

of Congress at the time the law was passed. A committee report issued by the committee that originally drafted the law as passed may be similarly useful; and a presidential statement issued at the time of the law's passage may also provide insight into what the statute was supposed to accomplish and what it was supposed to mean. However, testimony of someone who is not part of Congress, even if part of the floor debate, obviously does not carry nearly the weight of authority that a committee report would carry. In between are a variety of documents of various weight.

3. *How to Find Legislative History Documents*

As you may have surmised, it can be very difficult to compile a complete legislative history that includes all of the documents generated during a bill's passage into law. That task will likely require the help of an expert government documents librarian. However, such a complete history is usually unnecessary, especially in the normal course of legal research likely to be needed by an LL.M. graduate working with an average U.S. law firm. Therefore, only the most important and commonly used methods of legislative history research are presented here.

Some of the most important documents can be found reprinted in the *United States Code Congressional and Administrative News* (U.S.C.C.A.N.). Another legislative history research tool is the *Congressional Information Service* (CIS). The CIS is more complete than the U.S.C.C.A.N., in that it provides three means of access to legislative materials and even provides a list of all relevant legislative materials for each public law since 1970. Furthermore, it provides abstracts of the public law and major legislative materials. Both the U.S.C.C.A.N. and the CIS are used by referencing the Public Law number issued when the law was passed. You may remember that Public Law numbers are listed after the statutes in the U.S.C., the U.S.C.A., and the U.S.C.S., and are therefore fairly simple to access. U.S.C.C.A.N. is included in computer databases. It often includes the most persuasive committee report, and is usually enough for most legislative history research purposes.

However, sometimes the federal statute at issue is long and convoluted and has been amended a number of times with the result that it is difficult to find the Public Law number for that particular issue, and thus difficult to research by Public Law number. For example, a refugee should be granted asylum if he or she is "unable or unwilling to return to, and is unable or unwilling to avail himself or herself of the protection of, [his or her] country because of persecution or a well-founded fear of persecution on account of race, religion, nationality, membership in a particular social group, or political opinion ...." 8 U.S.C. § 1101(a)(42)(A). However, perusing the pertinent Westlaw U.S.C.A. material shows that not only is the statute very complicated, but also it has been amended a number of times. It is difficult or impossible to determine from the U.S.C.A. annotations when the "well-founded fear of persecution" language was added or what Congress intended that language to mean at the time. Research into pertinent A.L.R. sections shows that this phrase is key to a grant of asylum. In addition to the U.S.C.C.A.N. database, Westlaw also has a legislative history database. Using a term search of asylum /s fear produced a short list of 42 congressional committee reports, a number of which provided helpful insight into the history of congressional concerns about the grant of asylum. Again, LEXIS has similar proficiencies.

4. *Controversies Surrounding Legislative History*

Like the canons of interpretation, a certain amount of criticism surrounds the use of legislative history in interpreting statutes. A formal report issued by the committee that drafted the statute can be quite valuable and authoritative if it discusses the problem the legislature was trying to solve in passing the law. However, many documents generated during the legislative process lack any real authority, though they are sometimes used as persuasive authority by an attorney or judge who is intent on making a particular argument. For example, in considering a potential law, legislators listen to testimony from many different witnesses, including ordinary citizens, lobbyists, and members of other branches of the government. Furthermore, members of Congress, during floor debate, will often voice their individual opinions, or even voice lobbyists' concerns—simply because they know that their remarks will be recorded and possibly used as legislative history in the future, even if they fail to persuade the rest of the chamber.

Still, as part of the process of determining what the legislative intent was in passing an act, some of this information can be helpful. For example, in one case, Judge Learned Hand used the subcommittee testimony of a U.S. Army officer to help describe what the committee's concerns were at the time the legislation at issue was passed, shortly after World War II.[35] In and of itself, however, such testimony lacks any real authority because it is *not* the voice of the legislature. It is for this reason that some jurists (most notably Justice Scalia of the U.S. Supreme Court) have become highly critical of interpretations based primarily on legislative history.[36] Therefore, in researching legislative history, and in considering an interpretation based on legislative history, be very careful to weigh the authority of the document being relied upon before you draw conclusions about the meaning of a statute.

5. *Interpretations Based on Public Policy*

The third and final method of statutory interpretation is to consider the policy reasons for the statute and what effect a particular interpretation might have on that policy. Courts generally approach this method gingerly, as overuse can easily result in the criticism that they have overstepped their role and are legislating rather than adjudicating. However, this method can result in an interpretation that makes the most sense, especially when used in conjunction with other methods. When faced with a difficult statute, most courts use all four methods. They begin by reading the statute and examining prior case law. They then consider canons of interpretation, relevant legislative history, and policy concerns. In *Burns v. Alcala*,[37] the Court was

---

[35] *Fishgold v. Sullivan Drydock & Repair Corp.*, 154 F.2d 785, 789 (2d Cir. 1946).
[36] *See, e.g., Crosby v. National Foreign Trade Council*, 530 U.S. 363, 390 (2000) (Scalia, J., concurring: "Of course, even if all of the Court's invocations of legislative history were not utterly irrelevant, I would still object to them, since neither the statements of individual Members of Congress (ordinarily addressed to a virtually empty floor) nor Executive statements and letters addressed to congressional committees, nor the nonenactment of other proposed legislation, is a reliable indication of what a majority of both Houses of Congress intended when they voted for the statute before us.").
[37] 429 U.S. 575, 575 (1975).

faced with deciding whether an unborn child should be considered a child for purposes of child welfare assistance. The Court began by considering (1) the definitional statute, which was silent on the subject; and (2) prior case law, which was unhelpful.[38] The Court then turned to a canon of interpretation, which helped some.[39] That interpretation was reinforced by legislative history, including committee reports and a presidential message to Congress recommending the legislation.[40] Finally, noting the policy concern for the needs of pregnant women and the desirability of adequate prenatal care, the Court considered the fact that Congress had provided funding elsewhere for pregnant women and their infants as further evidence that it did not intend to duplicate that aid with the statute at issue.[41]

Statutory interpretation has been an issue of debate in the United States, at least among commentators, and new approaches are often considered, generally with the goal of limiting judicial activism. One issue that has been discussed is whether Congress should consider legislation on statutory interpretation, how Congress might collect the information it would need, and what such legislation might possibly contain, but nothing is currently pending.[42] Furthermore, given the underlying common law skepticism of codification discussed in Chapter 1, the author believes it unlikely that Congress could agree on such legislation or (in the absence of a large scandal) have any motive for passing such an act.

VI. INTERNATIONAL LAW AND TREATIES

As the globe shrinks, international law becomes increasingly important.[43] LL.M. candidates who are interested in studying American law are most aware of how globalization is affecting the legal profession, and most aware of the United States influence in this area.[44] It is hoped that knowledge of how to find and interpret U.S. legal authority will prove useful; nevertheless, attorneys who will be practicing in an international arena must also be capable of researching the law of multinational organizations, such as the United Nations, the World Trade Organization, the European Union, and other regional organizations, as well as the law of other countries.

[38] *Id.* at 579-80.
[39] *Id.* at 581.
[40] *Id.* at 582.
[41] *Id.* at 583.
[42] *See, e.g.*, Nicholas Quinn Rosenkranz, *Federal Rules of Statutory Interpretation*, 115 Harv. L. Rev. 2085 (2002); Richard A. Posner, *Reply: The Institutional Dimension of Statutory and Constitutional Interpretation*, 101 Mich. L. Rev. 952 (2003).
[43] *See generally* Detlev F. Vagts, "The Impact of Globalization on the Legal Profession," in *The Internationalization of the Practice of Law* 31-42 (Jens Drolshammer & Michael Pfeiferk eds., Kluwer Law Int'l 2001).
[44] *Id.* at 35.

A. Researching International Law Online

The Internet has dramatically changed international legal research.[45] Although international law sources have traditionally been difficult to identify and locate, many are now widely available through the Web sites of the United Nations and other international organizations. The United Nations Web site, *www.un.org*, provides much free information, including Security Council resolutions made since 1946, but a subscription is required to get access to the full text of resolutions from the General Assembly, Security Council, and Economic and Social Council, as well as other documents. However, many libraries worldwide are depositories for the U.N.'s CD-ROM service. The World Trade organization's Web site, *www.wto.org*, gives some background information, and makes available the basic documents governing the WTO's operations but, like the United Nations, makes access to decisions available only by subscription.

LEXIS and Westlaw are also valuable resources for researching international law. On LEXIS, simply choose the "International Sources" database, and choose from among a number of sub-databases, including U.N. documents, Celex (the legal site for the European Union), GATT, NAFTA, and U.S. treaties. Westlaw provides similar resources. Both sites include international journals, news sources, and case law interpreting international law, from U.S. as well as other courts. Some particularly useful non-fee Internet legal Web crawlers and research sites include *www.washlaw.edu*, *www.law.cornell.edu*, *www.law.harvard.edu*, *www.hg.org*, and *www.asil.org*.

B. U.S. Interpretations of International Law

Although treaties that the United States has signed and ratified are federal law, U.S. case law interpreting those treaties is also binding authority and must be considered when predicting how a U.S. court is likely to decide a problem involving an international treaty. Sometimes the interpretations of treaties can be surprising. For instance, as discussed previously, U.S rules of discovery give much broader power to attorneys than is given in most other countries, and these differences have caused international friction. The Hague Convention on the Taking of Evidence[46] attempted to resolve some of these differences.[47] However, the U.S. Supreme Court has held that the Convention's principles are permissive, not preemptive, and therefore do not displace normal discovery rules.[48]

Case law can also be inconsistent: U.S. courts may interpret a treaty in inconsistent ways. For instance, the United Nations Convention on Contracts for the International

---

[45] Morris L. Cohen & Kent C. Olson, *Legal Research in a Nutshell* 316 (8th ed. 2000).
[46] Hague Convention on the Taking of Evidence Abroad in Civil or Commercial Matters, *opened for signature* Mar. 18, 1970, 23 U.S.T. 2555, T.I.A.S. No. 7444.
[47] *Société Nationale Industrielle Aérospatiale v. United States Dist. Court*, 482 U.S. 522, 530 (1987).
[48] *Id.* at 539-40.

Sale of Goods (CISG)[49] stipulates that a court should consider all of the circumstances as well as the parties' subjective intent in interpreting a contract. This provision seemingly conflicts with the parol evidence rule, a common law principle stating that when a contract is written, oral evidence that varies the terms of that contract should not be considered. This conflict has been at issue in at least two cases in the United States, with differing results. In one case, the Fifth Circuit postulated that even if the CISG applied rather than Texas law, it did not necessarily displace the parol evidence rule.[50] In a later case, the Eleventh Circuit held that the CISG applied and therefore displaced the common law rule.[51] Thus, when researching how international law applies in a U.S. context, be sure to research case law interpreting it with the same care and diligence you would any other U.S. statute. (Incidentally, the Eleventh Circuit case is now widely known and so another decision side-stepping international law, like that of the earlier Fifth Circuit case, would be unlikely.)

EXERCISES

A. *Statutory interpretation*

Read *United States v. Scrimgeour*, 636 F.2d 1019 (5th Cir. 1981), and then answer the following questions in one or two detailed and specific but concise paragraphs:

1. What method or methods of statutory interpretation did the court use to interpret 18 U.S.C. § 1623?
2. How does this compare with generally accepted methods of statutory interpretation in your country?
3. Do you think the methodology was reasonable? What about the result? Why?

B. *Researching statutory law*

1. More "use or carrying"— coordinating statutory and case law research

Your client, Mr. Malcolm Woodrow, is charged with the "use or carrying of a firearm in connection with a drug trafficking crime." The applicable statute, as indicated by the Federal Prosecutor, is 18 U.S.C. § 924(c)(1)(A). Malcolm, a convicted felon, tells you that he wanted to purchase a gun to protect himself and his property, but could not legally do so because of his prior convictions. So he decided to buy the gun illegally. He approached his acquaintance, Max, and asked if he could buy a gun from him. Max said yes, that he would acquire a gun, and since Malcolm had no

[49] *Opened for signature* Apr. 11, 1980, S. Treaty Doc. No. 9, 98th Cong., 1st Sess. 22 (1983), 11 I.L.M. 671, *reprinted in* 15 U.S.C. app. 52 (1977).
[50] *Beijing Metals & Minerals Imp./Exp. Corp. v. American Bus. Ctr., Inc.*, 993 F.2d 1178 (5th Cir. 1993).
[51] *MCC-Marble Ceramic Ctr., Inc. v. D'Agostino*, 144 F.3d 1384 (11th Cir. 1998).

money, said that Malcolm could pay for the gun with illegal drugs. Malcolm later gave Max 24 doses of OxyContin, a prescription pain killer that has a high street value. Malcolm had a prescription for OxyContin because he suffers with severe back pain, but wanted the gun so badly that he was willing to sell some of his pills. In exchange for the pills, Max gave Malcolm an unloaded pistol. Malcolm was immediately arrested, because Max was a government informant. Is Malcolm likely to be convicted of this crime?

2. The man with the alligator bags (researching wildlife protection statutes promulgated in accord with an international treaty)

Your client, Mr. Lionel Boudreaux, has an alligator farm, and sells tanned alligator hides. Wanting to expand his business to include the sale of finished articles, he contacted a French firm that turns the hides into purses. The French firm agreed to make purses out of Boudreaux's alligator hides, but also wanted him to buy some of its ready-made Nile crocodile bags. Boudreaux agreed, and imported some of the crocodile purses to sell along with his alligator bags in his new leather-goods shop, relying on the representations of the French firm that the only crocodile used was taken legally under Egyptian law. He has now learned that Egyptian law prohibits the export of the particular species of crocodile used to make the bags, and is concerned that he may have violated U.S. conservation law by importing the crocodile bags. Your research in secondary sources has suggested the following issues to research in federal statutes. Find the statutes and answer the questions:

a. Is Boudreaux violating U.S. law by importing wildlife from a country that prohibits its export?
b. What civil and criminal penalties might he face?
c. Are the crocodile bags subject to forfeiture?
d. If so, might he have an "innocent owner" defense against forfeiture of the bags (so that he can send them back to France and ask the French company to reimburse him)? Locate a case that answers this question by relying on legislative history (look for a case involving parakeets). Cite both the case and the legislative history document.
e. What international treaty led to the promulgation of these statutes?

3. Researching U.S. bankruptcy law

You are a new associate. The partner you work for has approached you with the following problem. Our new client is a large bank, Moneypenny Bank Ltd. ("Moneypenny"). It does business in Tobango, a large, sophisticated island and sovereign entity in the Pacific Ocean, and has extended that business to the United States. Moneypenny extended a loan for more than $24 million (U.S.) to an international company incorporated in the British Virgin Islands and doing business in Tobango. The major shareholder of that company, Arthur Flybinight, a United States citizen, personally guaranteed the loan. Paragraph 15 of that guarantee provides:

> This guarantee and all rights, obligations, and liabilities arising hereunder shall be construed and determined under and may be enforced in accord with the laws of

> Tobango. I hereby agree that the Tobango Courts shall have jurisdiction over all disputes arising under the guarantee and irrevocably appoint Rabbitt & Warren of 1001 Hutchhouse, Tobango, to be my agent for the purpose of accepting service of the process hereunder.

When he executed the guarantee, Flybinight lived and operated his company in Tobango. Under the loan agreement, Flybinight was to satisfy the loan in full within one year. Instead, facing personal debts of more than $200 million, he traveled back to the United States and filed personal bankruptcy under Chapter 7 of the United States Bankruptcy Code.

Moneypenny's first law firm filed a proof of claim in U.S. bankruptcy court in the amount of $37 million, which accounted for its share in a second, separate $150 million syndicated bank loan. However, Moneypenny did not file a proof of claim for Flybinight's personal guarantee of the $24 million loan, nor did it object to the U.S. bankruptcy court's order discharging all of Flybinight's debts. That order included the following standard injunction: "All creditors whose debts are discharged by this order . . . are enjoined from instituting or continuing any action or employing any process or engaging in any act to collect such debts as personal liabilities of the above-named debtor (in accord with 11 U.S.C. § 524(a)(2))."

Moneypenny has just learned that Flybinight's wife remained in Tobango with $30 million, and wants to know if there will be any problem pursuing that money in Tobango to satisfy the $24 million loan. Your law partner remembers something about U.S. bankruptcy law, but is relying on your gaining knowledge of the extraterritorial reach of U.S. bankruptcy law. Be sure to research case law and secondary authority (especially law review articles) in addition to statutory authority. **Hint: the easiest way to approach this problem is to find one of the law review articles on point and scavenge its citations to find mandatory authority.**

a. Cite a case on point
b. Cite one or more law review articles on point
c. Could Moneypenny argue a fraud exception to the injunction and re-open the bankruptcy? Under what statute?

C. Administrative law

The following exercise requires research into administrative law materials. The most efficient approach may be to use a combination of Westlaw or LEXIS and the appropriate agency Web site.

1. Petitioning for asylum

Tatiana, a citizen of Belarus, applied for and was granted a nonimmigrant student visa to study in the United States at New York University. Before she left Belarus, she was a member of a group that demonstrated against the current administration, and was threatened with imprisonment by the Belarus KGB. Since that time, the political situation has deteriorated and she is afraid to return home—her father was fired from his job because of Tatiana's activities, her parents' phone is tapped, and the letters she sends her family disappear en route.

a. What federal statute authorizes foreign citizens to petition for entry as a nonimmigrant in order to study or teach?
b. What regulation concerning documentary requirements states that a nonimmigrant like Tatiana must present a valid passport and a valid visa in order to be admitted into the United States?
c. What regulation sets out the necessary qualifications for admittance? (I.e., what regulation indicates that Tatiana, as a student, needed a J1 visa?)
d. What statute enables the Secretary of Homeland Security to set such regulations?
e. 8 C.F.R. § 208.1 sets out the requirements for asylum. Does Tatiana seem to be qualified for a grant of asylum? Why?
f. How must Tatiana go about petitioning? Is there a handbook that explains the process?
g. If Tatiana's petition is denied by both the Immigration Judge and the BIA, is there case law that indicates a court might question the Agency's findings of fact? (I.e., can you find a case on point?)

D. International treaties

1. Convention on Contracts for the International Sale of Goods

Max, a retailer of ceramic tiles in Miami, Florida, went to a ceramics show and was thrilled by some Italian tiles. He was sure that his customers would love to buy them, so he and the Italian manufacturer started negotiating. At the show, he and the manufacturer's salesman reached an agreement about what kind of tiles, how many, and how much they would cost. Then the salesman had Max sign the Italian manufacturer's sales form. Max could not read Italian, but the salesman assured him that the Italian was the same as the agreement they had reached in English. When the tiles arrived in Miami, the entire order was wrong and Max refused to pay for them. The Italian manufacturer is now suing him. Under Florida law, Max's evidence about an oral agreement would be precluded by something called "parol evidence," meaning that if the parties intended a written agreement to state their entire contract, then oral evidence about agreements before the writing are inadmissible. However, your partner thinks that this agreement might be covered by the Vienna Convention on the International Sale of Goods, and wants to know:

A. Does the Convention cover this agreement?
B. If so, can Max use evidence of the oral agreement in his defense? (In researching this issue, be sure to look for both the text of the Convention and interpretive case law in the United States.)

BIBLIOGRAPHY

Berring, Robert C., & Elizabeth A. Edinger. *Finding the Law.* 11th ed. West Group 1999.

Berring, Robert C., & Elizabeth A. Edinger. *Legal Research Survival Manual.* West Group 2002.

de Soto, Hernando. *The Mystery of Capital: Why Capitalism Triumphs in the West and Fails Everywhere Else.* Basic Books 2000.

Fine, Toni M. *American Legal Systems: A Resource and Reference Guide.* Anderson 1997.

Greenawalt, Kent. *Legislation Statutory Interpretation: 20 Questions.* Foundation Press 1999.

Mazzoni, Cosimo Marco, ed. *A Legal Framework for Bioethics.* Kluwer Law International 1998.

Mersky, Roy M., & Djonald J. Dunn. *Legal Research Illustrated.* 8th ed. Foundation Press 2002.

CHAPTER 8

Rewriting and Style

I. UNITED STATES LEGAL WRITING RHETORIC

A. The Ideal

The ideal American legal writing style is clear, concise, and easily read. The reader should understand everything easily upon the first reading, find that the statements of law are based on thorough research, and find the arguments both easy to follow and convincing. The goal of either a law firm memo or a court brief is to convince the reader of two things quickly and completely: (1) that the writer thoroughly understands this particular area of law, and (2) that the writer has correctly applied the law to the facts of the problem at issue. If the writing is complicated or difficult to understand, the reader will not be convinced of either these two things.

Typically, the reader has very little time, suffers a great number of distractions, and is annoyed at having to read another legal document. The reader wants you, the writer, to explain your case quickly, completely, and convincingly so that she can get back to the other cases she is considering. Similarly, if the document you are writing is intended to persuade a court, the court wants to know right away what it is you want and why your client is entitled to that relief. Arguments in these kinds of documents must be clear, well-grounded in law, and easy to follow so that the reader (1) constantly knows where you are in your argument, (2) knows where you are going, and (3) finds it difficult to argue against your legal reasoning. Complicated sentences, long words, and elaborate introductions will frustrate this aim. Keep your sentence structure simple and eliminate fancy words. Get directly to your point. Let the reader know, at every stage, where you are and where you are going, using transitional phrases and sentences.

If you come from a culture in which the rhetorical style is intended to be a slow, gentle, polite, and gradual leading of the reader, you may find this very American style abrasive or at least uncomfortable. However, this directness has its own underlying civility. You are, in a sense, telling the reader that you know he or she is very busy, so you will take up as little of his or her time as possible by stating immediately what you want, and explaining simply and convincingly why your arguments should be accepted.

B. The Reality

This being said, much American legal writing is poorly done. Often this is due to the writer's lack of skill or lack of time. However, occasionally ambiguity and lack of clarity are an advantage. For example, a bill may be more likely to be passed into law if it can be interpreted in more than one way; likewise, a contract may be more acceptable to both parties if its ambiguity makes it more flexible. Occasionally, a client expects complicated language from an attorney, and may feel cheated because the will the lawyer drafted is so easy to understand that he wonders if he could have written it without the lawyer's help. Nevertheless, these are exceptions to the rule: Most people want a will that expresses their wishes simply and thereby avoids problems for their heirs.

Most people also understand that good, clear writing takes a lot of effort. Writing well will ensure success in a U.S. LL.M. program and make you a more attractive candidate for an internship with a U.S. law firm, if that is your aim. Furthermore, it will help you communicate effectively with U.S. attorneys in your future career, wherever that may be.

II. REWRITING

Ernest Hemingway reputedly said, "There is no such thing as good writing. There is only good rewriting." The only way to achieve good, clear, easy-to-read writing is through rewriting and then more rewriting. Rewriting begins by reorganizing and restructuring the document so that it follows a logical order and leads to logical conclusions. It amounts to giving the document a good, strong skeleton so that it can stand up well. Once the document is reorganized, it must be edited. Editing involves redrafting paragraphs and sentences for clarity and precision, and includes correcting grammar, citation, spelling, and punctuation errors. Editing gives the work muscle so that it can convince the reader of its strength. Finally, proofreading is necessary to spot any errors missed previously, to polish the work, and to give it a professional appearance. With documents, as with a job interview, a professional appearance is important.

III. REORGANIZATION

Reorganization should be done first on a large-scale, macro basis, and then on a small-scale, micro basis. First, examine the overall structure of the document to verify that it is basically well organized. Make any improvements needed — cutting and pasting is quite easy with a word processing program like Microsoft Word or WordPerfect. Once the large-scale reorganization is done, then work on small-scale reorganization.

One of the easiest ways to verify that the overall structure of your document is sound is to reverse-outline it. On scratch paper or in the margin, note the subject of each paragraph; then examine the sequence of those subjects to verify that it is both appropriate and logical. If the document uses headings and categories, verify that the headings and categories are accurate, clear, and in a logical sequence that helps guide the reader through the document. For example, the preceding section explained that there are three components of rewriting: reorganization, editing, and proofreading. The reader expects that this paragraph or section will discuss reorganization, followed by sections on editing and then proofreading. If, however, after explaining the existence of the three components, this paragraph discussed topic sentences, followed by editing, the reader would be confused because the sequence promised was not delivered. The reader would wonder what happened to reorganization and proofreading, and why topic sentences are being discussed instead of being included as part of editing.

Some documents, like an objective legal memo, a memorandum of points and authorities, or an appellate brief, have headings and an organizational structure mandated either by custom or by court rules. Other documents, like law review articles or custom-drafted contracts, will require more thought about organization. Nevertheless, the goal is always to use the organization that is best for the reader. This chapter uses the objective legal memo to give a specific example of how to reorganize, on both macro and micro scales, but the principles discussed here apply to all legal writing.

A. The Macro-Organization of an Objective Memo

The structure of a law firm memo is repetitive and designed to help the reader understand and follow an objective analysis of a legal problem. The first heading (Issue) introduces the reader to the legal problem, and the next (Short Answer) gives the final answer, to which the entire rest of the document will lead. These sections also introduce the reader to the most necessary legal terminology and the governing rule or rules. The "Facts" section gives the reader the necessary factual background. The "Discussion" section should first explain the governing rule and how it has been used in different cases. After explaining the governing rule, the discussion section then shows how that law applies to each specific fact given in the facts section. The "Conclusion" section summarizes the discussion section. It should be more developed than the short answer, but essentially repeats the same information.

In rewriting, first check to verify that each section of the memo is properly identified. Verify that all five sections are properly titled and their contents generally appropriate. The most important part of the objective memo is the discussion section; therefore, it invariably demands the most effort. If more than one legal issue is being addressed, each issue should be numbered and titled exactly as it appears in the issue section, and each should have its own rule and application. So, if the issue section lists two questions, so should the discussion section.

As an example, assume that you are writing an office memo about the firm's client John Zidane. Mr. Zidane slide-tackled Mr. William Beckham in the course of a recreational soccer game and Mr. Beckham's knee was injured as a result. Although the players' league normally permits slide-tackles, the referees of this particular game had prohibited them because the playing field was unusually slippery and they wanted to reduce the risk of injury. Mr. Beckham is now threatening to sue Mr. Zidane, and you have been asked to analyze the case. Assume that your objective memo has the following issues:

ISSUES

1. Is our client, John Zidane, liable for battery because he slide-tackled William Beckham in a recreational soccer game?
2. If he is not liable for battery, is Zidane liable for negligence?

Notice that these two issues are mutually exclusive: Mr. Zidane may be liable for one or the other cause of action, but not both. This strategy is called "arguing in the alternative," and it is used often. The corresponding discussion section would look like this:

DISCUSSION

1. Is John Zidane liable for battery because he slide-tackled William Beckham in a recreational soccer game?
   Battery is defined as . . . (explanation of battery).
   Mr. Zidane . . . (explanation of how the law applies to Zidane's facts, concluding that Zidane either might or might not be liable for battery).
2. If he is not liable for battery, is Zidane liable for negligence?
   Negligence is . . . (rule).
   Mr. Zidane (application).

B. Reorganization of the Discussion

The writer's first goal in an objective memo is to convince the reader that she understands the law. A clear, coherent, and complete explanation of law is the only way to do this. However, the most common error in the discussion section is to discuss first one case and how it applies to the problem, and then another case and how it applies to the problem, or even the reverse: to discuss one or two facts from the problem and then an authority, then another one or two facts and another authority. This mixture of rule and application is confusing and makes it difficult or impossible for the reader to gain a complete understanding of the law, leaving him unconvinced that the writer understands either the law or how it applies to the problem. For example, the following is the beginning of a discussion section from an actual LL.M. student's first closed memo. The problem dealt with a seamstress's failure to deliver the plaintiff's wedding dress in time for the ceremony. The student was asked to analyze whether the plaintiff could request damages for her emotional distress, in addition to the usual damages for breach of contract:

The proper claim for damages, for being compelled to miss the appointment at the beauty salon; for getting late to church; for the bridesmaids' appearance; for their lack of participation in the wedding ceremony and for their inappropriate attire, is to be brought through a breach of contract action. Mrs. Singer's failure to deliver the made-to-measure dresses before July 17 caused Ms. Manning to suffer mental pain, anguish, grief, fright, humiliation and injury. To this effect, the "wrongful act of the defendant entitles the plaintiff to recover although no actual damage be alleged or proved, and the form of the action may be ex delicto, the tort being a violation of legal duty involving as one of its elements a breach of contract."[1]

This example shows four basic problems, two involving organization and two involving editing. First, the writer failed to state the applicable rule and its components. Instead, she began by reiterating some of the facts in such a way that the reader feels as if he is being thrown into the middle of something, and has to figure out the beginning and the end on his own. Second, case law and application were mixed together so that the reader cannot tell where one ends and the other begins. Third, archaic language from one of the cases was quoted inappropriately, when it should have been paraphrased. Finally, the convoluted structure of the sentences makes them difficult to understand.

Another similar example:

Manning argues that Singer intentionally breached the contract to ruin her wedding and wants to claim damages for the pain and embarrassment she suffered. However, E. Allen Farnsworth opines that there has been a judicial reluctance to impose damages that are greatly disproportionate to the consideration to be paid by the party in breach of contract in order to avoid unjust compensation.

Again, the reader is confused because the applicable rule is not stated and the discussion of facts mixed with a discussion of law is confusing. A better beginning is as follows:

Generally, the victim of a breach of contract cannot recover damages for emotional distress resulting from the breach, but some exception may be made where the contract's special nature means that its breach is particularly likely to cause emotional distress. This exception, however, does not apply to contracts that involve purely commercial interests, as shown in prior Arizona cases.

This third example begins by stating the underlying background rule and its exception. It then introduces the cases that will be discussed in the following paragraphs and indicates how they relate to the underlying rule.

It is tempting, after discussing each authority, to explain how it applies or does not apply to the facts of the problem. Although this type of thinking may help in

[1] Citations are omitted from all examples for purposes of clarity.

prewriting, this structure leads to a series of dissociated discussions of various authorities, none of which explains to the reader the underlying structure of the law. The only sure way of convincing the reader that you understand both the law and how it applies to the problem is to begin by stating the underlying rule and identifying its components, then explaining how each component is interpreted in case law, and finally explaining how that law applies to the facts of the subject problem. Therefore, to ensure that a rule section is well organized on a macro level, first verify that the rule was stated and that the rule is followed by (1) the explanation of the rule and (2) a detailed demonstration of how the components of the rule operate. The client problem should not even be mentioned until all of the applicable law has been explained.

C. Small-Scale Organization of the Rule Section

Once rule and application sections have been rigidly separated, examine the rule section and verify that its organization provides the clearest possible explanation of the applicable law. Generally, it is best to use a deductive structure to explain the legal principle. As explained earlier, begin with the basic underlying legal premise. Then explain each of the components of that premise, going into the most detail on the components that are difficult to understand and those that are most at issue in your case. Finish the rule section by using factual examples from case law to illustrate how that component works in different factual contexts. The structure of the rule section can be visualized as a triangle with the broad-scoped, general, major premise at the top, the explanations of components in the middle, and the narrow-scoped, precise, and on-point factual illustrations on the bottom of the triangle (see Figure 8-1).

FIGURE 8-1
RULE SECTION STRUCTURE

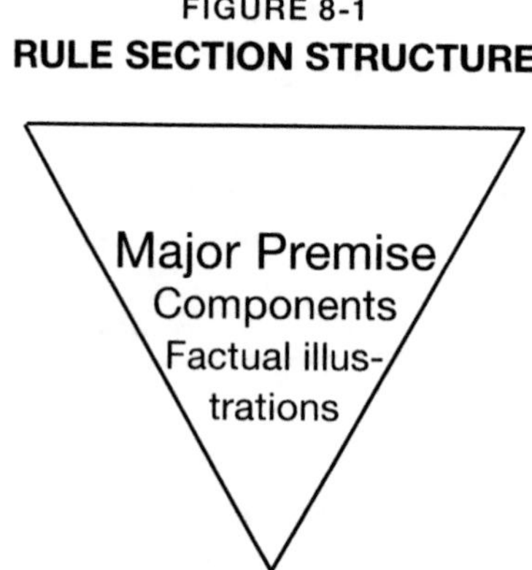

1. *Use of Case Law and Avoidance of Laundry Lists*

After mixing rule and application, the next most common error is to give incomplete explanations of case law or to list cases one after the other without explaining why they are important or how they illuminate the underlying legal rule. This is the "laundry list" approach. When cases are strung one after another without much explanation, the reader gains very little understanding of what they reveal about or add to the law.

In organizing the sequence of components, begin with the components that are easily established, assuming they need explanation, and end with the one component that is controversial, not so easily explained, or not so easily established given the facts of your problem. When there is only one problematic component, this sequence means that the reader still remembers the discussion of this component well when he starts reading the application. In contrast, if there is more than one difficult component, then work out a logical sequence for explaining them and tell the reader in advance that this is what you will be doing. Use the specific facts of one or more cases to help explain those components. One good way of doing this is to use cases that demonstrate both what establishes that component and what does not. This gives the reader the clearest understanding of how the rule operates. One cannot fully understand x until one also understands not x.

For example, the Harris gun-in-the-boot example in Chapter 3 begins with a statement of the predicate criminal statute: the use or carrying of a firearm in connection with a drug-trafficking crime. It then breaks the statute into three components. The definition of using or carrying is the component at issue, and the cases discussed define and exemplify those terms. Each case is introduced not by its name, but by what it adds to the definition of using (not x) or carrying (x). The first Supreme Court case described defines *using*. Next, *carrying* is defined in two cases, one from the Supreme Court and one from the Fifth Circuit. Finally, the facts of a second Fifth Circuit case, which are much like that of the problem case, are described to further demonstrate the meaning of carrying. By the time the reader begins the application section, he thoroughly understands what the statute means — that using and carrying are two different things — and he probably already sees on his own that Harris was not using the gun, but had carried it. What remains is for the writer to explain exactly this, in the application section.

2. More Than One Problematic Component

If there are two rule components that are at issue in the client problem, it may be easiest for the reader to have them divided into two separate issues, beginning with the issues section (as illustrated with the John Zidane example). Explain the necessary legal background at the beginning of the first rule section, and then refresh the reader's memory of that background at the beginning of the second rule section.

3. Sequence of Cases

The sequence in which cases are discussed depends on a number of considerations. As explained earlier, to a great extent the sequence should be determined by the component that the case addresses. However, if more than one case defines a component well, begin with mandatory authority, if you have any, because that will be the reader's most immediate concern. Discuss persuasive authority after mandatory. Similarly, discuss higher authority before lower. However, there are no hard-and-fast sequencing rules, because the best sequence is always that which addresses the reader's needs as they arise.

4. Paragraphs Discussing Cases

As a general rule in discussing a case, after explaining which component the case addressed and what the court said about that component, discuss the operative facts, issue, holding, and rationale of each important case—in that order—so that the reader thoroughly understands what happened in the case and why the court decided as it did. Depending on how important the case is to your analysis, you may need to discuss more or less of it, possibly including procedural history. The discussion of a case may range from one sentence to several, or even several paragraphs, depending on how relevant it is to the client problem or to the explanation of underlying law. To reiterate, it is most important to begin with a sentence or sentences explaining how the case relates to the underlying legal principle. Generally, it is equally important to discuss the operative facts. Remember that to a common law mind, a legal principle in absence of the facts to which it was applied means little or nothing.

5. Incorporating Secondary Authority

If you have helpful secondary authority that provides clarification of the primary authority, work it into the discussion of those primary sources.[2] Do not leave it until the end of the rule section. Instead, use it to support, supplement, and explain the rationales of the cases you discuss, at the same time and in the same paragraph. Usually, secondary authority is best used to further explain primary authority. Putting it at the end of the rule section forces the reader to go back and reread earlier parts of the rule section, something that is both annoying and confusing. Therefore, it is generally best to merge discussions or mentions of secondary sources into appropriate portions of the discussion of primary authority. Citations ensure that the reader will immediately recognize what is mandatory, primary, and secondary authority, so no overt explanation of the ranking of authority is needed.

For example, suppose you need to explain why the court decided that one must use the retail cost of a farmer's truck for purposes of a bankruptcy reorganization cramdown, rather than the wholesale value.[3] The Supreme Court's explanation is difficult to follow, but you have found a law review article that beautifully discusses the underlying bankruptcy laws and policies, and this case especially, and why the retail value is chosen rather than wholesale.[4] After giving the facts, holding, and slim rationale of the case, you would add the clearer explanation from the law review article, so that the reader gets a better understanding of the case and why the court decided the way it did.

---

[2] See Chapter 2: Primary authority includes cases, statutes, regulations, and constitutions; secondary authority is everything else.

[3] *Associates Commercial Corp. v. Rash*, 520 U.S. 953, 956 (1997) (interpreting 11 U.S.C. § 1325(a)(5) (2002).

[4] *See, e.g.*, Chris Lenhart, Note, *Toward a Midpoint Valuation Standard in Cram Down: Ointment for the* Rash *Decision*, 83 Cornell L. Rev. 182 (1998).

The following is an outline for a rule section based on the soccer slide-tackle problem, assuming it took place in New Jersey:

Issue 1: Is Zidane liable for battery?
Major Premise: Battery requires four elements: (1) A voluntary act, (2) with the intent to cause a harmful or offensive contact with the other person, (3) a harmful or offensive contact results, and (4) the other person did not consent.
Components: In the context of a recreational sport, a reckless or intentional offensive contact will probably not constitute a battery unless it is particularly egregious, because players impliedly consent to some such contact as part of the sport. *Crawn v. Campo*, 608 A.2d 465, 467 (N.J. Super. Ct. Law Div. 1992).
Factual Illustrations: A high-school soccer player was found not liable for battery. *Cunico v. Miller*, 2002 WL 339385, at *5 (Cal. Ct. App. Mar. 05, 2002) (unpublished opinion). Although the player, a forward, had kicked and injured the opposing team's goalie in an attempt to make a goal-kick, the court found the player not liable because the act was within the range of normal activities for a soccer game. *Id.* In contrast, however, in a recreational soccer game, a player could be tried for negligence because his slide-tackling of another player was against the rules of the old-timer's league that sponsored the game, even though slide-tackles are normally permitted in soccer. *Lestina v. West Bend Mut. Ins. Co.*, 501 N.W.2d 28, 33 (Wis. 1993).

D. Small-Scale Organization of an Application Section

1. *Structure of the Application Section*

The organization of an application section either parallels or mirrors that of the rule section. Like the rule section, each component of the underlying rule should be addressed in the application section, either in the same or reverse order, whichever will be easiest for the reader to follow. Whereas the rule section discussed the facts of specific cases, the application section should compare the specific facts of those cases to the specific facts of the problem at hand, and explain the legal implications of that comparison. Thus, the structure of the application section will either be the same kind of deductive triangle as the rule section (Figure 8-2, structure A), or it could be the inverse—a triangle with the point and the major premise at the bottom (Figure 8-3, structure B). In some ways, the second, inverted structure is more elegant and concise, because it does not require the writer to restate the basic premise more than once in the application section. This reverse-order format usually leads to a more concise result, as demonstrated in the following outlined application sections.

FIGURE 8-2
APPLICATION SECTION STRUCTURE A

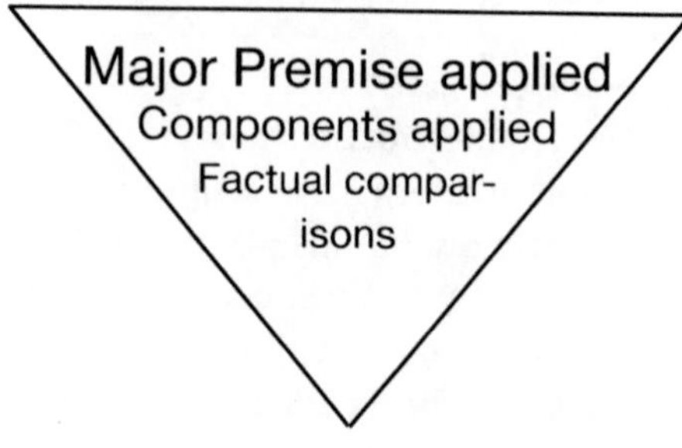

FIGURE 8-3
APPLICATION SECTION STRUCTURE B

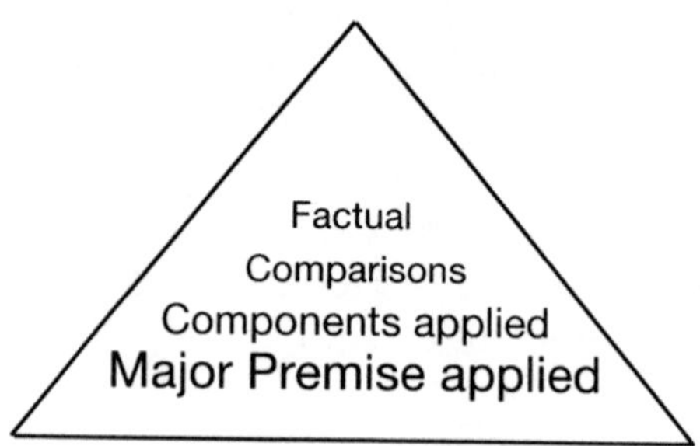

Outlines of Application Section for Zidane's Battery Claim

Example 1: Same Order as Rule Section

Major Premise: Zidane's slide-tackle of Beckham could qualify as battery because it was a voluntary act committed with the intent to contact Beckham and actually resulted in bodily contact.

Component: The question is, however, whether Beckham impliedly consented to the slide-tackle as part of the sport of soccer.

Factual Comparison: Zidane's slide-tackle of Beckham is unlike the situation in *Cunico*. In *Cunico*, the behavior complained about (an attempted goal-kick) was an expected part of the game. In this case, the behavior complained about was prohibited. Zidane's situation is more like that in *Lestina*, in that slide-tackles were prohibited in both games. However, the issue in *Lestina* was whether Lestina could be tried for negligence, not whether he was liable for battery. Furthermore, in the Zidane-Beckham game, the prohibition against slide-tackles was not as clearly defined, because the Zidane-Beckham league generally allows slide-tackles, though the referees of this particular game had prohibited them. In *Lestina*, slide-tackles were always completely prohibited. Although the elements of battery are otherwise present, Zidane has a reasonably strong argument that Beckham had impliedly consented to slide-tackles, and that therefore Zidane's act did not rise to the egregiousness required in the context of a contact sport. Therefore, it is unclear whether a court will find Zidane liable for battery.

Example 2: Reverse Order

Factual Comparison: Zidane's slide-tackle of Beckham is unlike the situation in *Cunico*. In *Cunico*, the behavior complained about (an attempted goal-kick) was an expected part of the game. In this case, the behavior complained about was prohibited. Zidane's situation is more like that in *Lestina*, in that slide-tackles were prohibited in both games. However, the issue in *Lestina* was whether Lestina could be tried for negligence, not whether he was liable for battery. Furthermore, in the Zidane-Beckham game, the prohibition against slide-tackles was not as clearly defined, because the Zidane-Beckham league generally allows slide-tackles, though the referees of this particular game had prohibited them. In *Lestina*, slide-tackles were always completely prohibited.

Component: Because of these differences, Zidane has a reasonably strong argument that Beckham had impliedly consented to slide-tackles, Major Premise: Although Zidane's slide-tackle of Beckham could possibly qualify as battery, because it was an intentional act and resulted in bodily contact, Conclusion: a court might conclude that Zidane's act did not rise to the egregiousness required in the context of a contact sport.

2. *Fact-to-Fact Analogy*

The most common error made in the application section is failure to compare specific facts to specific facts. Instead, the writer merely inserts the parties' names into the statement of the rule, concluding that each component is either established or not. This is commonly referred to as conclusional or conclusory analysis. For example, the statement that "Mr. Zidane is liable for battery because he hit and injured Mr. Beckham" is a conclusion of law. It does not mention the specific facts of the case, nor does it give the underlying rule, nor does it compare those facts to the facts of another case. Instead, a fact-to-fact comparison should be more like the following paragraph. Assume that this is the application section of the Zidane-Beckham negligence claim, and that the major premise — negligence — requires proof of (1) a duty to do or not to do something, (2) breach of that duty, (3) causation, and (4) damage.

Mr. Zidane injured Mr. Beckham by slide-tackling him in a recreational soccer game. Similarly, the plaintiff in *Lestina* was injured by a slide-tackle, but that league, aimed at old-timers, had prohibited slide-tackles in an effort to avoid these kinds of injuries. The *Lestina* defendant was held liable for negligence because the league rules had created a duty not to slide-tackle, and the defendant's violation of that rule caused Lestina's injury. In contrast, the league in which Mr. Zidane and Mr. Beckham play does not prohibit slide-tackles, though the referees in this particular game had told players to avoid them. Therefore, even though his slide-tackle caused Mr. Beckham's injury, because Mr. Zidane had little or no duty to avoid slide-tackling other players, his action was not a breach of duty, and it is unlikely that he will be found negligent.

Notice that the application sample paragraph compares and contrasts specific facts of both cases. The specific facts of *Lestina* are compared to the specific facts of the Zidane-Beckham case. This fact-to-fact analogy is the heart of common law analysis. Although one can find instances in which American attorneys argue without using fact-to-fact analogy, those arguments are never as convincing to a common law attorney as ones in which good deductive logic is combined with strong factual analogy. The preceding example demonstrates a reverse-order application. It begins with a fact-to-fact analogy and then mentions all the elements of negligence in reaching a conclusion: duty, breach, causation, and damages.

E. Reorganization of the Facts

The facts section should explain who the parties are and how the problem between them arose, in a chronological narrative. It should give the reader as clear a picture as possible of how the parties relate to each other and how each behaved. The only way to do this is to include every relevant detail and to be meticulously accurate about those details. After you have drafted and rewritten the discussion section, return to the facts section and verify that every single factual detail mentioned in the application section is presented first in the facts section, plus every additional detail that helps the reader picture the parties and follow the events. It may be helpful to the reader for you to end the facts section with a short statement of the client's legal problem that refers back to the issue, as in the Harris example illustrated in Chapter 3.

F. Reorganization of the Conclusion

The most common mistake in drafting the conclusion section is to make it too short—a mere one- or two-sentence repetition of the short answer. The short answer is a one- or two-sentence answer to the issue question. In contrast, the conclusion should concisely summarize the entire contents of the memo: the issue(s), the rule(s), your conclusions as to how they apply to the facts of your problem, and why, in one or two well-developed paragraphs.

G. Picturing How Sections of a Law Firm Memo Work Together

The goal of macro and micro organization is to make the document work together as a whole. In the case of a law firm memo, this marriage between organization and function is easily pictured. The issue and short answer sections are previews of coming attractions. The facts section tells the client's story, including all details that will help the reader picture exactly what happened. The rule section is a tool kit, and includes all the law needed to solve the legal problem raised in the issue and facts sections. The application section combines the details of the facts section with the law discussed in the rule section to reach a logical conclusion about the legal implications of the client's situation. The conclusion summarizes it all, giving a definite and well-explained answer to the issue and fulfilling the promise made in the short answer. Other types of legal documents are not always so tightly and elegantly organized, but one of the ways to ensure that a document is well organized and well crafted is to consider what each separate section contributes to the whole and review how they all fit together.

IV. EDITING

A. Paragraphs

1. Paragraph Structure

Just as all sections of a document work together to support the whole, so should each sentence work with the others in a paragraph. Each paragraph should be approximately five to seven sentences long and should discuss only one topic. The first or second sentence of the paragraph introduces and defines this topic, which is why it is often called a topic sentence. The first sentence should also refer back to the previous paragraph, thus providing a transition from one topic to the next. The transition should accurately reflect the relationship between the two paragraphs, and may also show how all of the parts of the analysis work together, as discussed in more detail later in this section. After the topic/transitional sentence, the sentences that construct the body of the paragraph explain and support the topic sentence. The paragraph then concludes with a sentence that summarizes the points made in the paragraph and leads into the topic of the next paragraph.

2. Topic Sentences

A topic sentence explains the basic point of a paragraph.[5] That point should be clear to the reader, and must be followed up by support. For example, a rule section

---

[5] John C. Dernbach et al., *A Practical Guide to Legal Writing & Legal Method* 144 (2d ed., Fred B. Rothman Publ'ns 1994).

topic sentence could be as follows: "Most states use a 'reckless disregard of safety' standard in recreational sports cases, but a few states use negligence instead." The body of the paragraph might then explain which states use which standard, that the state involved in the Zidane-Beckham slide-tackle case has not yet decided which standard it will use, and that therefore both standards will be discussed. Now the reader will be expecting to see an explanation first of the reckless disregard standard, and then of the negligence standard. To signal the reader that this expectation is about to be fulfilled, the first sentence of the following paragraph might begin: "In those states that have adopted the 'reckless disregard of safety' standard...." After discussing recklessness standard, the writer then transitions to negligence: "Negligence is the alternative standard in states that have rejected recklessness in recreational sports cases." The body of the paragraph that follows will support this topic sentence by explaining the negligence standard.

One of the problems with the student examples given in § III.B is that neither paragraph contains a topic sentence — neither paragraph mentions damages for emotional distress, the issue in the case. Neither paragraph makes a point. If the reader asks, "What are you trying to tell me?," she will receive no answer. The first example begins by stating that a claim for damages must be brought through a claim for breach of contract. It then says that defendant Singer's act made plaintiff Manning unhappy. The third sentence is a quotation which says, in convoluted terms, that some unidentified plaintiff should get damages even though there was no actual damage because a contract was breached. Thus, these are three disjointed sentences, no two of which are on the same topic, and none of which addresses the main issue of the memo. The second example is similarly disjointed. It consists of two sentences on two different subjects, neither of which addresses emotional distress damages. Therefore, in addition to being ineffective because they mix rule and application, these paragraphs are ineffective because they lack topic sentences.

Topic sentences must make a point, but to be effective they must also be easy for the reader to understand. Rewriting sentences for clarity and precision is addressed later, but an easy way to test the subject matter of topic sentences is to extract them from the memo or brief and see whether they accurately outline your analysis. Thus, reverse-outlining serves two purposes: It tests the logic of the document organization, and it verifies that each paragraph contains a topic sentence. Once you have verified that each paragraph contains a topic sentence and that each topic sentence accurately states the point of the paragraph, the next rewriting issue is to work on transitions.

3. *Transitions*

Transitions are devices that guide the reader from one subject to the next. They are also called signposts, a term that more accurately describes their function. Law can be complicated to explain, with multiple issues, each of which may have subissues. Asking the reader to follow you as you explain a legal theory and how it applies to a specific factual problem can be like hacking through a dense jungle. The reader will get lost unless you leave signs to guide her carefully through that jungle: "Straight ahead, reader . . . turn left now . . . watch out for that tree root . . . okay, we're almost at the end." Essentially, there are three kinds of transitions:

1. Transition sentences that bridge from one idea or paragraph to another
2. One-word or -phrase transitions that show how one idea relates to another
3. Linking words that help the reader.

The purpose of all three of these devices is to keep the writing flowing smoothly from sentence to sentence and paragraph to paragraph.[6]

a. Transitional Sentences

A transitional sentence from one paragraph to another fulfills three functions: it Reviews the topic of the previous paragraph, Introduces the topic of the current paragraph, and explains that topic's Legal Significance.[7] You can remember the elements of a good transitional sentence with the mnemonic RILS. As indicated in the first part of this section, a transitional sentence is usually also the topic sentence of the paragraph. Earlier, the following was used to demonstrate a topic sentence: "Negligence is the alternative standard in states that have rejected recklessness in recreational sports cases." This sentence is also a good transition because it reviews the previous topic (the recklessness standard), introduces the current topic (negligence), and explains the legal significance (some states use negligence instead of recklessness in sports cases).

Transitions should usefully describe the relationship between ideas presented in sections or paragraphs. They should not merely stick two ideas together like a verbal form of glue. For example, "In another case" is usually not an adequate transition from a paragraph describing one case to a paragraph describing another. Instead, an effective transitional sentence tells the reader how the two cases are related and why it is helpful to discuss them. Usually this can be done in one sentence, but occasionally even a clause will work.

b. Word or Phrase Transitions

An effective transition accurately shows the relationship between ideas. A RILS transitional sentence fulfills this function, but sometimes a transition can be made simply through the use of a word or phrase, especially when transitioning from one sentence to another rather than one paragraph to another. Different types of phrases and expressions show different types of relationships. Common relationships include similarities, differences, enumerations (numbering), cause and effect, temporal relationships, and others. Figure 8-4 lists a number of possible relationships, followed by several transitions that can be used to express that relationship.[8] It is a useful reference when searching for an appropriate transitional phrase.

---

6 Henry Weihofen, *Legal Writing Style* 151 (2d ed., West 1980).

7 Bryan A. Garner, Speech at Legal Writing CLE seminar, New Orleans, 2001. *See also* Bryan A. Garner, *The Winning Brief* 97-109 (Oxford Univ. Press 1999).

8 *See* Mary Barnard Ray & Jill J. Ramsfield, *Legal Writing: Getting It Right and Getting It Written* (3d ed., West Group 2000).

FIGURE 8-4

Relationship	Transition
1. Signaling similarity	similarly, analogously, as; likewise; again; also
2. Signaling contrast	not . . . but; conversely; however; in contrast; nevertheless; to the contrary; while; yet; still; though; although
3. Introducing conditions	although, even if, if, only if, provided that, unless, when, whenever, whereas, while
4. Introducing causation	because, if, since[9]
5. Introducing results	if . . . , then; when . . . , then; accordingly; as a result; consequently; hence; so; so that; therefore; thus; it follows that
6. Introducing examples or explanations	as if, as though, for example, specifically, namely, for instance, as an illustration, that is, particularly, in particular
7. Signaling a list	first, second, third, etc.[10]
8. Signaling an amplification or addition	both . . . and; either . . . or; neither . . . nor; additionally; in addition to; also; and; furthermore; next; last; nor; or; besides; another reason; likewise; equally important
9. Describing temporal relationships	after, afterward, as, as soon as, as long as, before, before this, during, earlier, later, meanwhile, now, once, since, simultaneously, subsequently, thereafter, at the same time, then, until, when, whenever, while, in the meantime, recently
10. Describing relationships of place	where, wherever
11. Summarizing	finally, in conclusion, in summary; in brief
12. To signal a concession	granted that, no doubt, to be sure, it is true, although

The most common mistakes inexperienced writers make is either failing to use an expression to denote a relationship, or using the wrong expression, so that the relationship is inaccurately described. A variation of this second mistake is using an

[9] Be careful. *Because* is a much stronger word indicating causation. *Since* should be used for causation only occasionally, as its primary use is to show a temporal relationship (i.e., "The world has been much less secure since September 11, 2001.").

[10] Not firstly, secondly, thirdly, etc., because they are ungainly and sound pretentious to American ears (you may well encounter this form in British English, though).

expression in an attempt to join two completely unrelated ideas. The second student example in § III.B makes this mistake. The first sentence describes the plaintiff's argument: Because the defendant intentionally breached the wedding-dress contract, the plaintiff wants emotional distress damages. The next sentence describes a leading scholar as saying that courts avoid awarding damages that are out of proportion to the cost of a breached contract. Even though the student joined the two sentences with the word however, they are on completely different topics, and therefore cannot be effectively joined together. The transition is inappropriate.

If you find that you are having trouble joining two adjacent sentences, and cannot find an appropriate transitional phrase, check to see if the problem is that the sentences are unrelated. If so, then one or both of them probably does not say what you want it to say and should be reworked. The preceding example could be reworked as follows:

> *Singer's breach of the contract to make and deliver the wedding dress on time caused Manning severe emotional distress, for which she wants damages. However, the general rule is that emotional distress damages are not awarded in a breach of contract suit.*

As rewritten, these two sentences are now properly joined by *however*, because the two ideas contradict each other.

A third mistake is to use cumbersome transitional phrases that impede rather than facilitate the progress of thought. For example, the phrases "Having proved our first point," and "This leads us to our second point" are verbose and pretentious. It is better to put the transitional phrase inside the sentence rather than at the beginning. In this instance, one could easily rework the sentences to show the enumeration: The reasons for x are dual. The first reason. . . . In addition to the first reason, the second reason. . . . Another example of this kind of construction is given in subsection A.3.a of this section, in the negligence/recklessness example of topic sentences.

c. Linking

In addition to transitional sentences and phrases, a third way to help the reader move from one sentence to the next is to repeat key words. This process is called linking. The writer links one sentence to the next by repeating a key word, and this repetition helps guide the reader along from one thought to the next. Linking is a very effective transitional device. In the sample paragraph on the Zidane case (§ III.C.5), the words slide-tackle, recreational soccer, negligence, and duty are used to link one paragraph, and sometimes one sentence, to the next. As an exercise, try to identify the linking words in this paragraph.

4. Paragraph Length

The minimum length for a paragraph in formal legal writing is usually three sentences—after all, one can hardly introduce a topic, substantiate it, conclude, and transition to the next topic in fewer than three sentences. Sometimes paragraphs in a letter are shorter than three sentences, but such short paragraphs are usually inappropriate in a formal memo or brief. If a paragraph is three sentences or less, check to see that the paragraph fully addresses the topic. Perhaps it assumes something rather than explaining it to the reader, or perhaps the rest of the subject was inappropriately allocated to a different paragraph. Everything should be in prose; there should be no lists. For example, the following excerpt from a student paper is a list, not an appropriate statement of the facts.

FACTS

- On April 23, Manning contracted with Singer for the latter to make ten made-to-measure dresses to be used in Manning's wedding ceremony.
- On May 15, Manning sent Singer a wedding invitation.
- During May and June, Manning had several telephone conversations with Singer regarding the dresses' progress. At all times, Singer reassured her that the dresses would be ready on time for the wedding
- On June 10, Manning and her bridesmaids had the first and final fitting for the dresses, which were still held together by pins.
- In a telephone conversation in early July, Singer told Manning that the dresses were almost ready and that she could pick them up the morning of the wedding day.
- On July 17, the wedding day, Singer and her bridesmaids went to pick up the dresses at 9:00 A.M., but they were still not ready.

These sentences should be joined together in paragraph form using transitions, so that they flow together smoothly. For more information on transitional devices, see §IV.3.

In addition to checking to see if any paragraphs are too short, check them to see if any are too long. As a general rule, a single-spaced paragraph should be no longer than approximately half a page. If any paragraphs are longer than that, break them into two smaller paragraphs. Sometimes you will notice that the paragraph is actually composed of two paragraphs, each on a slightly different topic; if so, all that is needed is to hit the "enter" key to separate them and perhaps add a transitional sentence or clause. At other times, however, an overly long paragraph mixes two topics together, and will require substantial revision to separate the two topics into two paragraphs. One effective way to check the length of a paragraph, as well as the structure of a sentence, is to read it aloud. If you are having trouble breathing by the time you get to the end of the paragraph, it is probably too long. If it sounds choppy, it may be too short.

B. Editing Sentences

1. Sentence Length

When you are considering how to revise a sentence, the most important question is whether the sentence says exactly what you mean it to say, as simply and clearly as possible. Any sentence longer than 3 lines (or 35 words) is probably too long and should be either simplified or broken in two. Do not make every sentence the same length, however, because that would make for monotonous reading. Occasional short sentences add strength. In persuasive writing, occasional short sentences can be extremely powerful: "Mr. Zidane did nothing wrong" is much more powerful than "Mr. Zidane should not be held liable for negligence because he did not breach his duty to behave in a reasonably prudent manner." The latter sentence may be appropriate in an application section, but the former carries much more punch and may well be extremely persuasive in a legal brief.

In addition to varying sentence length for readability, you will also want to vary sentence structure. Some sentences may be very simple, and others will have to be more complex in order to accurately express the relationship between two separate ideas. Two types of complex structures are often used to do this. A compound sentence joins two sentences with a conjunction such as *and* or *but*: "The boat did not sink, but it leaks."[11] Alternatively, one could use a conjunctive adverb to join two separate sentences: "The boat did not sink; however, it leaks badly." A complex sentence may join the same two ideas, but it does so in such a way as to show a more exact relationship between those ideas: "The boat did not sink, even though it leaks." The latter sentence uses the subordinating conjunction *even though* to express the relationship between leaking and sinking, and it adds more information about the writer's attitude toward the boat. Instead of joining two sentences ("The boat did not sink" and "It leaks"), the subordinating conjunction changed the first sentence into an independent clause and the second into a dependent clause: "even though it leaks" is no longer a sentence with a separate subject and verb.

2. Sentence Structure

Complex and compound sentences can add interest and accuracy to your writing. However, complex and compound sentence structures can also lead to problems. If, upon rereading a complex sentence, you find it difficult to follow, begin the revision process by identifying its underlying structure. Standard English word order is subject-verb-object. Problems often occur when a sentence fails to follow this order, or when it has so many modifying phrases that the underlying structure is obscured. The first student example on page 199 begins: "The proper claim for damages, for being compelled to miss the appointment at the beauty salon; for getting late to church; for the bridesmaids' appearance; for their lack of participation in the wedding ceremony and for their inappropriate attire, is to be brought through a breach of contract action." When faced with such an awkward sentence, identify the main subject, verb, and object, or subject and predicate, and then rearrange the sentence so that they appear in the usual order, eliminating unnecessary modifying phrases.

In this case, the subject is "the proper claim for damages," and the predicate is "is to be brought through a breach of contract action." The sentence, without the modifying prepositional phrases, is thus: "The proper claim for damages is to be brought through a breach of contract action." Unfortunately, this still says little or nothing about the law. Nor does it say anything about Maria Manning's situation, which was

[11] Lynn B. Squires et al., *Legal Writing in a Nutshell* 69 (West 1996).

what the prepositional phrases attempted to do. The sentence apparently was trying to do two separate things, and accomplished neither. A reworking of these ideas could be "Singer's breach of the contract ruined the wedding day Manning had planned for herself, causing her to cry before, during, and after the wedding. Because of this, Manning would like to claim both emotional and contract damages." Thus, if a convoluted sentence joins two or more ideas, separate them, analyze the relationships between them, and then use accurate conjunctions,[12] conjunctive adverbs,[13] or subordinating conjunctions[14] to rejoin them in a more effective way. A grammar handbook can help you reformulate sentences. Those written for legal writers are particularly helpful.

3. Paraphrasing and Using Language Consistently

One of the most difficult writing issues for most non-native English-speaking LL.M. students is knowing when and how to paraphrase rather than quote. As a rule, it is always better to paraphrase, except when a quotation is particularly illustrative or important. As explained in Chapter 3, a legal argument is an extended syllogism. A syllogism is effective only when the terms used do not vary. If terms vary, then the syllogism is not proven, as when Socrates was turned into a cat.[15] He may still have been mortal, but the syllogism did not prove him so, because the first premise of the syllogism was that all men are mortal, not all cats. It is much easier for the reader if the writer uses the same terminology consistently, rather than confusing him by changing terms just because those were the exact terms that the authority used. Furthermore, quotations are almost never a good fit with what the writer has to say. Usually, to express herself exactly, the writer needs to paraphrase an authority carefully, not quote it.

Because they wish to discuss a court's opinion as accurately as possible, many students are afraid to use their own words. The result is usually stilted and often incomprehensible. For example, in the Manning memo excerpted earlier, students were given three cases and a secondary authority. Though all the cases deal with the same issue, they use different terms to refer to emotional distress damages. One case used emotional pain and suffering, another non-pecuniary damages, and the third mental anguish. The modern term, however, is emotional distress damages, and the memo is much easier to follow if the memo writer uses that term consistently. In researching an area, be sensitive to language use. Then, when writing, use the most current language and substitute it for older language as needed. Occasionally, one might find there is too much repetition, in which case a synonym might be substituted, but repetition is preferable to reader confusion.

[12] Common coordinating conjunctions include *and, but, or, nor, for, yet,* and *so.*
[13] Common conjunctive adverbs include *as a result, besides, consequently, however, moreover, nevertheless, therefore, thus, also, otherwise, besides,* and *yet.*
[14] Common subordinating conjunctions include *after, although, as, because, before, if . . . then, that, when, where, whether, while, until,* and *unless,* among others.
[15] Chapter 3, § I.

C. Editing Details

1. Paragraph and Sentence Format

The first word of a new paragraph should be indented five spaces. Most word processing programs, such as Microsoft Word or WordPerfect, will automatically indent this amount if you hit the "Tab" key. Again, as with paragraph length, this differs from letter format. In a letter, it is perfectly acceptable to indicate the start of a new paragraph by skipping a line; however, this is inappropriate in formal legal writing where everything is already double-spaced. Similarly, sentences should be separated by two spaces so that the eye can easily pick up the end of one sentence and the beginning of the next. Although most U.S. word processing programs do this automatically,* if you are using the English program in a non-English-based software package, you may need to do it manually. Do a test printout to verify spacing before turning in any assignments.

2. Word Choice

It is best to use plain, familiar words. Though it is tempting—especially if English is not your first language—to use words such as *aforesaid, herein,* and *notwithstanding* because you see them in casebooks, *this, that, here,* and *despite* are much simpler, are easier to understand, and will make your writing clearer and stronger. Another common error is to use *said* as an adjective: *said contract, said defendant,* and the like. *Said* is the past tense of the verb *to say,* and should only be used as a verb. Using it as an adjective is pedantic jargon. Avoid all such legalese terms, and strike out all other unnecessary words and phrases. Typical unnecessary phrases include introductions such as "it can be seen that" or "it would seem that" or the infamous "it is important to note that." Others include wordy prepositional phrases like "in close proximity to" and redundant phrases like "personal friend." (I certainly hope that all my friends are personal.) In his Redbook, Bryan Garner gives convenient lists of legalese terms and other wordy phrases, and also lists a number of simple substitutions.[16]

In addition to using ordinary language, it is best to refer to people by their names and not dehumanize them by substituting client, plaintiff, defendant, appellant, or appellee unless otherwise instructed to do so. Readers can easily become confused and not know which plaintiff you are talking about: Is it the client, or one of the plaintiffs in one of the three or four cases discussed in the rule section? Furthermore, in the United States, clients have a right to everything in their attorney's file. No client would want to discover a memo written by his own attorney in which he was referred to as the client, the plaintiff, or the defendant.

Another simple way to improve writing style is to use the active voice whenever possible. In a sentence that uses the active voice, the action moves forward from subject

---

* You may have noticed that only one space is used between sentences in book publishing, in contrast to formal legal writing.

[16] Bryan A. Garner, *The Redbook: A Manual on Legal Style* 190-92 (West Group, 2d ed. 2006). Other helpful, similar texts include Mary Barnard Ray & Jill J. Ramsfield, *Legal Writing: Getting It Right and Getting It Written* (3d ed., West Group 2000); Alan L. Dworsky, *The Little Book on Legal Writing* (Fred B. Rothman 1992); Strunk & White, *The Elements of Style* (Macmillan, current ed.); and others.

through verb to the object of the sentence: "The jury awarded the plaintiff $55,000."[17] In contrast, the passive voice uses some form of the verb *to be*, resulting in a less-active sentence: "The plaintiff was awarded $55,000." The easiest way to spot passive voice is to look for the past tense of the verb *to be* plus a past participle (e.g., "was awarded"). If you find this, rewrite the sentence using the actor as the subject of the sentence (e.g., "the jury awarded"). Using the active voice makes your writing more active, more immediate, and therefore more exciting and interesting. However, sometimes the passive voice is appropriate, especially when the actor is unknown or unimportant or when you want to emphasize the recipient of the action instead of the actor.

3. Grammar

a. Verb Tenses

When polishing formal legal writing, be sure to check all grammatical issues—grammar-check programs help to a certain extent but are far from infallible. Inexperienced legal writers often have difficulty using consistent verb tenses. When writing about case law, use the past tense. In the application section, show how the law applies to the problem at hand by using the present or conditional tense: "In Mr. Zidane's case, unlike Lestina's, Mr. Zidane should not be liable because Mr. Beckham should have anticipated that he might be slide-tackled."

b. Articles

Another common grammatical problem for non-native English writers is distinguishing between definite and indefinite articles. Use *the* when the exact object is important, but *a* or *an* when it is not: "She rode an elephant while traveling in India." In this sentence, it does not matter what elephant she rode. In contrast, in the sentence "She was riding the elephant Jumbo when he went berserk," *the* refers to a specific elephant. The correct choice of definite or indefinite articles is often idiomatic and therefore quite difficult. If it is a problem for you, you might want either to look the topic up in a grammar book and learn the technical details, or to develop an ear for the choice by listening to fluent native speakers and noting the choices made by good native writers (depending on your personal learning style).[18]

c. Possessive Form

For some reason, many people find the possessive form confusing, and try to avoid it by using needless prepositional phrases. For example, *the defendant's car* becomes *the car belonging to the defendant.* This is a shame, because the possessive form in English is quite simple to learn and use. For a singular object, simply add an apostrophe + s: *defendant's car* refers to the car owned by one defendant. With a plural object that ends in an s, merely add the apostrophe: *defendants' car* means that more than one defendant owns the car. If a singular object already ends in an s or x sound, you should still add both the apostrophe and the s: *witness's* (though some people now omit the

---

[17] *Id.* at 144.

[18] For a detailed explanation of article use, see Anne Enquist & Laurel Currie Oates, *Just Writing: Grammar, Punctuation, and Style for the Legal Writer* 263-73 (Aspen Law & Bus. 2001).

final s in this instance). If you do not know your reader's preference, use the traditional form with the final *s*.

d. Capitalization

One issue that confuses inexperienced legal writers is when to capitalize the word *court*. The general rule is to capitalize all proper nouns (and full titles): United States Congress, United States Court of Appeals for the Fifth Circuit. When referring to the United States Supreme Court, capitalize the word *Court*, even if you omit the rest of the title, because you are using *Court* as a short form of a proper noun. Otherwise, do not capitalize *court*. The only other time *court* is properly capitalized is when it is used to refer to a specific court in which a document will be filed, and again it is capitalized because it is a short form of the proper noun. For example, in a memorandum of points and authorities, you would capitalize *court* when referring to the court in which you are filing the memorandum. Unless your legal research and writing course includes an advocacy problem, the only time *court* should be capitalized is when you are referring to the United States Supreme Court, or when it is the first word of a sentence.

e. Collective Nouns

A collective noun is a noun that represents a collection of persons or things regarded as a unit. Because the entity is regarded as a unit, it takes a singular verb when the noun refers to the collection as a whole, and a singular pronoun:

The Supreme Court ended its [not their] session without granting certiorari to any labor law cases.

Congress is [not are] in session.

Nevertheless, a collective noun may take a plural verb when it refers to the collection as separate persons or things:

The Student Bar Association have all gone home.

The latter, however, sounds awkward and Anglicized (the British commonly use this form). For an American audience, you may well want to rework the sentence:

"All the members of Congress have gone home" is better than "Congress have gone home."

f. Punctuation

Properly used, punctuation helps the reader by breaking thoughts into easily understood components and indicating relationships between ideas. Grammar and spell checkers will catch some errors—be sure that your computer is set for United States usage—but they will not catch all errors.

Commas

One common error is to omit the last comma in a series. For example, the sentence "Carrots, potatoes, and rutabagas are all root vegetables," properly contains a comma after the word *potatoes*. The comma indicates to the reader that all three nouns are given the same weight. Another common error is to omit a comma that sets off an introductory phrase: *In an action for negligence, the plaintiff must prove duty, breach, causation, and damages.*

Commas are relatively easy to learn to use, and many sources give clear explanations of when they should be used. Commas help clarify sentences by giving the reader a pause. Lack of such pauses often creates ambiguity. Therefore, omitting a comma is often worse than adding superfluous ones. Occasionally, however, commas are inappropriate. Commas should not separate subject from verb in a sentence.

Quotations

Another common punctuation error is failure to use quotation marks, failure to use them correctly, or failure to quote accurately. Quotation marks must be used every time you use the same words as the original source, and failure to do this amounts to plagiarism. For quotations, material must be copied word for word and punctuated exactly as it was in the original. If you make any changes to the quoted material, you must indicate those changes as described by rule 5-5.4 of the Bluebook or rules 48.0-50.4 in the ALWD. The most commonly applicable rules are summarized in Figure 8-5 and in the next paragraph. In American usage, the ending quotation marks come after (not before) commas and periods: The court held that "[i]n an action for negligence, the plaintiff must prove duty, breach, causation, and damages."

Both the ALWD and the Bluebook have very rigid rules about the content of a quoted passage, and you need to refer to one or the other source carefully until you learn these rules, which are only summarized here. In general, any change to the original language must be indicated with either an ellipsis or brackets. In the previous paragraph, the brackets indicate that the original sentence capitalized the letter *i;* the author changed it to a lowercase letter in keeping with correct sentence structure, but the sentence is otherwise exactly as it appeared in the original. The reader will know if language is omitted from the beginning of a sentence by the fact that the first letter following beginning quotation marks is not capitalized, so no ellipsis is needed. However, if language is omitted from the middle or end of a sentence, indicate that fact with an ellipsis. An ellipsis is not three dots. It is three dots and three spaces. When language is omitted from the end of the sentence, the ellipsis is followed by the original ending punctuation, and then quotation marks: "In an action for negligence, the plaintiff must prove . . . ." Note that nonlegal style guides may state different rules about ellipses at the ends of quoted material. Legal writers should follow the Bluebook/ALWD rules, to maintain the accuracy and specificity demanded in legal writing.

Semicolons, Colons, and Dashes

Typically, non-native English writers are unfamiliar with semicolons, colons, and dashes, and so do not take advantage of these useful punctuation marks. Semicolons act as "supercommas" in a complex sentence, and thus can help the reader sort things out. Therefore, they can join or juxtapose two logically related sentences:

Mr. Zidane did not intend to slide-tackle Mr. Beckham; he slipped on a patch of mud.

FIGURE 8-5

Change to original material	Action and indicia needed	Example
1. No change	Quote exactly; use quotation marks.	"Mary had a little lamb."
2. No change, but quoted material is longer than 49 words	No quotation marks. Instead, indent both sides one inch and type single-spaced. Citation is on first line of text following the quotation, not within the quotation itself.	Mary's complaint was as follows: Someone took my lamb. I looked under the hayloft, but I only found Jack, fast asleep. Then I looked in (29 + more words). *Mary Jones v. Michael Brown*, 23 So. 2d 5 (__La.__ 1997).
3. Adding words for clarity	Use brackets around the addition.	"Despite Mary's emotional plea that the lamb be returned, [the court] found that the animal properly belonged to Little Miss Muffett."
4. Adding or changing a letter within a word, usually at the beginning of a quotation	Use brackets around the addition or change.	The court was explicit when it said, "[T]he lamb belongs to Miss Muffett."
5. Omitting language from the beginning of a quotation	See 4. if changing the case of a letter; otherwise, just use quotation marks as usual. No ellipsis.	
6. Omitting language from the middle of a sentence	Mark the omission with an ellipsis.	Mary said, "That judge is . . . ridiculous!"
7. Omitting language from the end of a sentence	Add a period after the ellipsis to represent the period at the end of the original sentence.	"Miss Muffett had paid Mary's father for the lamb . . . ."
8. Indicating that a significant mistake in the quotation appeared in the original	Insert [*sic*] immediately after the mistake.	"This list of regulations are [*sic*] necessarily incomplete."

Furthermore, a semicolon is used at the end of each element in a list if any one element in that list contains a comma:

The Company warrants for one year that its forklifts (1) are free from defects in material and workmanship; (2) have the capacity and rating set forth in the Company's catalogs, provided that no warranty is made against corrosion, erosion, or deterioration; and (3) meet all relevant federal safety standards.

Colons are used to introduce a list (as with a statute) or between two sentences if one sentence sets up an expectation in the reader's mind that the next sentence fulfills. For example, the relationship between the Zidane/Beckham sentences above becomes a bit clearer when a colon is used rather than a semicolon:

Mr. Zidane did not intend to slide-tackle Mr. Beckham: He slipped on a patch of mud.

The colon indicates that Mr. Zidane did not intend to slide-tackle Mr. Beckham, and that the collision between them was caused only by Zidane's slipping on a patch of mud.

Dashes are used instead of commas to set off an interrupting phrase or comment. They add drama and perhaps a note of informality or humor, as they make the phrase stand out on the page. Although dashes are good tools, be careful not to overuse them. On a typewriter, a dash is formed by two hyphens; most word processing programs allow you to set an option that automatically changes two hyphens to the true (correct) typographic dash. Note that there are no spaces around a dash.

Mr. Beckham has decided not to pursue the action further—litigation would be too expensive.

The defendant's action—both understandable and humane in this case—cannot be rightly condemned.

Mrs. Zidane thought the intruder might be a burglar—or her husband.[19]

g. Issues of Style

Although one should avoid legalese and try to write as simply and clearly as possible, there are still certain formalities to legal writing in the United States. When you are writing as a professional, your tone should reflect that professionalism. Contractions and slang are inappropriate, as are rhetorical questions and usually the first person. Contractions (can't, don't, and etc.) may be appropriate for a letter, where the desired tone is a bit more informal, but are not appropriate in formal legal writing. Naturally, slang expressions are also inappropriate, as are slashes: and/or, s/he. A rhetorical question is a question mixed into a normal paragraph and that implies an answer: "Is it reasonable for a softball player to go out of his way to run into an opposing player?" Questions like this make writing sound either confrontational or somewhat juvenile, and do not convey the professional tone desired, though they may occasionally be appropriate in an advocacy context.

In an office memorandum or brief to a court, the goal is to keep the reader's focus on the analysis, not on the writer. The goal of an office memorandum is to convince the reader of your authority, and that is most easily established if the focus is on the writing, not the writer, which is why you avoid *I* or *we.* Similarly, in a memorandum of points and authorities or a brief to the court, the goal is to persuade the reader (i.e., the judge) that objective analysis shows that the law is in your client's favor. Again, you want the focus off yourself. Therefore, avoid *I, me,* and *my.*

[19] Mary Bernard Ray & Jill Ramsfield, *Legal Writing: Getting It Right and Getting It Written* 105-06 (3d ed., West Group 2002).

h. Citations

Citations are an absolute must in the United States, and U.S. attorneys and judges are obsessive in this regard. Any reference to another source must be thoroughly documented, and the exact page cited. In an office memorandum, this means that every sentence in the rule section should be followed by a citation, unless there is a strong reason not to do so. Some authorities and instructors allow citations every three sentences if the writer is referring to exactly the same page of exactly the same source, but one could always simply use *id.* in this situation. It is often better to err on the side of caution and have too many citations rather than too few. The only sentences in a rule section that do not take citations are those that show entirely your own thinking. Furthermore, your instructor may require any sentence in the application section that refers to an authority to be followed by a citation, and possibly every fact in the fact section to be followed by a reference to a page of the case record. The only place in an office memorandum where a citation is usually inappropriate is in the short answer.

Generally, in objective memos, each citation lists only one source. Law review footnotes, in contrast, often use string citations: a number of citations appearing together and separated by semicolons, all listing authorities that state the same thing. However, though it is appropriate in a law review article to demonstrate that you have found every single authority on a subject, string citations are generally undesirable in an objective memo.

This obsessive citation habit can make writing difficult. The best approach is to place citations after the substantive sentence. Think of the citation as a separate sentence that follows your substantive sentence, not something that is part of it. The following sentence is awkward and difficult to read: "In *Bourque v. Duplechin*, 331 So. 2d 40, 43 (La. Ct. App. 1976), the court held the defendant, Duplechin, liable for negligence." As simplified, it becomes: "In one case dealing with softball, the court held the defendant, Duplechin, liable for negligence. *Bourque v. Duplechin*, 331 So. 2d 40, 43 (La. Ct. App. 1976)." Rewritten this way, the emphasis is on the writer's point about the case, not on the citation itself. This way, the reader's eyes will register the citation, but will be able to skip over it without reading, in order to follow the author's train of thought without interruption.

At least one commentator has been trying to persuade lawyers and courts to allow all citations to be listed as footnotes, rather than keeping them in the text where they slow the reader down.[20] Originally, citations were placed in the body of the text because typewriters could not easily formulate footnotes. Now that word processing has eliminated this technical limitation, it is to be hoped that textual citations will eventually be eliminated as a result. However, if you are prohibited from putting citations in footnotes, construct your sentence so that the citation is contained in a separate citation sentence immediately following the substantive sentence.

---

[20] *See, e.g.*, Bryan A. Garner, *Speaking & Writing: Unclutter the Text by Footnoting Citations*, 33 Trial 87 (Nov. 1997).

V. PROOFREADING

The best way to proofread is in two stages: first, ask someone else to proofread a document for you and point out errors; then do it again yourself. The sequence is important, because the author needs time away from the paper to gain objectivity, and that time can be spent productively by having someone else proofread the paper in the intervening period. With regard to the first step, in a law firm, generally the supervising attorney will act as a proofreader. In a law school setting, to avoid honor code problems, ask the instructor whether you can use a proofreader and who that could be. Some instructors allow students to proofread each others' papers; others do not, but will encourage students to ask friends who are not taking the course to proofread.

Once the document has been proofread by a disinterested person, the author needs to proofread it again herself. Because a proofreader is disinterested or even friendly, he reads only to spot errors, and does not read as critically as the eventual reader will. Having gained some objectivity during the time the paper was being proofread by someone else, the author may now be able to discover that sentences or thoughts that at first seemed so well done are not as well written as she thought, or that she forgot something important.

If you absolutely cannot find a proofreader, then—once you have rewritten, edited, and polished the document—print it out and leave it alone for at least 24 hours. The intervening time helps you gain objectivity about the work, and will help you see exactly what you have written, not what you think you wrote. In addition to checking again for clarity, punctuation, and everything else, be aware that computer spell checkers cannot pick up inappropriate words. For example, one of the Manning student memos contained the following sentence: "*Therefore, what must be determined is what makes a contract special such that emotional damages will be awarded for its breach, and whether the breach of a contract to sew a weeding [sic] dress is that kind of contract.*" Most people do not wear special clothes for *weeding* their gardens, though many women want elegant *wedding* dresses. The error here occurred because the writer (1) failed to leave the memo alone for a day, (2) failed to proofread a hard copy, or (3) failed to have another person check it for him. The computer cannot tell that the writer meant *wedding* rather than *weeding.* Only a human reader could discern the error, but the error is embarrassing and makes the writer appear to be less than professional. To be sure that everything is the best you can possibly make it, give yourself time and space to proofread objectively before turning in a project.

EXERCISES

1. *Citation:* Put the following citations in Bluebook or ALWD form, or explain what additional information would be needed to do so.
   a. Mark Browning v. Abraham Fies, et al., 1912 Ala. App. Lexis 354-1 (Ala. Ct. App. 1912).

b. Farmers Insurance Exchange v. Henderson, 313 P.2d 404 (Ariz. 1957).
c. Patricia J. Williams, 22 Harv. C.R.-C.L. L. Rev. 407 (1987).
d. Mei-Ian E. Wong, note, The Implications of School Choice for Children with Disabilities, 103 North Dakota Law Review 827, 830 (1993).
e. Treaty on the Non-Proliferation of Nuclear Weapons, 21 U.S.T. 483, 729 U.N.T.S.

2. ***Punctuation:*** Correct the punctuation errors in the following sentences.
   a. Based on articulable suspicion, the police officer told the suspect to stand still frisked him and found cocaine in the man's shirt pocket.
   b. President John Kennedy said, ask what you can do for your country.
   c. He said that *the very integrity of the judicial system* (something) *depends on full disclosure of all the facts.* (everything in italic is a quotation).
   d. Once we recognized that the "reasonable man" is almost the same as a "*bon père de famille*", U.S. negligence law made more sense.
3. ***Grammar:*** Correct the grammar errors in the following sentences.
   a. In *Lestina*, the defendant slide-tackles the plaintiff and injured him.
   b. The court ordered that the car of the defendants be seized.
   c. Congress are debating this issue as we speak.
4. ***Word choice:*** Improve the following sentences by replacing legalese terms and eliminating unnecessary phrases.
   a. It is important to note that while the aforesaid plaintiff was signing said contract, his close personal friend was already making it impossible to perform.
   b. The defendant was found guilty by the judge and was sentenced to thirty years without possibility of parole.
5. ***Paraphrasing and sentence structure***: Rewrite the following quotations, using simpler sentence structure and more current terms.
   a. "A limitation more firmly rooted in tradition is that generally denying recovery for emotional disturbance or mental distress, resulting from a breach of contract, even if the limitations of unforeseeability and uncertainty can be overcome."
   b. "The plaintiff's special or ulterior purpose in making the contract was disclosed at the time it was entered into and thereby became incorporated into it and thus afforded a substantial basis for the assessment of mental damages."
   c. "The special circumstances having been known and assented to by each of the contracting parties, each is deemed to have contracted with reference to them, and the party who breaches the contract may justly be held to make good to the other, whatever damages, general or mental, he has sustained which are the reasonable and natural consequences of the breach under the known circumstances with reference to which the parties acted in making the contract."
6. ***Transitions:*** Make corrections, add transitional words and phrases, or change language to make the following paragraphs flow more smoothly.
   a. On Mardi Gras day, George Furman boarded a streetcar in New Orleans and sat down in the rear of the car. He had been to all the parades and wore a pile of beads around his neck. He had a bag of plastic go-cups. Like the beads, they had been thrown to him by people on the parade floats. Three teenage boys, Robert Boudreaux, Michael Beckham, and John Joseph boarded the streetcar. The three boys wore stockings over their heads and carried cans of beer. They were

obnoxiously loud and drunk. Boudreaux, who was very tall and muscular, turned to Furman and demanded, "What you lookin' at?" The two other boys gathered in behind Boudreaux, blocking Furman's exit through the aisle. Furman thought it best not to antagonize this group of teenagers. He averted his eyes and kept quiet. This proved to be a mistake. Boudreaux started screaming, "Answer me when I speak to you!" Furman did the smart thing. He gave them some beads. They gave him some beer. Everyone started yelling happily "let the good times roll."[21]

b. In a breach of contract claim, to recover for mental damages, the contract must be of such a nature that its breach causes mental distress for reasons other than a pecuniary loss. What makes a contract special is that the parties during the negotiation of the contract, should knew that the emotional distress is a natural consequence of the breach. This means that the emotional distress had been in the contemplation of the parties as the probable result of the breach.

7. ***Paragraph organization and topic sentences:*** Reorganize the following paragraph, reworking sentences and using transitions as needed.

   In *Lestina*, a soccer player slide-tackled another player and injured him. The court found him negligent because the old-timer's soccer league had banned slide-tackles. Id. Similarly, a softball player was found to be negligent because he ran off the baseline into the second baseman and injured him in a move that was blatantly against the rules of the game. Generally, defendants in recreational sports cases are found negligent if the act that caused the plaintiff's injury was a wrongful breach of the rules of the game, the plaintiff's type of injury was unanticipated in that particular sport, or the level of violence was generally higher than is customary for the particular league of players involved. Lestina. However, in a women's high school soccer game, the goalie could not bring suit when she was injured by a member of the opposing team who kicked her while attempting a goal kick. Cunico.

8. Using the guidelines in this chapter, rewrite, edit, and polish the closed memo assignment from Chapter 3.

[21] Adapted from Helene S. Shapo, Marilyn R. Walter, & Elizabeth Fajans, *Writing and Analysis in the Law* 152 (3d ed., Foundation Press 1995).

CHAPTER 9

Advanced Objective Writing

INTRODUCTION

Chapter 3 introduced U.S. legal reasoning and objective legal writing. Chapter 8 showed how to polish those skills into an office memo of the style used in U.S. law firms. Chapters 2, 5, 6, and 7 discussed U.S. legal research. This chapter will explain how to synthesize all this into the scholarly research project. Like an open memo, scholarly writing requires objective, critical analysis, but is aimed at a broader audience and is designed to be published in a U.S. law review or similar publication. A scholarly research project may also be part of an LL.M. program, as a thesis or seminar paper, or may be used as part of an S.J.D. application. Most LL.M. programs in the United States have an advanced writing requirement of some sort.

The other two styles of writing commonly used in U.S. law firms are termed *persuasive writing* or *advocacy* and *preventive writing.* These are explained in detail in Chapters 11 and 12, but in general, persuasive writing is writing that argues on behalf of a client, as in a memorandum of points and authorities or an appellate brief (*not* a law office memorandum of the type described in Chapter 3). These documents are submitted to a court and are the attorney's primary means of arguing the client's case. Advocacy requires the same fundamental, objective analysis as objective writing, but that analysis is then reworked, emphasizing arguments that favor the client and rebutting opposing counsel's arguments. Preventive writing is used in drafting legislation, wills, and contracts. It is also used in legal memos addressed to the client, explaining what activities are legal or illegal, to help the client avoid transgressing the law. The purpose of preventive writing is to create a legal relationship between two parties or to avoid potential litigation. This chapter focuses on scholarly writing, but the organizational methodology can be used for any objective writing project, whether it is a long, involved open memo or an LL.M. thesis. With some little adaptation, the same methods are also used for persuasive writing.

I. TYPES OF SCHOLARLY ARTICLES

Scholarly articles can be divided into two generic types: those that are intended for publication, and those that are not. Although this bifurcated classification is used here to help describe and explain expectations in the U.S. law school and law review market, the division has no real substance. At the LL.M. level, the writer of the article is a professional, and whether or not the article is likely to be published, the goal is to make it of publishable quality.

A. Seminar Papers and Thesis Papers

Many LL.M. programs include a substantial writing requirement. The student must write a graded scholarly paper, somewhere between 30 and 90 pages in length, for which he or she receives credit. A *seminar paper* is written in the context of a course. A *thesis* is a paper of substantial length written for credit under the direction of a particular professor, rather than as a course requirement. Different law schools use different names to refer to the same kind of paper: in addition to *thesis, independent study project, directed research project,* and other terms are used.

In either case, whether it is called a seminar paper or a thesis, the topic of the paper is individual to the student. The professor and the particular student reach an agreement about what the subject of the paper will be. Even if the paper is a seminar paper, no other student in the class will be writing on the exact same topic. A seminar paper is usually somewhat shorter than a thesis paper, and may be somewhat smaller in scope. The thesis, in addition to being larger in scope than a seminar paper, may include an oral defense, though this is unusual in the United States.

Whether a seminar paper or a thesis, usually the professor expects the student to suggest a topic, which the professor then accepts, rejects, or modifies. Once a topic is agreed upon, the student is generally expected to meet with the professor one or more times before the project is due, so that the professor can verify that the student is headed in the right direction and making good progress. Though the requirements vary from professor to professor, many professors want students to submit (1) a bibliography, (2) an initial outline, and (3) a first draft of the paper before submitting the final project for a grade. At these interim points, professors usually give students very helpful advice on how to improve the paper. Even if you do not feel that the advice is helpful, it is wise to do your best to follow it. As a professional writer, your job is to please your audience. In this instance, your audience is the professor who will be grading the project. Thus, even if the professor does not demand interim submissions, it is best to determine his expectations, and advisable to meet with him to verify that the project is progressing in accord with those expectations.

B. Law Review Articles

As mentioned earlier, seminar papers and theses are patterned after published articles. Furthermore, LL.M. candidates often have an opportunity to publish either a thesis or an article written specifically for a law review associated with a law school and run by student editors. Because having one's article published is a great honor in the United States, these publications are a valuable way of building one's résumé. Therefore, it is helpful to understand a bit about the types of articles published in law reviews, as well as about the U.S. law review system.

In general, law school law reviews publish four different types of articles: articles, book reviews, comments, and casenotes. Articles are written by scholars and practitioners who submit their work for publication. Usually, when deciding whether to publish a particular article, the student editors consider not only the merit or worthiness of the article, but also the prestige of the author. Therefore, most articles in law reviews are written by legal scholars of some stature. On occasion, however, an LL.M. candidate can place a thesis article with a law review if the topic is timely (or "hot") and the article well-written.

Some law reviews solicit book reviews either from professors at their law schools or from another scholar in the same field of law as the book being reviewed. These book reviews are at times very good secondary authority, and quite useful to someone researching the field. It is unlikely that an LL.M. candidate will be asked to write one, because the reviewer is by definition someone who is very knowledgeable in that particular area of law.

The remaining two types of law review articles — comments and casenotes — are usually written by J.D. students. Though law reviews sometimes publish LL.M. students' comments, if you have a choice, it is preferable to publish an article rather than a comment because it is a stronger résumé-builder. The casenote informs law review readers about a significant case, and provides a thoughtful and original evaluation of that decision. Often it is the first piece of scholarly writing required of a law review member, or is used as the subject for a writing competition: the student who writes the best casenote on a prescribed case becomes a member of the law review. Some law reviews dictate the structure of a casenote, issuing very strict guidelines about what is to be included. Even if they do not do this, however, a casenote is usually organized into four parts: an introduction of the case, its background, an analysis of the decision, and a conclusion. The introduction describes the case and its holding, and plainly states the writer's opinion of that holding. It also provides a road map of the note. The background gives preexisting law and explains the effect of the case. Analysis of the decision may either criticize the decision or explain why it is effective. (Usually, the more effective casenotes criticize the decision.) Finally, a short conclusion summarizes the analysis and invites the reader to take up the issues raised where the writer ended.[1] A law review comment is broader in scope and more sophisticated than a casenote, and can take a variety of forms. Its purpose is to analyze a particular, limited area of law. Often, the only way it differs from a seminar paper or article may be in length and scope of subject: a seminar paper is typically the shortest (30 to 45 double-spaced pages), a comment of moderate length (50 to 70 double-spaced pages), and a lead article the longest (80+ pages). The supervising professor or editor of the journal usually dictates the length of the work.

[1] Elizabeth Fajans & Mary R. Falk, *Scholarly Writing for Law Students: Seminar Papers, Law Review Notes and Law Review Competition Papers* 11 (West Group 1995).

II. SUBJECT CHOICE AND DEVELOPMENT

It is not enough to approach a professor and simply say, "I want to write my paper on intellectual property." The professor is most likely to respond with, "What area of intellectual property, and what do you want to say about it?" In other words, the professor expects the student to suggest both a narrow topic and an approach to that topic. Both of these will require some preliminary investigation of the field. Often, the most difficult part of writing a scholarly paper is finding something worth saying. The writer must find a subject that is interesting to both herself and her audience, and the subject must be manageable. Furthermore, the writer must develop something original to say about that topic (see discussion of the thesis statement in § III. A of this chapter). It is not enough merely to research an area of law and write a summation of that research.

A. Identifying a Particular Issue or Narrow Area

First, you must identify a particular issue or area on which to write. Assume that you have chosen a specific area of law: wetlands law, perhaps, or mergers and acquisitions. You must then narrow that field down to a specific question or aspect. You can research an interesting but too broad subject systematically to look for a manageable aspect of it. One good way is to peruse the table of contents of a casebook or treatise for possible topics, and then pick two or three tentative topics and see what kinds of articles have been written on that topic.

If you hope to eventually publish the article, find a topic of current interest, something known as a *hot topic*. To do this, one can research in two ways: through conversation with colleagues and professors, or through reading items of current interest. Talk to your professor, mentor, and other students, and scan legal and other news sources for current issues in that area. Your aim is to identify the current concerns of academics and practitioners. For example, the "Summary and Analysis" section of *United States Law Week* or the legal news section of one of the online research services might contain a short article that sparks your interest.

Many LL.M. candidates from outside the United States choose comparative topics: topics comparing one area or aspect of U.S. law to the law of the student's home country. This is a natural consequence of their studies. These can be very successful research papers, and are often welcomed by U.S. professors, but they have their own challenges. Comparing law from two different countries is pointless if it leads merely to a "gee whiz, they're different" conclusion. A good comparative paper must say something more: It must present and support a thesis statement — your own point of view — about this area. In researching and writing these types of papers, explore various analytical approaches from among those described in subsection B to develop your own viewpoint. This will help you narrow down and develop your topic, organize your paper, and develop a thesis statement. Some questions you may ask are: Why does U.S. law differ in this respect from the law of my country? Which is the more effective approach? Is the effectiveness of the approach closely tied to the legal culture in which it developed? Would one jurisdiction benefit by borrowing portions of the other approach?

Before finalizing your choice of topic, especially if you hope to publish it or if your reader expects originality, do a preemption check. Search law reviews and other scholarly materials to make sure your topic has not already been exhaustively explored, and that you will be able to find something original to say about it. Although you will eventually need to have a thesis statement, do not obsess about developing one before you research your topic. The thesis statement should be derived from your research, not imposed upon it.

B. Approaches to Articles

Most scholarly articles, whether law review articles, theses, or seminar papers, take one of approximately nine approaches. Non-U.S. LL.M. candidates, because of their prior training in a different legal system, often find themselves drawn to comparative law topics. The approaches commonly used in law review articles are easily adapted to comparative law topics, and may help you develop topic suggestions.

1. One of the most common approaches is to analyze law in an area that is confused, in conflict, or undergoing change. Very often courts will disagree on how to approach a particular issue, leading to a split in authority. In these kinds of articles, the author presents both sides of the controversy and the policy implications of each. In doing so, she presents and analyzes the most important cases on each side to illustrate the split, and then resolves the conflict or problem, offering a solution that she feels will best advance "goals of equity, efficiency,"[2] or other aims.

   In terms of comparative law, an article like this could compare conflicting ways in which in which different legal systems deal with the same issue. For example, the duty of good faith and fair dealing is part and parcel of the process of contracting, according to many civilian jurisdictions. At common law, however, there is no such duty until or unless a contract is in place. A paper discussing this conflict would analyze each theory, show how it developed, set out the policy grounds for each, explain how and when each is used, and then perhaps advise international practitioners on how to counsel clients involved in international transactions, or propose a way to harmonize the law of both systems.[3]
2. The law reform article argues that a legal rule or institution is unjust, inequitable, unfair, or incoherent. The article presents and analyzes the legal rule at issue, discusses case law or factual instances to illustrate the inequity, and rebuts opposing arguments. The writer then shows how the legal rule or institution should be changed. A comparative paper along these lines would criticize one country's approach, using

[2] *Id.* at 6.

[3] *See, e.g.*, Nadia E. Nedzel, *A Comparative Study of Good Faith, Fair Dealing, and Precontractual Liability*, 12 Tul. Eur. & Civ. L.F. 97 (1997).

another country to illustrate how the legal rule or institution from the other could solve the problem.[4]

3. The legislative note analyzes proposed or recently enacted legislation, often section by section, offering insights, background information, comments, and criticisms. It usually predicts how the legislation will be received and what the likely consequences will be—both good and bad. If your country has recently enacted new legislation, you might compare it to similar legislation in the United States, and predict whether the change will be good, bad, or mixed. One such study, originally written by an LL.M. candidate for the author's legal research and writing class, compared the U.S. Foreign Corrupt Practices Act to other proposed treaties. That study, expanded to article length, was published in one of the author's home-country law reviews.[5]
4. Interdisciplinary articles present another option. In an interdisciplinary article, the author shows how insights from another field, such as economics, sociology, psychology, or other behavioral field, can explain a legal problem or provide a better legal solution. For example, one study used behavioral science and sociology to explain why the enforcement of contracts was problematic in some post-Soviet republics.
5. In the theory-fitting article, the author examines developments in an area of law and develops a new legal theory or new explanation of the law.
6. Articles can be written on subjects that are related to law, but which are not themselves traditional substantive law, such as the legal profession itself, legal ethics, legal language, legal argument, or legal education. For example, another of the author's LL.M. candidates was fascinated by ethical considerations and billing practices of lawyers in the United States as compared to his home country. The article that developed out of his project, like the article on the Foreign Corrupt Practices Act, has been published in a law review.[6]
7. Some articles and scholarly projects either create a debate or build on a preexisting one. These types of articles usually begin with a short history of the debate ("In an influential article in *W. Law Review*, Professor X argued Z. Critics, including professor Y, attacked her view, arguing A, B, and C. This article offers D, a new approach to the problem of Z.").[7] For example, in the late 20th century, Professor Rodolfo Batiza argued that Louisiana law was based on French law,[8] while Professor Robert Pascal argued that it was primarily Spanish.[9] The argument went back

[4] *See, e.g.*, Rebecca Trail, *Note, The Future of Capital Punishment in the United States: Effects of the International Trend Towards Abolition of the Death Penalty*, 26 Suffolk Transnat'l L. Rev. 105 (2002).

[5] Guido Acquaviva, *La Legislazione Statunitense in Materia di Lootta alla Corruzione de Fronte agli Ultimi Sviluppi Internazionali*, 15 Diritto del Commercio Internazionale 625 (2001).

[6] Peter Eggenberger, *License to Bill = License to Kill? Ethical Considerations on Lawyers' Fees (with a View to Switzerland)*, 20 Penn State Int'l L. Rev. 505 (2002).

[7] Fajans & Falk, *supra* note 1, at 7.

[8] Rodolfo Batiza, *The Louisiana Civil Code of 1808: Its Actual Sources and Present Relevance*, 46 Tul. L. Rev. 4 (1971).

[9] Robert A. Pascal, *Sources of the Digest of 1808: A Reply to Professor Batiza*, 46 Tul. L. Rev. 604 (1972).

and forth for several years until it was answered by yet a third scholar, Richard Kilbourne, in a book arguing that Louisiana law is a mixture of both French and Spanish law, with an ever-increasing common law influence.[10]

8. Legal history is another category of scholarly articles. A study of the origin and development of a legal rule or institution may help explain its current operation or shortcomings.[11] A comparative study could explain how and why a legal theme or principle developed differently in different legal systems, even though they have common roots, and then explain why one may be more efficient than the other.
9. Empirical studies are often very valuable. In an empirical study, the author collects data and analyzes it to see if it fits with current opinion or legal theory, or to gain other insights into how the law operates. Recently, two scholars collected and analyzed hundreds of promissory estoppel cases (something that is not too difficult to do in an age of computerized databases). The theory had been that damage awards made in such cases were based on reliance. The authors discovered, to their surprise, that typically courts had difficulty in measuring reliance damages, and based awards on expectation instead.[12]

C. Unanticipated Research Problems

When choosing a topic, make sure that it is something for which research is feasible. If the resources you will need are available only in your home country, and you expect that you will neither be returning home nor be able to have someone send them to you, then choose a different topic on which to write. Before suggesting a topic, do some preliminary research to verify that you will be able to obtain the requisite resources. Occasionally a topic that originally seemed to be a good choice becomes impracticable because there simply are not enough resources or authorities available. Be sure to arrange your time so that you can adjust your topic if necessary, if your first choice appears to be unfeasible after a certain amount of research. If your project is a seminar paper, advise your professor immediately if you run into research problems, so that the two of you can adjust or amend the topic as needed.

III. THE CONTENTS OF A SCHOLARLY ARTICLE

A. Thesis Statement

When asked what distinguishing feature makes a good scholarly article, U.S. law professors and law review editors universally say that a good article has a *thesis*

---

[10] Richard Holcombe Kilbourne, Jr., *A History of the Louisiana Civil Code: The Formative Years, 1803-1839* (1987).
[11] *See, e.g.*, James E. Viator, *Give Me That Old-Time Historiography: Charles Beard and the Study of the Constitution, Part II*, 43 Loy. L. Rev. 311 (1997).
[12] Edward Yorio & Steve Thel, *The Promissory Basis of Section 90*, 101 Yale L.J. 111 (1991).

statement—in other words, it makes a point and the body of the paper supports and proves that point. A *thesis statement* is not the same as what is commonly referred to as a *thesis*, which refers to a long paper written as part of a degree requirement. Instead, a *thesis statement* explains the point the paper is making; it is like a topic sentence, but stronger. This statement of purpose may or may not be something you are used to, but it is consistent with all other types of legal writing. For example, an interoffice memo discusses the answer to a specific legal issue or issues. The answer is first presented in the short-answer section, then explained thoroughly in the discussion section, and reiterated in the conclusion section. Thus, it is a thesis statement. The same is true in advocacy: The arguing attorney first explains to the court why his client should win, then explains why that remedy is justified under the law, and then concludes with a final request for that remedy. The entire brief is organized around the fundamental argument or thesis.

Similarly, U.S. scholarly legal writing consistently demands that the writer tell the reader, early on, the purpose or point of the work, and how that point will be substantiated. The underlying message is that the reader's time is valuable and that the writer will take care not to waste it. Thus, any good piece of writing contains a thesis statement. In a law firm memo, the thesis statement is the short answer. The entire body of the memo is written in support of that short answer. Similarly, in a scholarly piece, the entire body of the piece is written to substantiate and support the thesis statement.

Sometimes the thesis statement is dictated by the choice of topic, particularly if the writer has a point or argument to make and researches with the sole purpose of supporting that argument. However, this usually is not the best way to begin a writing project, because it leads to opinion-based research rather than objective research, and therefore the reader may reasonably question whether the author's opinion is well grounded. More often, a writer will choose a topic based on his or her own interest, and will not develop an opinion or thesis statement until late in the prewriting stage.

In choosing a topic, consider carefully what type of thesis statement it is likely to generate, and whether that sort of point is one you are interested in making and your reader is interested in reading. For example, a casenote written about a case that was well written and well decided will ultimately say nothing more than "I agree." In contrast, a casenote written about a controversial or important but poorly reasoned case could have a much more important point to make about the law in that particular area.

Many LL.M. candidates write scholarly papers that compare some facet of their home country's law to U.S. law. A paper that merely makes comparisons is pointless to write, and therefore pointless to read because its thesis amounts to "See, they're different"—to which the reader's natural response is "Of course they're different, so what?" Thus, writing five pages on U.S. law, five pages on the law in your country, and then reaching some conclusion is not enough to constitute a well-written, well-thought-out paper with a definite thesis. However, a paper that compares two different countries' laws on a particular subject can be successful if it makes a statement about those differences, analyzing which facets are advantageous and which disadvantageous, or even the differences of which a practitioner needs to be aware.

Once you have chosen your topic and done a bit of research, develop a working thesis statement, and then revise it as your research broadens. In the final paper, the polished thesis statement is introduced in the very beginning of the article. The body of the paper then explains the support for the thesis statement, and concludes that the thesis statement is justified, based on the research and analysis done in the body of the paper. Thus, the thesis statement is used throughout the paper.

B. Basic Organization of a Scholarly Paper

Although there are a number of approaches for the thrust of a scholarly paper, the fundamental organization is surprisingly consistent, whether the paper is a seminar paper, a comment, or an article. The basic structure consists of four parts:

1. introduction
2. background
3. analysis
4. conclusion

The introduction presents the thesis statement and explains how the article is organized. If the article is very long, this introduction may be preceded by a table of contents. It may also include a table of authorities. The background section explains how the law developed in this area. It should be specific and comprehensive, and not assume that the reader has any knowledge of this area of law. The background section should, however, avoid irrelevant detail. Like the rule section of a law firm memo, it should explain the law, not merely list cases one after another, and it should discuss the facts of those cases to help illustrate how the law works (or perhaps does not work). The analysis, like the application section of a law firm memo, is the focal point of the paper. It should be original and closely reasoned, building to a convincing conclusion.

C. Footnotes

In a scholarly article, the author wants to demonstrate to the reader she is familiar with all the relevant literature on the topic, as well as avoid any possible plagiarism. The way to do this is through substantial citation. In scholarly articles, the citations are given in footnotes, or occasionally endnotes, and are not put in the body of the text. If you examine almost any article in a law review, you will notice that on average, one-third of the page is devoted to footnotes. Thus, a 70-page article may well have more than 400 footnotes.

1. String Citations

Having been introduced to the almost obsessive use of citations in law firm memos, it should come as no surprise that the same obsessive use is present in scholarly articles. In fact, publishers and audiences of scholarly articles are probably even more obsessive in demanding substantial verification derived from broad research and shown by citation. You might cite only the most authoritative source in a law firm memo, but when writing a scholarly article on a similar subject, you may well cite as many authoritative sources as you can find that make the same point. These long lists of sources are known as *string citations.* For example, the following footnote cites first Professor Palmer's article describing Louisiana's use of the civilian concept of *culpa in contrahendo*[13] and then lists four Louisiana cases, thus further substantiating Professor Palmer's point:

> Vernon V. Palmer, *Contractual Negligence in the Civil Law—The Evolution of a Defense to Actions for Error,* 50 Tul. L. Rev. 1, 42 (1975); *see, e.g.,* Davilla v. Jones, 418 So. 2d 724 (La. Ct. App. 1982), *rev'd,* 436 So. 2d 507 (La. 1983) (discussing *culpa in contrahendo*); Coleman v. Bossier City, 305 So. 2d 444, 447 (La. 1974) (same); Snyder v. Champion Realty Corp., 631 F.2d 1253, 1254 (5th Cir. 1980) (same); Morris v. Friedman, 663 So. 2d 19, 23 n.8 (1995) (same); Gray v. McCormick, 663 So. 2d 480, 486 (La. Ct. App. 1995) (same).[14]

2. *Discursive Citations*

In addition to having more citations than open memos, scholarly articles are likely to contain discursive citations as well as substantiating ones. *Substantiating citations* provide support for the point made in the text, as with the Palmer footnote just discussed. *Discursive citations* and the parenthetical notes that follow them create a sub-dialogue with the reader on topics that are somewhat tangential to the main topic of the article, and usually contain introductory signals to tell the reader why the material is being cited. Some scholars like discursive citations; some do not, believing that if something is important, it should be included in the text of the article, and that if it is not important enough to be in the text, then it should be left out. Other scholars believe that discursive citations help show the breadth of the author's research and allow her to introduce and discuss subjects that are slightly tangential to the topic of the article, but still very interesting to the reader. Be sure to determine your supervisor's view on the subject before either using or avoiding discursive citations.

A fuller explanation of signals is available in both the Bluebook (Rules 1.2 to 1.5) and the ALWD (Rules 45.0 to 47.3), so only a quick summary of them is included here. Introductory signals include positive signals that precede authority that further supports the author's point and adds an extra breadth or dimension beyond merely substantiating the text. In addition to positive signals, there are also introductory signals that indicate negative or contradictory authority. Positive signals include *see* (cited authority clearly supports the proposition); *see, e.g.* (cited authority provides examples of the proposition); *accord* (before a list of other authorities that support the proposition in addition to the first one cited); *see also* (cited authority constitutes additional source material supporting the proposition but not as strongly as source previously cited); and *compare [and] with [and]* (comparison of the authorities cited

---

[13] *Culpa in contrahendo* is a civilian concept that serves a function similar to that of good faith or promissory estoppel in U.S. common law: It provides for liability for misbehavior in the context of contractual negotiations. Although the concept exists in most civilian jurisdictions, its scope and definition vary widely from jurisdiction to jurisdiction.

[14] Nedzel, *supra* note 3, at 143 n.266.

will offer support for or illustrate the proposition). Negative signals include *contra* (cited authority directly states the contrary of the proposition); *but see* (cited authority clearly supports a proposition contrary to the main proposition); and *but cf.* (cited authority supports a proposition analogous to the contrary of the main proposition).

The following quotation is a sample of a positive discursive footnote, and similarly discusses *culpa in contrahendo.* In this example, however, the footnote discusses the German interpretation of the concept. The short discussion included in between the two citations provides details that the author felt were not important enough to be included in the text, but might interest some readers:

> *See, e.g.*, Friedrich Kessler & Edith Fine, Culpa in Contrahendo, *Bargaining in Good Faith, and Freedom of Contract: A Comparative Study*, 77 Harv. L. Rev. 401 (1964). Under German law, the concept of good faith has grown from a general clause concerned with how to perform contracts (BGB § 242 provides that "the debtor is obliged to perform in such a manner as good faith requires, regard being paid to general Practice") into a "super control norm" for the whole civil code, as well as for large parts of German law outside the code. Horn/Koeth/Leser, German Private and Commercial Law 135 (1982). The provisions in the U.C.C. dealing with good faith were inspired by the German Civil Code. E. Allen Farnsworth, *The Eason-Weinmann Colloquium on International and Comparative Law: Duties of Good Faith and Fair Dealing under the Unidroit Principles, Relevant International Conventions, and National Laws*, 3 Tul. J. Int'l & Comp. L. 47, 51 (1995).

This footnote, which begins with a *see, e.g.*, introductory signal, helps the reader understand exactly how important *culpa in contrahendo* is in German law. It also ties the German concept to the U.S. Uniform Commercial Code. Therefore, the footnote adds to the richness of the reader's understanding of the topic. It was not included in the body of the article because the topic of the section was the development of the concept generally in Europe, and therefore, though useful and interesting, these details about German law were somewhat tangential to the topic discussed.

Signals indicating contradiction show that the author is aware that some authorities challenge his textual point. If such authorities exist, the author should also explain why he rejects the contrary argument, and why it is unimportant or misguided. As a general rule, however, if you are faced with an authority that contradicts your point, you should explain in the body of the text why you reject that contrary opinion. Negative signals are more appropriately used to subtly add further support to the author's point. In the following example, the author uses a negative signal to compare the scope of the Swiss interpretation of *culpa in contrahendo* with analogous concepts in the United States and France. Although the signal is negative, the content of the footnote does not undercut the author's argument. Instead, it enriches and deepens the argument. The text of the article explains that under United States law, a defendant who has been found liable for a breach of a precontractual promise may be faced with greater damages than he would under French law, and that therefore the French concept is narrower in scope. The footnote points out that in comparison, the scope of liability under Swiss law may be greater than that in France, and hence more like the U.S. standard. Thus, the function of the footnote is to broaden the reader's knowledge of how various jurisdictions award damages in precontractual liability cases. Again, this conversation with the reader was not included in the body of the text, because the author considered it somewhat tangential to the topic being discussed:

> *But see* Ben-Dror, *supra* note 16, at 178 n.210. While civilian standard of damages in *culpa in contrahendo* cases is "negative" interest, the Swiss Code of Obligations gives the judge the discretion to award compensation at a higher rate than the reliance interest if he deems it equitable to do so.[15]

Footnotes are the norm in scholarly writing, in contrast to law firm memos and court documents, which traditionally use textual citations (citations that immediately follow the text of a sentence). As explained earlier, there is a movement to put all such citations in footnotes, regardless of the particular type of legal writing, but so far, the idea has not reached broad-based acceptance in practical—as opposed to scholarly—writing. Similarly, there is some controversy regarding discursive footnotes. Some editors object to long, tangential, textual footnotes, feeling that if the author's point is that important, it should be in the body of the paper rather than a footnote; conversely, if the point is not important enough to be in the body of the paper, it should be omitted entirely. Generally, you will not be expected to include extremely long discursive footnotes in a seminar paper, but you may want to have some in an article intended for publication.

D. Plagiarism Warning

The previous discussion presented two of the three purposes of citations. First, citations substantiate the author's assertions, providing both authority and bibliography. Second, discursive footnotes and citations (often those preceded by introductory signals) permit the writer to express ideas that are somewhat tangential to the topic, further substantiate points made in the body of the text itself, or even make humorous asides to the reader. The third purpose of citations and footnotes is at least as important as the first two: By attributing material borrowed from other sources to those sources, they avoid plagiarism. Sadly, each year a number of LL.M. candidates in the United States are accused of plagiarizing other works in writing a scholarly paper.

Just as it is against most U.S. law schools' honor codes to copy another student's paper, it is also against the honor code to copy or even use material from a published source without attributing that use to the original authority with a citation. If you quote language from a source, you must quote exactly, word for word, use quotation marks, and follow the quotation with a citation. Quotations must be exact, even down to the punctuation used in the original authority. Paraphrased material must also be identified with citations. Furthermore, this obligation applies both to textual material from other sources and to citations and footnotes from other sources. For example, cutting and pasting a footnote from another source without reading those sources is

[15] Nedzel, *supra* note 3, at 150 n.307.

also plagiarism subject to sanction. Sadly, when LL.M. candidates get into trouble for honor code violations, the problem is usually not that they have copied from another candidate (which almost all understand is a violation), but that they have used material from one or more *published* sources without attributing that material to the original source. Most honor codes treat the two violations as equally sanctionable. Thus, failing to cite published sources in a work submitted either to a professor or to a journal can lead to sanctions as severe as expulsion from the program. Do not let this happen to you. Take the time to properly cite all your sources. Though it may be difficult at first, it quickly becomes a habit.

IV. TIME MANAGEMENT AND RESEARCH STRATEGIES

A. Avoiding Procrastination

For many, the most difficult problem is preventing procrastination and thereby ensuring that the finished product will be thoughtfully researched and carefully written. Sometimes, the larger and more important the project, the more daunting and difficult it can be to get started. American attorneys often joke among themselves about procrastination and how widespread it is among us. Jokes aside, it is a serious problem, and is the underlying cause of many of the malpractice suits in the United States. Prior to teaching international LL.M. students, the author had been under the impression that it was a problem primarily among U.S. lawyers and law students. Unfortunately, the disease of procrastination seems to be either highly contagious or worldwide: The truth is that when we are busy, it is easy to find reasons to put off projects until the last possible moment. Almost anyone can research and write well, given enough time. The converse is also true: Almost no one can produce a well-researched and well-written project at the last minute.

To avoid procrastination, begin by mapping out a timetable: approximately one-third to one-half of available time should be spent researching the problem, and one-half to two-thirds writing, revising, and polishing the project. Then subdivide that time: Divide the research allocation into portions for Stages 1, 2, and 3 — recognizing that prewriting is part of Stage 3 research and that further research may be necessary once you start writing. Then divide the writing time allocation into writing, rewriting, editing, and polishing. Remember to allow at least 24 hours between editing and polishing, so that you can read a hard copy of the final product objectively, and spot spelling, grammar, and citation mistakes that you missed in previous revisions. Write your timetable on a calendar, and stick to it as closely as possible, revising as needed if you find that certain portions of the project take more time than anticipated.

Regular meetings with the supervising professor are another way to avoid procrastination, in addition to verifying that the project will meet her expectations. If you know you have to show Professor Smith your bibliography next Monday, you have a definite deadline by which the majority of your research must be done. The same is true of outlines and first drafts.

B. Research Strategy

Researching for a scholarly article is very much like researching for a memo. Begin by analyzing your question, generating terms, and researching in secondary authority. Then move to primary authority, and from there update. Continue until you find that most research trails lead back to the same sources. The only difference between researching for a scholarly article and researching for a law firm memo is that research for an article should be much broader based, and very, very thorough.

To maintain focus, it is helpful to begin each research session by reviewing an initial project statement. The initial project statement fulfills the same purpose that the initial issue statement does in researching a law firm memo: It keeps you on target, and helps prevent your research from wandering off on any number of tangents. The project statement can include both your topic and your preliminary thesis statement, theory, or purpose in pursuing this subject. It might even include a generic outline, such as the one at the end of this subsection. You can then organize your research easily as you progress.

Furthermore, it is not only necessary, but vital that you keep a research log—one that includes citations so you can locate authorities quickly and easily should you decide to use them. At first, keep track of everything that seems useful. Once you have focused your project and perhaps further narrowed your topic, you may find that you want to eliminate sources, but do not eliminate things you may need later. This is the time to become a pack rat, storing sources away until you are ready to periodically examine and analyze them.

GENERIC PROJECT OUTLINE[16]

I. Introduction
   A. Why you chose this subject
   B. Preliminary thesis statement: what you intend to do with this subject
II. Background
   A. How the subject developed
   B. Changes that occurred during its development
   C. Why it developed the way it has
III. Analysis
   A. Current state
      1. Advantages
      2. Disadvantages
   B. Changes suggested in commentary
      1. Advantages
      2. Disadvantages
IV. Your ideas for change
   A. Advantages
   B. Defects

---

[16] Gertrude Block, *Effective Legal Writing for Law Students and Lawyers* 231 (5th ed., Foundation Press 1999).

C. Storing and Organizing Research for Larger Projects

One efficient way of storing sources is to alphabetize reprints of the sources (with citation information) in a large accordion folder. On the front of the reprint, note why you kept it—what portion or portions of your project it addresses. Westlaw and LEXIS now have ways for you to keep notes about your reprints, but you may well find it faster and easier to use handwritten notes on sources because the handwriting stands out and you can recognize it quickly. You might even develop a colorful system of signals to indicate more important sources. For example, a yellow asterisk indicates an important source, and three yellow asterisks indicate something that is absolutely integral to your paper and must be incorporated before any other source. This way of organizing sources becomes very useful once you start to write the first draft. It helps you avoid having to research your own research and makes it easy to find materials when you need them during the writing process.

Hard-copy reprints are preferable to sources stored in computer files because they help with prewriting. All of the sources are easily accessed, easily seen, and easily stacked into piles according to which portion of the project they address. With a computer file, you can see only one screen at a time, which makes it much harder to synthesize different resources.

D. Reorganizing Research: Pre-prewriting

Once you have collected a certain amount of information, read it, analyze it carefully, and sort it into piles according to your preliminary outline. This will help you determine if you are lacking resources in one or more areas of your project. If something seems irrelevant, put it aside, perhaps in a tentative reject pile, but do not throw it away until after you have started writing and have ascertained that it is definitely irrelevant. Continue developing your notational indicators so that you will be familiar with your resources and have them well organized when you begin writing the first draft. As you read and analyze your authorities, read not just for content, but for rhetoric and tone as well. One of the mistakes inexperienced scholarly writers make is to accept commentators' opinions blindly and unquestioningly. Sometimes, although the research for a law review article was very well done, the author's opinions (thesis statement) can be questioned. The writer's opinion will be reflected in her word choices, and should be stated clearly in both the introduction and the conclusion. Ask yourself whether the author is writing from a certain political bias that might be coloring her interpretation of the research and, if so, whether you agree with the conclusions made. Especially if the author is a student, the thesis might be naïve and aspirational, not realistic or practical.

As you read through and organize your sources, take notes in more depth, and engage the material. A good way to do this is to keep asking yourself a number of questions:

- What are the specific legal principles in the area you are researching?
- How are they organized?
- What components of those principles are habitually litigated?
- Do the authorities agree, or is there a split in authority?

- If there is a split, what is the basis for that disagreement?
- What policy concerns are at issue?
- Which source or sources best explain the principles and policies concerned?

Furthermore, are there flaws or holes in the analysis? Is a particular article biased, or has it failed to prove its interpretation? Is that bias or interpretation justified? If not, perhaps the article is still useful because of the breadth of its research, rather than its conclusions—though you will want to be careful how you use it.

V. THE WRITING PROCESS

As with the research, the writing process for a larger scholarly work is very similar to that for an objective memo, though it takes more effort. Again, the most important part of the writing process may well be the prewriting. It is while prewriting that one develops the substantive worthiness of the project; as explained earlier, prewriting begins during the research process and may influence or extend the research. Writing, rewriting, editing, and polishing make the project reader-worthy and of professional, publishable quality. However, without substantial prewriting, you are likely to end up with a disorganized, unoriginal mass that lacks a thesis statement, or lacks solid support for the thesis statement. Even more likely, you may well find yourself stuck in the middle of the project, recognizing that it is not going well but finding yourself unable to remedy it.

There are four common consequences of failing to do enough prewriting. First, a writer may start the first draft before he fully understands what he is writing about, but by then be too attached to the draft to objectively pull it apart.[17] Second, by diving right into a draft, the writer does not give himself enough time or intellectual space to encourage creativity, so the final product is not nearly as insightful or imaginative as it could be.[18] Third, writing and sharpening sentences before verifying the solidity of the project's underlying structure wastes valuable time. Fourth, one may be so self-critical during the writing process that one develops "writer's block" and becomes unable to complete the project.

To avoid these problems, begin prewriting by reading through your authorities again slowly and carefully, taking more notes as you go about ideas that occur to you and that you want to develop in your final project. Like any growing thing, it takes time for the germ of an idea to grow into a paper, and those germs (or seeds) usually will not develop while they are in your head. The point of prewriting is to get your ideas out on paper, usually in a relaxed and haphazard fashion, where you can see them and begin to organize them. Once you have something on paper, often your thinking will take the ideas further, and you will gradually be able to make sense of the ideas and develop them into a thesis. After you have read through your authorities thoroughly, verify that

[17] Bryan A. Garner, *The Winning Brief* 4 (Oxford Univ. Press 1999).
[18] *Id.*

they are in keeping with the subject and scope of your topic and then begin the prewriting process in earnest. There is more than one way of prewriting, just as there is more than one type of writer.

A. The Natural Writing Process

To further understand the need for prewriting, it helps to have some view of the natural writing process. Writing can be divided into four steps, each undertaken by a different character.[19] These characters include the madman, the architect, the carpenter, and the judge. The madman, in charge of prewriting, is full of ideas, and spits them out in no particular order. His enthusiasm may carry him away. Often, rather than writing full sentences and paragraphs, the madman produces copious notes, jotting down ideas and possible approaches to a problem.

Once the madman has finished generating ideas, the architect takes over, making connections between ideas and planning a structure in which to present them. This is the conversion from notes or a free-form outline to a well-developed linear outline. The architect gives the project a beginning, a middle, and an end, and organizes the madman's ideas into a logical order.

After the madman and the architect have completed their work, the carpenter steps in. The carpenter actually builds the project — the first draft — using the structure developed by the architect but adding further detail and substance. The carpenter puts everything into words, incorporating authorities and keeping track of where to find those authorities so that citations will not be difficult to polish at the revision stage. At this point, the project need not be in complete sentences, but all of the ideas should be placed appropriately, and an attempt made to formulate grammatically correct sentences. However, do not spend an inordinate amount of time polishing a sentence that just will not go. Leave that problem to be resolved at a later stage, and just note to yourself that it is a problem.

Only after the carpenter has completed her work should the judge be allowed to examine it. Obviously, the "judge" stage is the rewriting, revising, and editing process. Often, the reason a writer has trouble is that he lets this "judge" criticize the writing too strenuously at too early a stage. Particularly if English is not your native language, be aware that you may tend to criticize your writing far too early in the writing process; this will substantially slow down your writing, stymie your creativity, limit your ability to generate an original thesis statement, and create a great deal of frustration.

The following explains four ways of prewriting, which you can try sequentially or mix-and-match as your project develops. Using notecards is a traditional method, but often ineffective for large legal writing projects. Unless you have used it for a long time, and are very comfortable with it, it might be better to focus on some other method. The second, outlining, is also a traditional method. It, too, however, has shortcomings. In particular, it can bring in the architect before the madman has finished his work. You should always have a well-developed outline before you start a first draft, but to

[19] Garner, *supra* note 17, at 4-5.

start prewriting with a rigid and detailed outline is a mistake, because it does not help you see various ways of organizing the project. Instead, you may find yourself locked into whatever outline first happened to appear in your head. The third method, free-form outlining or cluster diagrams, works well for many writers. This method allows you to approach outlining flexibly, thus giving your creativity and insight time to grow before you get locked into a rigid organizational structure. The final method, doing a preliminary "dump draft," works for those people who feel they simply must sit down and start writing immediately. Combinations of these methods can also be helpful: Many people feel most comfortable by starting with a dump draft and then developing an outline that organizes the good ideas from the dump draft; this is an effective way to first exercise the madman and then bring in the architect. You may want to experiment with the different types of prewriting to see which method works best for you.

B. Prewriting

1. Notecards and Preliminary Notes

The time-honored way of prewriting is to write each individual idea or principle on a small notecard, along with citation information (see the following sample). When it is time to begin organizing them, spread the cards out on a table and arrange them in a logical order. The disadvantage of this with a legal project is that it is difficult to allocate little bits of information appropriate to the size of the card. Furthermore, if you do not have a copy of the full authority on which the idea is based, it is easy to misinterpret the noted material on the cards, because it is taken out of context. Nevertheless, some people find this a very comfortable way to work because it disciplines them into summarizing important points and allows them to be very flexible until they have found a good way to organize those points. They then go on to formulate an outline from the notecards, and finally fill out the outline in a first draft.

To adapt this method to a legal project, it might be easier to use paper from a full-size legal pad instead of actual notecards. When you find a useful source, jot the title and citation information at the top of the paper, and your ideas or important information from the source on the paper. Then attach the paper to the front of your reprint of the source with a staple or a paper clip. Note where the ideas from one source overlap with those from another, and keep those two sources together to help in developing an outline.

Franklin A. Gevurtz, *The Globalization of Insider Trading Prohibitions*, 15 Transnat'l Law. 63 (2002).
Insider trading prohibitions generally accepted worldwide: goal is to promote deep and liquid markets.
Explains the explosive growth in nations prohibiting trading on insider information concerning stock, and analyzes effectiveness by comparing scope, behavior, definitions, and methodology of laws. Interesting & detailed comparison.
Note: look up interesting empirical study, Utpal Bhattacharya & Hazem Daouk, The World Price of Insider Trading, note 5.

2. Outlining

Outlining is probably the most traditional way to prewrite a scholarly work of any kind, legal or otherwise, and is an ultimate necessity in any writing project. The traditional advice is to simply sit down and organize your ideas into a sequence of topics, subtopics, and sub-subtopics. As mentioned earlier, the difficulty with this method is that it lacks the flexibility of some of the other prewriting methods, and may make it more difficult to recognize that something originally labeled as a sub-subtopic should really be a separate major topic. Generally, it is best to use one or more of the other prewriting methods first, and from there develop an outline. That way you do not lock yourself into any particular organization until your ideas are fairly well developed.

Insider Trading[20]

I. United States: Broad, vague
   A. 17 C.F.R. § 240.10(b)-5 (1998): Unlawful for any person, directly or indirectly, by the use of any means or instrumentality of interstate commerce, or of the mails or of any facility of any national securities exchange, . . . (device, scheme, to defraud) & (untrue statement) . . . in connection with the purchase or sale of stock
   B. *Chiarella v. United States*, 445 U.S. 222 (1980) (printer's employee): liability ltd. to fiduciary duty
   C. *United States v. O'Hagan*, 521 U.S. 642 (1997) (attorney profited from knowledge of client's potential tender offer for Pillsbury): misappropriation theory OR fiduciary duty.

II. Japan: Narrower, list of prohibitions
   A. Shoken Torihikiho (Securities and Exchange) Law No. 25, art. 190-2(2): Facts trigger prohibition, including management decisions about issuing securities, reductions in capital, stock splits, etc.

III. Germany

a. Organizational Paradigms for Comparative Projects

Comparative projects, whether comparing different countries' laws on a particular subject (as in the preceding sample outline) or comparing different approaches (as with a split or disagreement in authority within the same country), lend themselves to three organizational paradigms. In the first paradigm, the article examines each law or approach sequentially, making points about its advantages and disadvantages as each alternative is discussed. This seems to be the way the preceding outline would be organized once completed. The underlying paradigm is more clearly set forth in the following diagram:

[20] Content of outline taken generally from Gevurtz, 15 Transnat'l Law. 63 (cited in sample notecard in subsection 1 *supra*).

Comparative Paradigm 1.
Preliminary thesis statement: Insider trading rules in the United States, Japan, and Germany each have strengths and weaknesses, but are an effective way to encourage investors' confidence in a market

Alternative A: the U.S. model
1. combination of statute and case law
2. point 1: broad
3. point 2: vague

Alternative B: Japan
1. Statute listing facts
2. point 1: narrow as compared to U.S.
3. point 2: much more specific, as compared to U.S.

Alternative C: Germany

A second way of organizing this kind of comparative project is to make your points the major subject headings, addressing each alternative in sequence in subheadings:

Comparative Paradigm 2.
Thesis statement:

Point 1: Broad v. Narrow approaches
1. Alternative A: U.S.
2. Alternative B: Japan
3. Alternative C: Germany

Point 2: Specific v. Vague approaches
1. Alternative A: U.S.
2. Alternative B: Japan
3. Alternative C: Germany

The same two methods could be used with a split in authority. With the first paradigm, you would view or explain each view or approach separately, describing its strengths and weaknesses.

Each of these two paradigms has strengths and weaknesses. The difficulty in organizing comparative projects according to the first method is that the writer may have trouble explaining—and the reader may have trouble seeing—the comparisons. The strength is that the reader gets a clear and comprehensive understanding of each alternative. In the second paradigm, it is easier to explain the comparisons to the reader, but more difficult to give her a clear understanding of each approach.

The third and best paradigm is to combine the other two methods. The first part of the paper explains each approach thoroughly. In the next section, each point is made as in the second paradigm. This is the most comprehensive, persuasive, and effective method because it parallels the rule/application organization of a law firm memo discussion section by providing the reader first with an objective and thorough explanation of each alternative, and then giving her detailed and explicit comparisons based on the previous explanations. It avoids the "five pages my country, five pages U.S., and conclusion" approach that weakens many LL.M. comparative projects, and also forces the writer to develop a thesis. However, the ultimate choice of organizational structure will depend on the project, your research results, and your particular way of thinking.

Comparative Paradigm 3.
Thesis Statement
Explanation of alternative approaches
1. U.S.
2. Japan
3. Germany
Comparisons
1. Point 1: Broad v. Narrow: U.S. v. Japan v. Germany
2. Point 2: Specific v. Vague: U.S. v. Japan v. Germany
Conclusions

b. Case Charts and Informal Diagrams

It can be difficult at first to get control of case law—to gain an understanding of what types of facts lead to what decisions. Lack of comprehension of case law and lack of analysis of it leads to laundry-list writing, which is as useless in a scholarly work as it is in a law firm memo. To assist in analysis of case law, you may want to do a case chart, as demonstrated in Chapter 3 § III.2. Alternatively, you may want to use an informal diagram to help you learn what facts relate to which legal issues. Write down the components of your rule on one side of the paper. Then, on the other side, list the operative facts of various cases and the holdings. Draw lines attaching the various facts to the various components, to help you visually analyze which types of details address which legal issues and what conclusions you can draw about those details.

3. Free-Form Outlining

Figure 9-1 is an example of free-form outlining as applied to paradigm 3 of the comparative insider-trading article. Notice that one free-form diagram has been used for the first, explanatory portion of the article, and another for the comparative portion. In free-form outlining, begin by writing the topic of your project in the very center of a piece of paper. As the various most important components of that topic appear in your mind, add them to the diagram circularly, like spokes of a wheel coming from the center topic. Because you are working in a circle, no one component is given a leading spot, so you need not decide at this stage which component is most important or should be discussed first. As you work, you will realize that there are points you want to make about each component. These points are added as branches of the appropriate component. This branching and re-branching process shows natural relationships among ideas. The final free-form outline looks something like a spider, but each branch may itself divide into two or more sub-branches. You then redraft your free-form outline into regular outline form, beginning with whichever component seems to be the logical starting point, and rearranging components as needed for ease of transition and best logical flow. Free-form outlining has an advantage over some methods of prewriting because it does not interfere with the creative madman.

FIGURE 9-1
FREE-FORM OUTLINE

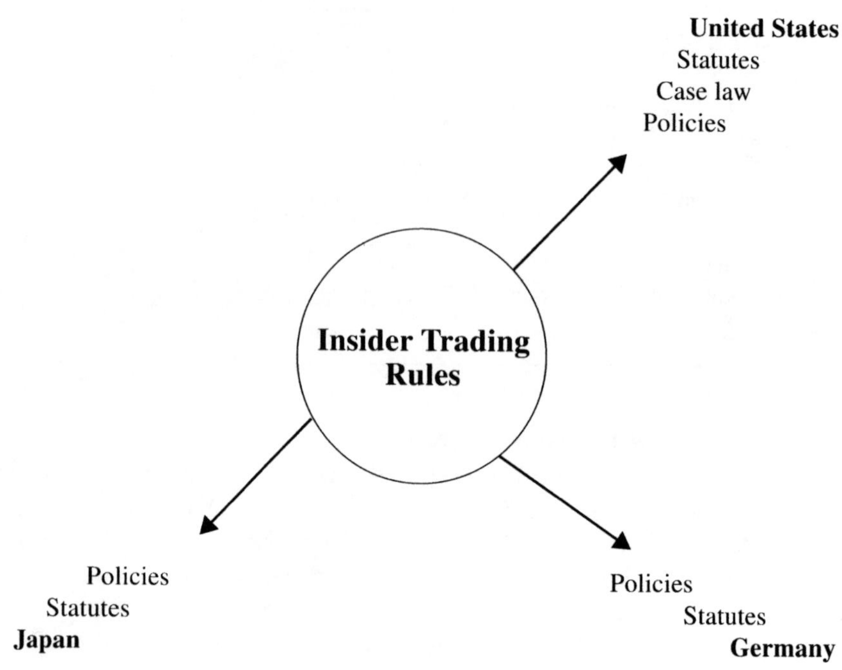

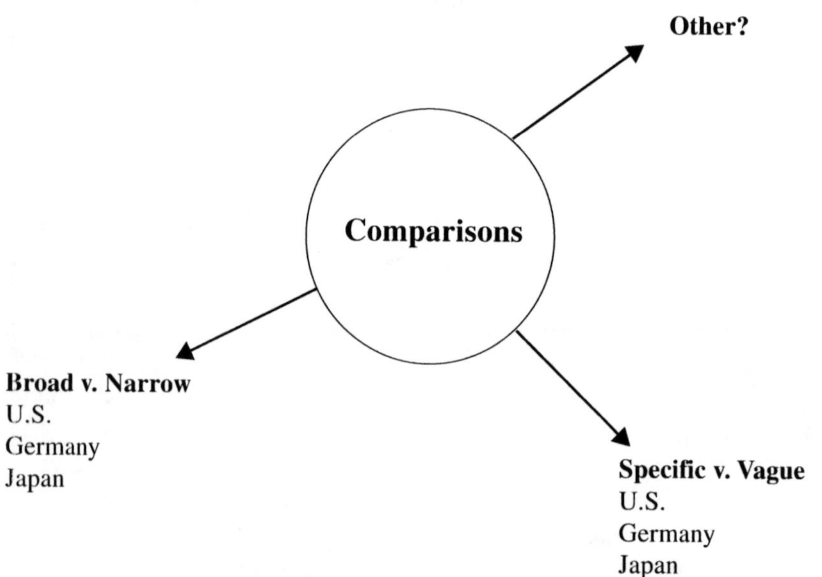

4. Dump Drafts

A *dump draft*, or *freewriting*, results when you focus on your topic and write down whatever comes to mind. Like a nonlinear outline, it allows you to give free rein to your creativity without fear of criticism. You need not concern yourself with grammar, style, or spelling. If English is not your native language, when you cannot quickly locate the English equivalent for a word, you can include the word that immediately comes to mind, as long as it will help you remember and communicate the idea to yourself. In general, though, it is best to force yourself to jot your ideas down in English whenever possible, assuming that the final project will be in English. Otherwise, you will face a translation hurdle in transitioning to the outline and then the first draft, in addition to the other difficulties inherent in any writing project. You will be the only reader of this stream-of-consciousness piece, so digressions and occasional non-English terms are fine and may even lead to fruitful ideas.

Once the dump draft is finished, look through it for any important ideas that emerged. Use them in organizing either a linear or a nonlinear outline. As you do this, you may develop more important ideas, which you can explore with further dump drafts.

5. Summary of the Optimal Prewriting Process

If you are experienced at scholarly legal writing, you may have your own methods of prewriting that work for you. However, if you were unsatisfied with your previous methodology or lack experience, try the following prewriting sequence, which is likely to produce good results for most people.

PREWRITING CHECKLIST

- ☐ 1. **Read all authorities** carefully, noting any thoughts, ideas, or important information on a separate piece of paper for each authority. Attach the notes to the authority.
- ☐ 2. **Create any case charts or cluster diagrams necessary to analyze case law.**
- ☐ 3. **Arrange your authorities according to the ideas they lead to.**
- ☐ 4. **Write a dump draft or nonlinear diagram.**
- ☐ 5. **Convert the results of item 4 into a linear outline.**
- ☐ 6. **Convert the linear outline into a first draft.**

C. Writing

Once you are ready to let the carpenter go to work — that is, when you are ready to write your first full draft — feel free to begin anywhere. Many people mistakenly assume that the proper way to write is to begin at the beginning, with the introduction, and then move sequentially through the outline to the conclusion. This is usually a mistake. To begin with, when you start your first draft, you may still not have the thesis statement well formulated. In fact, you probably will *not* yet have it well developed. If you were to write the introduction first, you would have to formulate some kind of thesis statement, and you would then slant the rest of the paper to conform to that statement. A better approach is to start somewhere in the middle. Begin with the first substantive subject of your outline, or anywhere that seems easiest. While you are working on the easier sections, you will probably think of resolutions to the problems you were having with other sections. Finally, once the substantive portion has been written, draft both the introduction and conclusion in accord with the actual content of the project.

1. *Problematic Sections*

While you are writing your first draft, you will probably find that although most sections resolve themselves as you go along, you seem completely unable to write one or two particularly difficult sections. If this is so, you probably need further research on those sections. Go back and reanalyze your research to see if this is indeed the problem, and do additional research as needed.

2. *Translation Problems with Comparative Topics*

Non-native English speakers who are writing comparative papers, in which they must explain, discuss, and incorporate the law of their home country, can run into severe translation problems. Often, the English language simply does not have equivalent terms. Even if it has the same terms, the meanings might be very different. Furthermore, it is difficult to change correct syntax in one language to correct syntax in another. As a result, one can become bogged down solving translation problems while the rest of the project suffers. The best way to deal with these problems is either to find a version of the law that has already been translated into English, or to run it through a computerized translating program (such as Babel Fish on AltaVista) and then adjust it as necessary for accuracy. Furthermore, it helps a great deal to work with a native English speaker, so you can check that the English version makes sense to the reader. Just be sure to obtain permission from your supervising professor, if necessary, to avoid honor code problems.

3. *Keeping Track of Citations*

It is absolutely necessary to keep track of authorities from the very first draft. Nothing is as frustrating as having to go back and spend several hours redoing research to substantiate an important statement. However, there is no need, in the first draft, to use proper citation form, and in fact it is inefficient to do so. Instead, create a working system of citation notes so that it will be easy, during polishing, to go back and correct the citation forms. To create a working system, simply assign each authority a very short identifier: a few letters or a word that will let you recognize the source. Then, when incorporating anything from that source into the first draft, footnote it immediately with the source identifier and the pinpoint page. For example, a reference to page 70 of the Gevurtz article mentioned in the insider trading illustration could be "Gev.70." Do not use *id.*, because you are likely to insert other sources during revisions, so that the *id.*s and their source identifiers will become separated and confused.

As with the problematic sections, if you find yourself needing to make a point but lacking authority for that point, you may have to do additional research on that issue, or perhaps rethink the point.

D. Rewriting

As with researching, prewriting, and writing the first draft, rewriting a scholarly article follows the same general approach as for a law firm memo: Check organization, content, transitions, and sentence clarity. Reviewing Chapter 8 may help, but the following summarizes some of the most important points and also gives advice particular to scholarly projects.

1. Organization

First verify that the paper is well organized. If you did enough prewriting, the basic organization should be quite sound, but there may be one or two subjects that should be rearranged, or paragraphs that are misplaced or duplicative. In checking organization, verify that the structure of the work flows from its substance: the parts of the whole must be congruent with some logical rationale, the paper must maintain the same organization throughout and not shift midstream, and each section must be internally logical in itself. Verify that the transitions from one paragraph to the next are smooth, and that each paragraph is logically structured and begins with a topic sentence.

2. Content and Scope

Next, verify that your background material is sufficient and your analyses accurate and well developed. Be sure that your points are meticulously documented, and that you have checked and read each and every authority to verify that it says what your article says it does. Make sure that conclusions neither underuse nor overshoot the evidence or authorities on which they are based. If your research at any point seems thin, recheck the authorities and search for further substantiation.

E. Editing

1. Signposts and Transitions

The point of the editing process is to make your project reader-friendly. Add or rework your signposts so that you give the reader clear and explicit explanations of what, exactly, it is that you are doing. The reader should be given explicit notice of the organization of the paper, not only by the road map given in the introduction, but also through the use of headings, section introductions, and conclusions.[21] Make sure that

[21] Fajans & Falk, *supra* note 1, at 73; *see also* Mary Barnard Ray & Jill Ramsfield, *Legal Writing: Getting It Right and Getting It Written* 327 (3d ed., West Group 2000).

your use of headings is consistent and that you follow a logical system of typeface changes to indicate sections and other subparts. Consider whether you will need a table of contents, and rework transitions so that they constantly reassure and remind the reader of where you are, where you have been, and where you are going. Use RILS sentence transitions, transitional phrases, and linking to help guide the reader.

2. *Paragraph and Sentence Structure*

In addition to working through signposts and transitions, rework paragraph and sentence structure to eliminate any unnecessary verbiage and make the writing as clear and concise as possible. Make sure paragraphs are of moderate length. A paragraph that is much more than half a page in length probably combines two or more topics, and should be broken into two or more smaller paragraphs. In contrast, a paragraph that is three sentences or less probably needs more development or substantiation. Sentences that were very difficult to formulate in the first draft should be reworked until they are clear and say exactly what you mean to say. One good way to test a sentence or paragraph for clarity is to read it aloud.

Now is also the time to convert your informal citation system to correct citation form and to verify that the information referenced is on the exact page cited. Although you will verify citation form again, in the polishing stage, citations are pesky things and it usually takes more than one revision to get them in shape. Start as soon as the article is in its final organizational form.

3. *Style and Tone*

Verify that the tone of your paper is professional by eliminating colloquialisms, legalese, and jargon; keep the reader and his interest level in mind as you adjust the language. The audience of a scholarly article may include, among others, experts in the field (including your professor) who are interested in accuracy and exhaustive research, scholars who want careful but creative treatment of a narrow topic, practitioners looking for new arguments they can use, judges who want to be brought up to date on the topic, editors who want excellence in their publications, and prospective future employers looking for excellent analysis and clear writing.[22] Ask yourself if your project addresses all these needs, or whether one or more aspects of it could be improved. Eliminate unnecessary passive-voice constructions, and use other methods to make your writing as easy and enjoyable to read as possible. This is not the time to sound pompous, nor is it the time to sound too jovial. You are trying to convince readers of the breadth of your research and the soundness of your arguments. You do not want to alienate them with stilted word choice, complex and convoluted sentence structure, or muddled thinking.

---

[22] Ray & Ramsfield, *supra* note 21, at 324.

F. Introductions and Conclusions

Introductions and conclusions are relatively brief in comparison to the body of an article, but anyone who has written one or the other knows that they take a disproportionate amount of time to write. They take longer to write because of their important functions and prominent positions: They create the reader's first and final impressions of the work.[23] An introduction establishes the context of a scholarly project. It identifies the topic of the paper, sets the topic within the larger context and scope of the subject, announces the thesis statement, indicates the support for that statement, and explains the organization of the work. Getting all this into an introduction is a feat unto itself, and will fulfill a reader's expectations, but will not attract readers unless they already have an interest in the topic. Therefore, above and beyond all these functions, an introduction should be captivating. Similarly, a conclusion that merely summarizes what came before is anticlimactic. You want the reader to leave excited about the subject matter and interested in exploring it further. Therefore, to end on a high note, you might suggest avenues for additional investigation, or emphasize the implications of your analysis and possible consequences of your suggestions.

There are several ways to attract readers to an introduction. You might begin with a narrative, throwing the reader into the middle of a riveting story that illustrates the importance of your topic. Alternatively, you might open with a striking quotation that sparks the reader's interest. A quotation can be effective if it is reflective and learned, or sometimes even impertinent, humorous, or provocative.[24] For example, an article on the death penalty began with the following poem, which also inspired the title of the article:

> My friend is a stranger, someone I do not know.
>
> A stranger far, far away.
>
> For his sake my heart is full of disquiet
>
> because he is not with me.
>
> Because, perhaps, after all he does not exist?
>
> Who are you who so fill my heart with your absence?
>
> Who fill the entire world with your absence?[25]

---

[23] Fajans & Falk, *supra* note 1, at 102.

[24] *Id.* at 105.

[25] Pär Lagerkvist, *Evening Land Aftonland* 119 (W.H. Auden & Leif Sjöberg trans., Wayne State Univ. Press 1975), quoted in Paolo Carozza, *"My Friend Is a Stranger": The Death Penalty and the Global Ius Commune of Human Rights*, 81 Tex. L. Rev. 1031, 1032 (2993). Lagerkvist was the 1951 Nobel Laureate.

Even if you cannot find an appropriate quotation with which to open your article, you might fulfill the same need to open quickly with a statement that grabs the reader's interest either with its criticism, its drama, or its humor.

Similar methods can be used to heighten the effect of a conclusion. Perhaps, instead of opening with a quotation, you will find one that is appropriate for your closing. It is generally best not to both open and close with a quotation, because the overuse usually seems stilted and artificial, but if you do use a quotation in a conclusion, look for a short quotation that is provocative, wise, or humorous, or that reinforces your own analysis:

> The greatest aspiration of this article, however, is that it should demonstrate the value of the study of comparative law. . . . [C]omparative law aims at "procuring the gradual approximation of view points, the abandonment of deadly complacency, and the relaxation of fixed dogma—and it permits us to catch sight, through the differences in detail, of the grand similarities and so deepen our belief in the existence of a unitary sense of justice."[26]

Alternatively, you might use a narrative about your personal relationship to the topic as an effective and forceful closing. Be very careful, however, with personal narratives: Unless they are well handled, they may end the article on too saccharine or emotional a note. Keep either quotations or personal narratives very short, and underplay any emotional language. Other ways to end forcefully are to end with a fresh perspective on a point made familiar in the body of the piece, or to invite the reader to explore the topic further in some slightly different direction, or simply to end with a blunt, forceful statement of your point.

G. Polishing and Proofreading

When you have finished editing the work, give yourself time to rest and regain some objectivity. Otherwise, you will continue to see what you want to see in the project, not what is actually there. Put the document away for at least 24 hours. If you have someone who is willing to read and comment on your work, and whose perusal of it will not violate the honor code, now is the time to let them see it. If the proofreader makes comments, consider those comments carefully and decide whether to incorporate them. Even if you do not agree with some of the criticisms, take another look at that particular section and see if the problem was caused by imprecise language, or if you can address the criticism in an alternative manner that solves the reader's problem but maintains your original point.

Use computer spell checkers and grammar checkers to eliminate as many errors as possible mechanically, but remember that only a final proofreading of a hard copy will enable you to spot typographical and other errors that the machine misses. By all means, avoid any "weeding dresses." Furthermore, go through the citations again to

[26] 1 Konrad Zweigert & H. Kötz, *Introduction to Comparative Law* 3, 3 (1987) (trans. Tony Weir).

verify citation form, and check for punctuation errors. Though these types of corrections seem minor, such flaws distract all readers and offend many. "They shake the reader's faith in your ideas,"[27] and can make him or her question your professionalism or ability.

H. Final Thoughts

Writing well is hard work in any language. For someone whose native language is not English, writing at a professional level is even more of a challenge. Nevertheless, the game is worth the chase. In the United States, a lawyer's success—or failure—is determined by the quality of his or her writing. Writing well leads directly to better opportunities and financial gain. Furthermore, writing well on a topic that interests you can be its own reward. The best moment comes when you finish the final proofreading of a project you have worked hard on and realize that the finished product is even better than you thought it was, and that you have surprised yourself with the accuracy and creativity of your insights. It is times like these when legal writing can truly be a satisfying endeavor.

EXERCISE

Research and write an open memo or scholarly article as assigned by your instructor.

BIBLIOGRAPHY

Block, Gertrude. *Effective Legal Writing for Law Students and Lawyers.* 5th ed. Foundation Press 1999.

Fajans, Elizabeth, & Mary R. Falk. *Scholarly Writing for Law Students: Seminar Papers, Law Review Notes, and Law Review Competition Papers.* West Group 1995.

Volokh, Eugene. *Academic Legal Writing: Law Review Articles, Student Notes, and Seminar Papers.* Foundation Press 2003.

[27] Fajans & Falk, *supra* note 1, at 81.

CHAPTER 10

Non-Fee Internet Legal Research

INTRODUCTION

Although Westlaw, LEXIS-NEXIS, Loislaw, and other commercial legal databases are becoming increasingly affordable because of market competition and improvements in technology, as it stands, many non-U.S. attorneys do not have access to these professional tools on a regular basis — they are simply too expensive. Furthermore, unless an attorney is in the United States, he or she may not have access to either the commercial legal research databases or a U.S. law library, but may still need to research U.S. law. Therefore, skill in using non-fee Web sites for legal research is important. As you may already have discovered, non-fee Internet legal research Web sites number in the thousands. Because they lack the sophisticated finding tools of the commercial databases, as well as the breadth of those databases, researching with non-fee Internet sites is not as efficient or thorough as it is with the commercial tools. Nevertheless, you can still do a lot. This chapter begins by explaining how to adjust the three-stage research strategy to non-fee Web sites. It then introduces some of the best (or most popular) U.S. non-fee legal research Web sites.

As was mentioned in Chapter 2, be aware that Web sites can change rapidly. In the interval between the first and second editions of this text, computer-assisted legal research (CALR) secondary research has become much easier and more efficient. To the extent that it is available to you at little or no cost, you may be able to use the same research strategies described in Chapter 5, rather than the strategies described below. Regardless, however, of cost issues, obtaining hard copies of your best sources (whether from the library or printed from a Web site) makes analysis much easier. Remember, as well, to carefully preserve citation information.

I. RESEARCH STRATEGIES

RESEARCH SEQUENCE REVISED FOR OPEN (NON-FEE) INTERNET RESEARCH

Stage 1 (same): Establish area of law, jurisdiction, and probable type of authority. Formulate initial research query, look for dictionary definitions of search terms, and generate synonyms. Plan research and do a limited search for secondary sources, especially if unfamiliar with the area of law.

Stage 2: in-depth search for primary sources.

a. If somewhat familiar with area of law, start with law-based search engines.

b. If very familiar, start with specific-authority database.

Stage 3: Update primary authority (alternate between Stages 2 and 3 as needed to verify a case before using it as the basis for a research trail); look again for secondary sources to help with interpretation.

Just as with any other type of research, it is necessary to plan before diving into research on the Web, to maximize the efficiency of limited research time. As usual, the first thing to do is analyze the problem and identify search terms and a possible query phrase or sentence. Consider what area of law is involved (tort, contract, bankruptcy), where you are likely to find appropriate authority (state or federal; statute, regulation, or case), and rephrase the search query as needed. List likely synonyms or alternate queries, using a legal dictionary, and plan research time, deciding which Web sites you want to try and in what order. The Legal Information Institute at Cornell Law School (*www.law.cornell.edu*) has an online legal lexicon that provides definitions, and Findlaw.com has *Merriam Webster's Law Dictionary* (1996) as its lexicon.

If the only research tools available are non-fee Web sites, modify the standard research strategy as follows: Instead of performing a thorough search for secondary sources in Stage 1, do a limited search—Wikipedia may be helpful in this regard. Then proceed directly to Stage 2, searching for primary sources, and Stage 3, updating. Finally, search again for secondary sources. The reason for altering the strategy is that secondary research is much more constrained and limited if one does not have access to commercial databases or a law library. State case law research is also very limited, because most non-fee Web sites that include state case law include cases dating only from 1990 or later. Shepardizing is also more difficult. If funding is available on a very limited basis, then use that funding wisely, perhaps for Shepardizing or Keyciting, or for obtaining a solid secondary source.

A. Stage 1 Research

The researcher's natural impulse, when starting a research project, might be to use one or more of the big search engines. Unfortunately, verifying the authenticity or value of anything one finds on the Internet can be difficult; when researching on non-fee Web sites, one must examine sources particularly carefully. This is especially true with the generic, non-law-based search engines like AltaVista, Google, Yahoo, or Ask.com. Any search with these engines is likely to generate a large percentage of useless results. Nevertheless, they can be used to search for background information.

Assuming that you have a search term such as "promissory estoppel," begin by using the Advanced Search feature. The search engines will give a choice of searches: *all of the words, using at least one word, the exact phrase*, or *excluding certain terms.* They may also allow you to limit your search based on the language, the file format, the date, or occurrences (where the language appears on the page). If given a choice, ask the search engine to include the domain information. This will further help exclude irrelevant and potentially virus-laden results.

Even with these advanced searches, the results from a generic search engine will probably be random and superficial at best, but they may yield some information that you can use to locate better authorities. For example, a search for "promissory estoppel" on Google, AltaVista, and Ask yielded more or less the same results on each: Wikipedia's definition (quite helpful), a definition from *law.cornell.edu* (thin, and the links did not work), a law firm's discussion of a law review article on promissory estoppel (lacking citations), a British law professor's explanation (slightly helpful), an explanation of Australian law, an LL.M. student's notes including an inaccurate example, incorrect definitions on "the K-Zone" and *law.com*, and a Web site offering forms for promissory notes (useless). It was difficult or impossible to find any substantive reference to the Restatement (Second) of Contracts § 90, which would have been most useful. Yahoo suggested a search for "elements of promissory estoppel," which produced, in addition to the previously listed results, a useful opinion from the U.S. Court of Federal Claims denying a defendant's motion to exclude testimony based on promissory estoppel. That opinion contains some useful discussion as well as citations. Generally, the best one can hope for is a well-written Wikipedia definition, or a law firm article for potential clients, giving a simplified explanation of the field, either of which you can use as a starting point, or at least a reference to an authoritative source.

Another approach, which is significantly more effective, is to use more selective search engines designed for lawyers. *Findlaw.com* is West Group's free Internet site. Among the advertisements, it contains a section for professionals, plus a topic list. The professional section includes another topic list. Choosing the Findlaw libraries entries leads to articles likely to be more relevant and substantial than one could obtain through the generic search engines. Other Web sites designed for attorneys can be similarly helpful. For example, the Center for Regulatory Effectiveness (CRE), a think tank established "to provide Congress with independent analyses of agency regulations," has a link to a very useful research tool called *fedlaw*, which was designed to be used by federal lawyers and employees. To access it, go the CRE's Web site, *www.thecre.com*, and use the appropriate link, or go to *www.thecre.com/fedlaw*. Another way to access fedlaw is through *firstgov.gov*: Link to the reference center, and then to laws and regulations where you will find a link to fedlaw. Fedlaw's *Topical and Title Index* contains useful links on a number of subjects and has simple search tools for all sources of U.S. federal law.

Alternatively, *lawsource.com* has links to a number of law review Web sites, many of which in turn have various of their articles online — but it will be difficult to locate a law review article on a particular topic. Additionally, *www.law.com* includes links to law firm Web sites that often have short articles discussing new and interesting developments in the law, though topic searching again will be difficult, and there will be few if any citations. *Alllaw.com* includes a legal topic index containing articles on legal topics for non-lawyers. Finally, *megalaw.com* has a topic index that lists secondary sources of various sorts. If, after a moderate amount of effort, you cannot locate any helpful secondary authority, then turn to searching for primary authority. Once having located primary authority, you may then be able to use other terms or links from it to locate secondary authority. Even with access to commercial databases and hard-copy libraries, research is very rarely a straightforward process, and backtracking is often required.

B. Stage 2 Research

If one has some knowledge of the area, the best starting place is either a .com or .edu legal research Web site, rather than a generic site or a search for secondary authority. As with secondary research, the databases designed for lawyers are often easier to navigate and more efficient.

1. Researching Statutes

Finding the text of codes, whether state or federal, is not difficult on non-fee Web sites, though they do not give access to annotations and their finding tools may be limited. The text of various codes is available through several search engines; *findlaw.com* and *law.cornell.edu* are both comprehensive and easy to navigate. Federal statutes can be found through Cornell's site, but also through the federal search engines, *www.fedworld.gov* and *www.firstgov.gov*. The two governmental sites are designed for public use, and it takes a bit of searching to link through to law, but they make available a vast amount of legislative and agency information. Furthermore, the "Reference Center" of *firstgov.gov* provides a link to fedlaw. All one need do is click on "Laws and Regulations" and choose the appropriate link from the pull-down alphabetical list. Because they specialize in legal research, the Cornell and fedlaw sites are easier to navigate.

Cornell and other legal search engines will also link the researcher to the official individual state Web sites, which are generally the only non-fee sources of the text of state statutes. Although a state Web site generally includes the entire text of that state's codes, the subject indexes and the simple Boolean finding tools on state Web sites are generally not as well designed as those for the *United States Code*. Therefore, a researcher may be forced to spend time searching through the text of statutes manually to locate applicable provisions.

2. Researching Regulations

If you know that the client problem involves federal administrative law, the most efficient approach is to search *firstgov.gov* or *washlaw.edu* for the appropriate agency's Web site. As explained in Chapter 7, searching the agency Web site first is often more efficient than using a commercial database. Although finding the correct agency can be an issue if you are unfamiliar with the United States executive branch, there are a number of ways to determine which is the appropriate agency for your problem. For example, suppose you want to research antidumping and countervailing duties, but are unsure of the correct agency involved. Washlaw.edu has a very useful "Agency Index." (One can access the same index through the Reference Center of *firstgov.gov*, under "Federal Agency Opinions, Manuals.") The "Agency Index" includes an Agency Guidance Table listing agencies in alphabetical order and containing links to each agency's publications, a chart of its structure, any forms it might supply to the public, opinions, manuals, its online library, and its directory.

Scrolling through the list, you might first think that the Federal Trade Commission would be the appropriate agency—but a quick check of one of the links indicates that the FTC is concerned only with domestic trade issues. Scrolling further down the list, the International Trade Commission (ITC) seems to be more appropriate. Checking the links there, the researcher quickly finds mention of antidumping and countervailing duty regulations, abbreviated by the agency as AD/CVD. Using the links provided in the Agency Table, one can transfer immediately to the ITC Web site and locate materials and ITC opinions there. Alternatively, by using the publication link provided by the "Agency Index," one can immediately download the ITC's handbook on antidumping and countervailing duties, which explains the agency's regulations in detail. Other links lead to AD/CVD forms, a list of petitions that have been filed, a chart explaining the organization of the ITC, and a directory with a link to statutes involving the ITC and including AD/CVD timetables.

3. *Researching Case Law*

The text of statutes and regulations is available through the non-fee databases, but case law research is more difficult without access to commercial databases or hard-copy libraries, because the only complete collections of state and federal cases are published by Westlaw and LEXIS. Due to copyright laws, they are not available on the free Internet. For example, the United States federal government publishes all Supreme Court cases in *U.S. Reports* and its predecessors. However, it does not publish circuit or district court cases. Those are published by Westlaw in the *Federal Reporter* and the *Federal Supplement*. Thus, although free databases can provide the entire range of Supreme Court decisions, their collections of circuit and district court cases are incomplete. To make things even more difficult, those collections lack citation information.

For example, Cornell's Legal Information Institute provides access to Supreme Court decisions, and is updated every 24 hours. In addition to doing a Boolean search of Supreme Court decisions, one can research them according to a simple subject index. In addition to searching individual federal circuit court databases, one can search opinions from all of the circuit courts at one time. However, none of the individual circuit court databases contains decisions prior to 1992, and many of them date from after that. Both fedlaw and Cornell's case law database include Boolean search tools, but they are of limited effectiveness as compared to Westlaw and LEXIS. Furthermore, once either fedlaw or Cornell's site has retrieved cases that purportedly include the search terms, those terms are not marked, and are therefore difficult to locate in the retrieved cases. Although you cannot Shepardize on the Cornell site, you can enter the case name as a search term and find cases that have cited it that way.

To locate case law interpreting a statute, once you have found the appropriate statute, you can use the statute citation as a search term in a case law database. Unfortunately, many state case law databases lack even the search tools that Cornell's has and are impossible to search unless one has the parties' names or a docket number. Furthermore, the majority of the non-fee state case law databases date only from 1990 or later to date, thus excluding much mandatory authority.

C. Stage 3 Research

One can update authority on noncommercial databases, though without the speed and efficiency of a Shepardizing feature. It is easy to locate current and pending federal regulatory law on agency Web sites, and one can check pending federal legislation through Thomas.gov or one of the other federal Web sites. Case law can be updated as described previously, by using the case name as a search term to search a database of the superior courts. For example, if the case to be updated was decided by the United States Court for the Southern District of New York, use the case name or its docket number from the lower court in a search to see if the case was reviewed, vacated, or reversed by the Second Circuit or by the United States Supreme Court. It is necessary—in fact, critical—to verify the validity of a case before using that case as the basis of future research: If the case is invalid, the entire trail of research based on that case will be invalid as well. This is why it was suggested earlier that when funding is limited, use it to either Shepardize or KeyCite the cases you have already found. Then print out the result so that you can research in the citing cases as well as research the citing history.

Finally, as mentioned earlier, look again for secondary authority that specifically discusses the authorities you have located. These materials will help you analyze the law found.

II. RESEARCH METHODOLOGY: BOOLEAN SEARCHES

If you have been working with Westlaw or LEXIS, then you have already been introduced to *Boolean* searches. George Boole was a 19th century British mathematician who developed a math-based way of defining logical relationships between terms. As of the time of this writing, the non-fee generic and legal Web sites do not have natural-language search capabilities and, as described earlier, their Boolean search features lack many of the sophisticated operators and connectors of the professional fee-based Web sites. Therefore, it may be more difficult and take more time to locate authority than you are used to if you have become accustomed to the fee-based sites. Whatever search engine or search engines you use, it is important to familiarize yourself with exactly how searches should be formed on that particular engine. If you use the wrong connectors, or use them incorrectly for that particular engine, your efforts will be fruitless.

To locate the connectors that any particular search engine uses, look for pull-down search menus or icons with names like *Advanced Search, Power Search, Search Tips*, or *Help*. In general, however, the two main Boolean operators or connectors are *and* and *or*. The following subsections give a short explanation of these and other connectors.

A. The *and* Connector

Connecting two words with *and* tells the search engine that both of your terms (or more, if all are joined with *ands*) MUST appear in all of the documents retrieved by the search. Some search engines recognize the word *and;* others look for the ampersand symbol (&) or a plus sign (+). Some engines may recognize both the word and a symbol. The *and* connector is restrictive. It narrows your search, making it more specific. If your search retrieves too many documents, then add more terms using *and* connectors. In contrast, if you find that a search has retrieved too few documents, eliminate one or more terms.

When using *and,* remember that although the search engine will retrieve documents with both terms, those terms may appear anywhere in the document. They are not necessarily going to appear close together. For example, if your search is *false and imprisonment,* you will get documents with both terms, but some documents may contain the word *false* four pages ahead of or behind the word *imprisonment.* This may make your results less specific than you intended.

Furthermore, although some search engines will limit the search to documents in which *false* appears before *imprisonment,* others may retrieve all documents that have both terms, regardless of the sequence in which they appear. If you want the terms to appear together or in a specific sequence, then see if the search engine employs *proximity indicators,* discussed in subsection E.

B. The *or* Connector

Connecting two words with *or* tells the search engine that at least one of the terms connected by that word must appear in the documents retrieved. Some search engines recognize the word *or*; others may look for a symbol. Thus, if you want to use this connector, you must check the search key to see which is required. In contrast to *and,* which is restrictive, *or* is inclusive. It widens your search, making it less specific: it will retrieve documents with either word as well as documents with both words. If you have synonyms in your search query, you may want to use an *or* connector so that the search engine retrieves documents with either or both words.

C. Problems with the Meaning of a Space between Words

Some search engines automatically treat words separated by a space as having the *and* connector between them. Thus, this kind of engine will read the search *false imprisonment* as *false* AND *imprisonment.* In this instance, the researcher probably wants both terms because *false imprisonment* is a term of art. Unfortunately, other engines will do the opposite, and interpret a space as the *or* connector. In this instance, the search engine would search for documents in which either word or both appear, again making the search much broader than desired. Therefore, before using a space between words, verify how the particular search engine you are using will interpret it.

D. Parentheses: Using *and* and *or* in the Same Search

Some search engines allow you to use both *and* and *or* in the same query, but you must use parentheses around the appropriate terms to tell the machine how to join the terms. Otherwise, such searches will be ambiguous and yield either too many hits, or frustrate the engine entirely so that it refuses to perform your search. For example, if your search was *false and imprisonment or kidnapping*, the search engine could search either for *false and imprisonment*, or for *kidnapping*, or both — which is probably what you want. However, it could also search for *false and kidnapping* as well as *false imprisonment*. It is unlikely that you would want *false kidnapping* cases; therefore, even if this search is not rejected by the machine, your results would, again, be far too broad. To avoid this, some search engines allow you to use parentheses: *(false and imprisonment) or kidnapping.*

E. Proximity Connectors

Proximity connectors are extremely useful. They tell the search engine how close you want two or more terms, and whether or not you want them in a particular sequence. To continue with the false imprisonment example, you would probably want the terms to appear one immediately after the other. Connectors that do this are called *order-dependent* proximity connectors. Other times, you may want the terms to appear in the same sentence, or in the same paragraph, but the exact order is not important. Furthermore, sometimes you may want your terms to appear in a specific part of the document: For example, you might want the name *Lestina* to appear in the title of the case, so that the search engine retrieves all cases with that title, rather than cases citing *Lestina.* This is termed *field searching,* because you are limiting the search to a certain field.

Non-fee search engines rarely include order-dependent proximity connectors, but you can often limit your searches to documents in which the terms appear fairly close together. At times, this is just as good or better than an order-dependent proximity connector. Search engines have different ways of allowing you to indicate how many words can appear between two terms. For example, Westlaw uses w/2 to indicate "within two words." Other search engines may use (2n) to indicate the same thing. Thus, *false w/2 imprisonment* would retrieve documents containing sentences such as "[t]he imprisonment was therefore false," as well as documents containing the phrase "false imprisonment." This automatic doubling of the search results would probably be helpful. Generally, if you want the terms to be in the same sentence, set the proximity connector to require that the terms be within 10 words of each other; if within the same paragraph, then require perhaps 30 or 50 words.

Different search engines have different ways of indicating a field search. Westlaw would use *ti(Lestina)* to indicate that *Lestina* must be found in the title of the document. AltaVista uses *title: Lestina* for the same purpose.

F. Quotations, Pluralization, and Wild Cards

If the search results should include an exact phrase, such as *false imprisonment* or *Foreign Sovereign Immunities Act,* some search engines will allow you to indicate that preference by using quotation marks: "Foreign Sovereign Immunities Act". The engine then searches only for documents that contain the exact phrase indicated. Be careful, however, not to overuse this feature, because it will be too restrictive. It may well exclude useful or even mandatory authority merely because the material is not exactly as phrased in the query. For example, the case you are looking for may state: "Under this Act, foreign sovereigns are immune from suit." However, because the exact title "Foreign Sovereign Immunities Act" is not mentioned, the case will not be retrieved in a quotation search. In this situation, a well-phrased query with proximity connectors would have worked better.

In such a situation, you want the search not only to account for the closeness of the terms, but also to allow variations of some of the words as well: *sovereigns* as well as *sovereign, immune* as well as *immunities.* Some search engines, like Westlaw and LEXIS-NEXIS, automatically look for both singular and plural forms of a word. Therefore, as long as you did not put the word in parentheses, it will look for both *sovereign* and *sovereigns.* Furthermore, some search engines permit a wild-card symbol that tells the engine to vary the ending of the word: *negligence* as well as *negligent.* Westlaw uses the exclamation mark (immun!), and AltaVista the asterisk (immune*). Therefore, a well-drawn search query on Westlaw could look something like this: *foreign w/10 sovereign w/10 immun! w/10 act.*

G. Getting the Most from a Search

To get the best use of and results from a search engine, you must familiarize yourself with the specific Boolean connectors it uses, as well as how it uses them. Because it is impractical to have to learn a system's methods each time you search, it is best to pick two or three different Internet sites and use them habitually so that you become very familiar with their connectors and operations. If, in the process of a research project, you find that none of your favorite sites is working, then try one or more new sites.

III. NON-FEE LEGAL RESEARCH WEB SITES

Essentially, there are three basic types of non-fee legal research sources on the Internet:

1. Legal research search engines, which support themselves by commercial sponsorships, and which include either a database of legal authority or hyperlinks to a wide variety of sources
2. Sites developed by law schools and other nonprofit organizations
3. Government Web sites

If you are limited to non-fee Internet research, you will need to be extremely careful to verify that you have found the best authority, because it will be difficult to verify or broaden your research results with secondary sources. Furthermore, research analysis will require more time and care without in-depth secondary sources to substantiate your conclusions about how a particular legal principle is interpreted by courts.

A. Legal Research Web Crawlers

The most popular U.S. legal research search engines are probably *www.findlaw.com*, which is run by West Group; *www.hg.org* (Hieros Gamos); and *www.megalaw.com*, associated with Aspen Publishing. The home pages of all three display a wide variety of options, interspersed with banners and advertisements. They all provide law-related search tools in addition to legal research, such as search tools for finding lawyers, law firms, court reporters, expert witnesses, and other things.

- *Findlaw.com*

  West Group's site is a good database for U.S. primary state and federal materials. It has some state materials directly online, obviating the need to hyperlink through to official state Web sites. It also has a reasonably good table-of-contents search tool, in addition to a basic Boolean search method. It does not have West's annotations, however, nor any way of KeyCiting or Shepardizing sources. For that, you will need access to (and money for) one of the commercial legal research Web sites. Findlaw was originally known as Lawcrawler, and can still be accessed under that name, but is now owned by West Group.
- Hieros Gamos

  Based in Texas, Hieros Gamos links to a massive number of legal databases and is the most international law research crawler of this group. It can be viewed in five languages (French, German, Italian, Spanish, and English), and includes access to the legal and governmental resources of 230 countries. If you are researching non-U.S. law, this may be a good site. For U.S. sources, however, one of the other sites may be less cumbersome.
- *Megalaw.com*

  Megalaw is a resource designed specifically for lawyers, and has a somewhat more professional appearance than Hieros Gamos. Like the others, it will search for law-related needs, such as expert witnesses, court reporters, and the like. Its legal research database links to several legal dictionaries, which can be useful. Furthermore, it has a good table-of-contents method for researching statutes, and links to law reviews, though one cannot access many of the actual articles online without paying a fee to Hein On Line (*heinonline.org*). Megalaw is associated with Loislaw and hence Aspen Publishers.

B. Law School and Other Nonprofit Organization Sites

Several of the major law schools have well-developed legal research Web sites. The most prominent is the one originally started by Cornell Law School, now a nonprofit organization titled the Legal Information Institute. Several of them have very interesting features, and they can provide efficient tools.

- *www.law.cornell.edu*
  Formally titled the Legal Information Institute, Cornell's is one of the best developed U.S. legal research databases on the Web. Through special arrangements with the Supreme Court, it posts searchable versions of Supreme Court opinions on the same day they are issued. Generally, with this site, the researcher can use either Boolean search methods or a well-designed table-of-contents method. It provides access to secondary sources through links to Findlaw and law firm Web sites, but these sources are not as good as law reviews.
- *www.oyez.org*
  Much narrower in scope than most sites, this site was originally sponsored by Northwestern University School of Law, and focuses solely on the Supreme Court. In addition to Supreme Court opinions, it also has 360-degree pictures of the Court itself, information on the Justices, and audiotapes of oral argument for a number of Supreme Court cases.
- *www.law.harvard.edu*
  Harvard Law School's library Web site has an International Law Resource site, which includes a useful annotated guide to law-related Web sites around the world. It also has an annotated guide to resources in Islamic law.
- *www.law.nyu.edu*
  NYU's law library page has a substantial catalog of links to international databases and information on those databases.
- *www.washlaw.edu*
  Washburn University's legal research Web site has a very useful index to a wide variety of federal and state governmental Web sites. Follow the links to electronic and online resources. It also has links to law review Web sites, which sometimes post their articles. Although the Boolean search tools provided are quite limited, this site still provides some useful access to secondary authority through its research guides and on its e-journals.
- *www.asil.org*
  The Web site of the American Society for International Law contains a marvelous, easily used springboard to various public and private international law sites.

C. Government Sites

1. Broad-Scoped Databases and Search Engines

- *www.fedworld.gov*
  Designed for the general public, this site is a comprehensive central access point for searching, locating, and ordering (or acquiring) government information. It can locate various legislative and agency Web sites, but because it is aimed at the general public, it is a bit cumbersome to sort through to legal sources.

- *www.firstgov.gov*

  Like fedworld, this central access site is also aimed at the public and is therefore a bit cumbersome for locating legal information quickly. However, it contains some very interesting and helpful information about the U.S. government that might otherwise be difficult to find. Through its "Reference Center," firstgov contains links to fedlaw, as described in § I.B.1.
- *www.thecre.com/fedlaw/default*

  Fedlaw, a federal lawyer's database, makes it easier to search the *United States Code* as well as other resources. The difference between this and the other central access sites is that this one is designed specifically for lawyers, and thus is easy to navigate.

2. *Specific U.S. Government Databases*

- *www.supremecourtus.gov*

  The U.S. Supreme Court's Web site.
- *www.uscourts.gov*

  This site provides access to the individual Web sites of U.S. courts, several of which have databases of their opinions as well as online access to local court rules. It also acts as a clearinghouse of information from and about the federal courts, including press releases, information on pending rule changes, and automated access to federal court records.
- *www.house.gov*

  The Web site of the U.S. House of Representatives, this site contains House schedules, rules, and links to member and committee pages. It also offers full-text searchable copies of the *United States Code* and the *Code of Federal Regulations,* and provides hyperlinks to a large number of Internet legal resources.
- *http://lcweb.loc.gov*

  The Web site of the United States Library of Congress provides access to a very wide variety of information, including useful access to copyright information and legislative files. It also accesses non-U.S. law through GLIN, the Global Legal Information Network.
- *http://thomas.loc.gov*

  A subsidiary of the Library of Congress's Web site, this site (named after Thomas Jefferson) gives easy access to much useful legislative information.

D. Generic Search Engines and Web Crawlers

Sometimes a generic search engine can be helpful either to make sure you have found everything possible from the Web, or to help in searching law firm sites for secondary research. These search engines include sites such as Google (*www.google.com*), Yahoo (*www.yahoo.com*), AltaVista (*www.altavista.com*), Ask (*www.ask.com*), Excite (*www.excite.com*), and Hotbot (*www.hotbot.com*). They will search everything except fee-based or members-only sites, so they should duplicate research you do on a number of the sites described earlier, and will also access sites you may have missed. Furthermore, some of them, such as AltaVista, have translating capabilities, which may be helpful as well.

EXERCISES: LOCATING AUTHORITIES USING NON-FEE CALR

A. *Secondary sources*

You want to learn about WTO trade remedies, especially subsidies and countervailing measures and cases involving measures taken by the United States against softwood from Canada and something called "zeroing." Using *Washlaw.edu*'s list of links to primary and secondary sources,

1. Look for background information about subsidies and countervailing measures.

B. *U.S. federal law*

Use U.S. governmental Web sites to learn about the U.S. administration's reaction to the controversy.

C. *International organizations*

What did the WTO say about U.S. use of zeroing in the softwood from Canada case?

D. *U.S. state law*

1. What states allow common law marriage? (Use Cornell's Legal Information Institute.)
2. Locate and cite the Massachusetts long-arm statute. (Hint: Use *findlaw.com*, *law.cornell.edu*, or other locator to link to the state's official legal Web site, and then use a term search involving *person, jurisdiction, court.*)
3. Locate the Illinois Good Samaritan Act.

CHAPTER 11

Persuasive Writing

INTRODUCTION: OBJECTIVE VERSUS PERSUASIVE WRITING

> Judges share the characteristics of other law-trained readers. Their attention is finite. They are busy and impatient with delay in getting to the bottom line. They generally focus more attention on the beginning and end of a document or a section than on the middle. They find facts engrossing. They want a road map. They value clear organization that sets out the rule of law.[1]

Nevertheless, documents written to persuade a court differ from memos written to advise a firm or client. In a law firm setting, the objective memorandum has several purposes: advising the partner or the client, identifying the strong and weak points of a case, and exploring the likely results of alternative theories of a case. A bench memo is a similar objective document designed to advise a court or "bench." Judicial clerks, normally young attorneys working as aides to judges, draft bench memos to advise their judges of the parties' arguments, to evaluate the legal basis and strength of those arguments, and to suggest a decision. All these documents have one overriding purpose: They are written to present an objective view of the law as it applies to a specific case. If well-written, they convince the reader that the writer understands the law and how it applies to the facts given.

Similarly, good persuasive writing must convince the reader that the advocate understands both the law and how it applies to the facts of her case. Thus, it is based on the same fundamental IRAC analysis as an objective memo. However, it must go one step further and persuade the reader (the judge) of the merits of the client's position. Thus, it differs from objective legal writing in focus. In accord with the adversarial nature of U.S. law, an advocate's goal is to persuade the judge that her client's view of the facts is more accurate, her choice of law more appropriate, and her

[1] Linda Holdeman Edwards, *Legal Writing: Process, Analysis, and Organization* 253 (2d ed. 1992).

analysis of how the rule should be applied is more accurate to the law and the facts than her adversary's arguments.

In the United States, courts depend on written arguments submitted by the parties' attorneys in writing, rather than on evidence presented at trial. More often than not, a case is won or lost on the basis of these written arguments, or, to use the vernacular, "on the paper." These written arguments are presented in a variety of documents, but among the most common are the *memorandum in support of (or in opposition to) a motion*, and the *appellate brief*. Because the case may be decided on the basis of these documents, it is vitally important that they be as persuasive as possible. They must both explain the facts and discuss the law, making no assumptions about what the judge does or does not know. Judges are usually legal generalists.[2] They may know a great deal about the rules of procedure that they use constantly, but they usually know a great deal less about individual areas of substantive law. They count on the attorneys to explain what the law is and how it governs the case, though they will certainly check and verify the attorneys' assertions, usually by using the citations provided in the attorney's *filing* (e.g., *brief* or *memorandum*).

The only facts of the case with which a judge (or jury) is familiar are those presented by the attorneys as evidence. Thus, a judge wants the advocate to present his case. The court expects the advocate first to describe the facts of the client's story; then to explain the law in a logical manner, using a step-by-step approach; and finally to explain why, under the law, the relief the client wants should be granted. While advancing his own arguments, the advocate must also rebut those of opposing counsel. Done in a respectful tone, this is not presumptuous, because the attorneys know much more about the case than the court will.

Drafting a persuasive document, especially something as complex as an appellate brief, can seem overwhelming at first. As with any large project, however, it is easier if it is broken down into separate tasks. Begin by determining what your final document will look like, the form it should take, and what it should include. Usually a law firm will have sample documents that it has filed in the past with that same court, which you can use as patterns. However, it is best always to check court rules in addition to using a template or pattern, to verify that the pattern complies with those rules. Review all the previous filings and evidence, marshalling established facts and allegations. Next, determine the legal principles that the court will be applying. Finally, outline the document; then write and rewrite.

After describing some of the basic types of form rules, this chapter describes with some particularity the most common filings. It then explains how to draft motion memoranda and appellate briefs. For a review of the civil trial process, see Figure 4-2 on page 104.

I. ISSUES OF FORM

The Federal Rules of Civil Procedure and the Federal Rules of Appellate Procedure set forth the basic requirements for all filings, and include some rules about form,

[2] Diana V. Pratt, *Legal Writing: A Systematic Approach* 252 (3d ed., West Group 1999).

appearance, and content. The appendixes to these statutes contain sample forms, which you can (and should) use in drafting documents. State rules are similarly codified, and usually are very much like the federal rules. Bear in mind, however, that these sample forms may contain archaic language that need not—and probably should not—be adopted.

These state and federal rules are supplemented by the local rules of each particular court. Local rules and sometimes forms or sample documents can be obtained from hard-copy formbooks in most law libraries, from clerks of court, and (most conveniently) from court Web sites. They are usually very specific, stipulating size of the paper to be used, type font and size, number of lines on a page, caption, heading, page limit, binding, and even the cover color of a brief. In federal appellate courts, typically the appellant's brief must have a light blue cover and the appellee's a red cover. Some courts require that several copies of the document be filed in hard copy, as well as one on disk. If the rules are not followed, a clerk of court may refuse to file the document, which can ultimately lead to sanctions or malpractice claims against both the filing attorney and the law firm.

Sometimes local rules are complicated, difficult to decipher, or incomplete. Therefore, when given an assignment to draft a filing, always ask either your supervisor or your support personnel for a sample document that you can use as a pattern. (The appendix to this chapter provides some illustrative samples.) Some employers will automatically give new attorneys a packet or disk of sample documents, and they may even have an office practice sheet, listing things they do or do not want in their documents. For example, one of the author's employers did not want the word *pled* used, and instead wanted *pleaded.* Another did not care, but wanted one or the other used consistently. Some employers or courts will allow you to use footnotes; others may not. Be sure to find out if there are any such preferences, and if there are, observe them. Furthermore, you should also verify with your supervisor how much time and effort he wants put into the project. Some clients and some issues may require a very in-depth, time-consuming approach, whereas others may only be able to afford (or have time for) a more summary approach.

As mentioned in Chapter 3, when you report to your supervisor and expect to be given an assignment, be sure to bring a pad of paper and pen to note down the exact assignment and any other information given. Furthermore, while you are there, interview your supervisor about the assignment. Try to get as much background information about the case or about relevant law as possible, without unduly burdening the supervisor or assigning attorney.

II. DESCRIPTIONS OF FILINGS

Some filings, such as complaints and answers, are in the form of a numbered list so that the opposing party can refer to each assertion individually. Because these filings are made before much discovery has taken place, their content is quite minimal, supplying only the basic facts required for the specific causes of action or defenses asserted. This is sometimes referred to as notice pleading: All the attorney is doing is putting the opposing side on notice as to what the issues will be. Others, such as a memorandum in support or an appellate brief, go into much more detail and involve careful research and analysis.

A. The Complaint

The *complaint* is the document filed by a plaintiff to commence a lawsuit.[3] It identifies the parties to the suit and establishes jurisdiction and venue.[4] It also identifies the cause(s) of action and requests specific relief from the court.[5] However, because it is the first document filed and counsel has not yet conducted discovery, the complaint need not contain an elaborate description of the facts of the grounds for relief, though it does require a good-faith belief on the part of the filing party (whether counsel or pro se) that he is entitled to such relief. Failure to reasonably investigate to ensure that the bringing of the lawsuit is not vexatious or frivolous can lead to sanctions imposed on the attorney, the party, or both under Fed. R. Civ. P. 11. A complaint is in the form of numbered "paragraphs," each containing one statement or assertion,[6] and should begin by asserting grounds for jurisdiction and venue.[7] After giving some factual background, the complaint presents one or more causes of action, and may plead them in the alternative.[8] As with all filings, it must be accompanied by a certificate of service. See the *Sendo v. Microsoft* complaint excerpted in the appendix to this chapter. Notice the assertion of jurisdiction on the basis of diversity, the introduction and assertion of background facts, and the listed causes of action (misappropriation of trade secrets, fraud, fraudulent inducement, etc.), and the remedies requested (attorneys' fees, jury trial, and various damages).

B. The Answer

The defendant, in response to the plaintiff's complaint, files the answer. It looks very much like the complaint because it tracks the complaint, paragraph by paragraph, admitting or denying each assertion.[9] It may also include defenses and counterclaims. Microsoft's answer to Sendo's complaint is excerpted in the appendix as well. Notice the title: in addition to answering each of Sendo's assertions, Microsoft is asserting affirmative defenses and counterclaims. In reading the answer, notice that Microsoft is careful to admit those things it would be pointless to deny (such as its own identity and citizenship and the fact that it had some contracts with Sendo), denies others (such as the misappropriation of trade secrets claim in paragraph 50), and gives a contingent denial, indicating lack of knowledge in yet other paragraphs. For example, in its first

[3] Fed. R. Civ. P. 3 (2007).
[4] Fed. R. Civ. P. 10(a) (2007).
[5] Fed. R. Civ. P. 8(a) (2007).
[6] *See* Fed. R. Civ. P. 10(b) (2007).
[7] Fed. R. Civ. P. 8(a) (2007).
[8] Fed. R. Civ. P. 8(a)(3) (2007).
[9] Fed. R. Civ. P. 8(b), 10(b) (2007).

paragraph, in reply to Sendo's assertion that it is a citizen of the United Kingdom, Microsoft states that it is "without knowledge or information sufficient to form a belief as to the truth of the allegations of Paragraph 1, and on that basis denies those allegations." After answering each of Sendo's claims, Microsoft asserts its affirmative defenses (including claiming that Sendo failed to state a claim and committed fraudulent misconduct itself, and claiming equitable estoppel as well). Finally, Microsoft asserts its counterclaims such as breach of contract, and presents its own prayer for relief.

C. Motions to Dismiss

Because trials are so expensive, motion practice is increasingly important. If successful, a pretrial motion to dismiss saves the client significant time and money. It is easiest to think about the standard for a pretrial dismissal if you imagine one party saying to the other, "Even if I did what you claim I did, you still can't sue me." This type of argument was known as a *demurrer* in archaic common law terms. Though the form is no longer used, the term still remains. You may remember that there are several types of motions that can be brought during the course of a lawsuit, including a pretrial motion to dismiss, a motion for summary judgment, a motion for judgment as a matter of law, or a motion for judgment notwithstanding the verdict. Though the exact title, purpose, timing, and content of motions vary, the basic format of a motion is usually fairly consistent. Normally, the motion consists of four documents:

1. The motion itself, usually no more than a page in length and containing a short description of why the case should be dismissed
2. The notice to the opposition of when and where the motion will be heard
3. A memorandum in support of the motion
4. A certificate of service

Often courts ask that a motion filing include a proposed order that the court could use to grant or deny the dismissal. The opposing party responds with a memorandum in opposition to the motion to dismiss.

Motion memoranda are very much like the interoffice memos you have already written, but are written persuasively rather than objectively. Courts often limit their length to a maximum of 15 pages but may grant a request to file a memorandum that is longer than the limit for good cause shown. If the memorandum is longer than the limit, the court may require it to have a table of contents or other finding aid. The language of the motion, as well as the language of the proposed order, may be fairly standardized.

In terms of pretrial or *12(b)* (from Fed. R. Civ. P. 12(b)) *motions*, if the defendant objects to jurisdiction, service, or venue, or if she has some defense that does not reach the merits of the case (such as the running of a statute of limitations), she can file a motion to dismiss before filing an answer.[10] If her objection is to personal jurisdiction,

[10] Fed. R. Civ. P. 12(b) (2007).

venue, or service, whichever she decides to file, she must include that objection in the first filing, or else the defense is waived.[11] If the pretrial motion to dismiss is accompanied by any evidence other than the parties' pleadings, such as an affidavit, it is automatically converted into a motion for summary judgment. The underlying issue may still relate to something other than the merits of the case, such as subject matter or personal jurisdiction, but the standard allows the court to look at evidence presented by the parties.

The appendix includes an example of a motion to dismiss and an excerpt of the memorandum in support, and the entire memorandum in opposition to the motion in the case of *Alexis v. Southern Natural Gas* (also known as *In the Matter of Denet Towing*). Defendant Southern Natural Gas is asking the court to dismiss some of the plaintiffs' claims in a maritime case. From the Memorandum in Support, you quickly learn that the plaintiff, Captain Alexis, was allegedly injured when the vessel he was captaining hit the defendant's submerged pipeline. The defendant owner of the pipeline argues that some of the plaintiff's claims are precluded by case law because they are contradictory to the purpose of maritime law. Specifically, in numbered sections, the defendant claims that non-pecuniary damages (such as loss of consortium) and punitive damages are barred by certain mandatory cases. In comparatively short opposing memorandum, the plaintiff argues that the cases cited by the defendant are not definitive, and are either contradicted by other cases or can be distinguished on their facts. Which of the two memoranda is easier to read? Which do you find more persuasive? Why?

D. Notice of Appeal and the Appellate Brief

If a party decides to appeal, he must first file a notice of appeal within the applicable indicates limits.[12] The notice of appeal is usually a short, one- or two-page document that lists the reversible errors the trial court allegedly made. If the appellant omits mention of an error, most courts will allow counsel to amend the notice, if done in a timely manner. Generally, however, an appellate court will consider only the issues raised in the notice of appeal. Once notice is filed and served, the appellant must file an appellate brief. An appellate brief is generally much longer than a motion and more complicated in form. The requirements for an appellate brief are usually very detailed and specific. In addition to a page limit of up to 30 pages (depending on court rules), an appellate brief includes a table of contents, a table of authorities, a statement of jurisdiction, a statement of the facts, a statement of the issues for review, and a statement of the standard of review, in addition to the discussion of the relevant law and how it applies to the case, and a statement of what relief is being requested. The rules may also require that the brief be filed on disk as well as in hard copy. Appellate courts, frustrated by attorneys' lack of care in complying with rules, require a certificate of compliance certifying that the brief complies with all of the rules.[13] Attorneys who fail to comply with rules may have their filings stricken by the clerk of court.

---

[11] Fed. R. Civ. P. 12(h) (2007).

[12] 28 U.S.C. Fed. R. App. P. 4(a)(1) (2007) (30 days for a civil appeal).

[13] Fed. R. App. P. 32(a)(7)(C) (2007).

III. DRAFTING MEMORANDA IN SUPPORT OR APPELLATE BRIEFS

Motion memoranda and appellate briefs are the documents in which the advocate sets forth developed legal arguments, rather than merely listing allegations or defenses. Judges are human, and a judge who is convinced of the equities of your client's position will be more receptive to your legal arguments.[14] Thus, persuasion involves giving the court both motivating and justifying reasons to decide in your client's favor. The motivating reasons stem from a careful explanation of the relevant facts, and the justifying reasons come from a logical step-by-step explanation of what the applicable law is and how it applies. In the language of salesmanship, one wants to give the judge logical (and legal) reasons for making an emotional decision, so the advocate appeals to both law (logic) and justice (morality and fairness). To do this, the advocate must relate his client's facts in a compelling manner, and then rebut opposing counsel's arguments as well as advance his own.

A. Prewriting

The first step in preparing either a memorandum in support or an appellate brief is to read and reread all pleadings and transcripts to select the issues to be argued.[15] Those issues will become points in the memorandum or headings in the brief. In preparing a motion to dismiss, the advocate's job is to carefully review the pleadings to look for irregularities in service, jurisdiction, venue, and other possible bases for dismissal prior to trial. The brief writer's job is to carefully review the entire trial court record, looking for unfair or erroneous rulings. Finding and framing issues is one of the most difficult tasks in persuasive writing, and it often requires much thought and broad knowledge of the law. The best approach is to list all issues that are conceivably possible, and later, after researching the law as needed, decide which issues to keep and which to omit.

Eliminate any issues that prove to be nonlitigable. Then research the remaining issues thoroughly, identifying and analyzing the underlying legal rules. Issues will stem from the interpretation of specific components of an underlying rule. Carefully and systematically consider each of these remaining issues from both sides. Taking your opponent's point of view will help you spot the weaknesses in your own position, as well as help you develop rebuttals to your opponent's arguments. Decide which are your strongest arguments and which the weakest. In the interest of focusing the court's attention on your best arguments, it is wisest to eliminate as many weak arguments as possible.

Just as with any other writing project, use prewriting techniques to arrange the remaining arguments in a sequence or outline that is both logical and persuasive — but remember that this preliminary sequence may change as you write and rewrite the

---

[14] Edwards, *supra* note 1, at 253.

[15] Gertrude Block, *Effective Legal Writing for Law Students and Lawyers* 191 (5th ed. 1999).

document. Begin to think carefully as well about how best to phrase those arguments so that they will be easy to understand, precise, and persuasive.

B. Format

Motions usually do not require any special language. There are, however, some requirements and habits of respectful language that are often used. For example, all courts use a specific form for the caption, and all courts give each case a docket number. For every court document, you will need to download the caption and fill in case name and docket number, or cut and paste the assembly from an earlier filing. Furthermore, you must follow court rules as to form.

Once the caption is in place, the document must be given a title, which is a plain statement of its purpose often written in all capital letters: PLAINTIFF'S MOTION TO DISMISS, DEFENDANT'S NOTICE OF MOTION TO DISMISS, or PLAINTIFF'S MEMORANDUM IN SUPPORT OF MOTION TO DISMISS, for example. Following the title is often an opening, designed to set a respectful tone. These leading phrases, like the title, are usually in all capital letters. The motion may start with "NOW INTO COURT comes . . . "; the notice with "PLEASE TAKE NOTICE THAT . . ." (after giving the name and address of opposing counsel, to whom it is addressed); and the motion memorandum with "MAY IT PLEASE THE COURT." There is usually no written requirement that these documents begin in this way, but this phrasing has become a convention. Again, the best way to verify what convention your employer wants you to use is to use another motion filed with the same court as a pattern, adjusting it as needed to the situation at hand.

Unlike the appellate brief, which has stringent form requirements, the form for memoranda in support is not usually rigid. Most pretrial memoranda contain only an **Introduction**, which includes needed factual details, an **Argument** (broken up by point headings), a **Prayer**, and the requisite signature and certificate. Generally, a motion memorandum should be short, and therefore does not need the extra subdivisions. Long memos, like appellate briefs, may use the following structure. Components standard in all motion memos are in bold; other sections that may be needed in long, complex memos are in normal type.

MOTION MEMO

- ☐ 1. Cover page
- ☐ 2. Table of Contents
- ☐ 3. Table of Authorities
- ☐ 4. Introduction
- ☐ 5. Question or Issue Presented, or just Issue
- ☐ 6. Statement of the Case (also called Statement of Facts or just Facts)

- ☐ 7. Argument, broken up by point headings
- ☐ 8. Conclusion (usually entitled a Prayer)
- ☐ 9. Rule 11 endorsement[16] and Certificate of Service

The only things that an appellate brief will contain that will not be in a motion memo are a separate statement of jurisdiction and a separate statement of the standard of review, as explained in subsection G of this section. The longer the document, the more clearly organized it must be. See the examples in the appendix at the end of this chapter (one is a short motion, the other is excerpted from a longer one).

C. Drafting Sequence

The drafting sequence for a motion memo or appellate brief, as with any larger project, varies from writer to writer and project to project. Generally, however, as with objective memos, it is easiest to draft the intensive rule and application discussions of law first, followed by the statement of facts (if needed), then to finalize the statement of issues or point headings, and to draft the introduction and conclusion last. In an appellate brief, begin with the statement of jurisdiction and standard of review, prior to the argument. The first, the statement of jurisdiction, is usually very formulaic, short, and straightforward. The second, the standard of review, will affect how the argument is framed, and so a good understanding of it is necessary before you draft the argument. However, for ease of understanding how these documents hang together, and because the components of a motion memo are slightly different from those of an appellate brief, the basic components will be described in the sequence in which they appear in the final documents.

SUGGESTED DRAFTING SEQUENCE FOR BRIEFS AND MOTION MEMOS

1. Statement of Jurisdiction
2. Standard of Review
3. Argument
4. Statement of Facts
5. Statement of Issues or Questions Presented
6. Introduction
7. Prayer
8. Table of Authorities
9. Table of Contents

---

[16] Required of all documents filed in U.S. federal courts: Fed. R. Civ. P. 11(a). See discussion infra in Section IV.

D. The Introduction and Question Presented

As with an objective memo, the introduction may be written last, once the writer has a very clear idea of the nature and contents of the document. The introduction is very important. It sets the tone of the memo. Its point is to tell the judge why the matter is before the court and define the type of decision the court is being asked to make. It explains the nature of the litigation and describes the motion before the court and the relief sought through the motion. It should also include enough factual information to explain how the controversy arose, and should summarize the parties' contentions. It should be short, interesting, easy to understand, and convincing.

The statement of question presented or issues is usually required as a separate section in an appellate brief, but is occasionally needed in a long motion memo as well. It summarizes an issue or issues the court must decide, phrasing them as questions. Traditionally, the question presented was a run-on sentence in the form of a question, into which the advocate tried to stuff both a factual framework and a legal question with only one possible answer. The following is an example of one such (poorly drafted) issue:

Whether Barndt Insurance can deny insurance coverage on grounds of late notice when Fiver's insurance policy required Fiver to give Barndt notice of a claim "immediately," and when in May 1994 one of Fiver's offices was damaged by smoke from a fire in another tenant's space, and when 10 months later, Fiver gave notice, and when Barndt investigated the claim for 6 months before denying coverage and did not raise a late-notice defense until 18 months after the claim was filed.[17]

Although the "whether" format is losing favor because of its inherent limitations, some attorneys and firms still use it.[18] Alternatively, an issue statement can consist of two or three short sentences setting the legal and factual basis of the controversy and ending with a question. The first sentence gives the legal principle, the second its application, and the third the question the court must answer to resolve the case:

The attorney-client privilege protects from disclosure only those communications that are kept confidential within the strict confines of the lawyer-client relationship. Eagle Company disclosed communications to a third-party insurance broker after learning of Rush Insurance Company's denial of coverage. Can Eagle Company now refuse to disclose these communications based on a claim of privilege?[19]

E. The Statement of the Case or Statement of Facts

The statement of the case or statement of facts is much like the facts section of an office memorandum, but the drafting technique used is very different. In an objective memo, the facts are those preliminary assertions supplied by the client or any other witnesses. In a filing, however, the only facts discussed should be those that are established in the court records, and the filing includes citations to the places in the record

---

[17] Bryan A. Garner, *The Winning Brief* 67 (1999).
[18] *Id.* at 47-79.
[19] *Id.* at 69.

where those facts are established. Furthermore, though both an objective memo and a filing require that the facts be told in a logical, easy-to-follow sequence, in a filing it is even more important that the statement of facts begin with a punch and then grab the reader's interest by telling a compelling story about people, emphasizing facts of record that are favorable to your client, neutralizing unfavorable facts, and humanizing your client.

1. Be Careful When Incorporating to-Be-Established Factual Assertions

In an appellate brief, the advocate relates the facts in the light most favorable to the client. However, in a motion memo, many facts are not yet established, and it might not even be appropriate to include a full *statement of facts*. Nevertheless, the reader will need some factual context in order to understand the nature of the controversy, and thus the advocate must incorporate some factual assertions. Furthermore, in deciding a motion to dismiss for failure to state a claim, the court assumes, without deciding, that the plaintiff's assertions are true, because a plaintiff's claim should not be lightly dismissed, and should be dismissed under this provision only if there is no possible way he could succeed at trial.[20] Therefore, in these cases, the plaintiff's memo will include the client's factual assertions relevant to the argument against dismissal, as well as the factual assertions needed for background detail.

For example, in the personal injury maritime case, the defendant, an oil and gas company, moved for dismissal of the plaintiff's loss of consortium and punitive damage claims. Excerpts from that motion, the memorandum in support, and the memorandum in opposition are included in the sample documents in the appendix at the end of this chapter. The defendant's memo minimized the facts, stating only that the plaintiff "was the master of the M/V OCEAN SCRAMBLER which allided with [defendant's] pipeline on July 5, 2000 and has sued defendants herein for damages along with his spouse, Bernell [sic]."[21] In contrast, the plaintiff's memo introduced the case with the following description incorporating established and to-be-established facts:

> Defendant Southern Natural Gas (SNG) owns a pipeline in Plaquemines Parish, Louisiana. When SNG's inadequately marked, inadequately covered pipeline ruptured and exploded, Captain Alexis and his crew were badly injured.

Incidentally, although the defendant's argument was strong and seemingly based on mandatory authority, the plaintiff won the motion. In addition to presenting underlying facts in an emotionally appealing way, the plaintiff's opposition memo pointed

---

[20] *See, e.g., Berkovitz v. United States*, 486 U.S. 531, 540 (1988).

[21] Note that this example was chosen because it illustrates how unfavorable factual assertions are treated in motion memos. However, it is not a well-constructed sentence: The misplaced modifying phrase at the end creates an ambiguity. As it stands, the reader can misconstrue the sentence as saying that Alexis is suing both SNG and his wife, Bernell. The sentence should have been broken into two sentences as follows: "Paul Alexis was the master of the M/V OCEAN SCRAMBLER which allided with a SNG pipeline on July 5, 2000. He and his spouse, Bernell, have sued the defendants for damages."

out not only that the courts were conflicted about the applicable legal principle, but also that the defendant had relied on dicta, and that granting the defendant's motion would lead to inequitable results.

2. *Use of Emotional Language*

Though its use is occasionally appropriate in persuasive filings, emotional language must be handled circumspectly, as in the preceding example. Use the facts to your client's advantage by appealing to emotions subtly rather than overtly, and maintain an objective tone. For example, to return to the wedding dress memo exercise discussed in Chapter 8, you may recall that Ms. Manning, the bride, wanted to sue Ms. Singer, the seamstress, for emotional damages when Singer breached her contract to sew ten formal dresses for Manning's wedding. In a memorandum or brief in support of Manning, rather than stating that Singer's breach of the contract was "outrageously callous and cruel, and completely ruined what was supposed to be the best day of Manning's life," it would be far more persuasive to state that "Singer's failure to complete the dresses on time left the wedding day in shambles and Manning in tears." The first uses emotionally laden conclusions, while the latter uses facts seemingly objectively, but in an emotionally appealing (and poetic) way. One cannot always be poetic, but being direct, strong, and clear, though understated, is more than adequate.

In addition to avoiding overly strident adjectives, avoid as well confrontational or 'conclusory' expressions. Statements such as "the evidence is convincing and uncontradicted that . . . ," "it is obvious that . . . ," and other pat phrases merely make assertions that insult the reader. Instead of explaining the writer's point, these types of expressions imply that the reader is stupid if she does not immediately reach the same conclusion without further explanation. As an advocate, your job is to explain and prove your case, not insist that the reader accept your assertions.

EXPRESSIONS TO AVOID

- "clearly," "plainly," "patently," "obviously," "undeniably"
- "The evidence is convincing and uncontradicted that . . ."
- "It is obvious that . . ."
- any similar expression

---

3. *Balancing Accuracy, Unfavorable Facts, and Organization*

In addition to being compelling but not overly emotional, the statement of facts must be scrupulously accurate, and every assertion should be supported by a reference to the exact page or pages in the record or transcript where the supporting testimony can be found, especially in an appellate brief. Courts can and do sanction counsel for misstatements, as described in § IV of this chapter on ethics rules. More important, though, an inaccuracy harms your credibility with the court and can thereby harm your client's chances. Opposing counsel will point out any misstatements and take advantage of them immediately. Therefore, it is important not to omit reference to unfavorable evidence, but to present it in a manner calculated to minimize the damage it might do.

Unfavorable facts can be deemphasized in several ways. One way is to discuss favorable facts first and bury the unfavorable ones in the middle of the explanation.[22] Another way to handle unfavorable facts is to describe them only briefly and broadly, while describing favorable facts in much more detail. A third method is to choose favorable words; some words have more positive connotations than others. One can call attention to evidence, if there is any, that the unfavorable facts were untrustworthy or contradicted. Finally, one can give minimal explanations of the facts, just enough to give the reader an understanding of the case. In the pipeline example, the defendant's memo minimizes the circumstances of the collision and uses the obscure verb *allided* to distance itself from a tragic factual scenario and focus more on seemingly favorable law rather than unfavorable facts. The defendant's memo follows the first half of the advocate's adage: "If you have no facts, argue the law; if you have no law, argue the facts." In contrast, the plaintiff's memo gives much more detail about the accident, creating sympathy for the plaintiff and antipathy toward the defendant.

When a full statement of facts is necessary, as in an appellate brief, the story should be told in a clear and orderly way. Context should generally be given first and details later so that the reader does not feel as if he has been thrown into the middle of the tale and must find his own way through the story.[23] As in an objective memo, chronological order is usually the most natural and best sequence for a detailed statement of facts in a persuasive memo or brief; however, the advocate may want to depart from it to emphasize certain facts and deemphasize others. Remember that the strongest position for anything is at the end, so be sure to save the strongest image for that spot without torturing the natural sequence. For example, the "wedding in shambles and Manning in tears" summation is a good ending sentence for a plaintiff's brief requesting emotional damages, because it leaves the reader with a vivid visual image of the plaintiff's emotional distress, and is a good transition to the argument that follows.

4. *Appellate Briefs: The Appellee's Statement of Facts*

The appellant is the party appealing the trial court's judgment, and therefore has the burden of introducing the case to the appellate court, explaining the facts, and establishing that the trial court made reversible errors. Very often, the appellee need not include an independent statement of the facts in the brief, and under some court rules is not even permitted to do so. To save time, trouble, and the court's patience, the appellee's brief might only point out errors in the appellant's statement of facts, unless the appellant's statement is completely inadequate, is badly confused, or raises issues of fact in addition to questions of law.[24] Otherwise, the appellee can simply state that she has no objections to the appellant's statement of facts, or she can explain limited

---

22 Henry Weihofen, *Legal Writing Style* 269-70 (2d ed. 1980).
23 *Id.* at 262.
24 *Id.* at 272.

objections: *"The Plaintiffs-Appellees object to the Statement of Facts in the Defendant-Appellant's brief in the following respects: . . ."*

Sometimes, however, the appellant's statement of the case is so slanted that the appellee is better off retelling the tale of what happened from her own side—which was, after all, the side that won in the court below. In this situation, the advocate must balance the appellate court's interest in saving time against the court's need to become familiar with the appellee's view of the facts.

F. Statement of Jurisdiction

An appellate brief always requires a separate section, usually a short paragraph, explaining why the particular court in which the brief is being filed has jurisdiction.

Statement of Jurisdiction

Appellant Evelyn Basilton appeals a final judgment granted by the United States District Court for the Western District of Texas. Notice of appeal was timely filed in accord with Rule 4(b) of the Federal Rules of Appellate Procedure. This Court's jurisdiction is therefore invoked under 28 U.S.C. § 1291.

The statement of jurisdiction explains to the court why the case is properly before it. In a pretrial motion, the case is usually not developed enough to warrant a jurisdictional statement beyond that provided in the complaint. Instead, jurisdiction may be the issue, as in a motion to dismiss for lack of subject matter jurisdiction or lack of personal jurisdiction. If the motion to dismiss is for failure to state a claim, the argument will explain why the claim allegedly fails: The claim is barred or not recognized in that jurisdiction, or the complaint failed to allege facts that substantiate one of the components of the underlying rule. Similarly, if the motion is for a dismissal on the ground of *forum non conveniens,* the argument will explain why the forum is inappropriate.

G. Standard of Review or Decisional Standard

In an appellate brief or motion memorandum, the decisional standard or standard of review is the best place to begin a working draft of the argument. Appellate briefing rules usually require a separate statement of the standard of review, often as a preface to the argument. In a pretrial motion, the underlying standard is usually that, even assuming that what the plaintiff alleges is true and actually happened, the plaintiff cannot or should not be suing in this court. The argument you develop must be based on the appropriate standard. Thus, even if a separate statement of the standard is not required, you will need to frame your arguments within the appropriate standard in both the brief and a motion memo.

Before drafting the argument, begin by researching the review standard, focusing on cases decided by the court in which you will be filing or its immediate superior, and looking especially for cases that yielded a favorable ruling. For example, if your memorandum is in support of a motion for summary judgment in an oil and gas case, look for a recent summary judgment case in which the judgment was granted; use the formulation of the standard from that case and cite it as authority. In general, the standard for granting summary judgment is that there are no material issues of fact and the movant deserves judgment as a matter of law.[25] It is an even better match if the favorable summary judgment case you find involves similar facts (such as an oil and gas issue for the preceding example). If, to the contrary, you are writing a memorandum in opposition to the same motion, look for a summary judgment case in which the judgment was denied.

As mentioned earlier, an appellate court subjects a trial court's decision on a pure question of law to de novo review. In other words, the appellate court grants no deference to the trial court's opinion, and is free to substitute its own opinion on the question of what the law provides in that jurisdiction.[26] The policy reasons supporting this standard are several.[27] To begin with, a question of law sets precedent that will affect future cases, whereas findings of fact affect only the parties to the case. Furthermore, appellate courts are unencumbered by having to consider evidence, and can focus more attention on legal questions. An appellate tribunal is usually comprised of more than one judge, so an appellate decision is usually a collaboration; therefore, legal questions are even more likely to be considered carefully and decided correctly in an appellate court. Under de novo review, appellate courts can affirm the trial court's decision using the trial court's reasoning, reverse it, affirm it on other grounds, or even take the opportunity presented by the case to announce a change in the law.

In contrast to the de novo standard applied to questions of law, appellate courts review a trial court's findings of fact only for clear error, because they cannot personally assess the witnesses' credibility and therefore must defer to the trial court's findings. This means that as long as the lower court's factual findings are plausible, the opinion must be upheld. Sometimes, however, a lower court's finding mixes law and fact. Negligence issues often do so. For example, a finding that mixes law and fact could be "Slide-tackling an opposing player in an old-timer's soccer league which prohibits them is inconsistent with the degree of care that would be exercised by a reasonable person under those same circumstances." Because this finding mixes fact and law, the reviewing court must decide whether to review it under a de novo standard or a "clearly erroneous" standard.[28] Depending on which side you were arguing for, in cases where it is unclear which standard should be used, you should argue for whichever standard is in your client's favor. In this instance, if you represented the defendant who was found negligent, you would argue for a de novo review. If you were representing the plaintiff who won in the court below, you would argue for a clear error standard, because you would have a greater chance of getting the trial court's decision affirmed under that standard. As a matter of habit, mixed findings in negligence cases are usually reviewed

[25] Fed. R. Civ. P. 56.

[26] Edwards, *supra* note 1, at 292-93.

[27] *United States v. McConney*, 728 F.2d 1195, 1200-01 (9th Cir. 1984) (en banc), for a discussion of the policy issues underlying the various standards in fact, law, and mixed questions.

[28] *Pullman-Standard v. Swint*, 456 U.S. 273, 289 (1982) (acknowledging that the jurisprudence of the standard used in fact/law mixed questions is in disarray).

only for clear error, but you would need to research the court's decisions to determine if this is the prevailing standard in your court.

A final standard of review that is commonly used is *abuse of discretion*. Generally, a trial court's rulings on questions of the admissibility of evidence, or its choices on how to manage a case, are reviewed only to see whether the court abused its discretion in making the ruling. The trial judge's duty in making such decisions is to refrain from acting unreasonably or arbitrarily. The policy rationales for the abuse-of-discretion standard include a trial court's practical need to be able to manage its caseload, judicial economy, the trial court's being the entity best able to assess the circumstances of the trial, the need for flexible rules to address all possible trial circumstances, and the need to support the trial judge's authority and control of the courtroom.[29] This is a very narrow scope of review, and it is much more difficult to argue for the reversal of a ruling based on this standard than for a reversal under de novo review.

The standard of review may be set forth in a separate section, as in the appellate brief. It should also be incorporated into the issues or point headings, whether you are drafting an appellate brief or a motion. Thus, as mentioned earlier, when researching the standard of review, look for an opinion that states the standard in a way that favors your case. Then phrase issues and point headings so that they accurately reflect the applicable standard. In a motion for dismissal based on a failure to state a cause of action or question to which a de novo standard would be applied, no special statement of the standard is needed: "[The defendants], pursuant to Federal Rules of Civil Procedure 12(b)(6), move to dismiss the loss of consortium . . . and punitive damages claims asserted by [the plaintiffs] because such claims are barred by the law of the Fifth Circuit and the United States Supreme Court." However, if you were questioning the trial court's findings of fact, you would incorporate clearly erroneous standard language: "The judgment should be overturned because the trial court's finding that Duplechin ran off the base line was clearly erroneous." Similarly, if the issue is to be reviewed for abuse of discretion, that standard would also be incorporated into the issue statement: "The trial court did not abuse its discretion by excluding the tire-expert's testimony because that testimony was based on untrustworthy science." The following is an example of a separate statement of the standard of review:

Standard of Review

The standard of review applicable to a summary judgment is de novo, meaning that the appellate court should apply the same test that the district court did. Bailey v. McDonnell Douglas Corp., *989 F.2d 781, 799 (5th Cir. 1993). A grant of summary judgment is mandated under Fed. R. Civ. P. 56 if there is no issue of material fact to be resolved at trial and the movant deserves judgment as a matter of law.* Little v. Liquid Air Corp., *37 F.3d 1069, 1975 (5th Cir. 1994).*

[29] Edwards, *supra* note 1, at 295.

H. The Argument

BASIC STRUCTURE OF AN ARGUMENT

Introduction: Umbrella paragraph

Issue or Point Heading 1

A. **Subheading**
Rule
Application

B. **Subheading**
Rule
Application

Issue or Point Heading 2

Rule
Application

The argument is the most important part of a memorandum in support or appellate brief, and corresponds to the discussion in an office memorandum; therefore, it is often the first portion drafted, and takes the most time and effort. The argument has two goals: to explain and to persuade. In addition to presenting the facts in a persuasive manner, the advocate must make his arguments clear and convincing. An argument must be clear and easy to understand if it is to be persuasive. Judges usually have very little time — and very little patience — for obtuse, convoluted reasoning. If they cannot follow your reasoning, they are unlikely to grant your request. Therefore, the most successful arguments are simple, strong, clear, direct, and well organized. They begin with a statement of the standard the court must use in making its decision, and then argue that under that standard, the law favors the client's position. In an appellate brief, the standard of review is usually stated in a separate section placed just in front of the argument, and then incorporated into the argument. In a motion, the decisional standard is simply incorporated into the argument. Each argument is divided logically into points and subpoints, and each point or subpoint contains both a rule section and an application section, just as does an objective memo.

1. *The Umbrella Paragraph*[30]

The first paragraph or two of the argument section in a motion memo or brief explains the rule and how the argument is organized. If the law is somewhat complicated, you might begin the argument with a short explanation of the legal background, reviewing the basic law in the area and defining needed terms, before you introduce the favorable rule and arguments. In addition to introducing any needed background law, the preliminary paragraph or paragraphs should help the reader by setting the legal context: (1) summarize the underlying rule of law; (2) explain the status of any

---

[30] Edwards, *supra* note 1, at 299-300.

components of that rule that will not be discussed; (3) assert the correctness of the ruling sought on the elements that will be discussed; (4) identify the relevant standard of review, if any; and (5) explain the order in which the points will be presented.

2. Point Headings or Issues for Review

A motion to dismiss requests certain relief from the court, and recites the grounds for that relief, but does not explain the underlying law or how the law applies to the case. Similarly, the notice of appeal assigns errors made in the trial court, but does not explain the legal issues raised by those alleged errors. The point headings in a motion memo and the issues in an appellate brief do explain the precise legal questions being raised.

In motion memos and appellate briefs, the argument is organized into *points* or *issues.* Each point or issue is one complete argument that relates to one component or part of the underlying rule. Each has a heading and may be divided into subheadings, all of which are set off by a special typeface. Each heading is substantively repeated in the topic sentence of the paragraph or series of paragraphs that follow it. The strongest argument is usually presented first, where it is likely to have the reader's closest attention. Weaker but still necessary arguments may be buried in the middle. If you have an argument relating to equity, consider using it at the end, so that you leave the reader with the impression that not only the law is on your client's side, but also fairness and justice. Each separate argument is supported by its own rule and application, just as is each issue in an objective memo. Because the court generally cannot allocate a great deal of time, brevity is strength in both motion memoranda and appellate briefs—but not at the expense of thoroughness and precision.

3. Formulate a Favorable Rule[31]

Framing points and issues for review is important, and the process begins at the prewriting stage. To formulate points or issues, you must first **identify the underlying legal rule.** This is not always simple in the United States, where rules are created mostly piecemeal from statutes and case law. The piecemeal formulation leads to ambiguity. Rules given in opinions are often loosely written, and many opinions do not even articulate the complete rule. Different opinions articulate the same rule differently, some fairly clearly and some not. Some opinions use language from earlier cases to articulate a rule, whereas others create an original articulation. In formulating a rule for an objective memo, one generally uses the language of mandatory authority, if there is any, or the strongest, clearest formulation of the rule if no mandatory authority is available.

Formulating a rule in an advocacy setting requires an additional step: identifying and stating the rule in a way most favorable to the client. If an objective analysis results in a favorable rule, you can break it into components and thereby formulate points and issues quickly. However, if objective analysis of a case seems to establish an unfavorable rule—one that is against your client's position—you cannot avoid mentioning the

---

[31] *Id.* at 254-61.

adverse case. In fact, ethical rules require that you disclose that authority.[32] Even if the rules did not require disclosure, you would lose credibility with the court if you failed to discuss adverse authority. Generally, however, the advocate can take advantage of the ambiguities inherent in common law to rearticulate the rule in the client's favor. There are two primary methods of doing this: either discount the troublesome case or distinguish it from your client's case.[33]

To **discount an adverse case**, read the opinion carefully to determine whether it actually is against your position: You may be able to see and recast the reasoning in the case in another light. In the gas pipeline motion, the defendant argued that two of the plaintiffs' causes of action should be dismissed, arguing that they were barred by a case that was mandatory authority. Plaintiffs' counsel read the case very carefully and was able to successfully argue that, contrary to the defendant's assertion, the higher court had not barred the cause of action at issue, but had specifically avoided deciding the issue. Therefore, the plaintiffs argued, the claims should not be dismissed.

If, however, the troublesome case is clearly not in your favor, you may be able to discount it with higher authority that will trump it. Research mandatory authority from a higher court, or more recent authority from the same court. If none is available, then resort to persuasive authority by surveying authorities from other jurisdictions. You may well find that courts disagree on this particular issue, and then you can argue that the court should adopt the interpretation that favors your client. This was a second strategy used by the gas pipeline plaintiffs' counsel. If the traditional interpretation is in your client's favor, you can argue that this is *settled law*, and that the troublesome case was not well reasoned enough to establish a change. In contrast, if several recent holdings showing a change in the law are in your favor, you can argue that this is a *modern trend*, and that the troublesome case shows outdated reasoning not in keeping with important policy concerns.

In addition to discounting the troublesome case, one can **distinguish** it on the facts. Using this method, the advocate argues that the client's facts are different from the facts of the troublesome case and that those differences are legally significant. Thus, the result of the adverse case should not apply to the client's case. To make this work, analyze the reasoning of the problematic case and find either language or implications that the law in the adverse opinion is meant to apply to factual scenarios unlike those in your client's case, for policy or other reasons. As a final argument, the gas pipeline plaintiffs' counsel further argued that the apparent reasoning in the adverse case, if applied to the client's case, would lead to unfair and arbitrary results that would be inconsistent with general tort law.

Using three different methods, the plaintiffs' counsel turned an adverse case into one that was in the client's favor, thus winning the motion. He reread and reinterpreted the case, argued that there was a split in authority, and argued that following the adverse case blindly would lead to unfair results. As with the gas pipeline case, usually, one or more of these methods will work so that you can develop a credible statement of the rule that is in your client's favor, even with adverse authority.

---

[32] *See* discussion in § IV of this chapter.
[33] Edwards, *supra* note 1, at 262-63.

4. Use the Favorable Rule to Develop Point Headings

Point headings and issues are not mere statements of general law. Instead, they are derived from a component or components of the underlying legal rule. Furthermore, each point or issue must be dispositive of your client's case. In other words, if you persuade the court of even one point, the court should grant your client the relief requested. Often, there will be points of law or legal issues that are in your client's favor and that need explanation, but which are not dispositive. These are relegated to subheadings. Once you have formulated the favorable rule, use it to frame the points or issues, then subheadings, and from there develop an organizational paradigm.

Distinguishing between Headings and Subheadings

In a case involving a conjunctive rule, each component of that rule may become an issue or point heading for the defense because each is required: If the defense establishes that any one component is lacking, defense wins. However, the plaintiff must establish all of the components; therefore, none is dispositive for the plaintiff, and each one that is at issue will be relegated to the level of a subheading. As you should remember, the elements of a cause of action for negligence are conjunctive. The plaintiff must establish all four: duty, breach, causation, and damages. Thus, a plaintiff's issue or point heading in a recreational soccer/slide-tackle case might be as follows. Notice that the legally significant language is italicized for emphasis, but would not be so in a real heading.

Plaintiff's Point Headings

1. *The trial court did not err in finding the defendant negligent because the evidence at trial established all of the elements of negligence.*
   A. *The trial court's ruling that the defendant had a* duty *not to slide-tackle was not clearly erroneous.*
   B. *The trial court's finding that the defendant* breached *the duty not to slide-tackle was not clearly erroneous.*
   C. *The finding that the defendant's slide-tackle was the* cause in fact *of plaintiff's injury was not clearly erroneous.*
   D. *The finding that the plaintiff was* injured *was not clearly erroneous.*

In contrast, the advocate for the defendant who had allegedly slide-tackled the plaintiff in a recreational soccer case would win if she proved that any one of the four components was not present. Thus, each component is a potentially dispositive issue or point. Defense counsel's point headings could be as follows.

Defendant's Point Headings

1. *Because slide-tackling is an accepted part of soccer, defendant had* no duty *to avoid slide-tackling.*
2. *Even if the defendant had a duty to avoid slide-tackles, the trial court erred in finding that he* breached *that duty by slide-tackling the plaintiff.*
3. *The trial court clearly erred in finding that the slide-tackle* in fact caused *the plaintiff's injuries.*
4. *The trial court clearly erred in finding that the plaintiff was* injured.

Because the clearly erroneous standard is a very difficult standard to reach, it would be very unlikely that a defendant would argue any but the first of these points. Under any given factual scenario, not all of the components of a conjunctive rule can be made into an issue or point, but when more than one component can be questioned, they are dealt with sequentially.

With disjunctive components, the issue would have to incorporate both components to be dispositive. For example, you might remember 18 U.S.C. § 924(c)(1) from Chapter 3, which makes it a crime to *use or carry* a firearm in connection with a drug-trafficking crime. The disjunctive components could form a dispositive issue: "Because Mr. Smith neither used nor carried the firearm, he should not have been found guilty of a § 924(c)(1) violation." Other point headings could be framed from the conjunctive components: "Because Mr. Smith was not trafficking in drugs, he should not . . . ." With a factor or totality-of-the-circumstances test, a point heading could not be based on only one factor, because one factor or circumstance will never be determinative of the case. Thus, discussion of factors or circumstances will be relegated to subheadings, as with disjunctive components or the plaintiff's subheadings described earlier.

Phrase Point Headings to Incorporate Facts and to Advance the Client's Case

A point heading is not a mere title or general statement of a legal principle. Instead, it is an argument derived from one component of the legal rule and is dispositive of your client's case. It is an independent and freestanding ground that entitles your client to the relief sought.[34] If the judge agrees with you on only this one component of the rule, that should be enough to entitle your client to the relief sought. A point heading must incorporate specific facts and advance your client's case. For example, the following are not good point headings because they are mere statements of law lacking any ties to the instant case:

The verdict was against the weight of the evidence.

A court lacking personal jurisdiction over the defendant is unable to render a personal judgment against him.

In contrast, the following are somewhat stronger point headings because they are tied to the instant case and address dispositive components of the underlying legal rules, though they are still not as specific as they might be:

The Jones Act and the Death on the High Seas Act are inapplicable to SNG.

All but Sendo's Breach of Contract Claim should be dismissed as a matter of law.

The best headings contain both a request for the specific ruling and fact-based justification under a component of the underlying rule:

Sendo's fraud counts should be dismissed as a matter of law because Sendo failed to plead them with particularity.

---

[34] Edwards, *supra* note 1, at 283 (citing Richard K. Neumann, Jr., *Legal Reasoning and Legal Writing: Structure, Strategy, and Style* 307 (3d ed. 1998); Helene S. Shapo et al., *Writing and Analysis in the Law* 283 (3d ed. 1995)).

[or, as reversed in the original]

Because Sendo failed to plead its fraud counts with particularity, they should be dismissed as a matter of law.

[or a second alternative]

Sendo failed to plead its fraud counts with particularity; therefore, those counts should be dismissed.

Determining Which Is the Strongest Point

The strongest point is the point with which the court is most likely to agree, not the one about which you feel most strongly or the one you feel is most morally justified. In addition to basing the organizational sequence on research into the underlying law and prewriting methodology described earlier, it is also wise to research the viewpoints of the judge or judges who will be deciding the case, so that you can take their interests and concerns into account.

Typography for Points and Subpoints

Headings and subheadings should be in different typefaces and/or styles, so that they act as signposts guiding the reader from one argument to the next. It is traditional to use all capital letters for point headings and italics for subheadings. However, using **bold** typeface may be more effective. Determine if your firm has a preference, but avoid using more than two different typefaces or styles for headings and subheadings, because they begin to get difficult to read and therefore may annoy your reader, the judge.

5. Supporting Arguments Using CRAC Analysis

An office memorandum uses IRAC analysis. In a motion memo or appellate brief, however, the writer wants to persuade the reader, and therefore uses CRAC analysis. As explained in Chapter 3, the major difference between the two structures is that CRAC analysis begins with a statement of the conclusion — in other words, a restatement of the point heading — rather than a statement of the issue. CRAC analysis is used rather than IRAC because when the judge knows where you are going, it is easier for her to understand and follow your argument. The restatement of the point heading is followed by the favorable rule formulated earlier, and an explanation and justification of the rule. Remember also to ground the explanation in policy as appropriate. This is the fundamental appeal to justice, fairness, and morality: "That court decided this way because it was fair and in the long-term interests of society to do so. The situation is the same here."

After you have explained and justified the rule, present any counteranalysis necessary to preempt opposing counsel's potential arguments. Then begin the application section by stating the factual conclusions you want the reader to reach. Follow this by applying the favorable rule to your client's facts, emphasizing the favorable facts and deemphasizing unfavorable facts, and explaining how the result accords with any policy concerns discussed in the rule section. Next, rebut opposing counsel's potential counterapplication, and finally restate your conclusion with up to a one-paragraph summation of the key points supporting it.

DETAILED OUTLINE OF AN ARGUMENT

Umbrella paragraph

First point heading

(rule section)
Restatement of point heading as a conclusion
Favorable rule analysis and explanation of the rule
Any counter arguments needed to preempt opposition

(application section)
Statement of factual conclusions about client's case
Application of rule to client's facts, emphasizing favorable facts
Any counterapplication needed to preempt opposition

(conclusion)
Restate conclusion, summarizing key points

This paradigm follows what the U.S. law-educated reader expects to find, in the sequence he expects to find it, and consistently produces a strong, persuasive argument. This does not mean, however, that the paradigm must always be followed slavishly. There are times when a slight variation may increase effectiveness. As a matter of habit, though, it is best to use this pattern for the first draft of an argument, and thereafter incorporate variations if they would either improve the flow of the document or increase its persuasive value. The following is part of a possible argument for Manning in the wedding dress example. Assume that Manning lost her request for emotional damages at trial, and is appealing that denial. Analyze the argument, locating and identifying the various parts of its structure. Consider how and where the argument preempts possible counterarguments, as well as whether and how it varies from the basic organizational paradigm and why it does so.

Argument

Emotional damages should be granted because Singer's breach of contract was the direct cause of Manning's emotional distress and Singer was aware of the personal nature of the agreement at the time of contracting.

Emotional distress damages are justified when the contract at issue has a special, personal nature so that its breach directly causes emotional distress and both parties are aware of this nature at the time of contracting. See Fogleman v. Peruvian, *Assocs., 622 P.2d 63, 65 (Ariz. Ct. App. 1980),* distinguishing Browning v. Fies, *58 So. 931 (Ala. 1912) (granting damages for emotional distress). The appellant, Ms. Manning, challenges the lower court's denial of emotional damages, because the contract for dresses for Manning's wedding was a very personal one and Ms. Singer must have been aware that breaching it would cause Ms. Manning emotional distress. This brief will first describe the nature of the contract and then show the parties' awareness of that nature.*

A. The contract for made-to-measure dresses for Manning's wedding was of a special nature such that its breach directly caused emotional distress.

Singer's breach of the contract to sew ten dresses for Manning's wedding caused Manning significant emotional distress because of the very personal nature of the contract. Emotional damages for breach of contract are usually denied out of concern that the plaintiff will be overcompensated. E. Allan Farnsworth, Contracts *§ 12.17, at 840 (3d ed. 1999). However, an exception is made if the contract is one for a personal service or special event such that its breach leads directly to emotional distress.* See id.*;* Browning, *58 So. at 934. For example,* Browning *involved a contract for the hiring of a carriage to take the plaintiff Browning and his family to a church for Browning's wedding ceremony. 58 So. 931. The defendant never sent the carriage, and as a result of this breach of contract, Browning and his family had to take a streetcar and arrived at the church 45 minutes late, hot, tired, and embarrassed.* Id. *at 933. Recognizing that this was a special type of contract involving an emotionally-charged event, the court granted emotional damages in addition to normal contract damages, at a time when mental damages were still somewhat unusual.* See id. *at 934.*

6. Handling Counterarguments

Knowing how to handle the opposition's arguments and potential arguments can be tricky. In general, it is best to define the argument in your own terms, rather than letting the opposition shape the argument.[35] Usually the old adage from American football applies: "The best defense is a good offense." This is one reason for beginning by formulating a favorable rule. After having explained your arguments, however, you may want or need to preempt those arguments opposing counsel is likely to raise. As a general rule, it is not effective to identify opposing arguments as such. In other words, avoid awkward sentences such as "The Appellee may argue that . . . ; however, . . ." Instead, disprove potential opposing arguments by proving your own position. In the preceding Manning example, opposing counsel is likely to argue that there is no Arizona case law granting emotional damages for breach of contract. The argument preempts this by explaining that prior Arizona cases can be distinguished on their facts.

In deciding which opposing arguments to address, try not to raise arguments the opposing party might not think to raise. When you must deal with such counter-arguments, though, try to avoid phrasing them better than adverse counsel will. Certainly, you do not want opposing counsel to define the issues unless you have extremely powerful arguments to counter them. Therefore, describe the opposition's potential arguments briefly and in general terms, and articulate your own position in much more detail. Never discuss a counterargument before setting out your own affirmative argument, because that allows adverse counsel to define the situation; your brief will have a defensive tone and therefore be much less effective. For the same reason, even if you are the appellee or respondent, it is best to draft your own brief before seeing your opponent's, so that you can develop affirmative arguments rather than just respond to

[35] Edwards, *supra* note 1, at 313-14.

adverse counsel's.[36] Then, after having read the opposing brief, adjust your reply as needed to counter any arguments you failed to consider in the first draft.

7. Organizing Arguments for Factor and Totality-of-the-Circumstances Rules

You will have to put a lot of thought into organizing arguments for rules that call for consideration of certain factors or consideration of the totality of the circumstances, because three different organizational paradigms can be used. Normally, the application section of an argument or discussion section mirrors the organization of the rule section. With factor and circumstances tests, though, the advocate may want to vary this structure. The application section can analyze each factor sequentially, or by party, or by theme. Depending on which factors or circumstances the advocate wants to emphasize or deemphasize, one or another of these organizational methods may be more or less persuasive.

As explained previously, each issue or point heading presents a dispositive question. Developing point headings for conjunctive and combination conjunctive and disjunctive rules is therefore straightforward: if you will win your ruling by proving that any one of the required components is not present, then each component becomes a prospective issue. If you must prove all of the required components, then each becomes a subheading. Logically, because both parties must prove all of the factors or all of the circumstances, individual factors and circumstances might be treated as subheadings, but the question is how best to organize and present them. Using an individual rule/application for each factor is generally not effective because it will confuse the reader. This would be the factor equivalent of a laundry-list approach. However, one could explain each factor sequentially in the rule section, and then apply each factor sequentially.

Arguments Organizing Factors Sequentially

(Dispositive issue or point heading): ***The ruling I'm requesting should be granted because the factors favor my client***

Rule explanation
First factor
Second factor
Third factor

Application section
First factor applied
Second factor applied
Third factor applied

[36] Bryan A. Garner, *The Winning Brief* 340 (1999).

For example, *Lestina* lists a number of factors that can be used to determine whether a participant's behavior in a recreational sport has been negligent:

> To determine whether a player's conduct constitutes actionable negligence (or contributory negligence), the fact finder should consider such material factors as the sport involved; the rules and regulations governing the sport; the generally accepted customs and practices of the sport (including the types of contact and the level of violence generally accepted); the risks inherent in the game and those that are outside the realm of anticipation; the presence of protective equipment or uniforms; and the facts and circumstances of the particular case, including the ages and physical attributes of the participants, the participants' respective skills at the game, and the participants' knowledge of the rules and customs.

Lestina v. West Bend Mut. Ins. Co., 501 N.W.2d 28, 33 (Wis. 1993). A factor-by-factor rule section would explain each of the factors, ostensibly describing how each factor was used in various cases. The application section would then compare the case law for each factor with the facts of the case at issue. This is a somewhat clumsy, bulky way of handling the application section. Unless there are only one or two factors at issue, the reader may quickly lose sight of the factors, what they mean, and which are in your client's favor.

As an alternative to factor-by-factor organization, one could organize the application section by party. In this approach, the application section could first explain how the factors favor the client, and then how they disfavor the opposition—being careful to deemphasize counterarguments. If there are a large number of factors, one might want to organize the factors by theme. For example, many states use a "best interest of the child" standard for determining which parent should be given custody. Statutes often list a great number of factors that are to be used to determine what is in the child's best interest. One could apply these factors to each parent: the first part of the application would discuss the interests served by awarding custody to the mother, and the second the interests served by awarding custody to the father.[37] Alternatively, the factors could be organized by interests that address the child's need for stability and those that address the child's need for a sense of control over his own fate.

Arguments Organized by Party

(Dispositive issue or point heading): ***Because the factors favor my client, the ruling I'm requesting should be granted***

Rule explanation
First factor
Second factor
Third factor

Application section
Factors favoring client

[37] Edwards, *supra* note 1, at 309-11.

Factors that seem to favor opposition (but why they are not as strong as those favoring client)

Factors Organized by Theme

(Dispositive issue or point heading): ***Because the factors favor my client, the ruling I'm requesting should be granted***

Rule explanation
First factor
Second factor
Third factor

Application section
First category of factors, and why they favor client (and not opposition)

Second category of factors, and why they favor client (and not opposition)

8. *The Prayer*

The purpose of the prayer of a motion memo or appellate brief is to ask the court for specific relief. Its function, therefore, is somewhat like a conclusion, but it must also include a request addressed to the court. Like opening words, closing words are critical. Sometimes the prayer or conclusion section of a motion memorandum can be very, very short: a mere one- or two-sentence restatement of your request to the court:

Singer's failure to timely deliver the dresses she had agreed to sew directly caused Manning severe emotional distress on her wedding day, and Singer must have known that this would be the result. Manning should be granted emotional damages. Therefore, appellant Manning respectfully requests that this Court reverse the trial court's denial of emotional distress damages and remand the case for a determination of quantum.

Often, however, especially for a longer memo, a little more may be necessary. In a few strong sentences or paragraphs, summarize the three or four reasons why the court should do what you urge, and respectfully state exactly what you are asking the court to do.

IV. A CAUTIONARY NOTE: ETHICAL RULES AND WRITING STANDARDS APPLICABLE TO ADVOCACY

The U.S. rules of professional ethics impose a dual duty to both client and court. This dual duty is usually described as requiring that counsel represent clients zealously,[38] but

[38] Model Code of Prof'l Responsibility Canon 7 (1981); *id.* DR 7-101; *id.* EC 7-1 [hereinafter Model Code]; Model Rules of Prof'l Conduct R. 1.3 cmt. (1983) [hereinafter Model Rules]. The concept of "zealous representation" embraces the traditional view that the interests of the lawyer's client are generally paramount to the interest in the administration of justice.

within the bounds of the law.[39] What surprises some attorneys from outside the United States is that a U.S. attorney is required to inform the judge of both law and facts that are adverse to her client's position. You may make any argument under the law or in a good-faith effort "for the extension, modification, or reversal"[40] of existing law, but you must reveal any "controlling" legal authority that you know to be "directly adverse" to your client's position and that opposing counsel has not disclosed.[41] Logically, even when opposing counsel has disclosed adverse authority, you will need to address those arguments; and even when the adverse authority is not controlling, you will usually want to discuss it so as to anticipate and refute your opponent's arguments.

In addition to this duty to disclose adverse authority, the Model Code also imposes a duty to inform the court "of all material facts," whether or not those facts are "adverse."[42] Thus, persuasive writing requires the development of somewhat different writing skills than objective writing: You want to present your client's position in the best possible light, emphasize favorable authority, distinguish unfavorable authority, and ask the court for specific relief.

Violation of these duties to accurately state the law and investigate facts has been sanctioned. For example, intentionally or unintentionally misstating the law, whether because of inadequate research[43] or failure to correctly analyze authority,[44] violates the lawyer's obligation to represent the client competently.[45] Failure to update statutes[46] or Shepardize cases[47] is also sanctionable. Such misstatements have led to severe disciplinary sanctions, including everything from a judicial rebuke[48] and requiring the attorney to pay his opponent's costs and fees,[49] to suspending the attorney's license to practice[50] and even disbarment.[51] An attorney's failure to investigate the facts of a claim has been similarly sanctioned.[52]

---

[39] Model Code, *supra* note 38, Canon 7; *id.* DR 7-102; *id.* EC 7-1; *see* Model Rules, *supra* note 38, R. 3.1 cmt.
[40] Model Rules R. 3.1 (1999); Model Code, DR 7-102(A)(2) (1983).
[41] Model Rules R. 3.3(a)(3) (1999); Model Rules of Prof'l Responsibility DR 7-106(B)(1) (1983).
[42] Model Rules R. 3.3(d) (1999).
[43] *E.g., Baird v. Pace,* 752 P.2d 507 (Ariz. 1987); *State ex rel. Oklahoma Bar Ass'n v. Hensley,* 661 P.2d 527 (Okla. 1983).
[44] *E.g., People ex rel. Goldberg v. Gordon,* 607 P.2d 995 (Colo. 1980); *Florida Bar v. Lecznar,* 690 So. 2d 1284 (Fla.1997); *In re Farmer,* 950 P.2d 713 (Kan. 1997); *In re Moore,* 494 S.E.2d 804 (S.C. 1997).
[45] Model Rules R. 1.1 (1999); DR 6-101(A)(1) provided that a lawyer shall not handle a matter "which he knows or should know that he is not competent to handle, without associating himself with a lawyer who is competent to handle it." Model Rules of Prof'l Responsibility DR 6-101(A)(2) (1983) required "preparation adequate in the circumstances." Rule 1.1 more fully particularizes the elements of competence. Whereas DR 6-101(A)(3) prohibited the "neglect of a legal matter," Rule 1.1 does not contain such a prohibition. Instead, Rule 1.1 affirmatively requires the lawyer to be competent.
[46] *E.g., State ex rel. Nebraska State Bar Ass'n v. Holscher,* 230 N.W.2d 75 (Neb. 1975).
[47] *E.g., Smith v. United Transp. Union Local No. 81,* 594 F. Supp. 96 (S.D. Cal. 1984); *Taylor v. Belger Cartage Serv. Inc.,* 102 F.R.D. 172 (W.D. Mo. 1984).
[48] *E.g., In re Winkel,* 577 N.W.2d 9 (Wis. 1998).
[49] *E.g., Wei v. Bodner,* 1992 WL 165860 (D.N.J. 1992).
[50] *E.g., People v. Boyle,* 942 P.2d 1199 (Colo. 1997); *In re Mekler,* 689 A.2d 1171 (Del. 1996); *In re Kovitz,* 504 N.Y.S.2d 400 (App. Div. 1986); *In re Disciplinary Proceedings Against Fischer,* 499 N.W.2d 677 (Wis. 1993).
[51] *E.g., State ex rel. Oklahoma Bar Ass'n v. Hensley,* 661 P.2d 527 (Okla. 1983).
[52] *E.g., Monument Builders of Greater Kansas City, Inc. v. American Cemetery Ass'n,* 891 F.2d 1473 (10th Cir. 1989); *White v. General Motors Corp., Inc.,* 908 F.2d 675 (10th Cir. 1990); *Hilton Hotels*

Furthermore, statutory and common law authorities impose professional standards for the form, organization, and style of writing of any document filed with a court.[53] Poor writing can lead to suspension from the bar in extreme cases,[54] dismissal of the complaint,[55] costs, reprimand,[56] and orders to take courses in legal writing.[57] Wordiness has been sanctioned,[58] as has poor grammar.[59] Although spelling and typographical errors do not usually lead to sanctions, they can be interpreted as indicators of a lawyer's general lack of competence.[60] Punctuation errors can have grave consequences when they change the meaning of a sentence. Inaccurate and incomplete citations or citations lacking pinpoint citations, when accompanied by other failings, can also lead to severe sanctions, including disciplinary proceedings.[61] Furthermore, when courts have local rules regarding page length and typographical conventions, some courts simply will not accept briefs that exceed the page limit; others refuse to consider the portion that exceeds the limit; still others have sanctioned attorneys for attempting to circumvent page limitations.[62]

The consequences of late filings can be harsh for both attorney and client. In one capital (i.e., death-penalty) case, an appeal was dismissed when a lawyer filed the notice of appeal three days late.[63] Similarly, in a civil appeal, a lawyer arrived at the court at 4:57 P.M. to file a brief.[64] However, he did not have all of the required copies with him, and the office closed at 5:00 P.M. Though his secretary arrived with the remaining few copies a few minutes after 5:00, the clerk refused to accept them, and the dismissal of the brief as not timely filed was upheld on appeal.[65] Although U.S. courts will usually grant extensions for good cause, a late filing and resulting dismissal can result in

---

Corp. v. Banov, 899 F.2d 40 (D.C. Cir. 1990); *Belich v. Szymaszek*, 592 N.W.2d 254 (Wis. Ct. App. 1999).

[53] Model Rules R. 1.1 (1999).

[54] *E.g., In re Willis*, 505 A.2d 50 (D.C. Cir. 1985); *Attorney Grievance Comm'n v. Myers*, 490 A.2d 231 (Md. 1985); *In re Wallace*, 518 A.2d 740 (N.J. 1986).

[55] *E.g., Greenberg v. Compuware Corp.*, 889 F. Supp. 1012 (E.D. Mich. 1995).

[56] *E.g., In re Disciplinary Action Against Hawkins*, 502 N.W.2d 770 (Minn. 1993).

[57] *E.g., In re Shepperson*, 674 A.2d 1273 (Vt. 1996).

[58] *E.g., TK-7 Corp. v. Estate of Barbouti*, 966 F.2d 578, 579 (10th Cir. 1992); *Morgens Waterfall Holdings, L.L.C. v. Donaldson, Lufkin & Jenrette Sec. Corp.*, 198 F.R.D. 608 (S.D.N.Y. 2001).

[59] *E.g., In re Disciplinary Action Against Hawkins*, 502 N.W.2d 770 (Minn. 1993).

[60] *E.g., P.M.F. Servs., Inc. v. Grady*, 681 F. Supp. 549, 551 n.1 (N.D. Ill. 1988).

[61] *E.g., Day v. Northern Ind. Pub. Serv. Corp.*, 164 F.3d 382 (7th Cir. 1999); *In re Shepperson*, 674 A.2d 1273 (Vt. 1996).

[62] *E.g., Columbus-America Discovery Group v. Atlantic Mut. Ins. Co.*, 56 F.3d 556 (4th Cir. 1995); *Douglas v. Sandoz Pharms. Corp.*, 2000 WL 33342286 (M.D.N.C. 2000); *In re Ramunno*, 625 A.2d 248 (Del. 1993); *Lawyer Disciplinary Bd. v. Turgeon*, 557 S.E.2d 235 (W. Va. 2000); *see* Judith D. Fischer, *Bareheaded and Barefaced Counsel: Court Reacts to Unprofessionalism in Lawyers' Papers*, 31 Suffolk U. L. Rev. 1, 31 (1997).

[63] *E.g., Coleman v. Thompson*, 501 U.S. 722, 727 (1991) (discussed in Fischer, *supra* note 62, at 23).

[64] *Fischer, supra* note 62, at 37 text accompanying n.286; *Olander v. French*, 680 N.E. 2d 962, 964 (Ohio 1991). See Motion of Appellants-Cross Appellees Requesting the Court to Retain This Appeal Under Sup. Ct. Proc. Rule VI, § 6 and for Waiver of Supreme Court Practice Rule IX, § 3(b); Robert C. Maier Aff. at 2 (filed Sept. 4, 1996), in *State ex rel. Olander v. French* (No. 96-1695) (Ohio Sup. Ct.). The author thanks Mary Beth Beazley of Ohio State University for relating this story on the legal writing e-mail list and for providing copies of the affidavits for this article.

[65] *Olander*, 680 N.E.2d at 964.

unnecessary hardship for the client and a subsequent malpractice suit against the attorney.

Although some of these sanctions may have been unusually draconian, the courts' concern is always that "when lawyers' writing does not meet the profession's standards of competence and public service, it harms both the profession and society by weakening confidence in the legal system and unnecessarily consuming court time."[66] Consequences of poorly drafted filings can range from loss of a profession to loss of credibility with the very court you most want to impress; therefore, it is most important to master legal research and writing skills.

DISCUSSION NOTES

1. *Locating court rules and samples*

A. Locate the local court rules for the United States Court of Appeals for the Second Circuit. How many copies of an appellate brief must counsel file? Cite the appropriate rule.

B. Locate Hawaii's Rules of Appellate Procedure. What is the maximum length of an appellate brief (if the party has not asked for leave to extend or exceed)? Cite the appropriate rule.

2. *Rewriting a statement of facts*

How would you rewrite the following statement of facts for an appellate brief in Manning's favor? In Singer's? (Assume that every fact was established at trial.)

FACTS

Ms. Manning and her nine bridesmaids hired Singer on April 23, 1999, to make dresses for Manning's wedding party. The dresses were to be completed before the wedding. Though Manning told Singer that the wedding was to take place in mid-July, she did not give Singer the exact date of the wedding. At the meeting in April, Singer took everyone's measurements and was given the fabric for the ten dresses.

From April until June 10, Manning and Singer maintained contact by telephone, and Singer assured Manning that the dresses were progressing normally. On June 10, Singer met with the wedding party for the final fitting. At that meeting, the gowns were held together with pins and none was wearable. Singer assured Manning that all the dresses would be ready in time for the ceremony. Manning spoke with Singer by telephone again on July 10 and mentioned the exact date and time of the wedding: July 17th at 1:00 P.M. Singer said that she was shocked that the date was so soon, and was, by that time, overwhelmed with work. However, she claimed to Manning that she was putting the finishing touches on most of the dresses and should still have them

---

[66] *See Fischer*, *supra* note 62, at 37.

finished on time, though it would be very difficult. She asked Manning to reduce the number of bridesmaids, but Manning refused. Although Manning asked to see the dresses, Singer assured her that she never let her clients see the work until the last stitch was in place.

However, none of the dresses was completed prior to the wedding, and some of the dresses were never finished. On the morning of the wedding, Manning and her bridesmaids arrived at Singer's shop at 9:00 A.M. Singer told them that although their dresses were still not ready, they were minutes from completion. She asked them to wait in the back of her shop, which was crowded, dirty, and uncomfortable. They waited there for three hours, and Manning missed her beauty shop appointments. She started screaming at Singer and crying.

Manning finally got her wedding dress at 12:30 P.M. She dressed quickly, but still arrived at the church ten minutes late. Five of the bridesmaids arrived at 1:00, too late to walk down the aisle with the bride and groom, but they stood by her side during the ceremony. Their dresses were unfinished and looked terrible. Furthermore, the two bridesmaids chosen to recite prayers during the wedding, as well as two others, were still waiting at Singer's sewing shop on Singer's representation that the dresses were nearly complete. Those four bridesmaids missed the wedding ceremony entirely and wore casual clothes to the reception. The bridesmaids felt humiliated as a result.

Manning cried before, during, and after the wedding, because of the problems with the dresses.

3. *Locating authority for a standard of review*

A. You are filing a motion for summary judgment in the Northern District of California. The substantive issue of the litigation is insider trading. Find and cite a N.D. Cal. summary judgment case involving insider trading and granting dismissal.

B. Similarly, you are defending against a summary judgment motion in the same case. Find a N.D. Cal. summary judgment case involving insider trading and denying dismissal.

4. *Formulating a favorable rule*

Reread the authorities for the DWI problem in Chapter 3, Problem B, pp. 98-99.

A. Formulate a rule for the prosecution.

B. Using the same authorities, formulate a rule for the defense.

5. *Rephrasing point headings*

Rephrase the following point heading to make it more effective:

> Whether the Michapo Sessatonkin Community Indian Tribe can sue the State of Arizona where it challenges the validity under federal law of two state fees imposed on petroleum distributors insofar as the fees are levied on distributors who make deliveries to the Tribe on its reservation even though neither of the two conditions essential to a federal suit have been met: the State has not consented to be sued, Congress has not abrogated the State's sovereign immunity, and the Eleventh Amendment bars the Tribe from suing the state?

EXERCISE

Draft a memorandum in support or in opposition to dismiss or an appellate brief as directed by your instructor.

APPENDIX TO CHAPER 11: SAMPLE FILINGS

UNITED STATES DISTRICT COURT
FOR THE EASTERN DISTRICT OF TEXAS
TEXARKANA DIVISION

SENDO LIMITED, SENDO INTERNATIONAL LIMITED, SENDO HOLDINGS PLC, and SENDO AMERICA, INC.,	)	
	)	Civil Action No. 502CV282
Plaintiffs,	)	
	)	Jury Trial Demanded
v.	)	
	)	
MICROSOFT CORPORATION, MICROSOFT LICENSING, INCORPORATED and MICROSOFT CAPITAL CORPORATION,	)	
Defendants.		

PLAINTIFFS' ORIGINAL COMPLAINT

TO THE HONORABLE COURT:

Plaintiffs Sendo Limited, Sendo International Limited, Sendo Holdings PLC, and Sendo America, Inc. (collectively referred to as "Sendo" or the "Sendo Group") hereby file this Complaint against Microsoft Corporation (hereafter "Microsoft"), Microsoft Licensing, Incorporated (hereafter "MLI"), and Microsoft Capital Corporation (hereafter "MCC") (collectively "Defendants") and would show the Court as follows:

I.

PARTIES

1. Sendo Limited is a company incorporated and registered in the United Kingdom. It is, therefore, deemed to be a citizen of the United Kingdom.

2. Sendo International Limited is a company incorporated in the Cayman Islands and registered in Hong Kong. It is, therefore, deemed a citizen of the United Kingdom.

* * *

5. Microsoft Corporation (hereinafter "Microsoft") is a company incorporated in the State of Washington with its principal place of business in that State. It is, therefore, a citizen of Washington.

* * *

II. JURISDICTION AND VENUE

8. This Court has jurisdiction over this matter pursuant to 28 U.S.C. § 1332 because this is a civil action where the matter in controversy exceeds $75,000, exclusive of interest and costs, and is between citizens of different States and in which citizens or subjects of a foreign state are additional parties.

9. This Court has general jurisdiction over Defendants because their contacts with this district are substantial and continuous. This Court also has specific jurisdiction over Defendants because (1) Defendants purposefully directed their activities to this district, have done business in this district, and purposefully availed themselves of the privilege of conducting activities within this district; (2) some of the events which give rise to the claims asserted in this action occurred in this district and the effects of Defendants' tortious conduct were felt in this district; and (3) the exercise of jurisdiction comports with fair play and substantial justice.

* * *

11. Venue is proper in this district pursuant to 28 U.S.C. § 1391(a) because Defendants are doing business in this district, and because Defendants are subject to personal jurisdiction in this district.

III. INTRODUCTION

12. This lawsuit is the result of Microsoft's master plan ("The Plan") to quickly obtain the technology necessary to enter and ultimately dominate the next generation mobile phone market, also known as 2.5G, created by the convergence of mobile phones and computers. The Plan to break into the 400 million units-per-year mobile handset market was created at a time when sales of Microsoft's core Windows and office software business were in decline.

* * *

16. Microsoft's Secret Plan was to plunder the small company of its proprietary information, technical expertise, market knowledge, customers, and prospective customers. Microsoft had been unable to successfully access the wireless market because the major handset manufacturers would not use their software. So instead, Microsoft gained Sendo's trust and confidence through false promises that Sendo would be its "go to market partner" with the Microsoft Smartphone platform, originally code named "Stinger." As a result of those false promises, Microsoft gained access to Sendo's hardware expertise and knowledge of the mobile carrier business.

IV. BACKGROUND FACTS

17. The Sendo Group was formed in August, 1999 to focus on the design, development, manufacturing, marketing and sales of new, high performance, feature rich mobile telephones for consumer markets worldwide. Sendo Limited designs and develops certain intellectual property relating to the design and configuration of mobile telephones.

Sendo International Limited owns certain intellectual property relating to the design and configuration of mobile telephones and accessories and regulatory and carrier approval processes, product pricing and customer specific order and marketing strategies.

* * *

49. As a result of Microsoft's numerous acts of unfair competition together with the cooperation and coordinated efforts of Marc Brown and MCC, Sendo has suffered undetermined damages and injury.

V.

CAUSES OF ACTION

COUNT I

MISAPPROPRIATION OF TRADE SECRETS

50. Sendo incorporates and re-alleges in full paragraphs 1 through 49 of this Complaint. The foregoing acts of Defendants constitute misappropriation of Sendo's trade secrets and unjust enrichment and enhanced value of Defendants' business activities to Sendo's detriment and injury.

51. Sendo has developed through the expertise and knowledge of its directors, managers, and engineers, and by trial and error, planning, and strategy, a number of trade secrets relating to its operation of a mobile telephone development and manufacturing business. Sendo has taken and continues to maintain reasonable efforts to maintain the secrecy of its trade secrets.

* * *

COUNT V

FRAUD

64. Sendo incorporates and re-alleges in full paragraphs 1 through 60 of this Complaint. The foregoing acts of Defendants constitute fraud.

65. Upon information and belief, Defendants intentionally made numerous false material representations to Sendo during the parties' business relationship knowing that Sendo would act in reliance upon those representations to its detriment. By way of example, Defendants promised to provide Sendo with further advances, under the Credit Agreement, and further technical support, if Sendo could secure a commitment from suppliers to place orders for parts and materials for the Z100.

* * *

COUNT XIII

FRAUDULENT INDUCEMENT

88. Sendo incorporates and re-alleges in full paragraph 1 through 87 of this Complaint.

89. Defendants made material, false representations of fact to Sendo to induce Sendo to enter into the NDA, SDMA, the Shareholders' Agreement, the OEM Embedded Operating Systems Licensing Agreement for Reference Platform Devices, and the Credit Agreement.

* * *

VI.
ATTORNEYS' FEES

91. Pursuant to the contracts and Texas Civil Practice & Remedies Code Section 38, Sendo is entitled to recover its reasonable attorneys' fees incurred in enforcing its rights. Sendo seeks the recovery of its reasonable attorneys' fees from Defendants.

VII.
JURY DEMAND

92. Plaintiffs request a trial by jury.

PRAYER

WHEREFORE, Plaintiffs Sendo Limited, Sendo International Limited, Sendo Holdings PLC and Sendo America, Inc., respectfully request that after a final trial hereof, the Court enter judgment in favor of Plaintiffs against Defendants on all counts, jointly and severally, and award Plaintiffs the following:

(1) All general damages;
(2) Special damages arising from Defendants' conduct, including, but not limited to, lost profits, loss of good will, reliance damages, and incidental damages;
(3) Defendants' profits arising from their tortious acts;
(4) Costs;
(5) Pre-judgment interest;
(6) Post-judgment interest;
(7) Attorney's fees;
(8) Exemplary damages; and
(9) Such other and further relief to which Plaintiffs may show themselves entitled.

UNITED STATES DISTRICT COURT
FOR THE EASTERN DISTRICT OF TEXAS
TEXARKANA DIVISION

SENDO LIMITED, SENDO	)	
INTERNATIONAL LIMITED, SENDO	)	
HOLDINGS PLC, and SENDO	)	
AMERICA, INC.,	)	
	)	Civil Action No. 5:02CV282 (DF)
Plaintiffs	)	
	)	Jury Trial Demanded
v.	)	
	)	Judge Folsom
MICROSOFT CORPORATION,	)	
MICROSOFT LICENSING,	)	
INCORPORATED and MICROSOFT	)	
CAPITAL CORPORATION,	)	

Defendants.

DEFENDANTS' ANSWER, AFFIRMATIVE DEFENSES, AND COUNTERCLAIM

Subject to their Motion to Dismiss and Motion to Transfer Venue,[1] Microsoft Corporation, Microsoft Licensing, Incorporated, and Microsoft Capital Corporation (collectively, "Microsoft") answer the Original Complaint of Sendo Limited, Sendo International Limited, Sendo Holdings PLC, and Sendo America, Inc. (collectively, "Sendo"), as follows:

I.
PARTIES

1. Sendo Limited is a company incorporated and registered in the United Kingdom. It is, therefore, deemed to be a citizen of the United Kingdom.

ANSWER: Microsoft is without knowledge or information sufficient to form a belief as to the truth of the allegations of Paragraph 1, and on that basis denies those allegations.

2. Sendo International Limited is a company incorporated in the Cayman Islands and registered in Hong Kong. It is, therefore, deemed a citizen of the United Kingdom.

ANSWER: Microsoft is without knowledge or information sufficient to form a belief as to the truth of the allegations of Paragraph 2, and on that basis denies those allegations.

* * *

5. Microsoft Corporation (hereinafter "Microsoft") is a company incorporated in the State of Washington with its principal place of business in that State. It is, therefore, a citizen of Washington.

ANSWER: Microsoft admits the allegations of paragraph 5.

* * *

[1] Microsoft incorporates into the answers set forth below the objections to Plaintiffs' Complaint set forth in its Motion to Dismiss and Motion to Transfer. To avoid repetition, Microsoft has not restated these objections in response to each allegation of the Complaint. By filing this Answer, Microsoft does not waive any rights asserted in those Motions.

II.
JURISDICTION AND VENUE

8. This Court has jurisdiction over this matter pursuant to 28 U.S.C. § 1332 because this is a civil action where the matter in controversy exceeds $75,000, exclusive of interest and costs, and is between citizens of different States and in which citizens or subjects of a foreign state are additional parties.

* * *

III.
INTRODUCTION

12. This lawsuit is the result of Microsoft's master plan ("The Plan") to quickly obtain the technology necessary to enter and ultimately dominate the next generation mobile phone market, also known as 2.5G, created by the convergence of mobile phones and computers. The Plan to break into the 400 million units-per-year mobile handset market was created at a time when sales of Microsoft's core Windows and office software business were in decline.

ANSWER: Microsoft denies the allegations of paragraph 12.

* * *

IV.
BACKGROUND FACTS

17. The Sendo Group was formed in August, 1999 to focus on the design, development, manufacturing, marketing and sales of new, high performance, feature rich mobile telephones for consumer markets worldwide.

ANSWER: Microsoft admits that Sendo Holdings PLC is a party to certain contracts with Microsoft. Microsoft is without knowledge or information sufficient to form a belief as to the truth of the remaining allegations of Paragraph 17, and on that basis denies those allegations.

* * *

V.
CAUSES OF ACTION
COUNT I
MISAPPROPRIATION ON OF TRADE SECRETS

50. Sendo incorporates and re-alleges in full paragraphs 1 through 49 of this Complaint. The foregoing acts of Defendants constitute misappropriation of Sendo's trade secrets and unjust enrichment and enhanced value of Defendants' business activities to Sendo's *detriment* and injury.

ANSWER: Microsoft incorporates and realleges its answers to paragraph 1 through 49 set forth above. Microsoft denies the allegations of paragraph 50.

* * *

COUNT XIII
FRAUDULENT INDUCEMENT

88. Sendo incorporates and re-alleges in full paragraphs 1 through 87 of this Complaint.

ANSWER: Microsoft incorporates and realleges its answers to paragraph 1 through 87 set forth above. Microsoft denies the allegations of paragraph 88.

VII.
JURY DEMAND

Microsoft requests a trial by jury.

AFFIRMATIVE DEFENSES

Microsoft asserts the following as affirmative defenses to Plaintiff's Complaint:

FIRST AFFIRMATIVE DEFENSE

Plaintiffs' claims are barred for failure to state a claim.

* * *

FOURTH AFFIRMATIVE DEFENSE

Plaintiffs' claims are barred by their own fraudulent misconduct.

FIFTH AFFIRMATIVE DEFENSE

Plaintiffs' claims are barred by the doctrines of estoppel and equitable estoppel.

COUNTERCLAIMS

COUNT I
BREACH OF CONTRACT

1. Despite Sendo's fanciful and unfounded allegations of a supposed Microsoft "Secret Plan" to harm Sendo, the failure of the Microsoft/Sendo Z100 Smartphone project is due solely to Sendo's many and various breaches (and ultimate wrongful termination) of the SDMA and other agreements, as well as Sendo's fraudulent course of conduct in repeatedly misleading Microsoft as to Sendo's financial situation, Sendo's progress in designing and developing the Z100, and Sendo's commitment to that project. On information and belief, Sendo's purpose of this misconduct was to deceive Microsoft so that Microsoft would continue to provide funding to Sendo (thus unknowingly throwing good monery [sic] after bad), which Sendo used to fund its other projects. These projects included, on information and belief, the design and development of a Nokia Smartphone, the Series 60.

* * *

7. As part of its scheme to defraud Microsoft and in breach of the SDMA and other agreements, on information and belief, Sendo diverted financial and human resources from its work on the Microsoft Smartphone to design and develop a rival Smartphone, the Nokia Series 60.

8. Microsoft has performed all conditions precedent under the contracts. Sendo's actions have caused damage to Microsoft. The foregoing acts constitute breaches of the SDMA and the parties' other agreements.

PRAYER FOR RELIEF

WHEREFORE, Microsoft demands a trial by jury and prays for an entry of judgment in its favor and an [sic] award Microsoft the following:

a. damages in an amount established at trial; . . . .

UNITED STATES DISTRICT COURT

EASTERN DISTRICT OF LOUISIANA

CAPTAIN PAUL ALEXIS AND	*CIVIL ACTION NO. 01-1993
MRS. BERNELL ALEXIS	*
	*SECTION T-2
VERSUS	*
	*JUDGE G. THOMAS PORTEUS, JR.
SOUTHERN NATURAL GAS COMPANY,	*
TENNESSEE GAS PIPELINE COMPANY,	*MAG. JUDGE WILKINSON
AND EL PASO ENERGY CORP.	*

****

MOTION TO DISMISS PLAINTIFFS' CLAIMS FOR LOSS OF CONSORTIUM AND PUNITIVE DAMAGES

Southern Natural Gas Company, Tennessee Gas Pipeline Company, and El Paso Energy Corporation pursuant to Federal Rules of Civil Procedure 12(b)(6) move to dismiss the loss of consortium, loss of society, loss of assistance and punitive damage claims asserted by Captain Paul Alexis and Bernell Alexis for the reason that such claims are barred by law of the Fifth Circuit and the U.S. Supreme Court.

Respectfully submitted

GRADY S. HURLEY (#13913)
JAMES E. WRIGHT, III (#13700)
RUTH B. SCHUSTER (#26506)
Jones, Walker, Waechter, Poitevent,
Carrère & Denègre, L.L.P.
201 St. Charles Avenue, 48th Floor
New Orleans, Louisiana 70170-5100
Telephone: (504) 582-8000
Facsimile: (504) 582-8010

Attorneys For Defendants,
Southern Natural Gas Company,
Tennessee Gas Pipeline Company and
El Paso Energy Corporation

CERTIFICATE OF SERVICE

I hereby certify that a copy of the above has been sent to opposing counsel, either BY HAND or by placing a copy of same in the U.S. mail, properly addressed, postage prepaid, this 10 day of August 2001.

UNITED STATES DISTRICT COURT

EASTERN DISTRICT OF LOUISIANA

CAPTAIN PAUL ALEXIS AND MRS. BERNELL ALEXIS	*CIVIL ACTION NO. 01-1993 *
	*SECTION T-2 *
VERSUS	*JUDGE G. THOMAS PORTEUS, JR. *
SOUTHERN NATURAL GAS COMPANY, TENNESSEE GAS PIPELINE COMPANY, AND EL PASO ENERGY CORP.	*MAG. JUDGE WILKINSON *

****

MEMORANDUM IN SUPPORT OF MOTION TO DISMISS PLAINTIFFS' CLAIMS FOR LOSS OF CONSORTIUM AND PUNITIVE DAMAGES

Defendants, Southern Natural Gas Company, Tennessee Gas Pipeline Company, and El Paso Energy Corp. (hereinafter collectively referred to as "defendants"), move to dismiss the plaintiffs' claims for loss of consortium and punitive damages. Paul Alexis was the master of the M/V OCEAN SCRAMBLER which allided with a SNG pipeline on July 5, 2000 and has sued defendants herein for damages along with his spouse, Bernell. In paragraph IX of the plaintiffs' Complaint, Bernell Alexis seeks recovery for loss of consortium, loss of society, and loss of assistance. That paragraph states:

> As a result of the above described accident, plaintiff Mrs. Bernell Alexis has suffered damages including, but not limited to, loss of consortium, loss of society, and loss of Captain Paul Alexis' assistance pursuant to general maritime law and supplemental state law, which damages together with related charges total TWO HUNDRED FIFTY THOUSAND AND NO/100 D ($250,000.00) DOLLARS, plus interest, attorneys' fees and costs, as nearly as can be presently estimated.

Further, in Paragraph X, plaintiffs seek recovery for punitive damages.

Plaintiffs filed their case pursuant to this Court's admiralty jurisdiction, specifically alleging jurisdiction under 1332, 1333 and Rule 9(h) of the Federal Rules of Civil Procedure. Their claims are governed by maritime law. Since the complaint designates Federal Rule 9(h) jurisdiction, the entire case must be heard in admiralty. *T.N.T Marine Service, Inc. v. Weaver Shipyards & Dry Docks, Inc.*, 702 F.2d 585 (5th Cir. 1983). State law may not be used to supplement or alter existing and established federal maritime law.

> Maritime law must maintain its uniformity and preempts state law when it is contradictory to maritime laws' purpose.
>
> * * *
>
> Maritime law specifically denies recovery to non-proprietors for economical damages. To allow state law to supply a remedy when one is denied in admiralty, would serve only to circumvent the maritime law's jurisdiction. Therefore, state law

> does not supply an alternative remedy to [plaintiff] when its claim was already denied in its proper maritime jurisdiction.

IMTT-Gretna v. ROBERT E. LEE S/S, 993 F.2d 1993, 1995 (5th Cir. 1993). The General Maritime Law of the United States is applicable and precludes recovery for the non-pecuniary damages of loss of consortium, loss of society, loss of assistance and punitive damages as alleged.

I. The General Maritime Law Precludes Bernell Alexis' Claim for Non-Pecuniary Damages.

The United States Supreme Court decision of *Miles v. Apex Marine Corp.*, 498 U.S. 19 (1990) and subsequent cases in the Fifth Circuit and the Eastern District of Louisiana, preclude recovery by Bernell Alexis for non-pecuniary damages alleged in the Complaint. The instant motion to dismiss should be granted and the plaintiff's loss of consortium, loss of society and loss of assistance claims must be dismissed with prejudice. The Supreme Court in *Miles* concluded that there was no recovery for loss of society in a Jones Act wrongful death claim since non-pecuniary damages are not recognized under the Jones Act. It has long been recognized that damages characterized as loss of consortium, loss of society, and loss of assistance, constitute non-pecuniary losses. *Sea-Land Services. Inc. v. Gaudet*, 414 U.S. 573 (1974).

Further, the Fifth Circuit has held that non-pecuniary damages are not recoverable under the general maritime law even as against non-employer defendant:

> The Supreme Court has clearly indicated its desire to achieve uniformity of damage recoveries in the exercise of Admiralty jurisdiction. Allowing [plaintiff] to recover loss of consortium damages would directly contradict the policy of uniformity emphasized and relied on by the Court in *Miles*.

Walker v. Braus, 995 F.2d 77, 82 (5th Cir. 1993); *Earhart v. Chevron USA Inc.*, 852 F.Supp. 515 (E.D. La. 1993) (loss of consortium and punitive damages were not recoverable in a suit brought against a non-employer defendant under the general maritime law).

In both the Fifth Circuit and the Eastern District of Louisiana, there have been a myriad of cases holding that the rule of *Miles* precludes the wife of a seaman from claiming loss of society and consortium under the general maritime law whether involving a death case or a personal injury case. *Michel v. Total Transportation, Inc.*, 957 F.2d 186 (5th Cir. 1992) (damages recoverable in a general maritime cause of action for personal injury did not include loss of consortium); *Murray v. Anthony J. Bertucci Construction Co., Inc.*, 958 F.2d 127 (5th Cir. 1992) (seaman spouse may not recover for loss of society damages under the general maritime law); *Mastrodonato v. Sea Mar, Inc.*, 2000 WL 339284 (E.D. La. 2000) (the uniformity sought by the Court in *Miles* is best served by a rule that denies loss of consortium damages against a third party just as they are denied against a seaman's employer); *Dufrene v. Dickson G & P International, Inc.*, 1999 WL 172931 (E.D. La. 1999) (the spouse of an injured seaman has no cause of action for loss of society under the general maritime law); *Ellender v. John E. Graham & Co.*, 821 F.Supp. 1136 (E.D. La. 1992) (the rationale in *Miles* extends to a non-employer); *Duplantis v. Texaco Inc.*, 771 F.Supp. 787 (E.D. La. 1991) (the general maritime law does not allow a spousal claim for loss of consortium); *Turely v. Co-Mar Offshore Marine*

Corp., 766 F.Supp. 501 (E.D. La. 1991) (dismissing the loss of consortium claims against the employer and non-employer defendant on the ground that there is no recovery for non-pecuniary damages under the general maritime law). Judge Lemmon's opinion in *Denet Towing Service, Inc.*, 1999 WL 329698 (E.D. La. 1999) is the only post *Miles* case in the Eastern District of Louisiana allowing a wife to recover for loss of consortium against a non-employer under the general maritime law. Judge Lemmon acknowledged that her *Denet Towing* decision is contrary to the weight of authority. *Id.* at *6. Since that decision was rendered, other courts in this district have chosen not to follow Judge Lemmon's departure from *Miles. See*, e.g. *Mastrodonato,* 2000 WL 739284 at *1 (in 2); *Diamond,* 2000 WL 805235 at *2.

The case at bar is an attempt by the spouse of a seaman to recover loss of society, assistance and/or loss of consortium which claims are specifically precluded by *Miles* and the cases which followed *Miles.* This suit is governed by the general maritime law which precludes recovery to Bernell Alexis for non-pecuniary damages and such claims should be dismissed as to all defendants in this case. Since the general maritime law is established in this area, there can be no application of any inconsistent state law.

II. The General Maritime Law Precludes Alexis' Claim for Punitive Damages.

The claim of Mr. and Mrs. Alexis for punitive damages is also foreclosed by the Supreme Court's decision in *Miles* as followed by the Fifth Circuit decision in *Murray v. Anthony J. Bertucci Construction Co., Inc.*, 958 F.2d 127 (5th Cir. 1992). *See also Anderson v. Texaco Inc.*, 797 F.Supp. 531, 533 (E.D. La. 1992). Punitive damages do not compensate for a loss but are imposed to punish and deter by virtue of gravity of the offense. *Molzof v. U.S.*, 112 S.Ct. 711 (1992). Accordingly, punitive damages have been held to be non-pecuniary in nature. *Anderson v. Texaco Inc.*, 797 F.Supp. 531, 533 (E.D. La. 1992). The post-*Miles* district court cases have concluded that punitive damages are non-pecuniary in nature and therefore are not recoverable under the general maritime law. *Anderson v. Texaco Inc. supra*; *Matter of Waterman Steamship Corp.*, 780 F.Supp. 1093 (E.D. La. 1992); *Bell v. Zapata Havnie Corp.*, 1994 WL 280 (W.D. La. 1994); *Guillory v. C.F. Bean Corp.*, 1994 WL 150738 (E.D. La. 1994); *Ledet v. Power Offshore Services, Inc.*, 1994 WL 150805 (E.D. La. 1994); *Poret v. Noble Drilling Corp.*, 1994 WL 150725 (E.D. La. 1994); *Sulliyan v. Crewboats, Inc.*, 1993 WL 841855 (E.D. La. 1993). Further, recent Eastern District opinions have recognized that the Supreme Court has never affirmed an award of punitive damages in an admiralty case in support of upholding the uniformity principal [sic] of *Miles* and denying recovery for non-pecuniary damages under maritime law. *In re: Diamond B. Marine Services, Inc.*, 2000 WL 222847 (E.D. La. 2000); *Galveston County Navigation Dist. #1 v. Hopson Towing Co.*, 92 F.3d 353, 358 (5th Cir. 1996).

Therefore, claims filed by a seaman or his wife for punitive damages under the general maritime law must be dismissed. *Bardwell v. George G. Sharp, Inc.*, 1995 WL 517120 (E.D. La. 1995) (punitive damage claims under the general maritime law are no longer supported by the law of this circuit under the uniformity principal [sic] set forth in *Miles*); *In re: Diamond B. Marine Services, Inc.*, 2000 WL 222847 (E.D. La. 2000); *Donaghey v. Ocean Drilling and Exploration Co.*, 1991 WL 999490 (E.D. La. 1991) (punitive damages are not available to seamen under the general maritime law). Even though state law is inapplicable, there is no state law recovery for punitive damages under the facts of this case since La. Civil Code article 2315.3 was repealed by the state legislature in 1996.

Conclusion

Paul Alexis and Bernell Alexis have no remedy for non-pecuniary damages as a matter of law. Under the law of the Eastern District of Louisiana, Fifth Circuit and U.S. Supreme Court, Mrs. Alexis' claim for loss of consortium must be dismissed. In addition, the punitive damage claims of Mr. and Mrs. Alexis must be dismissed since such claims are not allowed under the general maritime law.

Respectfully submitted,

GRADY S. HURLEY (#13913)
JAMES E. WRIGHT, III (#13700)
RUTH B. SCHUSTER (#26506)
Jones, Walker, Waechter,
Poitevent, Carrère & Denègre,
L.L.P. 201 St. Charles Avenue,
48th Floor New Orleans. Louisiana
70170-5100
Telephone: (504) 582-8000
Facsimile: (504) 582-8010

Attorneys For Defendants, Southern Natural Gas Company, Tennessee Gas Pipeline Company and El Paso Energy Corporation

CERTIFICATE OF SERVICE

I hereby certify that a copy of the above has been sent to opposing counsel, either BY HAND or by placing a copy of same in the U.S. mail, properly addressed, postage prepaid, this 10th day of August 2001.

UNITED STATES DISTRICT COURT

EASTERN DISTRICT OF LOUISIANA

IN THE MATTER OF THE COMPLAINT OF DENET TOWING SERVICE, INC., AS OWNER and OWNER *PRO HAC VICE* OF TUG OCEAN SCRAMBLER, her engines, tackle, appurtenances, furniture, etc., PRAYING FROM EXONERATION FROM OR LIMITATION OF LIABILITY	CIVIL ACTION *NUMBER: 00-2029 c/w* 00-2032 and 01-1993 *SECTION: "B" (2)* *JUDGE: IVAN L.R. LEMELLE* *MAGISTRATE:* *JOSEPH C. WILKINSON, JR.*

OPPOSITION TO DEFENDANT SOUTHERN NATURAL GAS' MOTION TO DISMISS LOSS OF CONSORTIUM AND PUNITIVE DAMAGE CLAIM

MAY IT PLEASE THE COURT:

Defendant Southern Natural Gas (SNG) owns a pipeline in Plaquemines Parish, Louisiana. When SNG's inadequately marked, inadequately covered pipeline ruptured and exploded. Captain Alexis and his crew were badly injured.

If Captain Alexis was not a seaman, or if the pipeline exploded on dry land, there is no question Mrs. Alexis could recover loss of consortium damages from third-party tortfeasor SNG.[1] Although SNG's pipeline originally was on dry land, SNG claims Mrs. Alexis cannot recover now because erosion uncovered SNG's pipeline, which presently is in the navigable waters of Romere Pass. SNG knew about the erosion and the hazard its pipeline posed to vessel traffic, but did not properly remedy the situation.

<u>Jones Act/Death on the High Seas Act Inapplicable to SNG</u>

SNG is not the Jones Act employer of Captain Alexis, SNG has not automatically paid lost wages or maintenance and cure to Captain Alexis, and SNG does not agree to be judged according to the Jones Act "featherweight" burden of proof to establish evidence of "even the slightest negligence" standard of liability. SNG therefore cannot hide behind the Jones Act case law precluding a seaman's family from recovery of loss of consortium and punitive damages from the seaman's employer.[2]

---

[1] *Kelly v. Bass Enterprises Production Company,* 17 F.Supp.2d 591 (E.D. La. 1998) (spouse of non-seaman injured riding boat which contacted allegedly improperly marked marine pipeline in Louisiana waters allowed to recover loss of consortium/loss of society damages); *Karle v. National Fuel Distribution Corporation,* 448 F.Supp. 753, 768 (W.D. Penn 1978); (awarding spouse loss of consortium damages against dry land pipeline owner); *Laird v. Hudson Engineering Corporation,* 449 F.2d 216, 219-220 (5th Cir. 1971) (against dry land pipeline fabricators).

[2] Inapposite Jones Act seaman-employer cases cited by SNG include *Miles v. Apex Marine Corp.*, 498 U.S. 19 (1990); *Guevara v. Maritime Overseas Corp.*, 59 F.3d 1496 (5th Cir. 1995) (*en banc*); *Michel v. Total Transportation, Inc.*, 957 F.2d 186 (5th Cir. 1992); *Murray v. Anthony J. Bertucci Construction Co., Inc.*, 958 F.2d 127 (5th Cir. 1992); *Dufrene v. Dickson GMP International, Inc.*, 1999 WL 172931 (E.D. La. 1999).

Likewise, this incident occurred on Louisiana territorial waters, so the Death on the High Seas Act (DOHSA) is by definition inapplicable to the case. Accordingly, DOHSA case law and analysis cited by SNG is inapplicable. Loss of consortium and punitive damages are appropriate pursuant to general maritime law supplemented by state law against non-employer third parties.[3]

Conflict in the Courts!

The *Miles* opinion did not address an action by a seaman and his wife against a non-employer third-party tort-feasor in Louisiana territorial waters. There is no question that prior to *Miles* the Alexis family could seek loss of consortium and punitive damages under general maritime law.

Many courts and commentators thoughtfully have studied the issue in detail, and found no reason to restrict a seaman's or his family's recovery against third-party tort-feasors by extending *Miles* beyond the seaman-employer relationship.[4] This is because third-party tort-feasors, unlike employers, are not required by statute to "trade off" automatic liability in return for a limitation on recoverable damages.[5]

Some courts, uncharacteristically, have not carefully analyzed the issue but simply applied *Miles* outside the seaman-employer relationship almost by reflex (possibly because the courts were not properly briefed by counsel.)[6]

In the zeal of advocacy, SNG counsel by selective quotation inaccurately suggests the Fifth Circuit has decided the issue, but the rest of the paragraph cited reads:

---

[3] *Denet Towing Services, Inc.*, 1999 WL 329698 at *4-*7 (E.D.La. 1999), copy attached as Exhibit "A:" *Misty Gerdes, et al. v. G & H Towing*, 967 F.Supp. 943 (S.D.Tex. 1997) (*Miles* does not bar non-pecuniary damages for seaman's family in suit against non-employer); *Strawder v. Zapata Haynie Corp.*, 640 So.2d 554, 561 (La. App. 3d Cir. 1994) (non-pecuniary and punitive damages available in seaman's family's suit against non-employer pipeline owner).

[4] *Denet Towing Service, Inc.*, 1999 WL 329698 at *2 (E.D.La. 1999) (citing six cases and law review article).

[5] *Id.* at *3-*5. See also *Kelly v. Bass Enterprises Production Company*, 17 F.Supp.2d 591 (E.D.La. 1998) (Louisiana citizens can recover loss of consortium damages from owner of pipeline their boat contacted in Louisiana waters). The *Kelly* plaintiffs did not have a seaman-employer relationship with the third-party tort-feasor marine pipeline owner, and recovered loss of consortium/loss of society damages. The Alexis family likewise does not have a seaman-employer relationship with third-party tort-feasor SNG.

[6] See Judge Clement's opinions in *Earhart v. Chevron U.S.A., Inc.*, 852 F.Supp. 515 (E.D.La. 1993) (*unopposed* motion to dismiss); *In re Diamond B Marine Services, Inc.*, 2000 WL 805235 (E.D.La. 2000) (citing her inapposite decision in *Carnival Cruise Lines v. Red Fox Industries, Inc.*, 813 F.Supp. 1185 (E.D.La. 1993) (incident apparently outside Louisiana territorial waters, plaintiff recovery controlled by DOSHA); and Judge Feldman's opinion in *Ellender v. Graham*, 821 F.Supp. 1136 (E.D.La. 1992).

Judge Feldman and Judge Clement respectfully disagree with Judge Lemmon's decision in *Denet Towing*, but Judge Barbier and Judge Fallon agree with Judge Lemmon's approach involving careful analysis of the issues and refusal reflexively to expand Miles beyond its facts. *Christopher Anthony Liner v. Dravo Basic Materials Co.*, 2000 WL 1693678 (E.D.La. 2000) (Barbier, Jr.); *Kelly*, 17 F.Supp.2d at 593-600 (Fallon, J.). Copy of *Christopher Anthony Liner* attached as Exhibit "B."

"*and without expressly so deciding at this time,* we acknowledge the strength of the argument that damages for loss of society *may* no longer be permitted in a general maritime wrongful death action involving the operator of a fishing boat."[7]

Dicta by one panel of the Fifth Circuit in a factually distinct case does not resolve the issue. The Fifth Circuit should directly address and resolve the issue, the only question before this Honorable Court is whether an injured man and his family living in a trailer in Boothville should have to appeal, or if the onus should be on powerful prosperous SNG.

Conclusion

Seamen like Captain Alexis are the special wards of this Court. They and their families at least should be able to recover the same damages that an ordinary Louisiana citizen can, or that Captain Alexis and this family could recover if he had been driving his pickup down the highway when SNG's pipeline exploded. Indeed, seamen and their families should be able to achieve even more generous recovery than non-seafaring Louisiana citizens under general maritime law (including punitive damages), particularly against non-employer third-party tort-feasors like SNG who create hazards in navigable waters.[8]

Giving talismanic significance to a victim's seaman status, to the advantage of a third-party tort-feasor, elevates form over substance and is repugnant to this Honorable Court's tradition of scholarship and justice.

Respectfully submitted,
TERRIBERRY, CARROLL & YANCEY, L.L.P.

MICHAEL M. BUTTERWORTH (#21265)
3100 Energy Centre
1100 Poydras Street
New Orleans, Louisiana 70163-3100
Telephone: (504) 523-6451
Facsimile: (504) 524-3257
Attorneys for Captain Paul Alexis and
Mrs. Bernell Alexis

[7] *Walker v. Braus,* 995 F.2d 77, 82 (5th Cir. 1993) (collision between two boats, *not* a marine pipeline explosion case).

[8] *Denet Towing Service, Inc.,* 1999 WL 329698, at *2 (E.D.La. 1999); *Christopher Anthony Liner v. Dravo Basic Materials Co.,* 2000 WL 1693678 (E.D.La. 2000).

CERTIFICATE OF SERVICE

I HEREBY CERTIFY that a copy of the above and foregoing has been served upon all counsel of record herein by hand delivery, facsimile transmission, or by placing same in the U.S. Mail, postage prepaid, this 10th day of December, 2001.

MICHAEL M. BUTTERWORTH

CHAPTER 12

Drafting Contracts

I. THE NATURE OF CONTRACT DRAFTING

The writer should so write that the reader not only may, but must, understand.— Quintilian

Earlier chapters introduced the first two types of legal writing used in the United States: objective writing used in law firm memos and scholarly articles, and advocatory writing used to persuade a court. This chapter presents the practice of preventive writing, the third style of legal writing. Preventive legal writing is used for contracts, legislation, and wills. Because of considerations of length, this chapter focuses only on the drafting of contracts, and specifically considers some of the concerns of international business transactions.

Regardless of whether she is drafting a will, a contract, or a legislative bill, the attorney's goal in this kind of writing is to avoid ambiguity and possible misinterpretation, and to plan for as many realistic contingencies as possible, thus making the parties' rights and obligations clear and preventing disputes and litigation. This writing must be thorough, precise, and as easy to understand as possible. Given the peculiarities of American English grammar, punctuation, word order, and precise use of language needed, this is a challenge for a native English speaker, and even more difficult for someone whose first language is not English.

Prepositions and imprecise use of language can easily cause problems. For example, one will provided that the remainder of the testator's property should be "divided equally between all of our nephews and nieces on my wife's side and my niece." This provision was poorly drafted. The heirs could not tell whether half of the property was to be divided among the wife's nephews and nieces (there were 22 of them) and the other half given to the testator's niece, or whether each person was to receive a 23rd interest.[1] Basing its decision on the exact definition of the preposition *between*, the court adopted the first interpretation, giving the testator's niece a one-half

[1] *Lefeavre v. Pennington*, 230 S.W.2d 46 (Ark. 1950).

interest. Had the testator wanted the property divided into 23 shares, the will should have used the word "among." When used precisely, *between* refers to a space between two objects, whereas *among* refers to something in the midst of a crowd. However, colloquial American usage no longer makes a definite distinction between the two terms, and most readers will not be aware of the difference.

In addition to problems created by inaccurate use of words, the author of a contract, will, or legislative bill wants to avoid problems created by improper word order, misplaced modifiers, or poor punctuation. For example, an insurance policy included the following definition:

> **"Insured"** means you and also: A relative. . . .
> **"Relative"** means:
>
> (a) your relative; or
> (b) anyone else, under the age of 21, in your care; who resides in your household.[2]

Litigation arose when the insured's son was involved in an automobile accident and the insurance company claimed that he was not covered because he was not residing in the insured's household at the time of the accident.[3] Both the trial and the appellate courts found that because of nonstandard word order[4] and improper use of semicolons,[5] the definition was confusing and ambiguous, and that it was "very difficult for the average person to read this policy and understand what is going on." Construing the ambiguity against the drafter of the contract (the insurance company), the court held that the contract did not exclude the son from coverage.

As can be seen from these examples, accurate use of language and punctuation is vitally important in preventive drafting. The drafter also wants to be thorough and ensure that all the most likely contingencies are covered as well. A great deal of litigation has been caused by failure of a contract to provide for an unanticipated occurrence. In these cases, a court may be able to fill in the gap in the contract either by resorting to underlying law or based on other language in the contract that indicates with some reliability what the parties would have agreed on had they

---

[2] *Auto-Owners Ins. Co. v. Sarata*, 33 Fed. Appx. 675, 2002 WL 753283 (S.C. Ct. App. 2002) (unpublished).

[3] *Id.*

[4] A modifying clause should be placed immediately next to the term it modifies. Thus, if the insurance company had wanted to exclude relatives not residing with the insured, the definition should have been as follows: " 'Relative' means someone who resides in your household and is (a) your relative; or (b) anyone else, under the age of 21, in your care."

[5] A semicolon indicates a stronger break than a comma and is usually used between independent clauses that are not otherwise related. It may also be used in a series between items that contain internal commas. Thus, the first semicolon in the original contract is properly used because it separates (a) from (b) and (b) has internal punctuation. In so doing, it excludes the clause "who resides in your household" from (a). The second semicolon, the one after the word *care,* is improperly used because there is no internal punctuation in the clause "who resides in your household." The primary problem with this insurance contract was the misplaced modifier, but the misused semicolon added to the confusion.

anticipated this problem. Many times, however, the latter is not so easily determined. If the contract is transnational in nature, the problem quickly can become more complicated because the parties and their attorneys may have different legal expectations.

In addition to having precise language, correct grammar and punctuation, and thorough consideration of as many realistic possibilities as possible, a contract must be consistent. Terms, headings, and provisions should all use the same language in the same way, the parties' duties should be consistent with the purpose of the contract and with other duties, and the consequences of breach or default should be explained clearly and treated the same way throughout the document.[6] Lack of consistency can lead to litigation.

Prevention, therefore, is the operative word in this kind of writing. It requires careful planning to cover all likely occurrences, and then careful rereading and editing. The drafter must be able to read his work as if he were his own worst enemy, looking for every available loophole and possible misreading. Reading and rereading the contract slowly and out loud may be the best way of locating potential problems. One can ask another attorney to help proofread, but the primary responsibility for accuracy and completeness will always remain with the drafter, because he best knows the client's wishes and situation. This chapter discusses a contract-drafting method used in the United States and provides a very basic checklist of provisions that a wide variety of contracts should include.

In drafting contracts, the attorney must balance the goal of preventing problems with the client's interest in having a private agreement that will satisfy both parties and be performed as drafted. Parties sign contracts because they want to do business. They do not sign them with the goal of litigating against each other in court after one or the other breaches the contract. Therefore, the client regards a contract as successful if it allows her to conduct business successfully with as little fuss and bother as possible. This aim can mean that the client's interest in having a short, clear contract must be balanced against — and may in some instances override — the attorney's concern that the contract cover as many contingencies as possible.

II. BACKGROUND AND PREPARATION

The process of approaching and drafting contracts can vary widely. In a large U.S. law firm, contracts may be drafted by a team of attorneys under the direction of one or more partners. Each firm or group may have its own system or method of going about the process, which a new associate learns as he or she becomes part of the group. In smaller firms, or for shorter contracts, one attorney may be responsible for the entire process, including client consultation, any negotiations with the other party's attorney, and actual drafting of the contract. Some clients want a contract that they can use

[6] Mary Barnard Ray & Barbara J. Cox, *Beyond the Basics, A Text for Advanced Legal Writing* 82 (1991).

many times, with many different contracting parties. These contracts are drafted with blank spaces so that the parties can simply fill in the appropriate names and dates. Examples of these kinds of contracts include the most common consumer contracts: sales, leases, insurance agreements, and others. These kinds of contracts are commonly called *form contracts* or *contracts of adhesion*. If the contract is long and complicated, or if it is a one-time transaction, the attorneys for both clients may work on drafting it. With complex contracts, attorneys may begin with a pattern contract containing clauses and phrases that have acquired legal significance through industry practice and judicial construction. Working with these kinds of contracts requires a background knowledge of the field so that one can determine which clauses in the pattern are mere legalese, and can therefore be simplified; and which are industry practice and must therefore be kept unchanged.

Regardless of the exact approach to a contract, all writing involves the same basic process: prewriting, writing, rewriting, revising, and polishing. In contrast with objective writing, however, the prewriting stage is probably much longer in preventive writing. One efficient method of drafting an entire contract is to subdivide the process into three steps, the first two of which are essentially prewriting:

1. The initial client interview
2. Preparation of an outline
3. Writing, rewriting, revising, and polishing the contract itself. Depending on the kind of contract involved, the process may require more meetings with the client, the other party, and the other attorney, as well as a substantial amount of negotiation as terms are agreed upon and settled.

A. The Initial Client Interview

The initial client interview is a time for the attorney to listen carefully, take careful notes, and ask as many questions as possible about the proposed contract. Some of the questions the attorney asks in the initial interview include the *purpose* of the contract, each party's *interests* and concerns, the anticipated *duration* of the contract, and the parties' *educational* levels. The answers to these questions will give the attorney some understanding of the scope of the project and the style of drafting needed. The attorney should also ask traditional journalists' questions, which will give him a more specific understanding of the content of the final contract: who, what, when, where, why, and how. From the answers to these questions, the attorney can begin to understand more about the client's business, what terms the parties may already have agreed upon, and what further information and negotiation will be required.

In addition to learning about the client's business, the attorney involved in an international transaction may need to consider the nature of the parties' transaction even more carefully than if the transaction were merely domestic. To begin with, the drafting of a sales agreement that pertains merely to a one-time event is quite different from an agreement that the client hopes will lead to a continuing relationship with the other party, even though both contracts involve exactly the same product, the same quantity, and the same price.[7] If the agreement is for a one-time sale, the attorney might use preprinted forms; if the client is hoping for a long-term relationship, though, the drafting and negotiating might be more balanced and conciliatory in style.[8] Therefore, the attorney needs to learn about the client's short-term and long-term goals.

Additionally, the attorney will need to become aware of both legal and cultural differences between the two countries involved, so that she can help the client negotiate as well as draft the contract in an effective manner. One party or the other may not be aware of business practices in the other country that will affect the transaction. For instance, the client, an American business executive, may not be aware that it is nearly impossible to deal with Argentine retailers without the use of an agent in Argentina.[9] The lawyer helping a client contract with a party from an Arabic country may need to be aware that Islamic law prohibits certain forms of interest as usurious; thus, commercial transactions involving parties subject to Islamic law may have to be structured differently than when the transaction involves only non-Islamic parties.[10] Contract law itself differs from legal system to legal system, and may affect issues such as the existence of precontractual obligations, when an offer is considered accepted, and what constitutes a breach of contract.

B. The Outline

Assuming the contract is such that one attorney will be doing most, if not all, of the drafting, after an initial discussion with the client about the contract and what it should include, the attorney carefully thinks through what is needed in the contract and prepares an outline. The outline includes not only the terms and conditions identified by the client, but also any other considerations the attorney wants to discuss with the client, based on the attorney's research into the parties' relationship, applicable law, and business trade practices. The attorney should research similar contracts and forms to help her envision what other contingencies and possible problems will have to be addressed. The client and the attorney may need to consider and discuss a number of legal questions, as well as a number of these practical considerations.

This initial outline is not to be seen by the other party, and therefore should include a frank assessment of the client's interests and concerns so that the attorney can discuss them with the client, particularly if the contract is for a one-time agreement rather than a form (adhesion) contract. If the contract is to be a one-time agreement, the attorney should determine what his client must have in the contract, and determine what the client is willing to give up if necessary to secure the other party's agreement. Even if the contract is to be a form that the client will reuse with a number

[7] William F. Fox, Jr., *International Commercial Agreements: A Primer on Drafting, Negotiating, and Resolving Disputes* (3d ed. 1998).
[8] *Id.* at 130.
[9] *Id.* at 131.
[10] *Id.* at 34-35.

of different clients, the attorney and client should discuss various possibilities, as well as the tone the client wants the contract to take. The attorney then reviews the outline with the client, taking notes and deciding with the client what should be included in the term sheet or draft contract.

C. The Term Sheet or Draft Contract

If the contract is for a specific transaction, rather than a form contract that the client will use many times, the attorney's next step may be to use the revised outline to prepare a preparatory document—either a term sheet or a draft outline—to be examined and considered by both parties.

It may be tempting to draft a contract or term sheet that focuses only on what your client wants from the agreement, ignoring or minimizing the other party's goals and attempting to obtain the most favorable terms possible for your client.[11] However, this approach is counterproductive. The other party will refuse to sign an unfavorable contract and may be offended if presented with one that ignores his desires, thus making it more difficult to come to an eventual agreement. Even if the other party fails to notice the unfavorable terms, they are likely to cause the disfavored party either to try to withdraw from the contract later or even to breach it. The client's ultimate goal is to achieve a working relationship with the other party. Therefore, a well-drafted contract takes all parties' interests and desires into account, so that they can all accept it with a minimum amount of time, effort, and friction.

The drafting attorney can, however, include terms that favor the client somewhat more than the other party but still take the other party's goals into account. Further, by drafting the original contract, an attorney is defining the situation and relationship between the parties from the start, and therefore has some initial control in favor of her client.[12] Take care, though, not to favor the client too much over the other party, or the other party may take offense and walk away from the agreement, as mentioned earlier.

1. *Term Sheet*

A *term sheet* is simply an outline of the proposed contract. Use of a term sheet may simplify and facilitate negotiation by placing format and essential terms before the parties and their attorneys without pressuring either party to adopt specific language; this deemphasizes some of the initial control concerns mentioned in the previous paragraph. Modifications made at a meeting of the parties are noted on the term sheet, and the draft of the contract is based on the result of those modifications. Attorneys who use the term-sheet approach sometimes find that it costs the parties less money, is faster, and leads to less combativeness than does preparing either a letter of intent or a preliminary draft.

---

11 Ray & Cox, *supra* note 6, at 85.

12 *Id.*, *supra* note 6, at 85.

2. The Letter of Intent

For complicated, long-term relational agreements, the parties may want to begin with a letter of intent, or document signaling that they have "agreed to agree." The reason for this preliminary document may be to help one or the other party obtain financing or governmental approval. These documents, however, can be tricky to negotiate and draft.

In most legal systems, a letter of intent is viewed as a mere preliminary document, and is not itself enforceable as a contract.[13] However, in the United States, these documents can take on a life of their own. At common law, letters of intent are traditionally not binding on the parties because they are considered an agreement to agree, but a computer search of any U.S. case law database will yield thousands of "letter of intent" cases, many of which have led to one or the other party being held liable for breach of contract.[14] For example, in one infamous case, the breach of a preliminary agreement for a corporate stock purchase led to an award of $7.53 billion, which was later reduced by agreement to $1 billion.[15] The determining factor is usually whether there is any indication of an intent to be bound, plus some specific obligation described in the document. Thus, negotiating parties who want to use a preliminary document may want to include language to the effect that it is merely evidence of a willingness to negotiate, and is not intended to constitute a binding contract. The difficulty with these types of disclaimers, however, is that they may weaken the document so much that a bank officer may find them an inadequate basis for a multimillion-dollar loan, or a government may find that the agreement is still too nebulous for it to grant approval.[16]

D. The Contract

After outlining, prewriting, and preparation, the final step is to prepare the contract, taking into consideration issues of word choice, avoidance of ambiguity, and clarity of expression. Like law firm memos and advocatory writings, contracts in the United States typically follow a fairly standard format. However, certain kinds of contracts take specialized formats, and in these situations the drafting attorney may want to use a similar contract as a pattern, adjusting it as needed.

1. Pattern or Formbooks and Other Resources

A pattern contract from a commercial formbook can be extremely useful as a drafting aid. This is distinct from the form contract discussed earlier. A *form contract*

[13] Fox, *supra* note 7, at 147.

[14] *See* Nadia E. Nedzel, *A Comparative Study of Good Faith, Fair Dealing, and Precontractual Liability*, 12 Tul. Eur. & Civ. L.F. 97, 118-20 (1997) (delineating some of the pitfalls of letters of intent).

[15] *Pennzoil Co. v. Texaco, Inc.*, 481 U.S. 1, 7 n.5 (1987).

[16] Fox, *supra* note 7.

is one that a client may use every day, and which includes blank spaces that the client and its contracting party can fill out as needed. In contrast, a formbook provides pattern contracts that an attorney can use to help draft a particular contract. Formbooks include all or most of the usual terms and conditions for that kind of contract, and may give explanations of underlying law and possible variations from which the attorney can choose the one that most suits the client's needs. However, each transaction is unique; pattern contracts are static instruments and use language, terms, and conditions that the parties to your contract may not want, or may want to change. Therefore, you will need to adjust any form or pattern to the unique characteristics of the transaction at hand. Because a contract must be internally consistent and unambiguous, if there are a number of these changes, or if the changes are significant, then you as the attorney will have to go through the entire contract scrupulously to make sure that everything works together. Furthermore, as mentioned earlier, you will need a strong understanding of industry practice and judicial construction. Rather than cutting and pasting from a form, if there are a substantial number of changes, it may be easier simply to use the form as a model, taking only those pieces that are entirely appropriate, but in effect drafting an entirely new contract.

A number of resources can help with drafting contracts for international transactions. The International Chamber of Commerce (ICC) publishes a series of model contracts that include a diskette of the contract text. Some of the titles are

- The ICC Model International Sale Contract: Manufactured Goods Intended for Resale
- The ICC Model International Franchising Contract
- The ICC Model Occasional Intermediary Contract
- The ICC Model Distributorship Contract (Sole Importer–Distributor)
- The ICC Model Agency Contract.

These publications include text of selected treaties (such as the United Nations Convention on Contracts for the International Sale of Goods (CISG),[17] advice on drafting the type of contract at issue, and the model contract.

In addition to formbooks, loose-leaf manuals and other sources can also be helpful. For example, Kluwer's three-volume loose-leaf series,[18] *International Business Transactions* (edited by Dennis Campbell and Reinhard Proksch), includes a disk of forms and documents for practitioners to adapt and use. The CD-Rom is updated annually, but the cost ($666.00 in 2007) is prohibitively expensive except for practitioners. Additional sources can provide a detailed overview of the process of drafting

[17] The ICC Model International Sale Contract (Manufactured Goods Intended for Resale) 32-58 (ICC 1997).

[18] Albert H. Kritzer, ed., *Contract Checklists, International Contract Manual* (Kluwer Law & Taxation Publishers 1991 & Supp. 2001).

international commercial agreements;[19] detailed insight into various issues such as choice-of-law clauses, sovereign immunity, dispute resolution, tax concerns, foreign corrupt practices treaties, and other specific concerns;[20] or insight into how the Unidroit principles have affected commercial contracts.[21]

Sales-of-goods contracts contain trade terms requiring special knowledge and careful use, such as *F.O.B.*, *C.I.F.*, and *F.A.S.* These terms are vitally important from a legal standpoint because they fulfill three separate functions: (1) they delineate which party pays for what portion of the transportation of the goods, and are therefore part of the price; (2) they allocate risk of loss; and (3) they set transportation requirements. Because these terms can vary in meaning from country to country, it is important that they be used specifically and carefully so that both parties to a transaction understand their risks and responsibilities. Although the International Chamber of Commerce has promulgated "Incoterms" to provide a standard set of terms for 18 major trading nations, even the countries that use those terms are not always consistent in their interpretation or use. Furthermore, use of the Incoterms may be confusing to a U.S. party that is accustomed to using the Uniform Commercial Code's very similar terms.[22] Thus, if you are drafting a contract for the sale of goods, be very careful to research the terms to be used, verify that both parties intend that those terms be used, ensure that they understand them, and then define the terms carefully and specifically in the contract.

2. *The Form of a Contract*

In general, no special form need be used to make a particular contract enforceable in the United States. Typically, a contract starts with a title, a date, and an introduction in which the parties and the substance of the contract are identified. It then gives a list of recitals or background information, possibly followed by a list of definitions, then the actual terms of the agreement, and finally, the signatures. This is the type of contract that will be explained in this chapter. However, a contract can be in the form of a letter or letters—one letter being the offer, and the other the acceptance—or it may have no particular formality or structure. An agreement to sell a house was once held enforceable between the parties, even though it was written on a dinner napkin![23] The checklist graph in Section III.F shows a generic United States contract structure, listing the types of terms and contingencies that usually must be considered and addressed in a contract.

---

[19] *See, e.g.*, William F. Fox, Jr., *International Commercial Agreements: A Primer on Drafting, Negotiating, and Resolving Disputes* (3d ed. 1999).

[20] *E.g.*, Michael Gruson, chair, *International Commercial Agreements* (Practising Law Inst. 1995).

[21] *E.g.*, Michael Joachim Bonell, ed., *The Unidroit Principles in Practice: Caselaw and Bibliography on the Principles of Commercial Contracts* (Transnational Publishers 2002).

[22] Fox, *supra* note 19, at 158-59.

[23] *Yarborough v. Anderson*, 242 So. 2d 11 (La. Ct. App. 1971).

III. DRAFTING THE CONTRACT

A. TITLE

B. DATE

C. Introduction
D. (Recitals)
E. (Definitions)
F. Terms (substantive provisions)
G. Signature and date lines
H. Witness signature lines

A. Title

Every legal document, including contracts, should have a title so that the reader can quickly ascertain its function.[24] Merely calling a contract an "AGREEMENT" is nonspecific and will not give the reader a clear idea of the purpose of the document. The title should be short and to the point, but it need not be on a separate title sheet unless the contract is extremely long. Examples of short but specific titles include BILL OF SALE, LEASE, SURETY AGREEMENT, IBERIA NATIONAL BANK HOME EQUITY LINE OF CREDIT, MORTGAGE, NOTE.

B. Date

Contracts must be dated so that the parties can know exactly when their obligations arise. Some contracts include the date at the top of the document, but many contracts include a blank date line at the end, by the signature lines, so that the parties can date the document themselves at the time of signature. There are any number of reasons why a signature date may change, so unless there is a specific reason to set a concrete date, it is often best not to date the contract itself, but to include a blank date line instead.

C. Introduction

An introductory paragraph or *caption* repeats the information given in the title. Whether or not it is given a heading, a contract introduction identifies the parties and

---

[24] Barbara Child, *Drafting Legal Documents: Principles and Practices* 109 (2d ed., West 1992).

indicates the nature of the agreement. The parties' names sometimes will be in all-capital letters, but not always:

> *This Iberia National Bank Home Equity Line of Credit ("Agreement") governs your line of credit (the "Credit Line") issued through Iberia Bank. In this Agreement, the words "Borrower," "you," "your," and "applicant" mean each and every person who signs this Agreement, including all Borrowers named above. The words "we," "us," "our," and "Lender" mean Iberia National Bank.*

Or, in a form contract:

> *"CONTRACT FOR SALE OF GOODS" between __________, a corporation organized and existing under the laws of _____ and having its principal place of business at __________("Buyer") and __________, a corporation organized and existing under the laws of __________ and having its principal place of business at ____________ ("Seller").*[25]

As you can see, in addition to repeating the information given in the title, the caption is the appropriate place to establish any short-form name(s) for the parties. For example, FAIRHOUSE RENTALS, INC ("FAIRHOUSE") indicates that the rest of the document will refer to this party as FAIRHOUSE. Alternatively, you could use the parties' contractual roles for short forms: FAIRHOUSE RENTALS, INC. ("LANDLORD"). You could also indicate that you are using first and second personal pronouns to refer to the parties, as in the preceding Line of Credit example. The use of "you" and "we" instead of impersonal third-person titles is most common in consumer contracts, such as mortgages, where it is important that a consumer who lacks any special legal or business background understand the document easily. If a short-form name is introduced, it should be used consistently throughout the document to avoid confusing the reader.

In common law jurisdictions, the introduction will often include a sentence saying that the parties "mutually agree" to the obligations described in the body of the contract, though the introduction does not and should not delineate those specific promises. The language referring to a mutual agreement is intended to indicate that each party has received consideration in exchange for its promises, and therefore that the contract is enforceable. *Consideration* is a common law requirement similar to the civilian concept of *cause*, but narrower in scope. *Cause* is the reason why a party agreed to be obligated. *Consideration* refers to the things or promises for which a party to an agreement *has bargained.* At common law, a promise is not binding unless and until the promisor is receiving something for which it bargained in consideration for the promise.

For example, in a sales contract, the buyer promises to pay money in exchange for the seller's promise to deliver the product, and the seller promises to deliver the product in exchange for the buyer's promise to pay money. The buyer's promise to pay is what the seller receives as consideration for the promise to deliver, and vice versa. Although things that qualify as consideration under common law also qualify as *cause* under civilian contract theory, not all civilian causes would qualify as consideration. For example, a promise to give someone something out of kindness or gratitude is

[25] *International Contract Manual* ch. 2, Preamble to the Contract.

unenforceable as a contract at common law because the promisor did not *bargain* to receive anything in exchange for its promise. In contrast, as long as the promise is made in the proper form, it may well be enforceable under civilian contract theory, because the promisor explained its reasons for making the promise.

When drafting an introductory caption, verify that the parties are accurately identified, their names are spelled correctly, and any short forms are introduced. Furthermore, verify that while the caption indicates the nature of the contract and that the parties mutually agree to it, the caption contains no specific terms that might create obligations for either party. The section explaining the terms of the contract is where all obligations should be explained, not the introductory caption.

D. Recitals

Background statements or *recitals* (the older term) may follow the introductory paragraph but are not always needed or used. In older contracts, recitals were conventionally introduced with the words *witnesseth* and *whereas*, but now this is often skipped entirely or replaced by a section titled "Background" or "Premises." A traditional example is provided in the ICC's Model Franchising Contract:[26]

WITNESSETH:
WHEREAS the Franchisor, as a result of extensive investments and practical business experience, has developed and owns a proprietary system (defined in Article 1 and hereinafter referred to as the System) relating to the operation of the business of providing __________.

WHEREAS this business is carried on under and otherwise uses (a number of) trade names and trademarks as set forth in part A of Schedule [1].
WHEREAS the Franchisor has built up a substantial reputation and goodwill in such trade names and trademarks which are associated with a high standard of products and services.
WHEREAS the Franchisor is willing to grant the Franchisee the right to and license to use the System, together with such trade names, trademarks and the shop signs, logos, utility models, designs, copyrights, know-how and patents [as] are designated in this Agreement (and which may hereafter be designated by the Franchisor in writing) as part of the System (as more particularly defined in Article 1 below) upon and subject to the terms and conditions set forth herein.
WHEREAS the Franchisee desires to operate a business using the System and the Proprietary Rights and to obtain a license from the Franchisor for that purpose, as well as to receive the assistance provided by the Franchisor in connection therewith upon and subject to the terms and conditions set forth herein.
WHEREAS accordingly, the parties have agreed to enter into the present franchise agreement (hereinafter referred to as the Agreement).

---

[26] The ICC Model International Franchising Contract 14 (2000).

The trend is to redraft these kinds of recitals in normal sentence form, without the archaic preface; however, some attorneys still prefer the old language, even though it produces sentence fragments rather than grammatically correct and hence easily read sentences. As redrafted, the preceding recital section might look like this:

BACKGROUND

The Franchisor, because of extensive investments and practical business experience, has developed and owns a proprietary system (defined in Article 1 and hereinafter referred to as the System) relating to the operation of the business of providing __________. This business is carried on under a number of trade names and trademarks, as set forth in part A of Schedule [1]. The Franchisor has built up a substantial reputation and goodwill in these trade names and trademarks, which are associated with a high standard of products and services. Furthermore, the Franchisor is willing to grant the Franchisee the right to and license to use the System, together with such trade names, trademarks and shop signs, logos, utility models, designs, copyrights, know-how, and patents as are designated in this Agreement (and which may hereafter be designated by the Franchisor in writing) as part of the System (as more particularly defined in Article 1 below), subject to the terms and conditions set forth in this Franchising Contract (the "Agreement").

The Franchisee desires to operate a business using the System and Proprietary Rights and desires to obtain a license from the Franchisor for that purpose. The Franchisor also desires to receive the Franchisor's assistance in connection with the System and Proprietary Rights, subject to the terms and conditions set forth in this Agreement.

Accordingly, the parties have mutually agreed to be bound by the following terms of this Agreement.

Recitals, whether in traditional form or in a modified modern form, are statements of factual information that give the background for the document. They present those facts about the parties that existed before the agreement, and because of which the parties came to be interested in coming to an agreement with each other.[27] They may also present preexisting facts that affect the agreement in one way or another.

Recitals should not discuss obligations that will arise once the contract is executed; if not carefully drafted, recitals may be interpreted by a U.S. common law court as expressions of intent and therefore part of the terms of the contract. If they are too specific, recitals may be interpreted as conclusive evidence of the facts they state rather than merely the background information that gave rise to the contract. For example, in one contract, a recital of claims of "approximately $94,000" barred proof of interest to be paid on the claims.[28]

[27] Child, *supra* note 24, at 126.
[28] *Detroit Grand Park Corp. v. Turner*, 25 N.W.2d 184 (Mich. 1946).

Therefore, do not put any promises or duties in the recital section—and before including a recital, consider whether it might be interpreted as proof of the facts it states. If you want to avoid this possibility, draft the recital in a more general manner or eliminate it altogether. You might also use a heading like "Background" instead of "Premises" or "Reasons for Contract."

E. Definitions

As with recitals, if the contract is fairly short and simple, try to avoid a definitions section: it can lead to inconsistencies and misinterpretations, and hence litigation. The greatest problem occurs when a term is given one meaning in the definitions section and is used with a different meaning later in the document, or when the definition given is ambiguous or inaccurately describes what the parties to the contract meant. A definitions section *is* needed when a number of terms are used in a particular way more than once in the document. The only way to know whether this is so is to draft the substantive provisions first, and then decide whether a definitions section is merited. When a definitions section is used, it is placed before the substantive provisions of the contract. Usually it is placed after any recitals, unless the recitals section contains terms that require definition, in which case the definitions section would precede the recitals.

To decide whether a separate definitions section is merited, ask yourself whether the contract uses several terms in an unusual or legally specific manner either in more than one section or throughout the contract. If so, then a definitions section makes the contract easier to read. When a specialized word is used in only one section of the contract, put the definition immediately before the first time the word is used, rather than having a separate definition section for only a few words.

If there is a definitions section, the words defined should be listed in alphabetical order, with each word followed by its definition. Whether or not it is in a separate section, the form and typeface of a definition sentence should indicate to the reader that this is a definition by putting the defined term in quotation marks (the most common method), or by italicizing, underlining, or bolding it. Whatever method you choose, use it consistently, as in the following example, again from the ICC Model Franchising Contract:

ARTICLE 1: DEFINITIONS

For the purposes of this Agreement, the following expressions have the respective meaning set forth below.
Business: the business of providing ______, when conducted in conformity with the System.
Confidential Information: means the information defined in Article 22.
Effective Date: as defined in Article 7.1.
Force Majeure: as defined in Article 26.

Drafting definitions takes skill and careful thought, first in deciding which terms should be defined, and then in drafting the definitions themselves. Generally there is no need to define a common word: If the reader is unfamiliar with the word, he or she can simply consult a dictionary. Words that justify a definition are those that are used in a manner different from common usage. Definitions are justified for technical terms or terms of art with which the user may not be familiar, but most commonly are used for familiar words that are being used in a way different from their usual meaning, as with the word *relative* in the insurance document described in § I. (In that case, *relative* referred not only to a member of the insured's family but also to anyone under the insured's care and living in his home.) Furthermore, if the contract is to be used for consumer transactions, definitions must be particularly clear, and any legal term of art should be defined.

To tell the reader that you are defining a word, use the verb *means* in the sentence. Then, with a word that is used in a manner different from common usage, decide whether the body of the contract uses that word in a more restricted sense than usual or in a more enlarged sense than usual. This type of definition is more accurately described as a *stipulation*, because it stipulates a certain meaning for purposes of the contract. An example of a *restrictive stipulation* is "In this agreement, the word *structure* means an office building of at least 20 stories." *Structure* could refer to a number of different types of buildings, but this definition limits the meaning, for the purposes of the contract, to tall office buildings. Another way of defining a restricted term is to use the words "*does not include*": " 'Structure' *does not include* any office building under 20 stories." Notice that these two statements are not quite the same in meaning. The "*means*" sentence limits structures to office buildings, but the "*does not include*" sentence could allow buildings other than office buildings, as long as they are 20 stories or taller. The most restrictive version would combine the two: " 'Structure' *means* office buildings only, but *does not include* any office building under 20 stories." However, in this particular instance, the first definition is short, clear, and to the point. Therefore, it is probably the best choice.

An enlarging stipulation expands the usual meaning, often using the verb *includes*. For example, " 'Structure' *includes* the lot or lots on which the office building stands." Stipulations can be both enlarging and restricting at the same time: "In this agreement, the word *relative* includes you, a relative, and anyone else both in your care and living in your home." (How does this stipulation enlarge the meaning of the word *relative*? How does it restrict its meaning? How does it change the tone of the original sentence quoted in § I, in the insurance example?) In addition to enlarging or restricting the normal meaning of terms, definitions can clarify the meaning of a contract in other ways. Consider, for example, these two sentences from the earlier caption example: "In this Agreement, the words 'Borrower,' 'you,' 'your,' and 'applicant' mean each and every person who signs this Agreement, including all Borrowers named above. The words 'we,' 'us,' 'our,' and 'Lender' mean Iberia National Bank." As you may have noticed, these definitions were so important to the contract that the drafter included them in the caption. Furthermore, the definitions are not really lexical definitions. Instead, they indicate synonyms or short forms referring to the parties *Borrower* and *Iberia National Bank*.

As with recitals, it is important that a definitions section not include any of the terms or conditions of the contract, because to do so would harm the organizational structure of the contract and make it harder for the parties to locate and understand their obligations. For example, a contract for the purchase of wine from a manufacturer might define "wine" as meaning "a beverage made from fresh grapes by natural fermentation." But, assuming that the parties intend for the manufacturer (the vintner) to make the wine for this contract in new French oak casks, as opposed to aging it in American oak or stainless steel casks, the definition of wine should not then go on to add this requirement as part of the definition. The French oak cask requirement is one of the vintner's obligations under the contract, not part of the definition.

Thus, definitions can be used to clarify what terms used in the contract mean, and can enlarge, restrict, or otherwise explain a specialized use. They should be set off, in some way, from the parties' obligations under the contract, either by special typeface or in a separate section.

F. Substantive Provisions (Terms)

CHECKLIST OF CONTRACT PROVISIONS[29]

- ☐ 1. Operating Clauses
- ☐ 2. Purposes or goals of contract
- ☐ 3. Each party's obligations
- ☐ 4. Statement of consideration
- ☐ 5. Payment arrangements: to whom, by whom, when, and how
- ☐ 6. Duration of the contract
- ☐ 7. Timing
- ☐ 8. Time for performance
- ☐ 9. Extensions: option to renegotiate or extent of flexibility
- ☐ 10. Automatic renewal
- ☐ 11. Termination Clauses
- ☐ 12. Termination and right to terminate
- ☐ 13. Notice of termination, *force majeure*
- ☐ 14. Contingency clauses
- ☐ 15. Default or breach
- ☐ 16. Notice of default or breach

[29] *See* Ray & Cox, *supra* note 6, at 89.

- ☐ 17. Determination of liability and responsibility between parties
- ☐ 18. Damages and remedies
- ☐ 19. Damages and liquidated damages
- ☐ 20. Other remedies (e.g., attorneys' fees, etc.)
- ☐ 21. Limitations of liability because of impossibility, *force majeure,* or other problems
- ☐ 22. Mediation, arbitration, or both before litigation
- ☐ 23. Procedures for mediation or arbitration
- ☐ 24. Choice of law and governing forum
- ☐ 25. Assignability
- ☐ 26. Permission for or prohibition of assignment of the contract to a third party
- ☐ 27. Methods for assignment, if permitted
- ☐ 28. Delegability (may one or another of the parties delegate duties to a third party?)
- ☐ 29. Methods of delegation
- ☐ 30. Miscellaneous Clauses
- ☐ 31. Assumption of good faith
- ☐ 32. Warranties or conditions
- ☐ 33. Incorporation of other documents
- ☐ 34. Severability of terms
- ☐ 35. Merger clauses (adoption or express rejection of subsequent modifications)

As indicated by the preceding checklist, the terms of the contract are contained in the main portion of the contract. They should be organized in a logical (often chronological) sequence and subdivided into sections, each with an informative heading that is numbered or lettered. Each division may itself be subdivided into organized subdivisions. The most common contract provisions are included in the checklist, which can be used as a pattern for an outline or term sheet as well as for the draft contract itself—but note that the headings should be changed appropriately as the document is polished.

When beginning the drafting process, start with the checklist or term sheet. Begin by separating each section in such a way that you can rearrange sections without difficulty, such as by putting each on a separate sheet of paper. If you are working on a computer, separate sections with extra blank lines so that it will be easy to cut and paste them.

As you draft each provision in a section, be careful to limit each provision to one subject only, and physically separate the provisions as you did the sections. Each provision should begin with an identifying heading and topic sentence, followed by the necessary supporting and explanatory statements. One reason to limit each provision to one subject is to help avoid ambiguous and conflicting provisions; another reason is to help you focus on drafting each provision in as clear and readable a way as possible. Yet another reason is to avoid burying a provision where a party is not likely to look for it. In addition to focusing on readability, be as thorough as possible by reviewing your checklist or term sheet to verify and reverify that every routine duty and every reasonable contingency is covered.

After completing the first draft of the substantive terms of the contract, reconsider the organization of those terms with the reader in mind. Although the checklist provides a preliminary organization, your contract may require a different sequence or may use subdivisions to help the reader locate various topics. Subdivisions are indicated when there are several provisions on the same basic topic. Each subdivision should have a general heading to help the reader understand the relationships among the various sections of the contract. The organization should help the reader follow and understand the document; thus, it is also the sequence most functional for the contract's purpose. Most of the time, a chronological organization is best: organize the provisions from beginning, to middle, to end of the parties' obligations. At this point, you should also decide whether to include a background or definitions section, and draft them if necessary.

Once the organization of the contract is relatively fixed, then reconsider language concerns. If sections or provisions were moved from place to place, they may have to be reworked for a smooth flow from previous provisions and to following provisions. Check section headings to make sure that they are informative and consistent with each other. You may also find that cross-references are needed; but, because cross-references make it more difficult to read a document, keep working on sequencing so that the need for cross-references is minimized. Verify once again that all routine duties and all reasonable contingencies are adequately covered.

After revising for logical flow and thoroughness, rethink each provision, testing to see whether it is specific enough to give the parties clear guidance, but not so specific that it becomes inflexible and difficult to comply with. Examine the tone of each provision. Some clients may prefer that the terms be drafted as specific promises, which gives a harsher tone to the document, but makes the obligations extremely clear: "The tenant will pay rent on or before the first day of each month." Others may prefer that terms be drafted as policies, which gives a softer tone: "Rent is due on the first day of each month." Make a decision as to which approach you will use, and use it consistently, or decide which terms should be phrased as promises rather than policies, for specific reasons.

1. Operating Clauses

The first section of the contract usually explains the goals or purposes of the contract, sets out the parties' rights and obligations, and generally explains how things will proceed when they are operating smoothly. A contract is generally organized in chronological order, but it may also follow the organization most likely to appeal to one or another party, or an organization designed to make the document easy to follow. The best organization achieves more than one of these goals at the same time.

For example, franchise agreements are usually drafted by the franchisor, which hopes that the potential franchisee will agree. Therefore, the document should appeal to the franchisee. The ICC model franchise agreement does this by first listing in general categories all the things that the franchisee will be granted: the franchise itself, rights and licenses to use the proprietary system, training, supplies, legal status as an independent business operator, and territorial exclusivity. Once the agreement has attracted the potential franchisee's interest with all these good things, it turns to the restraints put on the franchisee, the term of the agreement, and the good-faith obligation on the part of both parties. It then explains both parties' obligations, how improvements will be adopted, and the specifics and details of the categories of things that will be granted to the franchisee. After this, it covers transfer (how the franchisee may transfer the agreement to a third party), *force majeure*, and other termination provisions. Thus, in addition to being in chronological order according to the life of the parties' agreement, the sequence proceeds from general to specific to make it easy to follow, and begins with those things most likely to appeal to the franchisee.

2. Termination Clauses

Termination clauses provide for the normal termination of the contract. They may include provisions for when the contract will terminate, how it will terminate, whether one party should notify the other that it is terminating the contract, and how that notice should be delivered. They may also provide for termination when one party, through no fault of its own, is unable to fulfill its obligations, as with *force majeure* or some natural calamity. *Force majeure* clauses are often included in the miscellaneous section, but could also be placed with normal nonfault-based termination.

International trade involves more risks; therefore, *force majeure* clauses in international trade contracts may be broader than in contracts that are purely domestic. These risks could include "war, riots, insurrection, invasion," as well as fire, flood, import or export prohibitions, strikes and labor troubles, and other problems.[30] Some *force majeure* clauses have also included forgiveness for "inflation beyond the expected rate." The U.S. Uniform Commercial Code Article on Sale of Goods allows parties to default on a performance that has become commercially impracticable.[31] Therefore, when drafting an international trade contract, one might want to include a provision either adopting this clause, or specifically rejecting it, even if the U.C.C. otherwise applies.

In addition to *force majeure*, international trade contracts may also depend on government approval. This may be especially the case in transactions involving the transfer of technology. Generally, because government approval is required before a contract can come into effect, these provisions are usually phrased as a condition precedent to the formation of a contract, rather than as nonfault-based termination clauses. The burden of obtaining permission is usually placed on the party in the

[30] Fox, *supra* note 19, at 166-67. *See also* Andreas F. Lowenfeld, *International Private Trade* 3 (1981); Joseph M. Perillo, *Force Majeure and Hardship under the UNIDROIT Principles of International Commercial Contracts*, 5 Tul. J. Int'l & Comp. L. 5 (1997).
[31] U.C.C. § 2-615.

country that must issue the permission.[32] A typical government permissions clause for a sale of goods contract is "Seller shall obtain all necessary permits, licenses, or permissions to export the goods. Buyer shall obtain all necessary permits, licenses, or permissions necessary to import the goods. This contract is not fully executed or enforceable until all such permissions have been obtained."[33]

3. *Contingency Clauses*

Contingency clauses provide for fault-based termination of the contract. They define what will constitute a breach of or default on the contract, and how that breach or default will be determined.

4. *Damages and Remedies*

Traditionally, many commercial contracts in the United States contain some kind of penalty or liquidated damages clause. A penalty clause is often used in contracts in which the time of performance is especially important, such as in construction contracts: "Builder shall pay Purchaser $xxxx.xx per day for each day the project remains uncompleted after x date." Liquidated damages clauses provide for a certain amount of damages to be paid by a breaching party, and often include attorneys' fees. For example, a liquidated damages clause from a mortgage note provides:

> If I am in default, the Note Holder may send me a written notice telling me that if I do not pay the overdue amount by a certain date, the Note Holder may require me to pay immediately the full amount of Principal which has not been paid and all the interest that I owe on that amount. . . . If the Note Holder has required me to pay immediately in full as described above, the Note Holder will have the right to be paid back by me for all of its costs and expenses in enforcing this Note to the extent not prohibited by applicable law. Those expenses include, for example, reasonable attorneys' fees.

Most commercial contracts contain some kind of dispute resolution clause, and increasingly these clauses provide for arbitration under the rules of some domestic or international arbitration association (usually either the rules of the American Arbitration Association [AAA] or the International Chamber of Commerce). The initial motivation for the incorporation of such clauses was the notion that arbitration was a less expensive and faster process for resolving commercial disputes than the legal system of any particular jurisdiction. However, because commercial arbitration is itself expensive and procedurally complex, most commentators strongly encourage drafters to incorporate some language urging renegotiation, mediation, or a mini-trial before arbitration.[34] To reiterate, the purpose of a commercial contract is to enable the parties to do business smoothly, with benefits accruing to both sides. When a dispute arises, it is usually to both parties' benefit to resolve it quickly, for minimum cost and time, and

---

[32] Fox, *supra* note 19, at 168.

[33] *Id.*

[34] Fox, *supra* note 19, at 171; Thomas E. Carbonneau, *Arbitration & Dispute Resolution* (1995); Gary B. Born, *International Arbitration & Forum Selection Agreements: Planning, Drafting, & Enforcing* (1999).

return to doing business together. Arbitration, which is a privately conducted trial, can be as long, procedurally complex, and costly as a traditional trial.

One increasingly popular dispute resolution mechanism is mediation. In mediation, a professional mediator remains neutral to the dispute. He or she endeavors to help the parties negotiate their own resolution to the controversy. The parties generally agree prior to the mediation that any information exchanged or offers made during mediation cannot be used or even mentioned should the mediation fail and litigation or arbitration result. This confidentiality helps encourage the parties to resolve the disagreement themselves: It allows them to make more generous offers and take risks that they might not otherwise take if the controversy were to lead to litigation. Resolutions reached in mediation are often preferable to any that an outside entity, whether an arbitrator or a court, could award for two reasons: (1) both parties agreed to the resolution, and therefore they are more likely to abide by it; and (2) because the parties know the facts of their situation better than anyone else, the resolution may be fairer and better tailored to the underlying problem than the one an outside judge or arbitrator would impose. If, after a reasonable number of mediation sessions, the parties realize that they cannot resolve the issue on their own, they can then resort to arbitration or litigation as otherwise provided by the contract. A mediation clause can be as simple as the following:

> *If the parties have a dispute relating to the interpretation or application of any part of this contract, and cannot themselves negotiate a resolution, they shall first submit to mediation with [naming a professional mediation service]. If, after three [or some other specific number of] mediation sessions, the parties mutually agree that mediation is unlikely to lead to resolution, the controversy shall then be submitted for binding arbitration.*

The various major arbitration associations each have drafted standard form arbitration clauses purported to be sufficient as dispute resolution clauses. For example, the AAA suggests "Any controversy or claim arising out of or relating to this contract, or any breach thereof, shall be settled by arbitration in accordance with the rules of the American Arbitration Association, and judgment upon award rendered by the arbitrator(s) may be entered in any court having jurisdiction thereof." The International Chamber of Commerce suggests "[a]ll disputes arising in connection with the present contract shall be finally settled under the rules of Conciliation and Arbitration of the International Chamber of Commerce by one or more arbitrators appointed in accordance with the Rules." If a contract drafter wants only a quick arbitration clause, any of these will suffice because the institution's underlying rules will supply missing details. However, most experienced international lawyers find that these simplistic clauses can lead to unanticipated problems in terms of choice of law, choice and qualifications of arbitrators, and other potential issues.[35] Most arbitration clauses also provide for a choice of forum (e.g., "Disputes under this contract shall be subject to the rules of the American Arbitration Association and any arbitration under this clause shall take place in New York City, N.Y."). Some international commercial contracts provide for litigation in the domestic courts of one party or the other, or in a third country regarded as neutral by the contracting parties. In the United States, the parties' choices as to forum or method of resolution will almost always be honored.

[35] Fox, *supra* note 19, at 173.

5. *Miscellaneous*

a. Housekeeping Provisions

Housekeeping provisions, usually collected in a section titled "Miscellaneous," often relate to the administration and enforcement of the contract. Often they include provisions related to choice of law, modification, liquidated damages, *force majeure,* and other matters,[36] though (depending on the contract) these provisions might better be placed elsewhere, as suggested in the checklist at the beginning of subsection F. Try to minimize use of a miscellaneous section, because the parties may not be able to anticipate in advance the types of terms it may contain.

b. Provisions for Modification

In drafting a contract between one party from a common law jurisdiction and one from a non-common law jurisdiction, one common law principle an attorney may need to be aware of and make provision for is the parol evidence rule. Generally, when there is a writing memorializing an agreement, that writing (the contract) will be enforced by a U.S. common law court as written. An example is the case concerning the settlement agreement mentioned earlier, in which the court barred the complaining party from presenting evidence of interest on the $94,000. When the parties have stated their agreement in writing, courts usually reject evidence of any prior or contemporaneous oral agreement that might alter the written document—though there are some exceptions, such as for fraud.[37] The court will not be able to consider any oral changes purportedly agreed to by the parties, and will limit itself to interpreting the "four corners" of the document.[38] This interpretive principle is inconsistent with the United Nations Convention on Contracts for the International Sale of Goods,[39] as well as with the commercial law of a number of jurisdictions. Therefore, a well-drafted international contract involving a party from a common law jurisdiction should include a provision that either specifically adopts or rejects this principle.

G. Signatures and Dates

Signature and date lines are usually put at the end of the contract, to signify that the parties have read the entire contract and agree to its terms, and also to indicate the exact date on which they agreed to be bound by its terms. Make sure that in addition to providing a line for each party's signature, you also type the party's name under that

---

[36] Thomas Haggard, *Legal Drafting in a Nutshell* 20 (Thomson West 2003).

[37] Paul H. Till & Albert F. Garguilo, *Contracts: The Move to Plain Language* 11 (1979), cited in Ray & Cox, *supra* note 6, at 87 n.26.

[38] *Black's Law Dictionary* 682 (8th ed. 2004); *see* Joseph M. Perillo, *Calamari and Perillo on Contracts* 124-49 (5th ed. 2003) (discussing parol evidence rule).

[39] CISG art. 29: "(1) A contract may be modified or terminated by the mere agreement of the parties. (2) A contract in writing which contains a provision requiring any modification or termination by agreement to be in writing may not otherwise be modified or terminated by agreement. However, a party may be precluded by his conduct from asserting such a provision to the extent that the other party has relied on that conduct."

line. The exact date of signing is important, because at common law traditionally no obligations, including the obligation of good faith and fair dealing, arise until the contract is enforceable.[40]

H. Notarization and Witnesses

In contrast with many other countries, notaries in the United States have comparatively little power. Their primary role is to authenticate documents: to verify that the person or persons who sign the documents are who they say they are and swore orally that the information contained in the document is true, usually under penalty of perjury. Often, notaries have the power to effectuate a transfer of automobile title, but they cannot transfer immovable property. A lawyer is needed for that task. Although each state requires examination and licensing, training of notaries public in most of the United States is minimal,[41] and notaries are often paralegals in an attorney's office.[42] Thus, though a number of states have statutes that require authentication of certain kinds of contracts, other than providing space at the end of the document for the appropriate authentication, very little is often necessary.

EXERCISE

Review JKL's pro forma invoice, which follows. JKL wants to update its invoice, in view of the fact that it needs to comply with the U.N. Convention on the Sale of Goods and the Unidroit principles. It also wants to have an arbitration clause so that any disagreements will be settled in New York, using U.S. law. Furthermore,

1. As an attorney, you notice that the agreement does not contain any provision for the parol evidence rule; this could be a problem if the U.N. Convention is to apply. Draft a provision indicating that all modifications must be in writing signed by the seller.
2. Update and verify shipping terms to avoid confusion over shipping/insurance/assignment-of-risk terms.
3. JKL has found that it sometimes sends the products but does not get paid. It wants to make sure that it will actually be paid before it ships expensive equipment. How would you amend the payment provisions? Without discouraging business?
4. Clean up any archaic, useless language.

---

[40] Charles L. Knapp, *Enforcing the Contract to Bargain,* 44 N.Y.U. L. Rev. 673, 674 (1967).

[41] *See generally* Michael L. Closen, *To Swear . . . or not to Swear Document Signers: The Default of Notaries Public and a Proposal to Abolish Oral Notarial Oaths,* 50 Buff. L. Rev. 613 (2002).

[42] Louisiana, because of its civilian heritage, requires more training and gives notaries public a bit more authority than other states. *See* James D. Johnson, Jr. & Susan L. Johnson, *A Basic Louisiana Notary Guide* (2d ed. 1997).

JKL Industries, Inc.

Export Experts

Export Sales Dept.
P.O. Box No.
Back Street and Michigan Avenue
Philadelphia, PA 18195

PRO FORMA INVOICE

Purchaser:

Compania Importa Taralia
Caja pochtaya 13
Taral City, Taral

Invoice Number: QV/100
Date: 12/15/2008

Purchaser's Inquiry Number: CIB-5312
Date: 12/04/2008

Item No.	Manufacturer's Number	Description	Quantity	Price in Dollars Unit	Total	Availability	Weight in lbs
1.	B400	Jack Elk Forklift	10	80,000	800,000.00	February	45,200
2.	AB4201	Supersize fork for Jack Elk Forklift	10	10,000	100,000.00	February	14,800
			Estimated total net weight: 60,000 lbs—27,000 kilos Estimated total gross weight: 66,700 lbs—30,015 kilos				

Total Mat'l Value F.A.S. vessel Phila. or NYC	$900,000.00
Estimated Freight Forwarder's charges	30,000.00
Estimated Consular charges	4,500.00
Estimated F.O.B. vessel	
Estimated Insurance charges	5,500.00
Estimated Transportation charges	250,000.00
Estimated C.I.F.	$1,190,000.00

TERMS

Delivery F.A.S. vessel Philadelphia/New York

PAYMENT
LETTER OF CREDIT

Conditions: Prices shown are those in effect at time of quotation. Prices in effect at time of shipment will prevail.

TERMS AND CONDITIONS

Any order resulting from this quotation will be subject to the following conditions:

1. Delivery dates are approximate. Seller shall not be liable for any delay in, or inability to complete, delivery because of any of the following causes: Acts of God, suspension or requisition of any kind; strikes or other stoppages of labor or shortage in the supply thereof; inability to obtain fuel, material, or parts; fire, casualties or accidents; failure of shipping facilities; any other cause, whether the same or a different character beyond Seller's control.
2. Prices indicated are based on the prices in effect as of the date hereof, subject to change in accordance with the prices in effect as of the date of shipment.
3. Products are not returnable for credit or replacement, unless authorized in writing by Seller.
4. If, for any reason whatsoever, this order or any part thereof is terminated by the Buyer, such termination shall be effected with the understanding that termination charges may result therefrom.
5. Orders for special products are subject to shipment of any overrun or underrun not to exceed 10%. The Buyer will pay, in full, for such overshipment, and in the event of an undershipment the Buyer will consider the order completed with such undershipment.
6. Goods manufactured by Seller shall conform to the description, shall be fit for the ordinary purposes for which such goods are used, and shall be free of defects in material and workmanship at time of shipment. THERE ARE NO WARRANTIES OF MERCHANTABILITY OR OTHERWISE, EXCEPT OF TITLE, WHICH EXTEND BEYOND THAT STATED ABOVE.
7. Seller's liability and Buyer's remedy for breach of warranty or otherwise is expressly limited to the replacement of any products sold hereunder which Seller determines, by laboratory examination, as non-conforming, provided said non-conforming products are returned F.O.B. Seller's warehouse within twelve (12) months of shipment hereunder. Seller retains the right to render credit for the purchase price in lieu of furnishing a replacement product.
8. IN NO EVENT SHALL SELLER BE LIABLE HEREUNDER OR OTHERWISE FOR LOSS OF PROFITS, SPECIAL, INCIDENTAL, OR CONSEQUENTIAL DAMAGES OF ANY KIND.
9. Shipments hereunder shall be at all times subject to the approval of Seller's Credit Department.
10. Whereas any covenants, conditions, and agreements contained and consigned in this contract shall bind and inure to the benefit of the parties and their respective heirs, distributees, executors, administrators, successors, and except as otherwise provided herein, their assigns.

BIBLIOGRAPHY

Bonell, Michael Joachim, ed. *The Unidroit Principles in Practice: Caselaw and Bibliography on the Principles of Commercial Contracts.* Transnational Publishers 2002.

Burnham, Scott J. *Drafting Contracts.* 2d ed. Michie 1993.

Child, Barbara. *Drafting Legal Documents: Principles and Practices.* 2d ed. West 1992.

Fox, William F., Jr. *International Commercial Agreements: A Primer on Drafting, Negotiating, and Resolving Disputes.* 3d ed. Kluwer Law International 1999.

Gruson, Michael, chair. *International Commercial Agreements.* Practising Law Institute 1995.

The ICC Model International Franchising Contract. International Chamber of Commerce 2000.

The ICC Model International Sale Contract (manufactured goods intended for resale). International Chamber of Commerce 1997.

Ray, Mary Barnard, & Barbara J. Cox. *Beyond the Basics: A Text for Advanced Legal Writing.* West 1991.

Appendix A: Preparing for and Taking Examinations

INTRODUCTION

Just as preparing for class is somewhat different in U.S. law schools, so is preparing for exams. If you know what to expect and how to prepare for an exam from the very first, you can make the best use of your study time. The following is one of three questions from an actual criminal law exam (with apologies to Tennessee Williams and Marlon Brando):

> Stanley is a weekend drunk who never drinks alcoholic beverages during the week. Each Friday, after he receives his pay from work and before he comes home, Stanley visits his neighborhood bar and consumes five or six shots of whisky, each followed by a beer chaser. Then, on his way home from the bar, Stanley procures a case of beer, which he consumes across the weekend, each weekend. For several years, Stanley's weekend drinking has been a source of concern to his wife, Stella, not only because she finds Stanley's inebriated state to be sinful, disgusting, and otherwise antisocial, but also because when in this state Stanley makes sexual advances to Stella's sister, Blanche, who lives with Stanley and Stella. Since Stella works all day each Saturday, Blanche tends to hide in her room so as to save herself from Stanley's advances.
>
> Last Saturday, Stella came home early, so Blanche, hot, tired, and uncomfortable, finally decided to come out of her room. In a drunken state, Stanley made a sexual advance, which Blanche rebuffed, saying "No, no, you're drunk, as usual." Stanley picked up his licensed and registered revolver, and in Stella's presence removed all but one bullet, spun the magazine of the revolver, pointed the barrel at his head, and depressed the trigger. This is called playing Russian Roulette. Luckily for Stanley, the trigger fell on an empty chamber. Afterward, he waved the revolver at Blanche and said the following words to her: "Blanche, I will play Russian Roulette again unless you have sex with me." Blanche said, "I don't want to, and I hate you, but all right, Stanley," and went to the bedroom with him.
>
> Stella immediately called the police and related what she believed to be Blanche's jeopardy. A police patrol car with two police officers arrived on the scene two hours later. They found Blanche on the floor dead of a gunshot wound, and

> Stanley on the floor of the bedroom with his pants unbuckled and unzipped, lying unconscious in a drunken stupor. Stella explained that Stanley fell while unzipping his pants and accidentally shot Blanche. An autopsy revealed that had a simple tourniquet been applied anytime within the first hour of the shooting, Blanche would have lived.
>
> You are an assistant district attorney responsible for screening cases and determining what crime or crimes should be charged. You are aware of the facts as stated above. Write the memorandum to the District Attorney explaining the reason you recommend for and against each of the crimes you considered. Be sure to relate any defenses you anticipate will be juxtaposed.
>
> Professor Raymond T. Diamond,
> Tulane University School of Law
> Fall, 1996.

The question is probably unlike any essay question you have ever had: Apparently Stanley fell while unzipping his pants, so he never raped Blanche, and if her shooting was accidental, then you do not have to be a lawyer to conclude that there was no murder. There seems to be no right and no wrong answer. So what is there to write about?

Typically, a grade in a U.S. law school course is based entirely on the student's performance on an examination. The students are issued exam numbers and are not to use their names anywhere on their exam answers, so that all exams are graded anonymously. The professor does not learn who wrote which exam until after he or she has finished grading all exams. This ensures absolute fairness in grading, but the fact that your entire grade for the course is based on one exam means that if you should happen not to perform well on that particular day, and your answers do not reflect your knowledge of the subject, there is little or nothing you can do to improve the resulting poor grade.

In addition to being the sole basis for the grade, a U.S. law school exam has a unique format. The traditional U.S. law school exam consists of one or more essay questions, possibly with some short-answer or multiple-choice questions, and lasts two or three hours. Extra time may be given to LL.M. candidates whose native language is not English. Usually one or more of the questions presents a hypothetical conflict between two or more people, and the examinee is asked to analyze all parties' potential claims and defenses. In other words, the essay portion of the exam tries to mimic a real lawyering problem: a client comes to a lawyer's office with a story and wants your legal evaluation of the problem. The only differences are that

1. In the real world, the lawyer must decide what area of law is involved, whereas on an exam, that issue is already resolved.
2. In the real world, the lawyer will have time to research the problem, whereas on an exam, the law student must rely on his knowledge of the coursework, and is under time pressure.
3. In the real world, the lawyer's answer will be a simplified explanation of the applicable law, whereas on an exam, the professor expects a professional assessment of arguments on both sides of each issue, in IRAC form.

These kinds of exams fairly effectively test whether the student learned the material presented in class, and also whether he or she understands how to use that information in a professional context.

If you are used to exams that merely ask you to parrot back to the professor the material taught in class, these kinds of exams are often very unsettling. Memorizing everything covered in class will not help you understand how to approach these kinds of problems. Furthermore, these kinds of problems typically have no right (or wrong) answers, so a different answering technique must be used. A systematic method for studying and writing these kinds of exams has been proven successful by generations of U.S. law students. This appendix first explains how to study for these kinds of exams (by preparing a course outline), and then explains how to write a successful exam answer.

I. OUTLINING AND STUDYING

A. Preparing an Outline

To prepare for the exam, one first outlines the material covered by the course, and then studies that outline, gaining skill in applying the material to various situations by working with old exams or with other students. Outlines consist of the underlying policy concerns of the area studied and analysis of each legal principle studied. Each element of each principle is defined, and facts from various cases are used to illustrate those elements. Generally, the names of cases, the year they were decided, and other details are unimportant and will not be tested — unless the case led to the development of an entire doctrine of law. Hypothetical problems (*hypothets*) the professor presented in class are often important because they illustrate how an element applies to different factual situations.

An easy way to start an outline is to follow the table of contents given in the casebook used by the course, and then to flesh it out with notes from class rewritten so that they illustrate the principles and definitions taught. Outlines for three-credit courses are usually no more than 40 pages long, and no less than 15. The student then studies the outline, which has distilled readings, lectures, and any extra information gleaned from treatises. One very effective way to study an outline is to rewrite it, shortening it to half its original length, and then to rewrite it a second time as a one-page outline.

Any U.S. law school bookstore demonstrates the free market at work. U.S. drugstores have 30 or more kinds of toothpaste, and U.S. law school bookstores often have almost as many varieties of commercial outlines, which they hope to sell to unwary law students. In some schools, students even sell their outlines to other students, claiming, "It's a good outline, I got an A with it!" Although hornbooks can be useful when you need extra help understanding a legal principle, beware of purchasing commercial outlines or other students' outlines. They are almost invariably a waste of money. There are three important reasons for preparing your own outline:

1. The process of preparing an outline forces you to learn the material.
2. Your outline will be specific to the class and the professor; a commercial outline is not.
3. Making your outline requires you to synthesize and apply the law, something you will be required to do on the exam.[1]

B. Studying and Practicing with Hypothetical Problems

In addition to preparing an outline, the student should also practice by (1) reworking the hypothetical problems covered in class; (2) inventing and solving her own hypothetical questions (this is best done with a small study group); and (3) working through prior exams that the professor has given. Most U.S. law schools keep old exams and model answers on file, where students can access them easily. Working through one or two prior exams is a good supplement to preparing an outline but cannot substitute for it. For some basic courses, the "Law in a Flash" cards are helpful in this regard because they provide amusing and memorable hypothets that will enable you to practice handling various legal principles, though they will not help you with information specific to your course. They are available for many of the basic U.S. law courses. It is best to begin this kind of study practice early in the semester, so that you master each principle as you deal with it in class. Do not wait until the week before the exam to learn how to handle hypothetical questions.

C. Sample Outline

Examine the following torts outline. It was written for the torts portion of an exam on U.S. law for international LL.M. students. Consequently, it is not nearly as detailed as an outline for a full semester-length torts course would be.

TORTS OUTLINE

Tort v. Crime: compensates individual, rather than vindicating society's interests.

Tort v. Contract: considered separate subjects in U.S., no continuum of obligation. (But see relational contract theory)

Types of Torts by Degree of Fault

[1] Ruta K. Stropus & Charlotte D. Taylor, *Bridging the Gap between College and Law School: Strategies for Success* 67-68 (Carolina Academic Press 2001).

Intentional Torts

Intent: Actor desires to cause consequences of his act, or believes that the consequences are substantially certain to result from it. (Black's & Restatement (2d))

Intentional tort:

1. a desire to bring about a result, cause a certain injury
2. or substantially certain injury will result from the act
3. usually inferred by circumstances, not admitted by defendant

Black's: the actor is expressly or impliedly judged to have possessed intent or purpose to injure. (accidentally pulled trigger while playing with gun v. intentionally pulled trigger while pointing at plaintiff)

Examples of intentional torts:

Battery: intentional, nonconsensual, physical contact with a person without consent & which entails an offensive touching.

Assault: intentional attempt or threat to inflict injury (battery) upon another person such that the plaintiff reasonably fears that the battery is imminent

False Imprisonment: nonconsensual, intentional confinement of a person without lawful privilege, for an appreciable length of time.[2]

Reckless disregard of safety: Recklessness is in between intentional & unintentional torts, and involves an indifference to consequences involving danger to life or safety to others. (Used in most states as standard for liability in recreational contact sports, other states use negligence, as in soccer slide-tackle case).

Unintentional Torts

Negligence:

Elements: duty, breach, causation, and damages

Duty: an obligation to take some action or refrain from acting to prevent harm to another and for failure of which there may be liability depending upon the circumstances and the relationship of the parties to each other.

Breach: failing to use that degree of care which would be exercised by a reasonable person under the same circumstances as the defendant. (reasonably prudent person standard)

[2] *Black's Law Dictionary* 636 (8th ed. 2004).

Causation-in-fact: the particular cause which produces an event and without which the event would not have occurred; the "but for" test.[3]

Damage: the actual loss or injury caused by the negligence or intent of another, involving harm to one's person or property. *Damages* refers to compensation awarded by a court for a number of different reasons.

Examples of negligence from caselaw:

1. Trolley line wires: injury not foreseeable. Dft. could not anticipate that mischievous boy would swing on wire & electrocute himself. (*Adams*)
2. Social host liability for accident caused by drunk guest. Supporting public goal: reducing drunk driving (*Kelly*)

Defenses:

1. Lack of any one of the elements
2. Assumption of risk (*Lestina*)
3. Comparative negligence (modern)
4. Superseding, intervening cause: "an occurrence or force which not only comes between the initial force or occurrence, but which also breaks the chain of causation between the initial occurrence and the ultimate effect so as to render the initial force or occurrence causatively harmless."[4]
5. Statute of limitations (varies in length from state to state)

Strict Products Liability: manufacturer is strictly liable in tort when an article it places on the market is unreasonably dangerous because of a defect that causes injury to a human being. Usually by statute, first stated in Restatement (2d) of Torts § 402A. In many states, SPL is limited to 3 exclusive theories: manufacturing, design, and warning defects. The purpose of strict liability is to place the burden of proof on the manufacturer, not the consumer.

Policy reasons for SPL:

(1) fix responsibility on the actor who can most effectively reduce the hazard.

The MFR can do this, the consumer cannot.

(2) distribute cost of injury: overwhelming to an injured consumer, but MFR can purchase liability insurance & spread cost by charging a bit more
(3) discourage MFR from marketing defective products
(4) make it possible for injured consumer to have a chance in court due to lower burden of proof

3 types of defects:

(1) Defect in manufacture: product differs from the MFR's intended result or other identical units and the difference is the cause-in-fact of plaintiff's injury. Example: case involving safety hasps that broke in bread truck

[3] *Id.* at 221.
[4] *Id.*

(2) Defect in design: when plaintiff proves that the product fails to perform as safely as an ordinary consumer would expect when used in an intended or reasonably foreseeable manner or if plaintiff proves that the product's design proximately caused his injury and the defendant fails to prove, in light of the relevant factors listed below, that on balance the benefits of the challenged design outweigh the risk of danger inherent in the design.

Factors that the finder-of-fact may consider include: Gravity of the danger posed by the challenged design, the likelihood that such danger would occur, the mechanical feasibility of a safer alternative design, the financial cost of an improved design, and the adverse consequences to the product and to the consumer that would result from an alternative design. Example: high-lift loader lacking side stabilizers, which tipped over & injured plaintiff.

(3) Defect in warning: product is dangerous because it lacks adequate warnings or instructions. Example: many drugs (warnings of side effects)

Defense: product must have been used in a reasonably anticipated manner & any alterations must have been caused by normal wear-and-tear. If one or the other of these is not the case, then the manufacturer is probably not liable. Example: tying up safety bar on lawn mower (class hypothetical)

II. TAKING U.S. LAW SCHOOL EXAMINATIONS

A. The Plan of Attack

Just as an outline is successful if it systematically and thoroughly analyzes and synthesizes the course materials, so will an exam answer be successful if it is approached in a systematic and thorough manner. When the professor calls start, many students initially feel that they have forgotten everything they ever knew about the subject. This is normal. Follow these steps in this order.

1. Read the General Directions

Take a breath and begin by reading the general directions carefully. In the course of preparing for the exam, you may have checked old exams, and found that this professor always gives the same directions, but read them over again anyway, just to refresh your memory and verify that nothing has changed.

2. Scan the Exam and Allocate Your Time

Scan the entire exam. Ascertain how many questions there are, the point value of each, and the format (does the exam consist solely of essay questions, or are there some short-answer or true/false questions?). **Divide your time accordingly, and figure out at exactly what time you should switch from one section to the next.** Note the time allocations on your exam, so that they are instantly available and so that you can verify that you are limiting your time appropriately on each question, and will be able to answer all of them. After you have budgeted your time, do not read through each of the questions carefully before beginning—just begin with one or another of them.

One of the most common errors students make is to become so engrossed in answering one question that they run out of time and are unable to complete the exam. Professors can give points only for things that actually appear on the exam; knowledge that is in your head will not count. You may have known the material, but because you failed to demonstrate that knowledge on the exam, you will be disappointed by the grade you receive. Thus, at some point during the exam, if you see that your outlined answer is going to take more time to write than you have budgeted, shorten or abbreviate that planned answer as appropriate, depending on the relative importance of the remaining questions.

3. *Apportion One-Third of Your Time for Reading and Outlining Essay Questions*

Of the time you have allotted for each essay question, allocate one-third of that time for reading and outlining your answer. In addition to answering all of the questions, it is important that they be well answered: organized, coherent answers are given higher grades. Often students argue that they do not have time to outline their answers, but this is a mistake. Just as professors cannot give credit for things not written, they will not give credit for answers that are so disorganized that they cannot be understood, or fail to address the question asked. An answer outline is not detailed. It need only be enough to provide you with a road map as you draft the answer. Therefore, it does not take up much time, and ensures that the answer given on the exam accurately answers the question asked.

4. *Read Each Essay Question Twice*

Read each essay question twice before you start to answer it. On the first read-through, underline key words that bring to mind concepts discussed in the course, and possibly note those concepts in the margins. Pay special attention to the question asked at the end. You should probably read it an extra one or two times before beginning your full second reading of the entire hypothet. As you read the entire hypothet the second time, think about the question that was asked, and how the facts given in the hypothet relate to it, and outline your answer on scratch paper as you read the question.

You might even *begin* by scanning the hypothet through quickly, just to find the exact question asked, and fix that question in your mind before even beginning the first careful read-through. This is the method the author uses most often. For example, in the sample criminal law exam question reproduced in the first part of this appendix, I would scan through the question until I found the words: "You are an assistant district attorney . . . crimes . . . and defenses." I would then know that I needed to look through the facts for elements of crimes and defenses.

5. *Highlight Clues and Note Key Concepts*

As you read, your brain will begin to warm up. You will notice facts that remind you of issues, arguments, policies and cases—in other words, your outline. When you see one of these clues, highlight or underline it, and jot down a key word so that you will remember what issue, element, or case was called to mind.

6. *Outline Your Answer*

After highlighting this way through both readings of the entire question, think about how you want to organize your answer. Jot down that outline on a piece of scrap paper. It may resemble the major components of your study outline, or it may be in a different order, addressing each issue raised in the hypothet as it is raised. Do not outline in detail, just sketch in major points and anything else that comes to mind which you are afraid you might forget to include as you get caught up in the writing process.

7. *Write Your Essay Answer with an Eye on the Clock*

Begin writing, using your outline as a guide and proceeding systematically from one issue to the next. Keep an eye on the clock to make sure that you are staying on schedule, and adjust your answer and writing style accordingly.

B. Writing the Exam: IRAC and CRAC

What professors want is an organized, straightforward, and thorough analysis of the exam hypothetical, which identifies each issue fairly raised by the facts given and explains how the concepts covered in the course apply to the facts given in the hypothet. Law professors do not usually care how eloquently the sentences are phrased, and one or two small grammatical or punctuation errors are not a problem. Simple and direct phrasing is best. Thorough analysis and organization are paramount. Professors usually grade exams by using a checklist of the issues that should be discussed in the exam answer. The more of those issues that are addressed in a professional manner, the higher the grade will be. What they do *not* want (and what they get, far too often) is a jumbled, rambling discussion of law only indirectly related to the hypothet, as the student tries to regurgitate every idea ever mentioned in the course in a blind panic to get something down on the exam paper. This section first explains how to write an answer to a hypothetical essay-type question. Next, it explains some of the more common errors in exam writing. Finally, it illustrates with a sample test and two answers, one good and one not-so-good.

When you sketch out your outlined exam answer, begin by outlining the big topics, usually in the order in which they are presented in the question itself. A simple method for writing effective law school exams, and for organizing legal writing in general, is to use the IRAC or CRAC methods used by generations of law students (see Chapter 3). IRAC stands for Issue, Rule, Application, Conclusion. CRAC is a variation of that, substituting Conclusion for Issue. With this method, you begin each paragraph of your answer by stating the issue or conclusion that is the subject of the paragraph. You then state the applicable principle of law in a neutral manner; explain how it applies to certain particular facts given in the hypothet; and conclude that one or more parties in the hypothet may or may not argue that the principle applies. If one or more parties could claim that the principle applies, be sure to search for and discuss arguments that the opposing side would make about why the principle should not apply. Conclude by stating which argument is stronger. You need not (and probably should not) conclude that one or the other party will definitely win or lose at trial.

C. Common Errors

Students who may understand the law, and who have correctly spotted the main issues, make five common errors in writing exam answers that may lead the professor to conclude that they have not demonstrated that knowledge—and thereby award a low grade. Those errors include taking sides, failing to explicitly state controlling law, failing to note the relationship between legal issues, mixing legal categories, and discussing irrelevant legal principles.

1. Taking Sides

A hypothetical exam is testing, among other things, whether you can function in an adversary system. This means that you must analyze arguments on both sides of each issue. Sometimes the professor asks you to explain the parties' claims and defenses, but other times her expectation that you will analyze both sides is understood and tacit. Professors write hypothetical questions in such a way that there is no right or wrong answer, only stronger and weaker arguments. To get the most points, not only must you identify the relevant issues, but also you must identify and explain stronger and weaker arguments on *both* sides of each issue.

2. Failing to Explicitly State Controlling Law

After identifying a legal issue, state the controlling principle in a neutral way. For example, after identifying that the first issue is whether some party was negligent, your rule statement might be: "A negligence claim requires proof of four elements: duty, breach, causation, and damages." After this, you would explain how specific facts from the hypothet either do or do not establish each of those elements. The most common error is to skip an explicit statement of the negligence rule. This is a mistake because it fails to prove to the professor that you actually know that rule. Furthermore, if you do not explicitly state the applicable principle before applying it to the facts, you may forget to include one component or another in your application. This does not mean that you need to continually repeat a statement of a principle. Once you have stated the requirements of a negligence claim, for example, you can refer back to that statement if you have to deal with other parties' potential negligence claims.

3. Failing to Note the Relationship between Legal Issues

Explaining how one legal issue relates to another shows the professor that you understand how all of these various claims work, and thus that you understand the principles taught in the course in their proper context. For example, on a torts exam, after dealing with a party's potential liability for battery in an IRAC paragraph, you could state that even if the court finds that party not liable for battery, he or she could be liable for negligence. Thus, not only are you transitioning from battery to negligence, and showing the professor that you understand that more than one tort claim can be brought against the same party, but you are also stating the new issue for your next IRAC paragraph.

4. *Mixing Legal Categories*

Be sure you stick to one topic in each IRAC paragraph. If you are discussing negligence, do not suddenly mix in a sentence dealing with a potential battery claim, or mentioning facts from the hypothet in such a way as to indicate battery rather than negligence. Mixing categories leads the professor to conclude that you are not sure about how the legal principles work in a real-life situation, and again will result in a lower grade.

5. *Discussing Irrelevant Legal Principles*

In a hypothetical exam question, the professor is interested in seeing you demonstrate your understanding of the current state of the law and how it applies in real-life situations. Thus, you should discuss all legal principles that are fairly raised in the facts given. You will need to compare and distinguish the facts given with any current case law you studied, so as to demonstrate to the professor that you understand which principles apply and how. What the professor is *not* looking for, however, is an essay on how the law developed, or on any principle not inherent in the facts.

Demonstrate to your professor every concern about the case that you, as a lawyer, would consider. For example, in dealing with a negligence claim, you would discuss the presence or absence of each element (duty, breach, causation, and damages). You should also discuss assumption of risk and other defenses covered in the course, mentioning that some states have replaced assumption of risk with comparative negligence, so that you would need to research the applicable statutes. You probably should not, however, discuss how negligence developed out of the common law "trespass on the case," nor should you discuss issues of civil procedure on a torts exam — unless, during class, the professor specifically discussed a point of civil procedure that relates to some aspect of torts and some fact given in the hypothet raises that issue.

D. Sample Torts Question and Answers

Review the torts outline in § I.C of this appendix, and then spend no more than half an hour writing an IRAC answer addressing as many issues as you can in that time period. This is a difficult, complicated question, quite typical of professors who find that difficult questions make it easier for them to grade. For the purpose of learning IRAC exam technique, there is no need to address every issue in the exam. Once you have written your own proposed answer, compare it to the two sample answers that follow.

SAMPLE EXAM QUESTION (TORTS)

After finishing his Dixie Long Neck beer, Bubba Boudreaux grabbed his mean-looking Navagar TEC-9 semiautomatic assault pistol, which he had outfitted with an extended magazine holding 50 rounds of ammunition, and went hunting. First he went out into the Cajun State Hunt Club's woods to shoot deer. He shot what he thought was a deer, but it turned out to be another hunter, Nat'lie Numskull, who had forgotten to wear her orange parka. The Hunt Club requires hunters to sign a promise that they will wear their orange parkas at all times while hunting. Nat'lie was slightly injured. Unfortunately, Bubba didn't realize at first that Nat'lie wasn't a deer and tied her up. It took her an hour to free herself from the ropes, jump down from the top of his car, and go for help.

After shooting Nat'lie, Bubba became upset. He kept thinking about his ex-wife, and the lawyer who represented her. Because of his divorce, he had developed a deep-seated hatred of lawyers and believed that they posed a serious threat to his well-being and that his ex-wife's lawyer was part of a conspiracy to break up his marriage and destroy him financially. He had become so unhinged that he went to a psychiatric social worker, but recently he had missed several appointments and stopped taking his medicine. The accident with the gun upset him so much that he started thinking about that lawyer, Dewey Cheetem. So, he stumbled into Cheetem's office on the 53rd floor of a local skyscraper. To the extent he could think, he wanted to scare the attorney or possibly wound him. Unfortunately, after wounding the attorney, the complex firing mechanism on Bubba's gun jammed and the trigger, made of unusually brittle metal, broke off. Boudreaux dropped the gun, but all 50 rounds fired while the gun spun around on the floor. When it finally stopped, seven more people had been injured, including Boudreaux himself.

Navegar had targeted the gun to "gun enthusiast[s] . . . people who enjoy shooting" as well as those who "dress up in military outfits, and go to gun shows." It had heavily advertised the TEC-9 in a number of gun-related magazines, describing it "as tough as your toughest customer." Since its manufacture, the gun has been banned in the state Penal Code, which states that TEC-9s and other assault weapons are particularly attractive to violent criminals, "serve no . . . sporting purpose for honest citizens," and "the proliferation of these guns poses a threat to the health, safety, and security of all citizens of this state." Boudreaux had purchased the gun legally at a gun show in a neighboring state, saying that he wanted to use it for hunting and target shooting, even though he was told that the gun was poorly suited for this purpose because it shoots inaccurately. He looked at a number of different guns at the gun show, but chose the TEC-9 because it looked "mean." He rarely reads, and may or may not have seen the advertisements. Assume that the Cajun state strict products liability statute recognizes defects for warning, manufacture, and design. Discuss the various tort claims and defenses of all parties.

EXERCISE

Read the following two student answers, jotting down your impressions of how they succeed or fail.

Answer 1. (adapted from an actual student's answer)

This case is about Boudreaux, Numskull, and Boudreaux's lawyer, as well as the defective gun that Boudreaux bought. The issue is whether any torts were committed.

First of all, I will split the case in three parts according to the number of plaintiffs' actions and defendants involved.

(a) When Boudreaux shot Numskull by accident, he clearly committed an unintentional tort. What kind? Well, it was certainly battery because battery is defined as the aggression or defense caused by a person who gets in physical contact with the victim. It is indifferent whether it was an intentional or unintentional tort, even though intentional torts at this point overlap with criminal behavior and might be the source of a criminal prosecution.

(b) Second, Boudreaux was clearly drunk and crazy. He was seeing a psychiatrist. Anyone who starts shooting people in an office building is clearly crazy. Furthermore, he had drunk several beers.

(c) Because this deals with a gun that breaks, strict products liability applies. Judge Traynor of the California Supreme Court is credited with developing the first strict products liability cases. The purpose of strict products liability is to put the burden of proof on the manufacturer who can spread the cost of any damages by charging more for his products.

Boudreaux will clearly lose.

Answer 2. (also adapted from an actual answer)

There are several injured parties in this problem and each has one or more potential claims or defenses. Each person's potential causes of action will be considered in turn.

Nat'lie

Nat'lie will want to sue Boudreaux for the injuries she sustained. She has three possible causes of action: battery, false imprisonment, and negligence.

(1) Battery is an intentional offensive or harmful contact with another person without that person's consent. The issue here is whether Boudreaux intended to commit a battery. Intent is a deliberate act evidencing either an active desire to cause an injury or bring about a result or an act deliberately done from which a certain injury is substantially certain to result. It is usually inferred by the circumstances, not admitted by the defendant. Here, although Boudreaux intentionally fired the gun, he did not intend to wound Nat'lie with it. Furthermore, he did not intend contact with any other person (he thought he was shooting at a deer). Thus, he could argue that he is not liable for battery. On the other hand, it is hard to believe that he could mistake a person for a deer, and he did intend the act of shooting. So it is unlikely that this argument will be successful.

(2) False imprisonment is the intentional unjustified confinement of another person against his or her will. Although Boudreaux unjustifiably confined Nat'lie against her will, again, the issue is intent, defined above, and for the same reasons, Boudreaux may argue that he should not be liable for false imprisonment.

(3) Negligence does not require intent. Rather, it is an unintentional tort requiring proof of four elements: duty, breach, causation in fact, and damages. Duty is defined as the obligation to observe that level of care which a reasonably prudent man in similar

circumstances would observe. In this case, a reasonably prudent hunter would not go hunting while drunk because it is foreseeable that he would be likely to injure himself or other people. Boudreaux breached this duty, causing Nat'lie injury. Boudreaux, however, could argue that his act was not the cause in fact of her injury, and that her injury was caused by her failure to wear her parka. This argument would probably not succeed, but it might reduce Nat'lie's damages under the doctrine of comparative negligence.

(The rest of the answer continues by discussing Cheetem's claims for battery, the other attorney's claims, and including both negligence and strict products liability claims against Navegar.)

COMPARING THE TWO ANSWERS[5]

a. Introductions

Answer 1 begins:

This case is about Boudreaux, Numskull, and Boudreaux's lawyer, as well as the defective gun that Boudreaux bought. The issue is whether any torts were committed. First of all, I will split the case in three parts according to the number of plaintiffs' actions and defendants involved.

This is a rather weak opening because it tells the reader nothing that is not already known and does not focus on the specific issues involved. Stating that the issue is whether any torts were committed is so broad as to be meaningless. "First of all" is misleading, because it is not followed by a second section; the use of the first person (*I*) is unprofessional in tone; the predicate is confusing because it is not obvious that the case should be split into three parts, nor will the reader understand how one can organize the answer according to the number of parties involved. It would have been better to organize the answer according to each party's potential claims.

Compare the opening paragraph in the second answer:

There are several injured parties in this problem and each has one or more potential claims or defenses. Each person's potential causes of action will be considered in turn.

This opening is stronger because it shows that the student planned before writing and it explains simply and clearly to the reader what to expect.

b. First Substantive Paragraphs

Answer 1 continues:

(a) When Boudreaux shot Numskull by accident, he clearly committed an unintentional tort. What kind? Well, it was certainly battery because battery is defined as the

[5] *See* Kenney F. Hegland, *Introduction to the Study and Practice of Law in a Nutshell* 145-72 (2003). The text following the footnotes tracks Hegland's materials on exam techniques quite closely, as they provide an excellent explanation of exam technique.

aggression or defense caused by a person who gets in physical contact with the victim. It is indifferent whether it was an intentional or unintentional tort, even though intentional torts at this point overlap with criminal behavior and might be the source of a criminal prosecution.

This paragraph is problematic. The first sentence "he clearly committed an unintentional tort" reaches a legal conclusion without explaining the underlying legal principle first or applying the components of that principle to the facts of the case. The rhetorical question "What kind?" is inappropriate in tone, just as the use of the first person was in the previous paragraph. Both examples display an approach that most professors would find too informal and colloquial. Although battery is defined in the third sentence, the definition is inaccurate. It completely misses the requirement of intent, fails to explain that the touch must be offensive, and adds the meaningless terms "aggression or defense." The elements of a battery are never applied to the facts of the case; instead, the final sentence inappropriately discusses the distinction between tort and crime, which is irrelevant. In comparison, the second paragraph of answer 2 is as follows:

Nat'lie

Nat'lie will want to sue Boudreaux for the injuries she sustained. She has three possible causes of action: battery, false imprisonment, and negligence.

(1) Battery is an intentional offensive or harmful contact with another person without that person's consent. The issue here is whether Boudreaux intended to commit a battery. Intent is a deliberate act evidencing either an active desire to cause an injury or bring about a result or an act deliberately done from which a certain injury is substantially certain to result. It is usually inferred by the circumstances, not admitted by the defendant. Here, although Boudreaux intentionally fired the gun, he did not intend to wound Nat'lie with it. Furthermore, he did not intend contact with any other person (he thought he was shooting at a deer). Thus, he could argue that he is not liable for battery. On the other hand, it is hard to believe that he could mistake a person for a deer, and he did intend the act of shooting. So it is unlikely that this argument will be successful.

This begins by fulfilling the organization promised in the introductory paragraph: it addresses Nat'lie's claims, discussing each in turn in an IRAC paragraph. The first issue discussed is battery, which is defined correctly. The problematic element, intent, is also reasonably well defined, and then applied to the facts given in the problem. The application addresses arguments on both sides and then reaches a reasonable conclusion.

c. Third Paragraphs

Answer 1's third paragraph is short:

(b) Second, Boudreaux was clearly drunk and crazy. He was seeing a psychiatrist. Anyone who starts shooting people in an office building is clearly crazy. Furthermore, he had drunk several beers.

Unlike the previous paragraph, at least this paragraph does not misstate the law. In fact, it does not mention any law. Instead, it begins by manufacturing facts. The question did not say that Boudreaux was drunk, simply that he had been drinking. Be careful with facts and make distinctions between the facts as stated in the problem and reasonable inferences that can be drawn from those facts. Do not jump to conclusions. In this instance, the student decided that Boudreaux should be liable and apparently assumed that his being drunk and crazy would be further proof, but the answer never explains the legal effects of being drunk or crazy in the context of an intentional tort. Drunkenness is sometimes argued as a defense against the ability to form intent, but is rarely successful. Insanity can be a stronger defense, but the problem does not provide enough evidence to prove that insanity is involved in this instance. In any case, the student took sides, thus missing possible defenses that Boudreaux might raise and losing several points as a result.

Always maintain neutrality. You do not care who wins, and by not caring, you are likely to win more points on the exam because you will be better able to address arguments on both sides of the issue.

In contrast to Answer 1, the third and fourth paragraphs of Answer 2 systematically discuss two more potential claims that Nat'lie might raise against Boudreaux: false imprisonment and negligence. Furthermore, as with battery, the discussion of negligence considers both Nat'lie's claims and Boudreaux's potential defenses.

d. The Final Paragraph of Answer 1

The last paragraph of Answer 1 deals with strict products liability, but neither defines the term nor explains how it applies to the facts given. Instead, it provides some historical background about the concept, and then mentions one of the policy reasons justifying it:

> *c) Because this deals with a gun that breaks, strict products liability applies. Judge Traynor of the California Supreme Court is credited with developing the first strict products liability cases. The purpose of strict products liability is to put the burden of proof on the manufacturer who can spread the cost of any damages by charging more for his products.*

This paragraph identifies an issue fairly present in the hypothet, but fails to define the concept or apply it to the facts of the problem. Instead, it discusses the history of strict products liability, which is irrelevant to the question asked and unlikely to gain any points from the grading professor. The answer then concludes with a non sequitur that further demonstrates that the student has chosen sides: *Boudreaux will clearly lose.*

In addition to taking sides, Answer 1 inaccurately restates the facts of the problem and usually fails to define legal concepts. When it does define legal concepts, it does so inaccurately. Furthermore, it rarely if ever explains how those concepts apply to the facts of the problem, and it reaches unjustified conclusions as a result. In two separate places, it discusses things that are completely irrelevant to the question asked. A final criticism of Answer 1 is that it fails to show relationships among the various issues and legal concepts. In contrast, Answer 2 demonstrates a good understanding of the difference between intentional and unintentional tort when it both defines the term *intent* relatively accurately and explains that battery and false imprisonment both require intent.

Having reviewed this analysis of both answers, now return to your own draft answer and analyze it to see if you spot any errors of the sort committed in Answer

1. When you take a practice exam, perform the same kind of analysis, until you become used to using IRAC systematically.

BIBLIOGRAPHY

Block, Gertrude. *Effective Legal Writing for Law Students and Lawyers.* 4th ed. 1992.

Dernbach, John C. *A Practical Guide to Writing Law School Essay Exams.* Fred B. Rothman Publications 2001.

Falcon, Atticus. *Planet Law School: What You Need to Know (Before You Go) . . . But Didn't Know to Ask.* 1998.

Hegland, Kenney F. *Introduction to the Study and Practice of Law in a Nutshell.* West 2003.

Munneke, Gary A., Jr. *How to Succeed in Law School.* 2d ed. Barron's Educational Series 1994.

Neumann, Richard K., Jr. *Legal Reasoning and Legal Writing: Structure, Strategy, and Style.* 4th ed. Aspen Law and Business 2001.

Stropus, Ruta K., & Charlotte D. Taylor. *Bridging the Gap between College and Law School: Strategies for Success.* Carolina Academic Press 2001.

Appendix B: Drafting Advisory Memoranda for Attorneys in the United States

On occasion, attorneys outside the United States are asked to advise an American attorney about their own country's law and how it applies to a given client's situation. Then, after working long and hard on a memorandum, they send it to their contact in the United States only to learn to their frustration that the contact could not understand the memo, found it confusing or convoluted, or did not even read it! Except for the last possibility (which is completely beyond the writer's control), most of these problems can be minimized if the memorandum is as much like the standard in-office memo prepared in the United States. The goal, therefore, is to make the American attorney who will be reading the memo as comfortable as possible. Thus, not only should it look similar to a U.S. in-office memo, with the same headings, but to the extent possible, it should reflect the same IRAC analysis, while explaining the unique characteristics of the non-U.S. law and legal system at issue. This appendix essentially builds on the material presented in Chapters 3 and 8 but builds on it in light of the types of concerns a civilian attorney is likely to have in preparing an advisory memo for a U.S. counterpart. An example of such a memo, using the wedding dress memo presented in Chapter 8 as adapted under Chilean law is given at the end of the section.

I. VISUALLY APPROXIMATE THE STANDARD U.S. OFFICE MEMO FORMAT.

The standard interoffice memo begins with a heading identifying the type of document (a Memorandum), and indicating for whom it was written, by whom, concerning which case, and the date, as shown in Chapter 3 and in the sample memo. After a bold line separating the heading from the body of the memo, the memo is divided into several sections by headings: Introduction, Issue, Short Answer, Facts, Discussion, and Conclusion. In order to make it easier for the U.S. reader to understand the memo, use the same headings if at all possible. Furthermore, in designing the document visually, leave plenty of "white space," i.e., space the sections so that the document looks easy to read. Attorneys in the United States are often overloaded with reading material, so if the document looks easily read because it is divided into smaller components with clear headings, attorneys are more likely to both read it and be able to dissect and understand what they read.

II. IN PRESENTING THE LEGAL ANALYSIS, APPROXIMATE (AS MUCH AS POSSIBLE) THE IRAC STRUCTURE USED IN THE UNITED STATES.

As explained in Chapter 3, the Introduction refreshes the reader's memory concerning the topic of the memo in one or two sentences:

> Ms. Maria Manning hired seamstress Sally Singer to make dresses for her bridal party. Singer's work was not timely, and several of the dresses were not ready for the wedding. This memo explores whether Manning has a claim for emotional distress stemming from Singer's breach of the contract under Chilean law.

The Issue states the legal question addressed, while the Short Answer answers that question in one or two sentences beginning with Yes, No, or Maybe:

ISSUE

Under Chilean law, does Manning have a claim for emotional damages against Singer, the wedding party's seamstress, because Singer's breach of her contract to produce ten dresses for Manning's wedding caused Manning distress on her wedding day?

SHORT ANSWER

Possibly yes. Recent Chilean Supreme Court case law (or more correctly jurisprudence) recognizes moral damages in a breach of contract lawsuit, and the facts of Manning's case are such that the breach of contract led directly to the emotional distress.

The Fact section then presents a narrative of the underlying and relevant facts, omitting all references to legal terminology and conclusions. The Discussion Section, which is the most important part of the memorandum, then first explains the applicable rule thoroughly, component by component, and applies it to the facts given in the fact section. The section then concludes with a short sentence or two and that rationale is stated again in the Conclusion section.

III. IN ADDITION TO APPROXIMATING THE STRUCTURE OF A U.S. ADVISORY MEMORANDUM, APPROXIMATE COMMON LAW METHODOLOGY AS MUCH AS POSSIBLE AS WELL.

The difficulty comes with the fact that many (if not most) civilian jurisdictions do not recognize case law, or do so but to a lesser extent than do U.S. jurisdictions. Thus, in the Discussion section, you may be tempted simply to explain each component of the applicable rule without any examples of how each is used. Furthermore, you will be tempted to avoid making any analogies in the application section as well. This would be a mistake — a common law attorney would likely not accept the explanation of the rule, nor could she understand how you reached your conclusions about how it would apply in this section. The best approach in the absence of authoritative case law is to supplement the explanation of law with examples drawn from a scholarly treatise or other authority, and then supplement the application section with analogies to those factual examples. Remember as well to argue both sides so that the reader can easily see the strengths and weaknesses of the client's position.

ADD AN EXPLANATION OF YOUR LEGAL SYSTEM'S METHODOLOGY AS NEEDED TO HELP THE U.S. READER UNDERSTAND THE DIFFERENCES.

In addition to using factual examples and analogies and arguing both sides, explain your legal system's methodology as needed so that the U.S. reader can more easily follow your reasoning. Remind him or her, probably at the beginning of the Rule section where you are explaining the context of the rule, of the extent to which your system differs from that of the United States: does your system officially recognize case law? Unofficially acknowledge it? Or is case law irrelevant?

IV. REMEMBER TO USE TRANSITIONS AND TO EDIT AND CAREFULLY PROOFREAD YOUR MEMO.

In addition to using the basic structure of a standard U.S. memo and a comparable analytic method, a successful advisory opinion is thoroughly edited so as to be as reader-friendly as possible. In editing, try to read the memo as if you were your audience. What additional information will the reader need in order to understand your point? Is everything phrased as simply as possible? Are the transitions carefully drafted so that you are accurately explaining the relationships between your ideas and flowing smoothly from one to the next? Have you verified that the grammar and punctuation are correct? Does the document look neat and professional? Logically, the more successful your memo is, the more likelihood that your U.S. colleague will want to hire you again in the future.

V. PROVIDING UPDATES ON A NUMBER OF TOPICS.

Sometimes a consulting attorney will be asked to give an update on a number of pending matters, rather than an advisory opinion on one case. In such a case, if there is a particular form the U.S. colleague prefers to use, by all means use that form. Otherwise, be sensitive to your colleague's desire for clarity and brevity in designing one. The standard memo heading is probably still appropriate, but instead of "Issue, Short Answer, Facts, Discussion, and Conclusion," the subheadings could be the titles of each case. The easiest way for most readers to locate a subheading is if they are bolded or bolded and underlined. Traditionally one might use all capital letters, but this is much harder on the eyes. Thus, the subheadings could be"**Abacus v. Martin, Beta v. Short, Conrad v. McDonald,**" etc. Then, for each update begin with a brief reminder of the substance of each matter and a short statement of any new measures taken. If nothing has happened in the interim period, state that fact in as short a manner as is appropriate, and use exactly the same language for each such non-active matter.

VI. SAMPLE MEMORANDUM: THE WEDDING DRESS IN CHILE.

In the spring of 2007, the author was given the honor of a Fulbright grant to teach at the Universidad de los Andes in Santiago, Chile. The following sample memorandum was developed under the auspices of that grant with the very capable research help of Ph.D. candidate Francisca Barrientos and is an example of an advisory memo using Chilean law to analyze the Wedding Dress problem. As you read it, note the explanation of the differences between Chilean and U.S. methodology, the presentation of the two jurisprudential cases, and the fact-to-fact comparison in the application section.

MEMORANDUM

TO: **George Gonzalez**

FROM: Chilean Attorney

RE: Client—Maria Manning: Contract Damages for Emotional Distress

DATE: May 12, 2007

INTRODUCTION

Ms Manning hired seamstress Sally Singer to make dresses for her bridal party. Singer's work was not timely, and several of the dresses were not ready for the wedding. This memo explores whether Manning has a claim for emotional distress stemming from Singer's breach of the contract under Chilean law.

ISSUE

Under Chilean law, does Manning have a claim for emotional damages against Singer, the wedding party's seamstress, because Singer's breach of her contract to produce ten dresses for Manning's wedding caused Manning distress on her wedding day?

SHORT ANSWER

Possibly yes. Recent Chilean Supreme Court case law (or more correctly jurisprudence) recognizes moral damages in a breach of contract lawsuit, and the facts of Manning's case are such that the breach of contract led directly to the emotional distress.

FACTS

Ms. Manning and her nine bridesmaids hired Singer on April 23, 1999, to make dresses for her wedding party. The dresses were to be completed before the wedding on July 17, 1999, at 1:00 p.m. At the meeting in April, Singer took everyone's measurements and was given the fabric for the ten dresses.

From April until June 10, Manning and Singer maintained contact by telephone. Manning even sent Singer an invitation to the wedding, although Singer never responded. Nevertheless, Singer assured Manning that the dresses were progressing normally. On June 10, Singer met with the wedding party for the final fitting. At that meeting, the gowns were held together with pins and none was wearable. Singer assured Manning that all the dresses would be ready in time for the ceremony. Manning spoke with Singer by telephone again in early July, and Singer assured her that she was putting the finishing touches on the dresses. Although Manning asked to see the dresses, Singer assured her that she never let her clients see the work until the last stitch was in place.

However, none of the dresses was completed within a reasonable time prior to the wedding, and some of the dresses were never finished. On the morning of the wedding, Manning and her bridesmaids arrived at Singer's shop at 9:00 a.m. Singer told them that their dresses were still not ready, but were minutes from completion. She asked them to wait in the back of her shop, which was crowded, messy, and uncomfortable. They waited there for three hours, and Manning missed her beauty shop appointments.

Manning did not get her wedding dress until 12:30, and was nearly ill with anxiety by that time. She dressed quickly and arrived at the church ten minutes late. Five of the bridesmaids arrived at 1:30, too late to walk down the aisle with the bride and groom, and their dresses were unfinished and looked terrible. Furthermore, the two bridesmaids chosen to recite prayers during the wedding, as well as two others, were still waiting at Singer's sewing shop on Singer's representation that the dresses were nearly complete. Those four bridesmaids missed the wedding ceremony entirely and wore casual clothes to the reception. The bridesmaids suffered emotional distress and humiliation as a result.

Manning cried before and during the wedding, because of the problems with the dresses.

DISCUSSION

As a civilian jurisdiction, Chile does not recognize *stare decisis*; nevertheless certain court cases (or more correctly jurisprudence), especially from the Chilean Supreme Court, are highly persuasive. Until recently, moral damages (the equivalent of emotional damages) were not available for breach of contract because the Chilean Civil Code does not expressly provide for them.[1] Article 1556 provides: *La indemnizacion de perjuicios comprende el daño emergente y lucro cesante, ya provengan de no haberse cumplido la obligación, o de haberse cumplido imperfectamente, o de haberse retardado el cumplimiento.* In English, this translates as "Damages for nonperformance, defective performance, or delayed performance are measured by the loss sustained by the obligee and the profit of which he has been deprived."[2]

The Chilean Supreme Court, however, recently began to grant moral damages. In the landmark case *Rafart con Banco*, decided in 1994, the Court granted Maria Rafart moral damages in a breach of contract suit against her bank. Rafart had opened a bank account with a bank that subsequently and wrongfully honored 36 checks forged on her account by a third party. Because of this, Ms. Rafart's credit rating was ruined. She demanded both compensatory and moral damages. The Supreme Court granted moral damages (in addition to compensatory damages), relying on two reported cases and referring to positive jurisprudence under the Civil Codes of France, Belgium, Spain, Switzerland, and Argentina.

In another, more recent case, the Supreme Court expanded on the reasoning first articulated in *Rafart con Banco*. In this case, the plaintiff Hugo Ruiz Ruiz sued two laboratories, his doctor, the Chilean Institute of Public Health, and the Chilean State Treasury. The defendant laboratories had performed an AIDS test, and erroneously reported that he was HIV positive. That result was confirmed by the Institute of Public Health, leading to the plaintiff's losing his customers and becoming a social

[1] Carmen Dominguez Hidalgo, 1 El Daño Moral 347 (2003).
[2] Trans. Author, *Compare* arts. 1994-1995 of the Louisiana Civil Code.

outcast. Eventually his anguish became so extreme that he attempted suicide. Finally, when he realized he exhibited none of the symptoms of AIDS, he had himself tested by an independent laboratory. The results of the new test indicated that he had never had the disease. The Supreme Court affirmed the award of moral damages, basing its reasoning on the Dominguez treatise cited above, and adding that new developments in society mean that the law must change in order to provide justice. Thus, reinterpreting Article 1556, the Court reasoned that moral damages are included in the concept of *daño emergente* (sustained losses).

There are significant similarities between this jurisprudence and Manning's situation. Ruiz's loss of his emotional stability when faced with a false positive AIDs test is like Manning's emotional distress when faced with a wedding ruined by poorly-made dresses that were untimely delivered. Admittedly, Ruiz's situation was more serious, but in both cases the defendant's defective or delayed performance caused the plaintiff serious emotional harm, harm that was directly related to the nonperformance. The facts of *Rafart* can similarly be compared to the case at issue: The devastation wrought by the bank's negligent handling of her account is similar to the emotional distress suffered by Manning as a result of Singer's negligent handling of her wedding dresses. Thus, Manning may be able to recover moral damages under Chilean law.

CONCLUSION

Although Chilean courts used to prohibit moral damages for breach of contract, current Supreme Court interpretation of article 1556 now allows for them, finding that they are included in the concept of *daño emergente*. Thus, because Manning's factual situation is similar to that in *Ruiz* and *Rafart* where such damages were granted, she has a colorable claim for moral (or emotional) damages.

INDEX